Published by Melbourne Books
Level 9, 100 Collins Street,
Melbourne, VIC 3000
Australia
www.melbournebooks.com.au
info@melbournebooks.com.au

Copyright © Paul Fleckney 2018

All rights reserved. No part of this publication may be reproduced, stored in a retrieval system, or transmitted in any form or any means electronic, mechanical, photocopying, recording or otherwise without the prior permission of the publishers.

Every attempt has been made to locate the copyright holders for material quoted and images printed in this book. Any person or organisation that may have been overlooked or misattributed may contact the publisher for correction in any future printing.

Original cover art: Voodoo and Dan Woodman
Cover design: Vanessa Neil

Title: Techno Shuffle: Rave Culture and The Melbourne Underground
Author: Paul Fleckney
ISBN: 9781925556315

A catalogue record for this book is available from the National Library of Australia

RAVE CULTURE & THE MELBOURNE UNDERGROUND

PAUL FLECKNEY

M
MELBOURNE BOOKS

For the ravers.

CONTENTS

9	Prologue
10	Introduction
21	Chapter 1 DANCING QUEENS
43	Chapter 2 PUNKS AND PINEAPPLE HEADS
66	Chapter 3 PLEASURE SEEKERS
92	Chapter 4 CHILDREN OF ECSTASY
116	Chapter 5 PURE RAVERS
141	Chapter 6 TECHNO RENEGADES
169	Chapter 7 GLOBAL VILLAGERS

198	Chapter 8 **MELBOURNE SHUFFLERS**
227	Chapter 9 **GATECRASHERS**
255	Chapter 10 **TWO TRIBES**
290	Acknowledgments
292	Interviews Conducted
294	Sources Consulted
306	Endnotes
314	Index
324	Discography
328	The Author

Prologue

Global Village, Footscray, 1995. The magic begins before you get in; standing outside in the queue, you watch the Coode Island cranes play Tetris with shipping containers while a woman in angel robes drops rose petals on your head from a second-floor window. When you walk in the door, it's like stepping into a fantasy realm. Inside the techno wonderland, you walk along fluorescent corridors lined with ancient gods and science fiction dreams of the future. There could be a thousand or ten thousand people here, it's impossible to tell. Everything that happens here belongs only here. Even the light cannot escape, sealed in by black plastic and silver tape. Lost in a labyrinth of desire, you feel neither fear nor discomfort, only wonder. Clanging metal rises above a pounding beat and shakes your whole body. Someone you have never met before hugs you. Every few seconds, an emerald green laser cuts through the blackness and fleetingly reveals the faces around you before they recede once more to the shadows. You have come home.

Introduction

A Time to Dance

Norfolk, England, 1984. Sunday evening. Dad pours a scotch, pushes back the settee and queues up a stack of 45s on his Pioneer. He plays the hits of his youth, tunes like 'Reelin' and Rockin'' by the Dave Clark Five, Cream's 'Sunshine Of Your Love' and 'Da Doo Ron Ron' by The Crystals. I dance wildly, burning my soles on the carpet as I slide into the furniture. I feel free and exhilarated. Dad looks on with adoration and amusement. I'll never get this close to him again. I stop to breathe; even my six-year-old limbs have limits. But as my heart beats like a bass drum, Dad gets up and puts on one last record. The bassline starts, the Hammond organ comes in and when Steve Winwood screams, 'Well, my temperature's rising and my feet are on the floor', I lose it. 'Gimme Some Lovin'' by the Spencer Davis Group is still one of my all-time favourite tracks. I flail around like a bird caught in a net and when the song finishes I beg Dad to play it again. Can life get any better than this?

For the next ten years, the answer was no. Schoolbooks, rules and peer pressure replaced freedom, fun and dancing. Music became strictly a listening experience. I played home-taped cassettes of heavy metal my friends had lent me and then on Sunday nights tuned into Radio 1 to hear the Top 40 countdown. In the last week of high school, I bought a cheap exercise book, wrote my name on the front and passed it round my classmates. It was now the English summer of 1994. These 'leavers' books' were our nineties version of Facebook, except the 'page' was made of paper and the 'likes' and 'comments' were written in pen. My friends filled my book with farewell notes, drawings and Nirvana song lyrics. Two months earlier Kurt Cobain had shot himself in the head. Many of my mates were still grieving. I lost the book years ago but there's one entry I'll never forget. An anonymous contributor took up a whole page, drew a large square and wrote underneath: 'This is how I will always remember you'.

Dork, nerd, geek, square; I've been called them all. I tried hard to be cool and popular but I was always one step off the beat. I didn't even know who Cobain was until I read his obituary in *The Times*. Sure, I had plenty of friends. But I always felt like I was on the edge of the group. I didn't belong. When I was seventeen, I found solace in alcohol, the Englishman's antidote to social awkwardness. Drinking didn't make me cool but after four or five pints I didn't care. What began with sipping Guinness and shooting pool in country pubs turned into all-night bingeing at friends' eighteenths and drunken joyrides through sleepy Norfolk villages. And then when I was bored of that, I went clubbing.

Never has something promised so much and delivered so little as the nightclub. I hadn't danced since those Sunday evenings in front of Dad's record player—I couldn't wait to feel free once again, moving my body to the sound of the beat. The first club I went to was called Peppermint Park. It was located in a three-storey mock Tudor mansion in the backstreets of Norwich. The dress code for men was strict and conservative: a long-sleeved shirt, tailored trousers and leather shoes. As a result, the queue to get in resembled a bad catwalk show for Ben Sherman or Ted Baker. At the door, the bouncers looked like football hooligans and behaved like bullies. They often turned me away for no reason whatsoever. When I made it inside, things weren't any better. The drinks came in cheap plastic glasses and were criminally expensive. There were always three times as many men as women and fights were commonplace. At the end of the night, I left with beer stains on my shirt, cigarette burns on my hands and ringing in my ears.

I learnt two things at Peppermint Park. The first is that the purpose of clubbing in nineties England was to get pissed and 'pull' the opposite sex. I was very good at the former and hopeless at the latter. Second, club disc jockeys (DJs) deliberately played bad music to drive the pissed-off punters to the bar where the real money was made. Surely, only the most dedicated clubber can stay on the dancefloor when R Kelly's 'She's Got That Vibe' comes on for the fourth time in one night?

But then in 1996, my brother Neil arrived home one day with a pair of decks, a mixer and a stack of 12-inch vinyl. Whenever my parents went out, the house shook to the sound of trance anthems like 'Café Del Mar', 'I Can't Help Myself' and Robert Miles's 'Children'. My friends James and Leon were DJs too, playing New York house classics from Masters at Work and Todd Terry. It wasn't the first time I'd heard this music. I remember sneaking away from my homework to dance to 'Theme from S-Express' on *Top of the Pops* when I was ten years old. But this time it was different. When I listened to nineties house and techno music it was as though I had awakened the six-year-old child cocooned inside. I loved it. It was magical.

Whatever Happened to Rave?

Brian Behlendorf, internet entrepreneur and technical guru behind the Burning Man festival held annually in the Nevada desert, provides an old but still useful definition of rave:

> In general practice, a 'rave' usually refers to a party, usually all night long, open to the general public, where loud 'techno' music is mostly played and many people partake in a number of different chemicals, though the latter is far from necessary. The number of people at the event is unimportant; it can range from 50 people to 25,000 people … A large part of the concept of raves is built upon sensory overload—a barrage of audio and very often visual stimuli are brought together to elevate people into an altered state of physical or psychological existence.[1]

For a shy boy brought up in a Christian household, rave was both a horror and a seduction. I'd read all the newspaper headlines back in 1988 about the 'evil of acid house' and watched the pantomime of moral panic play out on TV. Not to mention hearing all those crazy songs on *Top of the Pops* with their bleeps, breaks and blatant ecstasy references. I loved the music but rave meant drugs. Drugs were bad. Therefore, I was bad. Even today, going out to a warehouse party or festival makes my stomach clench.

But rave also promised a sense of community, belonging and freedom of expression—ideas that intrinsically appealed to an outsider like me. From the safety of my teenage bedroom, rave looked and sounded like a reimagining of sixties idealism and hippie counterculture, something that resonated strongly having grown up listening to Dad's record collection of Dylan, Donovan and Joan Baez. Techno was folk music for the nineties, or so I thought, replacing lyrics with beats to protest against the ills of mainstream society and culture. Rave was what I'd been searching for. There was only one problem: I was five years too late.

In 1996, I moved to Nottingham to attend university. *Trainspotting* was screening at the cinema and with it came 'Born Slippy', Underworld's bleak and brilliant techno-homage to a crumbling society. At night, after a few beers at the Union bar, I'd return to my room, put on my techno and fall asleep. While my subconscious crossfaded the 4/4 beat into my alcoholic dreams, in real life rave continued to elude me. Clubbing meant commercial venues with cookie cutter names, fusty carpets sticky with lager and cheesy 'choons' chewed up and spat out of tinny speakers. As I stood at the bar, drunk, bored and a little bit terrified, watching short, skinny men with shaved heads trying to pick up or pick a fight, I wondered to myself whatever had happened to rave. Sure, I went to a few good clubs. I even had what one might call a near-rave experience in Coalville, a Midlands town as drab and industrial as its name suggests. Passion was loud, frenzied and thrilling but as I danced amid a throng of sweaty youth, I felt like a voyeur. I didn't see rave in front of me but instead its rotting carcass, pumped full of steroids and strapped to a subwoofer to give the illusion of life. Rave in England was dead, suffocated under a blanket of commercial genres, punitive laws and the hegemony of alcohol. An entire subculture that in later years would define my generation had passed me by. I felt a weird nostalgia for a time I'd never experienced, amplified by a music that evoked a thousand happy faces dancing in a field and having the time of their lives. It's hard to put this feeling into words; thankfully, I don't need to—just dim the lights, turn up the bass and put on Orbital's 'Belfast'.

After university, I got a job, met a girl, followed her to Melbourne, got married, quit my job, got divorced and had a premature mid-life crisis. I was thirty-two. It was thirteen years since I'd heard that echo at Passion of what rave might once have been like. I couldn't remember the last time I'd stepped inside a club. And my techno collection had shrivelled to two or three commercial trance compact discs (CDs) I used as backing tracks for my gym workout. Rave was a distant dream that I'd long ago given up hope of finding. And then I met Kim.

'A Big Playground'

'It was like a big playground, a crazy adventure.' Kim McClelland went to her first rave in Melbourne in 1997, the same year I went to Passion. The difference couldn't be starker. The Melbourne rave scene was at its peak. 'The rave scene blew my mind in every way possible,' Kim says. 'You'd walk in and there'd be thousands of people all doing their thing with no authority and no expectations. You could do what you want, say what you want, be who you want and stay up all night.' Kim says going to a rave in the nineties was like 'coming home'. A home where she belonged.

'As a kid, I was always different,' Kim tells me. When she was eight, Kim moved from Bangladesh to a small Victorian country town where she was bullied because of her skin colour and unusual accent. Her world changed when she attended an alternative school for years 11 and 12. 'Everyone had piercings or dyed hair and it was free dress so all these kids wore amazing clothes,' Kim recalls. 'So when I moved to Melbourne for university I was already on this pathway of individuality, music and creative expression. I was hungry for it.' The rave scene fed her appetite. She describes an 'intensely creative space' where people danced in crazy outfits and when walking into a warehouse was like stepping into 'another dimension'.

For Kim and thousands like her, going to a dance party in Melbourne during the nineties was a monthly or weekly ritual that, for a few precious hours, allowed them to be free. Free from a society whose adult, conservative and mainstream values jarred with their youthful ideals for a better world; free from a system where an individual's worth was measured only in terms of his or her capacity to produce and consume; and free from a culture where the rich and the beautiful gained exclusive entry while the disadvantaged were left queueing behind the velvet rope. Rave became a sanctuary for society's outcasts. They called it PLUR: Peace, Love, Unity and Respect. Regardless of age, race or gender, people bonded through a shared love of all-night dancing and techno music. Rave celebrated individuality and free expression within a community of likeminded people. It was different, inclusive and beautiful. And above all, it was fun.

As I listened to Kim's stories, I realised she'd encountered exactly what I'd spent my teenage years searching for. I felt like I'd been cheated. While I'd been dodging the punches and the puke, getting drunk on cheap beer, and dancing to commercial shite in my school shoes, she'd tasted a euphoria I could only dream of and a freedom I couldn't imagine.

Techno City

Kim arrived late to the scene. Her friend Brewster B. had been there from the start, first as a punter and then as a DJ. Born in England, Brewster moved to Melbourne as a kid. With his baseball cap, piercing blue eyes and cheeky grin, he radiates a childlike fascination with the world that belies his fifty years. In 2013, he and his partner Cathy visited Kim and me while we were staying in a whitewashed village high in the Andalucían mountains of southern Spain. One night, as we sat under the stars eating tapas and drinking rioja, Brewster thrilled us with stories from the early days of Melbourne rave, spinning tales of clashing promoters, clueless police and crazy car park capers. I was enthralled. If Kim had struck a match on my skull, Brewster squeezed the bellows to get the fire roaring. Little did I know it then, but that night as I scribbled in my journal, I had embarked on a four-year journey into the Melbourne rave and techno scene. Through writing about rave, perhaps I could finally participate in a subculture that had evaded me for twenty-five years.

Back in 1984 when I was dancing in my lounge room, 10,000 miles to the south Brewster was bopping to italo disco at the Waltzing

Matilda Hotel in Springvale. He found the music fun, fluffy and lightweight but every once in a while he heard a record that 'pushed the envelope' and tweaked his interest. One night in 1987, he chatted to DJ Peter Mac in the booth. Peter told him about Mandate, a club in St Kilda where the DJs played 'really interesting' music. That night after Peter had finished his set the pair drove up the Princes Highway, parked the car on Carlisle Street and climbed a flight of steps above a shop into two knocked-together Edwardian apartments. 'I walked into Mandate at three in the morning with Peter and I'd never been in a club before where you couldn't fucking see!' Brewster says. 'It was so much smoke from a smoke machine and a strobe that you couldn't see more than a couple of inches in front of your face.' But his real problems began when the smoke cleared. Everywhere he looked, topless men surrounded him. Of course the clue had been in the club's name but Brewster had been too naïve to prise the two syllables apart. 'I thought I'd stumbled into some kind of gay bondage den,' he tells me. 'I completely freaked out. I'd never really met a homosexual man before. In the 'burbs of Springvale someone wouldn't be openly gay.'

Peter led the panicked Brewster to the DJ booth. Safe from the terror of the dancefloor, Brewster marvelled at the strange new sounds emerging from the speakers. Since the sixties, gay clubs around the world have led the way in playing innovative electronic dance music. Melbourne was no exception. 'It was like early acid stuff and house,' Brewster recalls:

> It was DJ Pierre and early Trax records. There was also stuff from Mantronix, 'Male Stripper' by Man 2 Man and 'Jack Your Body' by Steve 'Silk' Hurley. It was all much more four-to-the-floor than italo disco, the kick [drum] was very prominent.

As Brewster walked out the door, he knew it was time to wave goodbye to Springvale. The underground beckoned.

'More than fashionable or trendy, "underground" sounds and styles are "authentic" and pitted against the mass-produced and the mass-consumed,' Sarah Thornton writes in *Club Cultures: Music, Media and Subcultural Capital*.[2] But it's more than being subversive; it's about doing it in secret. Members of the underground, she explains, revel in being 'in the know': a thrilling and enviable sensation that they are part of something that is inaccessible to others.[3] The underground is like that childhood den or pack of cigarettes that no-one else knew you had. Underground music is difficult to find and its success is driven primarily through live playing as opposed to extensive radio airplay or television appearances. But while members of underground subcultures often practise unlawful acts such as taking recreational drugs, committing petty crime, and illegally occupying private property, it's not the law but the media they fear most. At any moment, television, radio or newspaper coverage could expose their precious scene to the dreaded 'other': in this case, the 'normal' or the mainstream.[4] As a result, undergrounds are fluid and contested spaces because what is underground today will inevitably become commercial tomorrow. In Melbourne, the underground occupies the inner city. One-time terrain of the working-class, by the seventies, middle-class kids were exchanging the neat green lawns and Sunday barbecues of their parents' suburbs for the grit and thrill of a post-industrial landscape.

The Melbourne rave scene evolved against a backdrop of a city undergoing significant social change. Formerly the manufacturing capital of Australia, by the late eighties, global economic restructuring had taken its toll. A recession in the early nineties compounded the misery, bringing a dip in economic confidence and a rise in youth unemployment. All of a sudden, a generation of young Melburnians saw their future disappear before their eyes. With little hope of job security or career progression, some looked elsewhere for fulfilment. Ironically, they found it in the abandoned factories and warehouses that once would have offered the employment opportunities they now lacked. Swapping tools for techno, they transformed these symbols of industrial decline into temporary nether realms of pleasure, places where the outside world could be momentarily forgotten. Bringing together homegrown talent and international influences, Melbourne's first acid house parties appeared in the summer of 1988–89. A decade later, rave had fizzled out in England but Melbourne kept the flame alive. Somehow, dance music, once the preserve of gay men and ethnic minorities, had overrun a rock'n'roll town. The scene even developed its own dance style: the Melbourne shuffle. On New Year's Eve 1999 over 20,000 ravers arrived at the docks to greet the new millennium. It was the largest ever rave in the southern hemisphere. The scene looked unstoppable.

But as the new millennium dawned, something had changed. For some, the scene had come of age. For others, it was a time to mourn the loss of innocence and accept that their big playground was a secret no more. Both groups agreed on one thing: they could never go back.

Get Ready

Techno Shuffle is an argon laser cutting through the mists of nostalgia for those who were there, and a cosmic voyage of discovery for the uninitiated. It's a tale that links three decades of American and British dance music history with Melbourne's own rich legacy of underground music and culture. A story that starts with a dozen people dancing in a shed and finishes with Melbourne Bounce and a billion hits on YouTube. Perhaps your only prior experience of this strange subculture is an occasional scare story in the media or an early morning encounter with a brightly dressed and sun-dazed raver trying to find their way home. Or maybe you are a member of today's EDM generation, for whom nineties rave is but a distant myth, a hazy phenomenon from the past that can only be interpreted by listening to 'old skool' techno or watching video clips of Mongolian teenagers shuffling in a car park.* Whatever your story, I invite you to come on a journey with me. We've waited a long time. It's time to come home.

In writing this book, I've tried to capture an authentic record of events, not a pre-recorded mixtape of well-worn myths. But trying to patch together a story from fragmented and conflicting memories that are a quarter of a century old is difficult. No two persons' truths are the same. Having not personally lived through the Melbourne rave scene frees me from the temptation to focus on my own experiences that undoubtedly would have been one-sided, disjointed and parochial. Instead, I have drawn much of the material for this book from interviews with people who were there. Some of them became multimillionaires while others were left penniless, damaged and broken. Together, they are the voice of the Melbourne underground.

Thank you for your patience. Get out your glowsticks, pull on your phat pants and sprinkle the baby powder on the floor. No dickheads please. If you listen hard, you can hear the music. We're going back, right back. Are you ready?

---

*   In this book, electronic dance music means all forms of electronically produced dance music—this can include, but is not limited to, disco, house, techno and trance. 'EDM' also stands for 'electronic dance music', although in this book EDM refers specifically to a commercial and often highly produced style of dance music that became popular in the US in 2012 and has since become a global phenomenon. See Chapter Ten for a more detailed discussion on EDM.

Chapter 1

DANCING QUEENS

This is Disco

Greenwich Village, New York, 21 June 1969. A dozen police officers are trapped inside the Stonewall Inn after a raid gone wrong. Out on the street, an angry rabble throws beer bottles and bricks that break the windows and bounce off the barricades. With each hurl, the Stonewall Inn's clientele of gay men, lesbians and drag queens unwind decades of oppression. Three men uproot a parking meter and thrust it like a battering ram against the door. The crowd swells and when backup police arrive, the scene deteriorates into a riot. Unable to sleep for the noise, local residents stand on their stoops and stare.

    A few doors down on Christopher Street, an after-hours underground gay haunt called the Haven throbs to a soundtrack of intense rhythm and blues and funky rock. There's no break in the music, just a barrage of wrist-pumping, body-shaking records. The man responsible for this rhythm overdose is a young amphetamine-fuelled Italian-American called DJ Francis Grasso. Out on the dancefloor, his disciples rejoice in the freedom to be themselves, twisting and jiving to a music that sings their joy and howls their heartache. This is what the Stonewall rioters are fighting for. This is disco.

* * *

Disco is the thread that ties sixties New York to nineties Melbourne. I don't mean the cheesy retro-rubbish that has you making letters above your head at your uncle's wedding. I mean *real* disco, born of hippie idealism and mixed with the angst of a generation that had grown up not only with Stonewall, but also Martin Luther King and the Vietnam War. 'Disco was the revolution,' Bill Brewster and Frank Broughton write in *Last Night A DJ Saved My Life*. 'Disco was secret, underground, dangerous. It was non-blond, queer, hungry. It was emancipation.'[1] But this freedom was temporary. As the disco tribe poured out of underground clubs into the cold morning light, they returned to a world that cast them as degenerate and undesirable.

The first discothèques had sprung up in cellars and subterranean taverns in occupied Paris during World War II. These discothèques often played jazz, which the Nazis despised as *Negermusik* (Negro music). 'To run a discothèque in wartime Paris was to participate in an act of civil disobedience,' Brewster and Broughton write. They continue: 'The discothèque's lasting reputation as a place where outlaws gathered was sealed in smoky basements in occupied territory.'[2] In seventies New York, gay and African-American minorities reinvented the discothèque as their own refuge from straight, white society.

The Disc Jockey, the Refugee and the Orphan

Prior to the Haven the DJ's role had been little more than a jukebox with a human face. DJ Francis changed all that. These days, synchronising the drumbeats between one track and the next to create the illusion of a single unbroken song is one of the first techniques any aspiring DJ learns. In the early seventies, however, beat matching was fiendishly tricky given the complexity of mixing live drumming: programmable drum machines and sliding pitch controls were still a decade away. Yet DJ Francis relished the challenge, as writer Matthew Collin explains:

> [He] would layer the orgasmic moans from Led Zeppelin's 'Whole Lotta Love' over a heavy percussion break, cutting the bass and treble frequencies in and out to heighten the energy level, segueing from soul to rock then on into hypnotic African drums and chants.[3]

DJ Francis matched his mastery of the decks with his immodesty. 'Nobody mixed like me,' he told Brewster and Broughton, '[n]obody was willing to hang on that long. Because if you hang on that long, the chances of mistakes are that much greater. But to me it was second nature. I did it like I walk my dog.'[4] DJ Francis bequeathed two gifts to dance music: beat-mixing and the egomaniac DJ.

DJ Francis persuaded the Haven's owners to install a stereophonic sound system and the world's first stereo DJ mixer. For these innovations, he owes a debt to Polish émigré and Holocaust survivor Alex Rosner. Around 1971, Rosner sold one of his sound systems to a shy Puerto Rican called David Mancuso. Raised in an orphanage in upstate New York, Mancuso recalls how Sister Alicia profoundly influenced his musical journey when she would put on records for the children to sing and dance to.[5] In his twenties, he hosted underground dance parties at his Greenwich Village home (known as The Loft) playing little known records from his eclectic collection of psychedelic rock, Afro funk, Latin and soul. In contrast to DJ Francis, Mancuso eschewed tight mixing and technical tricks in favour of letting the music tell a story or create a mood.[6] His parties were invitation-only and alcohol free, bringing together gays, straights, blacks, whites, poor and rich in an intimate environment where longstanding social and racial barriers faded away.[7] By 1977, The Loft had spawned dozens of copycat discothèques throughout New York's five boroughs. One of them, a former truck garage in the Hudson Square district of Manhattan, became the empire of Mancuso's most talented and ultimately tragic disciple: the inimitable Larry Levan.

Dirty Disco and the Velvet Rope

The Paradise Garage is the ancestor of all modern dance clubs and Larry Levan, a heroin addict who died of heart failure at thirty-eight, inspired a generation of DJs. At the Garage, patrons fucked on the dancefloor, indulged in a plethora of drugs and drank the acid-spiked punch.[8] And all the time watching over them was Levan, ready to churn them up or wind them down with his twists, turns, peaks and drops. A black, gay man playing to a black, gay crowd whose enthusiasm for hard drugs and sex almost matched his own, the Paradise Garage was New York underground 'dirty disco' at its finest.

Levan (born Lawrence Philpot) redefined the DJ's role even more than DJ Francis and helped cement dance music as a credible genre. Every Saturday night from 1977 to 1986, Levan played 'disco, soul, gospel, rock, reggae, European electro-pop [and] even German *kosmiche* synthesiser epics like Manuel Göttsching's *E2:E4*—all sixty minutes of it'.[9] Whereas earlier DJs had played album tracks, Levan took advantage of the newly available 12-inch single format that offered extended playing time and better sound quality—ideal for the dancefloor. He set a standard for taste making, mixing, remixing and set building that few have surpassed. Many of his remixes remain classics to this day: tunes such as the disco anthem 'Is It All Over My Face' by Loose Joints and Skyy's 'First Time Around'. 'He really was an engineering genius as far as sound was concerned—they even have speakers named after him,' Paradise Garage co-owner Mel Cheren told Collin. 'He was brilliant. He wasn't an easy person but most artists aren't.'[10]

In New York in the late seventies, Paradise Garage was the place to go if you were African-American, gay and male; for everyone else, it was Studio 54. For young hedonists hell-bent on having a good time Studio 54 was like heaven, except harder to get into. It was the place to be seen and the scene to be part of. Studio 54 was bigger than Paradise Garage, with brighter lights, better sound and more commercial music; Gloria Gaynor's 'I Will Survive' became a club favourite after it was 'discovered' by resident DJ Richie Kaczor.[11] 'Studio 54 was nice, but it was really for the uptown, glitzy crowd,' DJ François Kevorkian told Brewster and Broughton.[12] In the balconies and alcoves, busty waitresses and bare-chested busboys plied celebrities with champagne and cocaine. The managers enforced a notoriously elitist and brutal door policy, setting a precedent for pretentious dress codes, power-tripping bouncers and velvet ropes that persists to this day. When I was nineteen, I queued for two hours in February snow outside a Nottingham nightclub wearing nothing more than a dress shirt and trousers only for a bouncer to turn me away because I wasn't handsome or rich enough. For this humiliating and potentially life-threatening experience, I can thank Studio 54.

For the disco purists sold on Mancuso's vision of acceptance and inclusion Studio 54 was too much. 'It was the beginning of disco becoming a business,' journalist Vince Aletti told Brewster and Broughton. 'I think it was destructive to have a velvet rope. It was completely against the idealism of disco and the community of disco.'[13] I see Aletti's point but can't help thinking that blaming the velvet rope for disco's demise is a sleight of hand. Mancuso's parties at The Loft were similarly exclusive, if not more so, given they were invitation-only. Perhaps instead this is an early example of a disgruntled old skool purist reacting to losing their secret underground scene to the mainstream. Yet things were about to get much worse.

From Night Fever to Fever Pitch

The early disco sound embraced a wide range of black music styles, including soul, funk, rock, Motown, and rhythm and blues. Disco as its own distinct and marketable genre didn't emerge until the release of *Saturday Night Fever* in 1977. If Studio 54 turned disco into a 'business', *Saturday Night Fever* made it a multi-million-dollar industry. Starring John Travolta and featuring music from Australian pop group the Bee Gees, the surprise global box office smash propelled disco into the public consciousness. The film's portrayal of white heterosexual youths seeking escape from their dreary suburban lives through dancing is admittedly some distance from disco's black, gay, underground roots. And yet this seems to be dance music's unavoidable destiny, as Matthew Collin explains:

> Black and gay clubs have consistently served as breeding grounds for new developments in popular culture, laboratories where music, drugs and sex are interbred to create stylistic innovations that slowly filter through to straight, white society.[14]

I suspect Collin uses *straight* in both senses of the word here: heterosexual certainly but also straight-laced, conservative and mainstream. No longer restricted to underground Manhattan clubs, disco had jumped the East River and landed in picket-fenced suburbia. Musically it had shifted too; gone were the soulful vocals and lushly orchestrated backing tracks, replaced with a four-on-the-floor beat and chauvinistic undertones. The revolution was over.

Freedom had been won. It was time to don a chest wig, wear a lime green shirt and make triangles in the air to 'YMCA'.

By 1979 a commercial and cheesier flavour of disco had taken over America's airwaves, charts and dancefloors. Eurodisco, also known as Hi-NRG, Euro pop or simply Euro, delivered a manufactured sound using synthesisers and drum machines in place of acoustic instruments. The definitive Eurodisco record is Donna Summer's 'I Feel Love', released in 1977 and produced by Italian Giorgio Moroder and Englishman Pete Bellotte. Summer was a black woman but the sound is unmistakably white.

But not everyone succumbed to the night fever. For God-fearing, rock-loving Middle America, disco was the devil's music. The hatred and hysteria reached fever pitch in July 1979 when Detroit DJ Steve Dahl organised a 'Disco Demolition Derby' at Chicago's Comiskey Park baseball stadium. Mobs of disco haters blew up 10,000 disco records and rampaged onto the field.[15] Chicago DJ RA Feutz was there:

> People were only charged a dollar to enter the park if they brought a record for the demolition. It was supposed to be a double-header game. Obviously the second game was cancelled due to the destruction and mayhem.

Author Simon Reynolds compares the scenes at Comiskey Park to the Nazi book burnings of 1933.[16] Witnesses observed white fans burning not just disco records but any black music.[17] Disco's brief reign was over and rock music reclaimed the ears of the American public. Yet dance music would have the last laugh. Six years after Comiskey Park, Dahl's hometown of Detroit gave birth to techno, a genre so far removed from traditional notions of musicality that if disco was rock'n'roll's bastard child, techno was Frankenstein's monster.

Ten thousand miles away in Melbourne, it was as if Comiskey Park had never happened. This will not surprise Australian readers.

We're used to inheriting the world's cultural cast-offs long after their sell-by date. While the vinyl popped and smouldered on a Chicago baseball field, Melbourne's disco explosion was about to ignite.

The Kings of King Street

New York, 1979. A young Greek kid from Melbourne's western suburbs waits in the queue for Studio 54. Behind him, a seemingly endless trail of people stretches along West 54th Street and around the corner onto 8th Avenue. He's spent the day at the Billboard Music Conference watching Larry Levan tear it up on the turntables. Now, wearing a knitted shirt and brown leather pants, Sam Frantzeskos is dressed for success. He approaches the bouncers, grins broadly and starts to chat. Whether it's on account of his boyish good looks, the not-from-round-here brogue or the high-profile company he's keeping, Sam passes through the velvet rope and into the pleasure zone. It's like nothing he's seen before. Multiple levels filled with illicit alcoves and bacchanalian balconies; huge lighting rigs hanging from the ceiling; and wave after wave of smooth raunchy disco floating above a sweaty sea of flesh. We're not in Footscray any more.

Hollywood has given us two templates for the nightclub boss: the villainous gangster with ties to the Mob or Mike Myers's sleazy portrayal of Studio 54 founder Steve Rubell in the 1998 film *54*. Sam Frantzeskos fits neither stereotype. The black curls of his youth are long gone but the wide smile and piercing eyes remain. Currently a respected Melbourne restaurateur, Sam is warm and self-assured. When we meet in 2015, he talks candidly with the air of a man who has nothing to hide. 'Studio was a game changer for me,' he tells me as we sit watching the Yarra wend its way around Herring Island. 'As soon as I walked into that place, I said to myself, "this is what I want to be doing."'

In 1976, Sam and brother George got their first break in the Melbourne nightclub industry when they bought Peanuts Gallery from Brian Goldsmith 'for just a few lire and the kiss of [his] ring'.[18] Peanuts occupied the basement of 459 Swanston Street in the city. After seeing Studio 54 in New York, Sam knew he had to find a larger venue to accommodate his vision. The brothers approached entrepreneur George Nelson Frew who offered them the old Commodore Hotels head office building at 60 King Street. 'When we opened Inflation Nightclub [in November 1979], technology in this industry had grown so much in a short time that we brought in a three-watt argon-neon laser,' Sam tells me. 'We also imported two holograms and dressed our female lighting operator in this glam silver jump suit with a headpiece and goggles.'

Peanuts had a single Thorens belt-driven turntable; the DJs announced the songs during the pause between tracks while they changed the records over. Having seen beatmixing in New York, Sam knew the Thorens had to go. He imported two direct drive Technics turntables (probably SL-1200MK2s) and a Citronics mixer and then instructed his in-house DJ, Noel Russell, to learn beatmixing. 'Before you knew it, every DJ on their night off would come and see Noel mix records,' Sam says. Noel and fellow DJs Peta Tollic and Paul Minchell played commercial disco in the Studio 54 vein. Yet Sam knew it was about more than just the music; the whole experience mattered. He hired Avairs Cizevski to build him a sound system. 'Not great in retrospect, but at the time it was pretty good,' Sam admits. Avairs also installed moving isolators, infinity walls and 500 pinlights. Sam based the interior design for Inflation on New York, New York, a club that soaked up the almost-beautiful and not-so-famous turned away by Studio 54. '[New York, New York] was a brilliant three-storey concept and since Inflation was also a three-storey building, it made the inspiration easy,' he explains. The main dancefloor was in the basement while the upper floors contained a café, private function rooms and a video lounge.

A few doors down from Inflation, Brian Goldsmith had opened Underground in a century-old bluestone factory in 1977.[19] *The*

Age credits Brian with having 'practically invented Melbourne's nightclub scene'.[20] While Sam looked to the New York underground music scene for inspiration, Brian chose the London Underground (aka the Tube) for his. 'There were lots of railway references,' says Timmy Byrne, who began his DJing career at Underground in 1980 and later became resident DJ:

> There was an old red carriage in the middle of the place. The front part of it was the DJ booth where the driver or guard would go and the rest of it was set up for fifteen to twenty people to have dinner in there.

Underground became a renowned celebrity hangout where Brian hosted people like Rod Stewart, Liza Minnelli, Harry Belafonte and John Travolta. 'Brian's wife was Rona Newton-John, Olivia's sister,' Timmy says, 'so, you had that sort of calibre of people coming through the venue.' Not to be outdone, at Inflation Sam entertained Grace Jones, Bette Midler, George Michael and the rock band KISS. It was all very decadent. Photographer Rennie Ellis visited Inflation in 1980. His images reveal a lost era of suits, furs, breasts and buttocks on the dancefloor.[21]

Today, King Street is lined with offices and fast food joints sandwiched between strip clubs and tacky bars. It's a 24/7 precinct catering for the overworked and oversexed corporate male during the week and the heavy-drinking working-class man at the weekends. Inflation lingers on although nowadays it markets itself as an 'Entertainment Complex', whatever that means. In the late seventies, however, King Street looked very different: quiet during the day and desolate at night. 'That area was the warehouse district ... it was the dark city part of town,' Sam says. 'Because it wasn't a brightly lit area, it meant that people could come dressed up.' In the seventies, most Melburnians had little time for black culture, whether of the homegrown Aboriginal kind or the imported African-American variety. And while thankfully the Melbourne Cricket Ground was never tainted with the acrid smell of burning vinyl, disco was still a dirty word for the mainstream crowd. Sam knew he had to safeguard his finely feathered patrons inside and outside the club. Whatever he did, it worked. 'We were just kids from the 'burbs living a fucking dream,' he says.

Italo Disco and the Melbourne 'Wog'

While Giorgio Moroder was busy taking over America's airwaves in the late seventies, back in his native Italy producers and DJs were cutting their own records because they couldn't afford expensive imports. Italo disco, as it became known, relied on drum machines, synthesisers and overdubbed English vocals to make experimental music with a pop music sensibility.[22] Originally intended for the local dance music scene, italo disco found an eager export market in Germany, Spain, France, Scandinavia, Japan, Canada, the United States (US) and Australia.[23] Writer Dan Sicko describes italo disco as the 'missing link' between disco and new wave in the US. When the US government lifted trade restrictions on importing records in 1980 disco-starved DJs and dance music audiences 'devoured' the new sound.[24]

'Italians and Greeks started disco in Melbourne,' Dominic Tenuta, co-founder of Snoopy's Discotheque in Brunswick, told *The Age* in 1986. 'They liked to dress up and show off. The Anglos were always in the pub and when they came here all they did was start fights.'[25] By 1982, 'Italian Disco Nights' had become the 'vogue' for Italian-Australian youth in Melbourne.[26] British-born Brewster B. felt like a minority whenever he went nightclubbing in Melbourne's southeastern suburbs:

> The music at discos in Melbourne in the early eighties was italo disco. A good eighty per cent of the crowd were Italians and Greeks. It was almost a turf war mentality within these clubs … the Anglo Aussies on one side of the club and the

Greeks and Italians on the other. We wouldn't cross to the other side of the dancefloor.

These Italian and Greek kids were the children of refugees who had fled post-war Europe in the fifties and sixties. The Australian government, at that time worried about the 'Asian invasion' from the north, pursued an aggressive immigration policy dubbed 'Populate or Perish'. When British immigrants failed to arrive in the requisite numbers, southern Europeans became the 'non-preferred' but 'have to have' alternative; they weren't 'quite white' but they were 'white enough'.[27] But not everyone agreed. Some of the Anglo-Irish majority called the new arrivals 'European refuse' or 'wogs'.[28]

Nineteenth-century British colonialists used the term 'wog' to vilify people of Arabic and Asian backgrounds. The word is possibly a contraction of 'western oriental gentleman' or 'wily oriental gentleman'. Australian diggers picked up the term from their British comrades in the trenches of World War I and brought it back home.[29] According to Greek-Australian actor George Kapiniaris, wog was a 'killing word', a reason to fight.[30] Melbourne's Italian, Greek and Yugoslavian communities were already marginalised from mainstream Australian society due to their higher rates of unemployment, lower paid jobs and poor English language skills.[31] Wog hardened these divisions. Stereotypically, the sons of southern European migrants drove 'wogmobiles', played 'wog ball' [soccer] and danced at 'wog clubs'. In Melbourne, the disco became a refuge for Mediterranean youth much like it had for gay men in New York a decade earlier.

Yet again, the marginalised 'other' had pioneered new forms of dance music. While young Greeks and Italians brought italo disco to the forefront of the Melbourne nightclubbing experience, another ostracised group found their own revolution in Hi-NRG and its derivative dance-pop. By the early eighties, Hi-NRG had become the 'lingua franca' of white gay dancefloors the world over.[32] Melbourne was no exception.

Hedonism and Heartache

For many in Melbourne's gay and lesbian community, the seventies was a time they'd sooner forget. Michael Hurley writes of unsolved murders, raids on bars and 'beats' and frequent police harassment.[33] Prominent gay or gay-friendly clubs in the late seventies included Pokeys at the Prince of Wales in St Kilda, Chaps and Babes at the Chevron in Prahran, the University Club on Collins Street and Sweethearts (later Mandate) on Barkly Street, St Kilda.[34] Venues advertised via word of mouth or the lesbian and gay street press. To gain entry into some venues, you had to knock or buzz and wait for a slot to slide open and a pair of eyes to check you over.[35]

On 24 June 1978, the Gay Solidarity Group organised the first Mardi Gras parade in Sydney to commemorate the nine year anniversary of the Stonewall riots.[36] The police attacked some revellers and arrested fifty-three.[37] The subsequent printing of the names, addresses and occupations of those fifty-three by the *Sydney Morning Herald* triggered marches and protests around the country, including in Melbourne.[38] The following June, 3000 people attended the second Gay Mardi Gras parade—this time without violence or arrests. While it lacked the gravitas of a Stonewall moment, it demonstrated that the mood was changing. In January 1981, the Victorian government decriminalised homosexual acts between consenting adults. And although the stigma of being queer did not disappear overnight—the Australian Medical Association kept homosexuality on its list of illnesses until 1984—gay and gay-friendly venues could now advertise more openly. In the seventies, gay nightspots had been scattered all around the inner city. From 1980, however, venues began to consolidate into two distinct gay and lesbian 'precincts': one in Collingwood and a larger hub centred on Chapel Street and Commercial Road in Prahran.[39] Never one to miss a beat, Sam Frantzeskos started a gay night on Wednesdays at Inflation in 1981. 'We brought the gays from south of the Yarra … No gay night had ever worked in the city. Later on they did. But we were a straight club doing a gay night.' Until one night in 1983 when suddenly, it wasn't any more. "'Fuck off you AIDS-infected faggot" was how the new door policy was communicated to me by the door staff when I arrived ready for a good night,' Chris Gill writes on Facebook. 'I never went back.'

The first reported case of AIDS in Australia was in Sydney in 1982. At that time, the disease was known as gay-related immune deficiency (GRID) or gay cancer. Andrew Peter Collins was a prominent DJ in the Melbourne gay scene during the eighties:

> In 1980, we were buoyant and enthusiastic ... We had the straight community behind us, we were finally getting out of that homophobic rut that was the seventies. It didn't last. By the mid-eighties, we were pushing shit uphill against the religious right, the politicians and the homophobes ... it's such a shame. To think what might have been if HIV had never happened.

Melbourne experienced its first AIDS-related death in 1983. In 1987, 523 people contracted HIV in Australia and 290 died the same year. 86 percent of the victims were gay or bisexual men.[40] Until the widespread availability of combination antiretroviral therapy in the mid-nineties, an HIV diagnosis was akin to a death sentence. Very few patients survived longer than two years. Hundreds of men died—sons, lovers, brothers and dear friends. Kim's uncle, schoolteacher Ken McClelland, was one of them. Ken had served time in Pentridge prison after police arrested him in his classroom for resisting the Vietnam War draft. One of Gough Whitlam's first acts when he became prime minister in 1972 was to free Ken and six fellow protestors.[41] In the eighties, Ken turned his attention to the growing AIDS crisis. A 'stalwart' and courageous campaigner, he set up the first teams of carers for AIDS sufferers north of the river.[42] Ken died from AIDS-related complications in his Northcote home in 1992, aged forty-seven.

The Alternative Lifestyle Organisation (ALSO) had been established in Melbourne in 1980 to address the needs of ageing gays and lesbians. The AIDS crisis suddenly gave the organisation a new impetus. ALSO issued media releases and held community meetings to counter the inaccurate statistics and misinformation emerging from the mainstream press.[43] They also raised funds to support AIDS victims and their families. For over a decade, the organisation's most lucrative fundraiser was the dance party.

Red Raw and Winter Daze

Australian history seems to place the birth of the gay dance party at the 1980 Mardi Gras post-parade party and subsequent Recreational Arts Team (RAT) parties at Sydney's Hordern Pavilion.[44] However, Michael Hurley reports that almost all of the national homosexual conferences between 1975 and 1983 ended with a dance.[45] In Melbourne, church halls and reception centres in South Yarra and St Kilda had been hosting regular 'camp dances' since at least 1969.[46] David (surname withheld) tells me he attended a Jackaroos party in 1979 in a condemned four-storey building on Flinders Lane. He had recently moved to Melbourne from the country. 'I remember they played disco music,' he says. 'It was quite an eye opener!'

In December 1982, ALSO threw its first dance party, called Raw Hide, at a warehouse in Little Grey Street, St Kilda. Seven-hundred men dressed up as cowboys for the all-male party.[47] In 1984, Raw Hide became an annual event on the Australia Day weekend in January. Two years later, ALSO partnered with the Victorian AIDS Council to launch a second dance party, called Winter Daze, on the Queen's Birthday weekend in June. The parties featured live shows and big budgets. One year, the organisers flew in international pop star Grace Jones.[48] Martina Navratilova attended the 1988 Raw Hide in a West Melbourne warehouse, just hours after winning the Australian Open women's doubles final with Pam Shriver.

Andrew Peter Collins played at dozens of ALSO parties along with Debbie Walters and Sydney disco legend Stephen Allkins. 'We weren't educating the crowd with new material,' Andrew tells me. 'We played whatever was current in the clubs ... we kept the music all girly and wonderful.' In 1989, the DJs earned $100 each ($200 in today's money) for an all-night shift. Today, superstar DJs can command up to $300,000 per set, even if some of them spend half the time watching football on their iPhone.[49] But back then it wasn't about the money. Some wouldn't even take it: 'I'd seen friend after friend die from HIV,' Andrew says. 'I refused to be paid because I had a conscience.'

In 1989, Raw Hide became Red Raw. By now, the parties were attracting almost 3000 patrons. ALSO added an annual New Year's Eve party and the Women's Own Warehouse party to its busy social calendar. Finding bigger venues to accommodate the growing crowds became an ongoing challenge for Geraldine Kirby's team of organisers. Between 1982 and 1992, ALSO used at least thirteen different locations for the parties: four warehouses in South Melbourne; Station Pier and the Melbourne Film Studio in Port Melbourne; Festival Hall on Dudley Street; a shed on the Maribyrnong riverfront in Footscray; and three different warehouses in what is now Docklands. ALSO furnished each venue with stages, bars, toilets, dancefloors and gender-exclusive 'fuck rooms'. While it meant extra work for the organisers, the excitement of exploring a new venue each time became part of the attraction.

By the late eighties, dancing all night to electronic dance music appealed to heterosexuals, as well as the usual clientele of gay men, lesbians, bisexuals and transgender people. ALSO welcomed straights' dollars but cautioned their attitude. One Red Raw flyer spells out 'Party Correct' and 'Party Incorrect' behaviour, the latter including 'Straight men trying to pick up women', 'Straights being sleazy' and 'Straight couples bonking'. The bottom of the flyer reads: 'Remember that ALSO parties celebrate lesbian and gay pride, not sexual liberation for everyone'.

In his book *Pleasure Consuming Medicine*, Kane Race argues that the gay dance party made a political statement of resilience and possibility:

> The massed bodies, decorations, lights, drugs, costumes and music combined to produce a powerful and widely accessed perception of presence, belonging, shared circumstance, and vitality at a time when the image of the gay man, dying alone, ostracized from family, was the publicly proffered alternative.[50]

Dance parties in the AIDS era engendered a mindset of living in the moment: have fun now because this could be your last time. My interviewee Marcus (surname withheld) exemplifies this attitude. He partied 'heavily' from 1975 to 2001, the first eleven years in London and from 1986 onwards in Melbourne. 'What happened with AIDS is that we became even more hedonistic,' he tells me over coffee. He sees in my face it wasn't the answer I expected. 'You name it, I've done it,' he laughs. Marcus attended pubs, clubs and private parties but it was the dance parties that lit up his social calendar: 'you wouldn't miss a Red Raw or a Winter Daze.' In 1998, Red Raw attracted a crowd of 6500, its largest ever.[51]

As the parties grew, they became more difficult to run. The organisers relied on unpaid helpers; without them, the overheads were prohibitive. But each year, the volunteer base shrank. 'HIV made such a dent in the number of talented people,' Andrew Peter Collins says. 'So many were dying or burning out ... those of us who were left were like slaves hauling pieces of marble to build the pyramids.' Andrew tells me they received little support from the straight dance music scene where people weren't dying of AIDS but were mortally afraid of it. 'People didn't want to work with poofters,' he says bluntly. By 2001, labour shortages and falling profits led the organisers to outsource the parties to an external events management company.[52] The format had outlived its role as a fundraiser but retained symbolic value for the gay community. Red

Raw lasted until 2007. Three years later, ALSO disbanded.

The dance party not only mobilised the Melbourne gay scene during a challenging period but it also became a first-rate prototype for rave. Many of my interviewees cite Red Raw and Winterdaze as important influences. The ALSO parties pioneered all-night dancing to electronic music in Melbourne and taught future rave promoters the value of attracting a mixed crowd and finding a new venue for each party.

The Six O'clock Swill

Alcohol had always made an appearance at the dance party. However, much of the twentieth century had been one long hangover from a powerful temperance movement that had held sway over Australians' drinking culture from the 1880s to the 1960s. In 1916, during World War I, the Victorian government introduced six o'clock closing for all hotel bars (it had previously been 11pm). Pro-temperance campaigners concerned about the impact of drink on the working classes leveraged wartime concerns about drunken soldiers and the patriotic need for self-sacrifice to win support for early closing.[53] The *Australian Christian World* claimed God had allowed the war so that 'Australia might realise the necessity for cleaning up the moral hearthstone'.[54] Interestingly, the 'moral hearthstone' only applied to the working class; those who could afford their own cellars or drank in private clubs were exempted from the rules.[55]

Each day, working men poured out of their offices and factories at five o'clock and indulged in an hour-long alcoholic binge at the nearest hotel before retreating to their suburban homes and housebound wives. It was like an evening with Don Draper compressed into sixty minutes. They called it the 'six o'clock swill'. John Brack's 1954 painting *The Bar* brilliantly captures the mood: a sour-faced barmaid stands with her back to a throng of grim middle-aged men downing schooners of beer. Journalist John Larkin recounts the experience:

ankle deep at 5.30pm in a morass of cigarette butts decomposing in slopped grog, a howling thirsty mass crawling over each other to demand fifteen beers each to drink in the last, desperate guzzling minutes.[56]

The term 'swill' was no accident; contemporary media compared the scenes to hungry pigs feeding at a trough.[57] In contrast to the farmyard scenes at the pub, dancing was typically a sober affair. Almost all of the discotheques at that time, venues like Bertie's, Sebastian's and the Thumpin' Tum, were unlicensed and open to all ages.[58]

By the sixties, the rise of commuting by private car meant the six o'clock swill wasn't just anti-social, it was lethal. In 1964, its supporters finally conceded that 'the hours of sale did not determine the quantity of liquor consumed; only the conditions and manner in which much of it was consumed'.[59] Two years later, the Victorian government ended fifty years of early closing when it extended regular trading hours until 10pm and permitted music venues to apply for a 3am cabaret licence. This was the era of Melbourne's first licensed nightclubs, places like Whisky A Go Go with its go-go girls in cages and satanic orgies on stage,[60] and a few suburban pubs with a 'disco' attached at the back. 'The nightclubs back then were very glamorous,' Brewster B. remembers. 'They all had raised dancefloors with handrails, flashing lights and parquetry flooring. It was all quite lush.' But the cabaret licence came with conditions, as Sam Frantzeskos explains:

> The cover charge for the entertainment was actually disguised as a food charge. You had to charge $3 or whatever and then you had to give [your patrons] a roast chicken and mash or fish and chips. Many ordered and ate the food but most didn't, leaving some dollars over to pay for the talent and security.

Further relaxation of liquor licensing laws in the eighties meant that many nightclubs could serve alcohol until 7am. Social engineering was out, the free market was in, and dancefloors everywhere became saturated with booze.

'Alcohol and Plenty of Sex'

Melbourne, February 2015. I ring the bell at Sean Kelly's apartment and his partner opens the door. 'He'll be ready in a few minutes, he's just getting up,' she tells me. It's 11am. She smiles and reads my mind. 'He still keeps nightclub hours.' Sean stopped DJing in 1989, but it seems the habit is hard to kick. His lounge room betrays the tell-tale trappings of having spent countless nights behind turntables: unidentifiable audio equipment in the corner, shelves of neatly stacked vinyl against the wall and a faint trace of nicotine in the air. As I strain to read the titles on the record sleeves, Sean appears, coffee in one hand, cigarette in the other. These days he's swapped DJing for day-trading; where once he played New York disco now he plays the New York stock exchange. My eyes wander around his spacious and beautiful home and I tell him they don't make apartments as big as this anymore. 'This was built in the early nineties,' he replies. 'It was one of the first apartments in the CBD.'

Melbourne hasn't always been a 24-hour city. Until the late eighties, the central business district was, as its name suggests, a bustling paean to Mammon in the daytime and practically a ghost town at night once the shops and offices had closed. In 1982, the city centre had 685 dwellings, compared to almost 30,000 in 2010.[61] In 1983, the central business district had two kerbside cafes; in 2016, Melbourne averaged ten coffee machines per city block.[62]

In 1980, Sean worked the bar at Inflation. He says straight clubbing in the eighties meant social drinking and picking up:

> You had different crowds but principally people went out to be friendly because the drug of choice was alcohol. So you'd have a few beers, you'd meet somebody and you'd go, 'What

are you doing tomorrow night?' It had a really heavy social angle to it … it was alcohol and plenty of sex.

At venues like Inflation and Chasers, artists and socialites clinked champagne glasses and snorted cocaine with fashion designers and Patrick Bateman stockbroker types flying high on a decade of glamour and greed. According to Sean, 'It was a music scene, it was a dance scene, a fashion scene. It was haircuts, photography, models.'

The eighties heralded the golden era of nightclubbing in Melbourne. In 1986, the Frantzeskos brothers sold Inflation and began work on a new club that would dwarf its competitors in size, cost and ambition. When the Metro opened in the former Palace Theatre on Bourke Street on 25 November 1987, it was Australia's first superclub. Sam hired celebrity architects Biltmoderne to transform the old theatre.[63] The redevelopment cost $10 million. 'In the design sense, what we actually built was superior to anything Studio 54 had,' Sam explains. 'We had the best architects, the best designers, we had the best people putting together a magnificent nightclub.' The lighting alone cost $1 million dollars and included fifty moving lights, a ten-watt argon laser and a robotic lighting rig that moved above the dancefloor. And then there were the numerous bars, VIP rooms and metres upon metre of velvet rope.

The Metro represented a new breed of clubbing that became the de facto Saturday night entertainment for a generation of Melbourne youth. Commercially oriented from the outset, throughout the eighties and nineties, Metro hosted fashion parades, MTV broadcasts and live music including dance music heavyweights The Prodigy, Chemical Brothers, Moby and Fatboy Slim.[64] But things didn't get off to a great start. The venue's 7am licence and superclub status attracted much attention, some of it unwelcome. One night, MTV filmed live from the club. Some parents watching at home recognised their underage children on the screen. 'I think the powers at hand wanted to make an example of us and so they sent about forty coppers in on a Saturday night "Gestapo style" to check IDs,' Sam tells me. 'They bolted the doors, turned on the cleaning lights and turned off the music. Out of nearly 2000 people they found eleven underage girls, all with false IDs.' The Liquor Licensing Commission tried to close them down just a week before Christmas. Sam and his partners successfully defended the charge but the damage was done: 'Channel 7 had publicised it pretty badly ... we lost a million dollars in revenue and then had to spend a ton of money to relaunch it.'

But the Metro had other enemies too. Its dazzling lights and glitzy decor could never seduce the Melbourne underground.

Chapter 2

PUNKS AND PINEAPPLE HEADS

Little Bands, Big Sound

St Kilda, December 1978. A southwesterly blows in off the bay, whooshes through the palm trees in Catani Gardens and buffets the crumbling mansions along Fitzroy Street. Everywhere is boarded up or closed, except for the fish and chip shop that sells heroin under the counter. Out on the street, the junkies share the cracked footpath with the drunks and prostitutes who call St Kilda home. On the corner of Grey Street stands the Seaview Hotel, formerly the George. In the late nineteenth century, the George had been Australia's finest hotel, serving the wealthy and the fashionable who sculpted St Kilda into their playground by the sea.[1] Now the hotel, like the suburb around it, was slowly withering away, like a ragged dowager clinging to the coat tails of her former glory.

On this cool summer night, a stream of young men and women climb a short flight of steps and head upstairs to the Crystal Ballroom ('the Ballroom'), a gilt-edged hangover from the hotel's Victorian heyday. The wooden floorboards creak and groan under a raucous capacity crowd. On the stage, a band plays angsty guitar-driven noise that rises above the cacophony of clinking glasses and chattering voices. This is definitely not pub rock. Instead, they call it punk.* Skinny art school students mingle with platinum blondes in fifties' ball gowns while mods in op-shop suits hang out with mohawked men, butch feminists and retro hippie chicks. These disenchanted middle-class kids mix alcohol and speed with over-the-counter cough syrup, antihistamines and 'effies' (pseudoephedrine). Meanwhile in the blood-spattered toilet cubicles, patrons inject coffee, LSD and heroin into their veins. Anything goes at the Ballroom. Anything, that is, except being mainstream. Welcome to the Melbourne underground.

A few miles away on Nicholson Street in North Fitzroy, the Primitive Calculators live in a converted shopfront next door to Whirlywirld, a four-piece led by Ian 'Ollie' Olsen and John Murphy. All day, people shuffle in and out of the Calculators' front room, forming bands on the fly and rehearsing with borrowed guitars, keyboards and synthesisers. Musicianship is by no means essential; what is more important is the willingness to try. Performing at venues like Fitzroy's Champion Hotel, Richmond's Tiger Lounge

---

*   Many writers refer to this period as post-punk, not punk. For example, Ian Andrews and John Blades write: 'The energy of punk, instead of ending in abrupt failure in 1977 ... opened up a range of musical possibilities, creating a large audience to new experiences—at least it did in Australia, and in many other parts of the world. This explosion of musical ideas after punk, roughly between 1978 and 1984, is generally known as post-punk.' (2009, pp. 36–37). However, David Nichols tells me nobody used the term post-punk until the nineties. At the time it was punk and then later new wave.

and the Ballroom, these 'Little Bands' (as they become known) play one or two short gigs before they are forcibly dismembered and reconstituted.[2] The bands' names are as inventive and confrontational as their music: Too Fat to Fit Through the Door, Jimmy Haemorrhoid and the Piles, Child Molester +4 and Thrush and the Cunts to name but a few. As night falls, the musicians and their hangers-on sit together in the Calculators' overgrown backyard. They smoke, drink and watch the sun set over a rust-red collage of iron rooftops, brick chimneys and dirty factories.

In the late seventies, Melbourne's inner north was a gritty, working-class district. A few years later, local residents would feel the suffocating squeeze of gentrification as economic restructuring robbed them of their jobs and replaced their workplaces with trendy warehouse conversions.[3] For now, however, the inner city still belonged to them. The Little Bands scene naturally gravitated towards this edgy urban milieu on the Yarra's northern banks, colonising tumbledown sharehouses in Richmond and Fitzroy. Richard Lowenstein's 1986 film *Dogs in Space* opens a window into this world of white punks, self-imposed communal squalor and heroin overdoses.[4]

And yet, on the other side of the river it was a different city. Stately elms screened the mansions and tennis courts of the old rich, the descendants of merchants and squatters who'd built their homes on the high ground here to escape smog and soot. These privileged suburbs were anathema to the punk scene and divisions soon emerged. Rowland S. Howard attended the Swinburne Community School in Hawthorn, a 'tiny school of 100 misfits'.[5] At sixteen, he was playing guitar in pioneering punk band the Young Charlatans with Ollie Olsen. Two years later he joined Nick Cave's band the Boys Next Door. Howard's song 'Shivers' is one of the scene's most enduring anthems and today he's lauded as a hero of the underground. A laneway in St Kilda even bears his name. But back then it was different. Shortly before his death in 2009, Howard recalled how territory became a weapon in the battle for the underground: 'the people in the Boys Next Door weren't welcome over the other [north] side of town,' he said. 'We were seen as phoneys and rich kids.'[6] Musician Philip Brophy also felt the venom of the North Fitzroy set when they accused him and his band Tsk Tsk Tsk of being rich kids from the 'other side of the river'. 'I come from fucking Reservoir!' Brophy exclaimed in the *We're Livin' on Dog Food* documentary.[7] Pronounced Rez-er-*vaw* or simply Rezzie by the locals, Reservoir was, and just about still is, a working-class suburb in Melbourne's north. It's a world away from the private school bastions of Camberwell and Kew that Brophy's accusers were probably alluding to. It seems that many wanted to claim the underground for their own, excluding everyone else. Fifteen years later, the rave scene would be no different.

Despite the rivalry, the punk scene coalesced around a core ethos. Firstly, it was aggressively do-it-yourself (DIY), sticking its middle finger up to the music industry with one hand while cashing a dole cheque with the other. 'What made that scene possible in Melbourne in the late seventies, more than anything else, was the legacy of the Whitlam government,' Calculators frontman Stuart Grant explained:

> They made the dole liveable. There were probably thousands of people all over Australia living on the dole and making up bands … it was like an arts grant.[8]

Meanwhile, freedom from the capitalist machine brought independence from the music industry and separation from mainstream society and culture. Musicians embraced 'anti-stardom anonymity' and shunned 'bloated musical overproduction'.[9] Finally, the scene was disposable in that the short-lived bands made very few recordings. If not for the fractured memories of those who witnessed it, it's almost as though punk never existed at all. Perhaps that's how they intended it—a unique phenomenon that occupied a narrow wedge of space for a thin slice of time. DIY, independence, disposability: these were punk's generous gifts to the Melbourne underground. However, I doubt anyone could have predicted punk's immense influence a decade later when the rave train came to town.

By the end of 1980, Melbourne's punk explosion was fizzling out. The Little Bands scene dissolved in 1981, dislocated and demoralised by drugs, drink and destitution.[10] The Boys Next Door waved goodbye to the Crystal Ballroom and flew to London. As The Birthday Party, Howard, Cave and bandmates Mick Harvey and Tracey Pew enjoyed commercial success selling the sound of the Melbourne underground to the world. Whirlywirlders Ollie Olsen and John Murphy also headed to Europe but followed a different flight path. Inspired by their shared fascination of electronic music and the increasing affordability of synthesisers, they formed a new project in Berlin. The name was Hugo Klang and the sound was techno.

'It's Basically Techno'

St Kilda, January 2015. I'm sitting in Ollie Olsen's housing commission bedsit gazing out through a long, narrow window that frames a postcard panorama of Luna Park and the St Kilda foreshore. Ollie tells me he was lucky to get this flat; just a few months ago, he'd been homeless. I'm shocked. Underground doesn't pay the rent. Tall and animated with a booming voice that bounces around his tiny flat, Ollie seems like a prized eagle trapped inside a birdcage. Next to my chair, there's a bird's nest of coloured wires and twiddly knobs that I correctly guess is a synthesiser. It's a habit Ollie can't give up. 'I have a freeform improvisation band called the Taipan Tiger Girls,' he explains. 'It's drums, guitar and me playing synthesiser and we improvise … I've gone back to my roots with electronic music.' Those roots have nourished the many branches of the Melbourne underground for the last forty years.

Ollie grew up in Norway and Melbourne. In 1975, he enrolled in an electronic music course at the Council for Adult Education (CAE) under the instruction of German avant-garde composer, Felix Werder. 'Werder studied with [Karlheinz] Stockhausen,' Ollie says. 'In fact, he was an enemy of Stockhausen's. They used to have terrible fights whenever they met up.' At the CAE studio, Ollie dabbled with analogue synthesisers like 'big Moogs' and the EMS VCS3, the same machines that psychedelic rock pioneers Pink Floyd, Hawkwind and the Byrds and had been using since the late sixties. He also studied *musique concrète*, a form of composition developed by French electroacoustician Pierre Schaeffer whereby an artist splices and rearranges pieces of magnetic tape to manipulate sound. Unable to afford a real synthesiser, Ollie built his own using Schaeffer's techniques:

> My father had bought this old tape recorder. I used to make a lot of pieces by cutting up tape and creating sounds, creating feedback loops, and recording feedback, creating oscillations, making the tape player feed back internally, and basically building my own synthesiser in a way, but out of collage.[11]

Australia has a rich legacy of experimental electronic music innovation dating back to 1945 when Percy Grainger developed his first 'Free Music' machine, a precursor to the analogue synthesiser.[12] In 1979, Kim Ryrie and Peter Vogel built the world's first digital sampler, the Fairlight CMI, which changed the sound of popular music.[13] Ollie drew on this electronic tradition with his early punk bands The Reals and Young Charlatans, but with Whirlywirld he shifted one step further into the unknown: 'I've always been interested in dance and music ... I loved disco even in the punk era. So, with Whirlywirld we started to use disco beats and basslines.' At the time, dance and disco were dirty words for 'serious' musicians but Ollie persevered nonetheless. For Hugo Klang, he upgraded his cassette recorder to a Roland TB-303 bass synthesiser and a TR-808 programmable drum machine. Combining his 303 sequences and 808 loops with John Murphy's live drumming and Alan Bamford's 'quasi-sampling', Ollie realised he'd stumbled upon a whole new sound.

'It's funny because when I hear the Hugo Klang stuff now, it's basically techno,' Ollie says. 'What we were doing is very close to acid house.' I'm intrigued and so I naïvely ask him where I can find it on YouTube. He smiles, shakes his head, ferrets around in a drawer and then hands me a home-recorded CD with 'Hugo Klang Live' scrawled on the front in black pen. He warns me that the two recordings, a live-to-air performance on Melbourne radio station 3PBS in March 1983 and a gig at the Trade Union Club in Sydney the following month, have poor sound quality. Unperturbed, I take the CD and think about how, in our present age of digital abundance, there is something thrilling about hearing music that can't be found at the click of a mouse.

Hugo Klang is genre-defying music filled with repetitive talking loops and cacophonous metallic noise interwoven with Ollie's gruff shouting, high-pitched wailing and vaguely political messaging. It's not easy listening. But beneath the vocals one can hear a dark, brooding electronic beat fortified with kick drums, crashing high hats and acidy bleeps and gurgles. At around eighty beats per minute (bpm), Hugo Klang lacks the danceable rhythm of modern techno, but speed it up, pare back the vocals and I'd dance to it. One track in particular, 'Mad Bakes the Problematic Head', seems a decade ahead of its time with its trancey crescendo, syncopated breakbeat and a trumpet thrown in for good measure. Ollie is right. It *is* basically techno.

Ollie wasn't the only ex-punk to experiment with electronic music in the eighties. Many avant-garde and post-punk bands integrated electronic music into their style, including Melbourne's David Chesworth (Essendon Airport) and Philip Brophy (Tsk Tsk

Tsk) and Sydney's Severed Heads. Industrial and noise groups were also early adopters of emerging electronic music technologies. Citing Whirlywirld and the Primitive Calculators as influences, Sydney band SPK blended electronically generated noise with subsonic rumbles and power tools to produce an extremely loud and 'genuinely evil' sound.[14] After Hugo Klang, Ollie too embraced the industrial and noise aesthetic, first with Orchestra of Skin and Bone and later with No. Critic Ian McFarlane praises No as the 'ultimate crossover act' on account of its 'confrontational fusion of hardcore energy, abrasive heavy metal guitar riffs, electro-funk beats and acid-house grooves'.[15] But the new sound didn't appeal to everyone. Producer Josh Abrahams recalls seeing No at the Prince of Wales in St Kilda in 1988:

> It was one of the few times that music has made me feel physically sick. It was so loud, it threw me against the back wall of the room. It wasn't loud in a clean way like techno can be; it was really all high mid-frequencies and Ollie screaming like a demon on stage. It was overwhelming. I stuck around for about half a song.

Ollie's experimentalism was a twisted thread in the finely woven tapestry of underground subcultures and inventive styles that evolved during the eighties. To take us into this world of crazy hairdos, fearless fashion and bleeding edge music, we need a time-travelling tour guide, somebody who was there from the start and saw it all. Enter Mad Rod.

The Professor of Nightclubbing

Melbourne, August, 2014. I'm at Lounge on Swanston Street, sipping a mineral water and waiting for Mad Rod. I'm nervous. Mad Rod is part of Melbourne's techno establishment; he ran Club Filter right here at Lounge for eleven years, making it Melbourne's longest running techno night. As I lose myself to the hyperspeed world of squabbling voices in my head, a tall and striking man approaches, dressed from cap to boot in Melbourne black. As soon as he smiles, my anxieties filter to nothing. Rod (he's dropped the 'Mad' nowadays) is warm, effusive and very talkative. His speech is uncensored, his mannerisms exuberant and his attitude positive and spiritual. The second time we meet, he gives me a miniature bronze Ganesh to watch over me as I write. I still can't decide whether it's a good luck charm or a hidden surveillance camera.

For Rod, the underground is not simply one's taste in music or clothes; it is a way of life and a state of mind in which one identifies with the alternative, champions the counter-cultural and rejects the mainstream:

> The underground is the supporter of the underdog, the alternative creative lifestyle people and the cultures they have helped to create and foster ... I am from the underground ... I live my life underground always.

Born in sixties St Kilda to 'bohemian type' parents, Singtoh Roddajun-Dogon was never going to be a normal kid. 'I'd been interested in electronic music since I was very young in the early seventies,' Rod says. 'Coming from a family with an arts background, I would listen to it at parents' houses and parents' friends' houses.' After exhausting the stock of 'BBC Doctor Who type records' at his local Coles supermarket, Rod scoured the shelves of Melbourne's independent record stores, places like Greville Records in Prahran and Collector's Corner on Swanston Street. He tells me he became an amateur distributor of experimental and 'extreme' electronic music, filling record store crates with rare and unheard imports. When I press him for examples, he cites the Krautrock-inspired noise of Einstürzende Neubaten or the early industrial sound of Throbbing Gristle:

> It's that really heavy mechanical sounding electronic music that could be made from not necessarily machines but from

> smashing a car. I went to this thing in Berlin in the eighties and there were these people running around with chainsaws hitting shopping trolleys and you had to get the fuck out of the way or you would have been killed. It was amazing! These guys were running around naked with flour all over themselves. It was avant-garde. It was industrial.

Rod attended the St Kilda Alternative School, an institution that prized experiential learning and student self-motivation over rules and regimentation. But even being able to smoke at your desk and wear make-up to school wasn't enough to rein in a free spirit like Rod. By his early teens, he'd traded in his formal schooling for an education from the underground:

> My first job was in a nightclub when I was thirteen. I worked as a cloakroom person, sometimes on the door, later behind the bar ... I am the product of a nightclub school. I am the professor of nightclubbing with many, many qualifications.

In the late seventies, Rod descended further into Melbourne's underground. He tells me he went to 'bizarre little venues' in disused houses and warehouses in Prahran, St Kilda, Fitzroy, Collingwood and the CBD: 'There were little clubs and bars and stuff from '79 to around '84 ... you had to know people there or you weren't getting in.' The city might have appeared empty to office workers heading home at 5pm but many of the laneways and fire escapes back then led to artists' squats, underground performance spaces and illegal clubs.[16]

Rod went to Mandate when it still had prison-themed decor, reflecting the then illegal status of homosexual acts between consenting adults. 'You'd hear the most incredible underground electro disco and see the most crazy, spectacular bizarre things like sex on the dancefloor ... and I'm just a really young teenager going, "Fuck! What's this?"' For a young man with a refined taste for the weird and eclectic, Rod had stumbled into his own personal heaven. He watched the Melbourne underground of the eighties evolve into a hive of intense creativity:

> Melbourne had these amazing subcultures. You could go to one club and it would be full of New Romantics or pineapple heads, people with huge hairstyles and all this intense make-up; and then you'd go elsewhere and there'd be some punk rock thing happening and then some gay sleazy disco thing going on somewhere else and then some really, modern, futuristic thing happening all in the space of one night … Melbourne was like a bad New York; bad as in good.

While these subcultures differed from each other in terms of fashion, philosophy and style, their willingness to experiment with new forms of electronic dance music bound them together. In the eighties, Melbourne's graffiti-strewn walls shook to the sounds of New York dirty disco and italo disco, New York electro à la Afrika Bambaataa, the English new wave synthpop of Depeche Mode, Human League and Soft Cell, and the proto-techno of Kraftwerk and its German industrial descendants. 'Of course, people had their niches', Rod says. 'But they crossed over. After all, a party's a party.'

Down at Inflation, it didn't take Sam Frantzeskos long to tap into the new zeitgeist. In 1982, he opened Blitz on Monday nights. Sean Kelly describes the crowd:

> Anyone who was in a non-nine to five job would go to Blitz night … New wave/New Romantic music brought in kids who were disenfranchised or not part of the mould because it gave them the scope to get dressed up … for these outcasts, Monday night became their thing.

The club's secluded location that had so impressed the gay disco crowd also suited the alternative kids. Inflation was still the coolest club in town. But a young man from the western suburbs had other ideas.

Sweltering Nights

Melbourne, October 2015. I'm chatting to Gavin Campbell in the open-air balcony at Cookie, high in the plane tree canopy above Swanston Street. Gavin is a survivor. A heroin habit in the eighties led to a 'spectacular fall from grace' in the nineties followed by a year-long stint in rehab. Yet here we are twenty years later and he's still DJing and releasing music on his own label. While others have burnt out, given up or died, Gavin is the proverbial grandfather who smoked and drank all his life and still lived to 84. He's shorter than I expected, with sunken eyes and a raspy voice.

Born in 1960 in working-class Footscray, Gavin is widely regarded as a founding father of Melbourne's club scene. In the late seventies, however, he preferred the St Kilda band scene, hanging out with the likes of Hunters and Collectors, The Reels and the Models. Gavin slowly developed a taste for dance music via 'daggy gay clubs' like Chaps and Babes at the Chevron and 'Eurotrash style discos with Top 40', of which Mickey's Disco was a prime example. Mickey's had a raised dancefloor with squares on the ground that lit up à la *Saturday Night Fever*. Gavin beams as he remembers:

> I [will] never forget the first time I went there ... I was walking through the club as 'MacArthur Park' was playing and as we stepped up to that lit-up dancefloor, the kick started and the song began. It was glorious.

Mickey's was located in the Sea Baths complex, a festering canker of seediness on the St Kilda seafront. Go to the Sea Baths today and it's hard to imagine its sleazy past amid the dull cafes, pricey restaurants and private gyms. And yet this architectural mishmash of Moorish domes and Spanish Mission parapets had once housed strip joint Whisky A Go Go and later hosted Bojangles nightclub where in 1987 Chopper Read shot and killed drug dealer Sammy Ozerkan.

Back in 1982, two of Gavin's friends started a club night

at Meridian, a 'shitty little disco' on the north bank of the Yarra, where Princes Walk is now. Paul Goldman and Brett Houghton were well known in the underground scene, having spun records to warm up crowds for The Birthday Party at the Seaview (formerly Crystal) Ballroom. The tiny club attracted a capacity crowd on four consecutive Tuesday nights until the owners shut it down. 'We were freaks and I think they must have got a little bit frightened,' Gavin says.

It may only have lasted a month, but Gavin couldn't get Meridian out of his mind. Lacking the funds or records to launch his own night, he asked his friend Craig N. Pearce to help him out. Craig obliged, found a venue and promptly installed Gavin as his door bitch: 'I was really grumpy about that because the club was my idea but I didn't want to miss out on being involved.' Swelter opened in September 1983 at Matilda's on the corner of Queen Street and Little Collins Street in the city. 'You'd have to go down into it,' Gavin explains. 'It was really atmospheric. No matter how sweaty it got, it was still cool, as in cold.'

Swelter was an instant hit. 'Swelter offers the best music of any new dance venue so far in Melbourne,' *The Age* declared just one month after it opened. 'The Motown and James Brown numbers mixed in with new black funk from England and the US make for a heady dance mix.'[17] Shortly after that review was published, Craig broke up with his girlfriend Andrea Treble and wanted to shut the club. But Andrea saw its potential and persuaded Gavin to keep it going. Following a two-week hiatus, they relaunched the club to a packed opening night in the summer of 1983. Meanwhile, Gavin had promoted himself from bouncer to DJ. Things didn't get off to the best start:

> On that opening night, I got on the turntables and I'm like, 'Oh my God, every song is so slow.' So I got them to ring the technician. The technician came all the way in from Frankston [40 km away] and just slid down the pitch

control and walked out. And I'm like 'there turntable, take that!' I had no idea what it was even for!

Gavin learned to DJ through trial and error. He believes that his focus on choosing the right songs to play in the right order set Swelter apart from the two-a-penny discos around town:

> The discos would just play one long stream of disco. It all sounded the same. There were great songs being played but not great nights of music where you became a fan of it. That's the sensibility that dance clubs like Swelter brought to the party.

Gavin's musical cravings left few genres unscathed. Every Tuesday night, he cued up Aretha Franklin and James Brown backed by Queen, Abba, Elvis Presley and—not forgetting his roots—the odd record from Hunters and Collectors or The Birthday Party. In using an eclectic mix of records to craft a story or create a mood, he was emulating the New York loft parties of his hero, David Mancuso. Gavin played non-stop for four hours from 9pm until 1am, which was the latest nightclubs could open in 1983. 'I felt like God,' he tells me. 'But by the end of the night I had a cracking headache because 45s only play for three or four minutes and so I was constantly changing records over.' I can't imagine God reaching for the Nurofen to treat a headache. But I *can* imagine Gavin up there in the booth, frenetically flicking through his record box and dropping discs onto the platter with a feverish Levan-like intensity.

Swelter attracted an industry crowd of designers, artists and fashionistas as well as a sophisticated gay crowd who Gavin says had grown tired of the 'girly music' on offer at commercial clubs. 'If you had dropped a bomb at Swelter and blew it up when it was a packed house, you wouldn't have a lot of the arts and entertainment industry in Melbourne,' he claims. Reporter Peter Wilmoth visited Swelter in March 1985:

The dress here is fantastic. More shoe-string ties, green and purple make-up, flowing evening dresses, boys in Western shirts and big, black coats with war medals pinned on them. Studded wrist bands. Cloth arm bands. Hair over eyes. Hair pushed back. No hair at all.[18]

Seditious Subterranean Beats

At its peak, Swelter pulled in close to 500 punters—not bad for a Tuesday. Gavin's success didn't go unnoticed. Sean Kelly had taught himself to beatmix while working at Inflation, practising in front of 'kids from Northcote' before the main DJs came on. After he unsuccessfully tried to take over Thursday nights, Sean and partner Mark Anderson launched Sedition in early 1985 at the Ballroom, by now renamed the Seaview Ballroom:

> A property developer had bought it and he had some young kids and the kids wanted to do something. So we met them and they said, 'Upstairs, we've got this huge ballroom. You guys can have it, we'll paint it, we'll fit it out, you take the door, we'll take the bar.'

Just a couple of years earlier, the Ballroom had witnessed the dying wails of punk. Now, its century-old floorboards bounced to the rhythm of high-energy beats two nights at week (*Beat* magazine founder Rob Furst ran a dance club on Saturday nights called Locomotion where Gavin DJed, among others).[19] At Sedition, the headliner was a young man named Guy Uppiah. Guy boasted an extensive collection of 12-inches from the disco era. When he left for London in the autumn of 1985, Guy left his records with Sean who promptly took over the decks. Due to liquor licensing constraints, Sean had to move the party from the Ballroom to the smaller Blue Room at 1am. Realising that Hi-NRG tracks wouldn't work in such a cramped space, he turned down the tempo and dialled up the soul:

'It would be Jocelyn Brown 'Somebody Else's Guy' ... it would be these beautiful soul tracks that were never anywhere near a radio.'

Sedition earned Sean $1000 a week for one night's work. More importantly, his profile in the Melbourne nightclub scene was on the rise. In October 1985, brothers Fab and Camillo Ippoliti invited Sean to run the music at their new club Subterrain (formerly Peanuts Gallery, later Industry nightclub) on Swanston Street. Prior to Subterrain, Fab and Camillo had managed Inflation for Sam and George Frantzeskos. With Sean and fellow DJ Warwick Purvis at the helm, Subterrain rapidly developed a reputation as the place to hear 'alternative' music from bands like Dead or Alive, Depeche Mode or The Cure. Sean expains: 'It was like, "I'm an isolated, alienated kid from the suburbs, this music appeals to me and now I can hear it in nightclubs" ... I became the weird DJ who played weird shit.' Things were about to get even weirder. In 1986, a young man from Adelaide introduced Sean to a crazy new sound called hip hop.

B-boys and Breakbeats

Much like any genre of popular music, hip hop wasn't really new at all. It had evolved from New York electro, itself a fusion of George Clinton-style funkadelica and the electrosynth krautrock of Kraftwerk. The title track from Kraftwerk's ground-breaking LP *Trans-Europe Express* had been a hit on New York underground dancefloors in 1977.[20] In 1982, Afrika Bambaataa and the Soulsonic Force reworked 'Trans-Europe Express' as 'Planet Rock', widely regarded as one of the earliest electro records. The song's 'science-fiction themed breakdance electro-funk' not only brought Kraftwerk to the attention of future techno producers (see Chapter Four), it thrust rap onto the world's music stage and paved the way for the hip hop phenomenon of the mid- to late eighties.[21]

Similar to rave, hip hop is not just a style of music, it's also a subculture. Its roots date back to the New York block parties of the early seventies when gangs of African-American youths gathered on the streets outside their homes. Hip hop's distinctive motifs originate from this 'block party' setting: the DJ, the MC, the sound system, rapping, breakbeats, graffiti and the b-boy (short for 'break-boy', as in breakdancing). Like fellow New York imports punk and disco, hip hop influenced the Melbourne rave scene significantly.

Hip hop culture had surfaced in Melbourne by the mid-eighties, most prominently in the graffiti domain, as 'writers' left their mark on trains, bridges and walls. In 1986, Sean Kelly started playing hip hop at Subterrain. The initial response was underwhelming:

> I started playing this hip hop stuff and it was all around 100bpm. LL Cool J's 'I Can't Live Without My Radio' is 89 bpm. To get someone to dance to that who'd only danced to 130 bpm was difficult ... it wasn't what they'd practiced at home.

Undeterred, Sean launched what he claims was Melbourne's first dedicated hip hop night on Thursdays at Subterrain. With a respectful nod to its New York roots, he called the club Harlem and hired writers to graffiti the sunken dancefloor. There was only one problem: Sean had about twenty hip hop records in his entire collection. 'I was playing album tracks, I'm not even waiting for 12-inches ... I didn't have enough material. There were four bands making the music.' Nevertheless, hip hop started gaining a wider audience in Melbourne. Chasers Nightclub opened its own hip hop night, Time Square, on Fridays. DJs Paul Siedle and Charlie Quay mixed in the latest cuts from Run DMC, the Beastie Boys and Salt-N-Pepa, in between scratching and rapping competitions. Back at Subterrain, Sean invited Gavin Campbell to guest DJ but it came with a condition: he had to learn to beatmix so he could mix hip hop into his sets. Gavin's new DJing skills couldn't have come at a better time. He was about to embark on a five-year journey that changed the Melbourne clubbing experience forever.

Razor Sharp

If you stop at the corner of Queens Road and Roy Street opposite Albert Park now, you'll find a knoll of unloved grass in front of black railings mounted with spear-like spikes. I like to think the sharp spikes are an ironic reference to the site's former use as Razor nightclub and not just a heartless measure from the local council to deter homeless people from sleeping in the park. We can but hope.

In 1986, Gavin Campbell had closed Swelter and was addicted to heroin. In an effort to go clean, he planned a road trip from New York to Los Angeles with friend Jules Taylor. Gavin knew Jules from the punk scene. She had played in several Little Bands, including Thrush and the Cunts. In 1983, Jules and partners Andrew Maine and Melbourne funk maestro Paul Jackson started an all-nighter on Friday nights at the Hardware Club, an 'old boys' men's club on Hardware Lane in the city. When Peter Wilmoth visited Hardware Club in 1985, he declared that patrons 'can rest easy that they are listening to the correct music, and talking to the correct inner city people and shopping at the correct second-hand American-wear shops in Greville Street'.[22] New York muralist Keith Haring painted the DJ booth and people had to bribe the door staff to get in.

'We started Razor to raise the funds for our trip,' Gavin says. 'We knew we were the coolest in town. Jules from Hardware Club, me from Swelter. Of course everyone would come. And then we'd just close it and go away.' Gavin and Jules approached the Light Car Club of Australia (LCCA), who owned a clubhouse at 46 Queens Road. Situated halfway between the city and St Kilda, Gavin pictured the beautiful Art Deco mansion as the ideal venue to soak up the Swelter and Hardware crowds and the St Kilda band scene. Like the Hardware Club, the LCCA had a 24-hour members-only licence that meant they could stay open long after other clubs were forced to shut at 3am. But most importantly, the club's members were desperate for cash. The LCCA ran the first Australian Grand Prix at Phillip Island in 1928 and organised six motor race meetings at Albert Park during the fifties, including the 1956 Olympic Grand Prix, won by Stirling Moss. Back then, the Albert Park race circuit included Queens Road. Perhaps seeking to secure a prime trackside location, the LCCA members moved their clubhouse to 46 Queens Road in 1961. But the Grand Prix had outgrown them and the race would not return to Albert Park during the LCCA's lifetime. By the time the Formula One World Championship took control of the Grand Prix in 1985 and moved it to Adelaide, the LCCA had become a debt-ridden anachronism.

Gavin knew about the club's financial troubles. Would the members be willing to hand over their treasured clubrooms to someone like him? Fortunately, luck was on his side:

> It just so happened that one of the girls behind the bar was listening in on the conversation and when we left, she said to the manager, 'The club they had before this, you had to bribe $50 just to get in and then pay to get in. You're going to make a lot of money if you do this on Friday nights for them'. So they rang us up and said yes straight away.

Gavin and Jules never took that road trip. When Razor opened on 10 October 1986, it became the coolest club in Melbourne and for five years represented the zenith (or should that be the nadir?) of the city's underground scene. Framed photographs of famous races lined the corridors and the rooms were named after champion drivers. Gavin and Jules hired art director Macgregor Knox and artist Siobhan Ryan to transform the members' dining room into a voodoo cave dancefloor. Every Friday night, they pulled up the curtains, rolled back the carpets and hung two-metre-high African masks on the wall. One of the masks looked like a Darth Vader head. 'He had red scanners in his eyes that cut through the smoke all night long,' Gavin says. 'He was the overseer of the dancefloor.' There was also a fur-clad devil with strobes for eyes and a voodoo lady with a Marge Simpson hairdo filled with flashing Christmas tree lights. 'The masks gave the dance room this incredible atmosphere ... we just had a cluster of mirror balls with pinspots on it, a smoke machine, a strobe and then these lights on the wall. Everything else was dark.'

Two floors above the dancefloor, the rooftop balcony stretched for the length of the building, with uninterrupted views of the park and the ocean beyond. The balcony was initially designed to provide a panorama of the Albert Park circuit (for the races that never eventuated). In the Razor era, the balcony hosted barbecues, band nights and a rooftop cinema, possibly Melbourne's first. 'We had a run of six or so really hot Friday nights,' Gavin remembers. 'We were screening *Robocop*. At dawn, the rooftop was still packed.' And because of the 24-hour licence, people partied well into the morning and watched the sun rise over Melbourne's leafy eastern suburbs. What a way to start the weekend.

At Razor, Gavin played disco, funk and soul. It was hard work. Playing four hours non-stop at Swelter was difficult enough but DJing until 7am was insane. So he brought in Paul Main and Tim Stammers to share the load. Tim had previously run an after-hours party at the University Club, a gay-friendly venue located on the seventh floor of a glass-fronted sixties office tower at 100 Collins Street (the building still stands but the club has long gone). A few months later, Gavin added Guy Uppiah, recently returned from London, to the Razor lineup. 'Eventually I realised what a shit hot DJ Guy was,' Gavin says. 'He was much better than me. But you couldn't tell him what to play. I never knew what was going to happen but it was always underground, really cool, black music.' Many other DJs claim to have played there, something Gavin firmly denies:

> There were four DJs at Razor and that's it ... that's how I always ran my clubs. I considered that if just one song was played that didn't belong then the night was ruined. I wasn't a purist but I didn't want to hear the shit that was played at Chasers or the Chevron.

In 1990, Gavin invited Paul Main and ex-Essendon Airport guitarist Robert Goodge to work with him on a remix of Yothu Yindi's 'Treaty'. One day Gavin had spotted a photograph of an Aboriginal ceremony with a Mushroom Records logo on it. He approached Simon Bayertz, Mushroom's head of A&R, to find out more:

> I knew straightaway what this meant because as a teenager I had a bit of a fascination with the dreamtime, I thought it was dark and mysterious … I said [to Simon] 'What about these guys? Who are they? Can we listen to something for a Razor remix?' and he said, well, the thing is, two albums have been made, and not yet recouped on what it cost to produce these albums, and that Mushroom wouldn't want me to remix this band … The walls went up. And so, I may as well say it now, I snuck the tapes out of the building.[23]

The original version of 'Treaty', reminding Prime Minister Bob Hawke of his 1988 promise of a treaty for Aboriginal people, had failed to chart. Razor's 'Filthy Lucre' remix toned down the protest element, brought in a disco backbeat and elevated Dr. Yunupingu's 'magical' Yolngu chanting to centre stage.[24] It peaked at number eleven in the Australian Recording Industry Association (ARIA) charts, becoming one of the earliest Australian-produced commercial dance music hits. 'Razor [Recordings] in 1988 was the first independent dance label in Australia,' Gavin claims. 'It was attached to the club and licensed to Mushroom … 'Treaty' came out in '91 but we made it in '90. We were flogging it at the club for six months before it was released.'

No Dickheads Please

It wasn't just the DJs who had a hard time getting into Razor. For the kids dancing to 'shit' at Chasers and the Chevron, Razor's velvet rope remained firmly in place. 'All I remember about Razor is that I was rarely allowed in,' says raver Nimmo Sandilands. His is a familiar story. Getting into Razor was a catch-22. You had to be a member but you could only apply for a membership card inside the club. That meant sweet-talking the door bitch, the glamorous and daunting Shaneen Allen. This was no problem for celebrities, industry types and interstate visitors. Everyone else, however, needed 'the right vibe about them'. I ask Gavin what the 'wrong vibe' was. He replies:

> Dickheads. Yobs. Bogans we call them now ... just people who were there only because it had a late licence. Later in Razor's life, a lot of Chevron types would come at 5am once it had shut and they wouldn't get in. But the staff would.

Gavin admits the members-only licence gave Razor the 'illusion of elitism'. But some weren't so easily deterred. One clubber tells me he gained entry by scaling the guttering and climbing onto the balcony.

Singer Kate Ceberano said one perfected the art of clubbing at Razor, a 'place where you practised flirting, drinking, dancing and socialising as an art form'.[25] Journalist Chris Johnston described Razor as 'a wonderland of celebrities, freaks, transvestites and fantastic music free from the tyranny of genre'.[26] Not everyone saw it that way. For Sid Sidney, admittedly a self-confessed Chevron type, once was enough:

> I went there and it freaked the hell out of me. It was too seedy, dark and dingy and there were too many Australian celebrities. There were all these stars you'd seen in films and I thought, 'What am I doing here?'

Razor's roll call of the rich and famous included Bono, Helena Christensen, Harry Dean Stanton (then in his sixties) and a highly inebriated Shane McGowan.[27] Stef (surname withheld) began working at Razor in 1989. He mixed cocktails on the rooftop and later looked after the pool tables, playing with the likes of U2 and

Lemmy from Motörhead. 'Razor was a pretty amazing club,' he tells me when we catch up in a city café in 2015. 'Anyone touring would come there. Michael Hutchence would walk in with Kylie and no-one would mob them or ask them to sign anything because everyone was too cool for school.' As well as the celebrity circus, Razor had its share of local characters. 'I met some really shady people on that balcony,' fashion designer Teresa Liano said. 'I'd just be like, "Woooah! Which hole did you crawl out of?" But that was part of the fun.'[28]

And yet for all its freaks, fame and fashion, it was the music that kept Razor rocking. Gavin first discovered house music in 1987. 'I was in the record shops all the time and I got all the early house records and threw them in when I could ... after a while, the house kind of took over Razor.' Sean Kelly also experimented with the new sound at Subterrain, which arrived just as he was running out of hip hop records to play. 'Thank God that house came along!' he laughs. And by God, he surely means Frankie Knuckles, the universally acclaimed Godfather of house music.

Chapter 3

PLEASURE SEEKERS

Move Your Body

Chicago, 1981, 1am on a Sunday morning. You're at an underground nightclub called the Warehouse. Situated two blocks to the west of Union station in the manufacturing district, you're literally on the wrong side of the tracks. Behind the decks stands Frankie Knuckles, a New Yorker who used to DJ with Larry Levan at SoHo gay club, the Continental Baths. Knuckles plays disco, soul and funk overlaid with thumping basslines, sampled black female vocals and a relentlessly pounding four-to-the-floor kick drum. His mixing is flawless, his track selection inspired. A thousand gay black and Latino men surround you, moving their bodies to the beat. The energy in the room is intense. It feels like the music is passing through your bones. You have six more hours before you suspend this alternative reality and face the outside world once more. It's time to knuckle down and dance.

'I had to re-construct the records to work for my dancefloor, to keep the dancefloor happy, as there was no dance music coming out!' Knuckles said in a 1997 interview. 'I'd take the existing songs, change the tempo and layer different bits of percussion over them to make them more conducive for the dancefloor.'[1] Knuckles edited and remixed records using a reel-to-reel tape recorder, much like Levan had done at the Paradise Garage. In 1984, he started mixing live TR-909 drum loops into his sets.[2] Although more technologically advanced than its older analogue cousins (the TB-303 bass synthesiser and the TR-808 drum machine), the TR-909 still produces a synthetic sound. This feature ensured its rapid obsolescence among pop music producers who sought a more authentic timbre but it was precisely the sound Knuckles was seeking. More than thirty years later, the TR-909 kick drum remains the definitive house music motif.

House music initially meant any music played at the Warehouse (hence the name). When Knuckles left in 1982, the owners renamed the club the Music Box and hired DJ Ron Hardy to take over. Hardy played his music loud and very fast, supposedly because when he was on heroin the music sounded slow.[3] Hardy's disciples developed a new form of freeform solo dancing called 'jacking' that simulated male fucking, thrusting and grinding. One could jack into a woman bent over, another man, a pole or even the wall.[4]

Under the stewardship of Knuckles and Hardy, house emerged as a new genre of dance music, a sexy and rhythmic reprogramming of disco, funk and soul. Like punk and hip hop before it, house was a DIY genre: anyone with the most basic gear could mix old sounds together to make something new. Along with the ubiquitous 909 kick, house music's most recognisable features include synthesised piano vamps, hissing hi-hats, handclaps and drum rolls.[5] In 1984, Jamie Principle recorded 'Your Love', one of the earliest house music releases. Released on Chicago's Trax Records, 'Your Love' seamlessly blends its unforgettable arpeggiated synth intro with a deep moody bassline and Principle's breathless singing. To me, it's the sound of the eighties.

House music crossed the Atlantic in 1986. Marshall Jefferson enjoyed UK Top 40 success with 'Move Your Body (The House Music Anthem)'. In January 1987, Steve 'Silk' Hurley's 'Jack Your Body' topped the British charts. That same month, presenter Alan Rados launched his new show 'House Music' in the wee hours of Sunday morning on Melbourne community radio station 3RRR. Rados's show and Paul Marinelli's Friday night program 'Dance Till Dawn' gave many Melburnians their first taste of house music. In all likelihood, both DJs sourced their vinyl from Central Station Records.

Central Station Records

In 1979, Italian migrant Giuseppe (Jo) Palumbo opened Central Station Records and Tapes in a tiny 'four metres by four' outlet in the Princes Gate Arcade, a strip of shops on the way down to platform 14 at the old Princes Bridge Station (where Federation Square is now).[6] He started out stocking Top 40 singles and albums but after a while, customers began requesting titles he'd never heard of.[7] As Jo enquired with his suppliers, he unwittingly stumbled into a legal minefield that would occupy much of his time, money and energy for the next two decades. In Australia, the big six major record companies (CBS, EMI, Festival, Polygram, RCA and Warner) weren't interested in catering to 'niche tastes' like electronic dance music.[8] 'The majors ... didn't want us to have dance music,' Jo wrote in 2017. 'They didn't get it. It was too gay, too woggy, too do-it-yourself and too new.'[9] Not only that, but copyright law permitted the majors to sue anyone who imported records that they (the big six) had not licensed for the Australian market. In the late seventies, that was most of the American *Billboard* Hot 100.[10]

Recall from Chapter One how 1979 was ground zero for Melbourne's disco explosion. As demand for US-pressed 12-inches intensified, Jo began importing directly from distributors in Miami and New York.[11] He sold his very first 12-inch to DJ Ken Walker. 'Jo and I became friends and I spread the word to other DJs,' Ken told Rell Hannah:

> The next thing you knew you had people queueing up to buy vinyl from him. The American and UK pressings sounded thirty or forty percent better than the local pressings.[12]

In March 1980, after the first of many legal challenges, Jo took the imports off the shelves and sold them under the counter or from the boot of his car, and only to trusted DJs and customers.[13] In between fighting lawsuits and relentlessly lobbying for copyright law reform, Jo worked tirelessly at growing his business. By 1982, he owned four shops in Melbourne: a dance music store on Chapel Street, a heavy metal shop called Metal for Melbourne on Flinders Street, and two stores in the City Square, one specialising in British 'alternative' music and the other selling dance music.[14]

In the early eighties, the City Square on the corner of Swanston and Collins streets was a vast grey concrete slab bookended by *Vault* (aka the 'Yellow Peril'), a giant yellow angular sculpture unloved by the public and scorned by the media.[15] The square also featured a graffiti board (where the water wall is now) and a marble area ('the Marble') where breakdancers would meet and compete. Promoter Richard Maher remembers the City Square as the 'heart' of Melbourne's emerging hip hop culture.[16] Jo sponsored breakdancing and DJing competitions in the square, bringing thousands of kids to the area and earning the respect of the council who welcomed any attempt to activate a place the public had rejected as 'barren, noisy and ugly'.[17] DJ Brewster B. was a regular visitor to the Square in the eighties:

> You used to be able to walk underneath what is now the Westin [hotel] and there was this big open arcade where the

shop was and loads of b-boys used to hang out there. It was this cool wannabe sort of space.

Melbourne was awash with dance music in the mid-eighties, thanks in part to the popularity of remix services like Disco Mix Club (DMC) that re-edited pop songs for the dancefloor. 'It'd be like ABC or Yazoo or something like that, and they'd just extend the intro and outro, cut out long bits of middle sections, the boring bits, and just make it more dancefloor friendly,' vinyl junkie Nimmo Sandilands explains. 'You had heaps of these agencies all around the world that were doing this kind of dance music.' Armed with bagfuls of the latest house cuts from Central Station, gay and gay-friendly clubs like Razor and Mandate gradually introduced Melbourne to the new Chicago sound. At first, Timmy Byrne wondered if house music was just another marketing label:

> The disco/dance music that I was buying sounded a lot like this music called house and I had some trouble getting my head around whether there was any difference between them ... and there wasn't really, it was only that the syncopated four-to-the-floor drum machine was right through house. But you could have the same tempo on a disco or dance release at that time yet it wasn't called house music.

In 1987, Central Station Records started publishing a separate house music chart as a supplement to its regular dance/disco chart. A few short-lived house music clubs opened during this period, such as Bauhaus at the Starwood Funk Club in St Kilda (run by DJs Paul Siedle and Nui) and The Drinkers Club at IDs Nitespot on Greville Street with John Course. But house rarely featured in *The Age* nightclub listings of the time. Not until it picked up a mischievous four-letter prefix.

Acid Trax

Acid house owes its existence to the misuse of a single piece of obsolete technology, our good friend the Roland TB-303 bass synthesiser. Designed to replace a bass guitar, the 303 has a one-octave keyboard and six knobs that control the pitch, resonance and other ways to manipulate sound. In 1985, Chicago musicians DJ Pierre, Earl 'Spanky' Smith and Herb Jackson tried to create a bassline to accompany one of Spanky's rhythm tracks.[18] This after all was the machine's intended purpose. But as they twiddled the knobs back and forth, the trio stumbled upon something altogether unexpected. 'No one [had] ever used this resonance control knob, which turns it from being like a normal bass sound into a squalchy [sic], filtered-type sound, which is the sound that it's become famous for,' Melbourne producer Steve Law told the ABC.[19] Recording as Phuture, DJ Pierre, Spanky and Jackson released their 303 explorations as 'Acid Tracks' in 1987.

English writer Simon Reynolds describes 'Acid Tracks' as 'somewhere between a faecal squelch and a neurotic whinny, between the bubbling of volcanic mud and the primordial low-end drone of a didgeridoo'.[20] Fortunately for Phuture and indeed for acid house, Ron Hardy at the Music Box was unperturbed by allusions to bowel movements, molten lava or mournful corroborees. He placed 'Acid Tracks' on high rotation—remarkable for a record that lasts eleven minutes and seventeen seconds.[21]

Ollie Olsen discovered acid house while working at Collector's Corner record shop. 'I thought the music was awesome ... it was Phuture's 'Acid Tracks', all the early Mr Fingers stuff, Tyree Cooper. It was fantastic.' Ollie says 'acid' is Chicago street slang for stolen music.[22] Tyree Cooper, on the other hand, claimed that acid house is 'just a name that fits because the music's crazy, it's weird and wired'.[23] Most people, however, will always associate acid house with drugs, a reputation no doubt enhanced by the Music Box's alleged practice of spiking the water with LSD.[24] And yet over in England, acid house fell in a love with another drug altogether, one that would come to define a new youth subculture.

The Love Virus

For a chemical that has caused so much contentment and controversy, ecstasy has disappointingly humble origins. In 1912, a group of German chemists developed 3,4-methylenedioxy-methamphetamine (MDMA) as an intermediate compound in their search for a new blood clotting agent. When World War I intervened, the chemists put their work on hold and MDMA lay forgotten for fifty years.[25] Then in 1966, Californian chemist Alexander Shulgin established a home laboratory to synthesise psychoactive substances.[26] It was the sixties after all. MDMA was one of over 150 'mind-altering drugs' he developed and subsequently tested on himself, his wife Ann and his friends[27]—Shulgin's zeal for scientific experimentation clearly didn't extend to the field of human ethics. Impressed by the heightened sense of emotional and empathetic connection that MDMA induced in his subjects, in 1977, Shulgin introduced the drug to his psychologist friend Leo Zoff. Over the following decade, American psychotherapists prescribed over half a million doses of MDMA to patients suffering from post-traumatic stress disorder (PTSD), drug addiction and 'marital difficulties'—the latter giving rise to the urban myth of MDMA as a marriage counselling drug.[28] In recent years, scientists have reaffirmed MDMA's efficacy in treating PTSD and believe it may also help autistic adults manage their social anxiety symptoms.[29]

MDMA proved too tempting to confine to the therapist's couch. By 1983, Texan clubbers could buy the drug legally over the counter in Dallas and Austin nightclubs.[30] The dealers branded MDMA 'Ecstasy' (or XTC) because they wisely thought it would sell better than 'Empathy'.[31] For centuries, worshippers of different faiths have exalted religious ecstasy, an altered state of consciousness that enhances spiritual awareness and is often accompanied by visions and euphoric sensations. If you've ever taken ecstasy, this may sound familiar. Ecstasy hitchhiked its way across the US to gay clubs in Chicago and New York (including the Paradise Garage) where it tempted punters to take a walk on the wild side. But by 1985, the honeymoon was over. That year, the US Drug Enforcement Agency criminalised MDMA, giving it the same 'street drug' classification as cocaine and LSD.

Ecstasy slowly drifted across the Atlantic, arriving like feel-good flotsam on British shores as partygoers returned from New York with tablets sewn into the seams of their suitcases or Sellotaped to their bodies. Very few of these tablets ended up on the dancefloor. Instead, most passed into the hands of a small Soho elite of music journalists, designers, models and pop stars who took ecstasy at private parties.[32] Outlawed in America and unknown in England, for the second time in its history MDMA faced extinction. And then, whether by chance or magic, the drug washed up on the sandy white beaches of Ibiza. After seventy-five years of travelling the world, the love virus had finally found the perfect host.

Sun, Sea and Smiley Faces

The Mediterranean island of Ibiza has long been a magnet for counterculture. Hippies arrived in the sixties, followed by queers and bohemians. The White Isle offered a 'liberal idyll' in contrast to the authoritarian regime on the Spanish mainland under General Franco.[33] In 1976, a young Argentinian named Alfredo Fiorito arrived on the island after fleeing the military junta that had seized power in Buenos Aires. Eight years later, Alfredo began a six-year DJ residency at Amnesia, a club located 4 kilometres inland from Ibiza Town and surrounded by fields and scrub. Alfredo mixed disco, pop and house music while a diverse crowd of locals and tourists danced in a place that British techno pioneer Adamski later described as a 'beautiful big Garden of Eden'.³⁴ Alfredo created the Balearic beat. Although it would later give its name to a subgenre of house music, Balearic originally meant a particular style of clubbing: open air, all-night and wildly hedonistic.³⁵

In 1987, four friends from London touched down in the heat of the Ibizan summer. Nicky Holloway, Paul Oakenfold, Danny Rampling and Johnnie Walker had heard about Amnesia from fellow DJ, Trevor Fung. What they didn't know was that over the summer of 1987 someone had slipped a little white pill into Amnesia's heady cocktail. 'We'd all been introduced into taking an E,' Walker laughs during the documentary *Pump up the Volume: The History of House Music*. 'I remember seeing Paul Oakenfold and Nicky Holloway skipping around the club hand in hand.'³⁶ Acid house had also arrived in Ibiza, courtesy of Alfredo. The English boys had heard acid house before in London but not while taking ecstasy. Putting the two together changed the game. Intoxicated by their Ibizan experience, they returned to London determined to keep the party going.

Get Right on One Matey!

London, November 1987. Acid house, the bastard child of a Chicago mother, drugged and given up for adoption in Ibiza, has passed into the care of two upstart DJs from England. In November 1987, Paul Oakenfold open Future, a self-styled 'Balearic' club, but he doesn't own enough house records to sustain a whole night and the club soon folds.³⁷ Danny Rampling fares better. In a tiny gym on Southwark High Street, his club Shoom attracts a capacity crowd of loved-up Londoners dining on a menu of house, pop and ecstasy. DJ Terry Farley was there: 'These people were in Gaultier suits one week and then the next they were very spiritual and …' he pauses, '"on one matey" as they say'.³⁸ In British raving lexicon, 'Get right on one matey!' is slang for taking ecstasy.

Over the English winter of 1987 and 1988 acid house kept a low profile. It was a halcyon time for those few in the know. But, as always, the marketers were only one step behind. In January 1988, London Records released *House Sounds of Chicago*. Sarah Thornton claims the record company invented the term 'acid house' in the sleeve notes.[39] Before this people had called it 'acid music' or simply 'house music'. The sleeve notes also emphasised the music's underground origins and its controversial drug connotations, seemingly in an attempt to entice curious youngsters to try their product. It worked. By the English spring of 1988 acid house was fast becoming the next youth subculture.

In May, Nicky Holloway opened the Trip at the London Astoria, a mainstream club on Charing Cross Road. Writer Matthew Collin claims that following the success of the Trip, scores of London clubs switched from funk to acid house overnight.[40] By July, hundreds of kids had traded their black suits and shoes for dayglo dungarees and t-shirts emblazoned with a yellow smiling face—the soon-to-be universally recognisable symbol of acid house. 'It was an unstoppable formula,' Collin writes. 'Ecstasy plus house music equals mass euphoria.'[41] They called it the Second Summer of Love, twenty-one years after their stoned and sex-crazed hippie parents had lived through the first one.

As the subculture grew, divisions emerged. The Balearic old timers from Shoom saw their precious little scene draining away, replaced with a rowdy mob of 'Acieeed!' chanting youths they mockingly labelled 'Acid Teds' (possibly on account of the latter's habit of taking teddy bears to parties). The Teds in turn regarded the Balearics as cliquey, elitist and wanting to keep acid house all for themselves.[42] By September it was clear who had won. Too big for the clubs to contain, thousands of people descended on London's abandoned warehouses and aircraft hangars.

The acid house explosion didn't escape the notice of Britain's notoriously scaremongering tabloids. Initially fooled into thinking that acid house was all about LSD, once they discovered the truth, they filled the front pages with warnings about the evil of ecstasy. Acid house incensed their moral outrage even further when they discovered many of the drugged-up dayglow army were underage. London's promoters could not have paid for better advertising, as Nicky Holloway explains:

> I'm sure that lots of people never heard about what was going on until they read about it in the daily newspapers and thought, 'ooh, we'll have to have some of that'.[43]

Thousands turned into tens of thousands. And then at some point in early 1989, people stopped calling the gatherings acid house parties. They had become raves.

We Call it Rave

The idea of dancing all night to heavily percussive music while under the influence of mind-altering substances wasn't discovered in England in 1988. Precedents for such behaviour date back millennia; many indigenous tribes still perform such rituals today, where psychoactive plants and fungi take on a 'religious quality'.[44] In Western culture, Nietzsche traces the history of singing and dancing crowds intoxicated by the 'narcotic draught' back through the whirling dancers of St Vitus and St John in the German Middle Ages to the Bacchic choruses of the ancient Greeks and the orgiastic festivals of the Babylonians.[45] He calls it the 'Dionysian impulse' after the Greek god of wine, theatre and religious ecstasy, who impelled his followers to lose their individual identity to a community of the dance. A god of ecstasy? Those Greeks really knew how to party.

More recently, New Age travellers had been touring the English countryside since the sixties, organising free music festivals at sacred sites and pagan landmarks. The sixties also gave us 'rave', meaning 'a lively party'.[46] In the mid-eighties rave came to denote an illegal warehouse party, often with a punk flavour and a DIY ethos.[47] Around the same time, West Indian dance collectives began hiring out warehouses and blasting out soul and reggae from homemade sound systems to crowds of youths alienated from white mainstream clubbing culture. The English rave scene of the late eighties unified these punk, hippie and sound system vibes under a pulsating soundscape of electronic beat-driven music and drug-fuelled hedonism.

Rave was counter-cultural in the beginning, appealing to people who lived outside the Thatcherite 'Greed is Good' mantra. But as it grew, it became a product of the system it was trying to circumvent. A flock of savvy young entrepreneurs soon realised they could make big money. Maximum individual profit from minimal upfront investment—this was Thatcherism 101. And while the acid house scene and the sixties hippie festivals shared a common interest in dancing all night under the influence of psychoactive drugs ideologically the two camps were distant. 'I don't think you can really liken the '60s to the '80s,' says Eton-educated Tony Colston-Hayter, a rave promoter tabloids dubbed the 'Acid House King'. '[It] was very much something else—it was totally non-political. It was the ultimate hedonistic leisure activity. It was about going out and having a good time.'[48]

By 1989 soaring demand and an increasingly well-informed police force meant London could no longer contain the rave beast it had awakened. As promoters looked further afield they found an entire country ready to exchange fifteen pounds for a 'disco biscuit' and a night of non-stop dancing. Suddenly, all England was awash with Aciieed.

20,000 People Standing in a Field

A petrol station on the M25, England, August 1989. You're sitting in the back of a car with two mates while another friend calls a mobile phone number from a payphone. You tremble with fear and excitement. You haven't dropped yet and everything around you seems freakishly normal. Your friend returns to the car and smiles. She lowers the handbrake and drives off in the same direction you've just come from. After twenty minutes you exit the motorway and become enmeshed within a tangle of country lanes and wheat fields. You count five or six church spires that mark the way, like unlit beacons on the path to paradise. As you turn a sharp bend, you see a fog of red lights in front. The car slows down. You can hear music. 'We're close,' your friend says. 'Let's roll.' She pulls out a small gram bag from her bra and takes out four off-white tablets. You hold yours up between your index finger and thumb and try to discern the logo in the centre but it's too dark to see. Not that you really care; it's always been good before. You wash it down with a gulp of Evian to cleanse the bitter aftertaste on your tongue. The cars ahead have stopped and people stand in the road chatting, hugging and sharing water bottles. Finally, you pass through a farm gate into a field. There's a makeshift stage in the distance, bright lights, a Ferris wheel, a cowshed and thousands of people. Welcome to the future.

I was eleven years old in 1989. I remember watching the *BBC News* and reading *The Times* headlines over breakfast, feeling horrified at the thought of drugged-up youths trampling through farmers' fields and forests. England's green and pleasant land had been the playground of my childhood. Many a day had I spent building dens, hiking over hills and playing hide-and-seek with my friends. I felt like these trespassers had trashed my backyard. But then in 1995, British indie band Pulp released the single 'Sorted for E's and Wizz'.[49] 'Oh is this the way they say the future's meant to feel? Or just 20,000 people standing in a field', Jarvis Cocker sang. When I heard that song, I realised that something inside me had changed. Far from disgusted, instead I felt a deep longing for something I'd missed, something I'd never get to experience.

* * *

As schoolboy entrepreneurs took the party to the Home Counties and beyond, they played cat and mouse with both cops and gangsters. 'The first big party I ever played at, I saw big bags of cash and drugs and sawn-off shotguns', Adamski recalled.[50] Back in London, warehouse party promoter Joe Wieczorek remembers when things started to go wrong:

> All of a sudden a promoter in East London decided he'd get security he knew and they were all from the Inter City Firm.[51] He opened the door … They'd found a way in and then they demanded £125, £150, £175, £200 … it was going up all the time. They'd say, 'You need ten men. You need twelve men.' That's the way it went.

Rave might have lost its innocence behind the scenes but it didn't matter to the hordes of youngsters dancing in the paddocks till sunrise. In August 1989, an Energy party attracted 20,000 ravers to a Surrey field.[52] As venues became harder to find and police and thugs closed in, the organisers were forced to innovate. Tony Colston-Hayter sent scouts out to farmers, telling them he wanted to hire their farm to make a film. He also used voicebanks that he progressively updated with new information as the night went on, and gave out membership cards so that he could claim he was organising private parties.[53] All of these cunning yet ultimately futile schemes found their way to Melbourne in the nineties.

In September 1989, Italian dance act Black Box released 'Ride on Time'. It became an instant rave classic and topped the UK singles chart for six weeks. Rave had crossed over into the mainstream consciousness. Things would never be the same again. Over the coming months, police crackdowns, government pressure, criminal gangs and a drop in ecstasy supply squeezed rave back inside the clubs.[54] Those who weren't yet ready to extinguish the flame teamed up with travelling free party sound systems like Spiral Tribe, Tonka and Exodus, or fled to the continent or Goa. In the midst of all this mayhem, a pair of raving refugees boarded a flight to Australia ready to start a new life. Or so they thought.

'It was Another Era'

The outskirts of Melbourne, January 2015. I'm on the back deck of a café overlooking the Yarra 75 kilometres upstream from the CBD. The river gently meanders past beautiful bushland, unrecognisable from the dirty brown sewer that squelches through the city. Heidi (aka Hydi) John sits opposite me. She's wrapped in a bright blue shawl, sipping a latte and rolling a cigarette. It's not hard to see why people call Heidi the mother of the Melbourne rave scene. When she smiles, which is most of the time, her eyes twinkle and her whole body pulsates with loving energy. Within seconds I'm under her spell. Richard John sits to her right, his wiry grey tresses tied up in a ponytail that keeps them off his worn, chiselled face. Heidi's speech is soft and warm, interspersed with a smoker's cough and frequent interruptions from her husband. As their wariness towards me fades, they reveal a deep and unabated passion for what they see as the true spirit of rave.

'We knew from the start it was another era, another stage in the evolution of the human being,' Richard explains. 'People suddenly coming together, separation was no more. Evolving, talking together, talking to black and white … like the Manifesto says'. He hands me a black and white photocopy labelled *ARTISTIC MANIFESTO: Melbourne underground development*. 'It's all in there.' And so it is. I skim through five paragraphs of New Age spirituality and philosophy that resonate to the rhythm of peace, love, unity and respect—or PLUR as it was called. Richard grabs the manifesto from my hand and reads aloud:

> Music and Dance have always been sacred throughout earth's history and they each have amazing powers—together, given the right circumstances, they can produce

miracles … we know the power of this most ancient tradition … evoking memories and emotions of the past and future, connecting us to something infinitely larger than ourselves yet within all of us.[55]

He pauses, and I look at them. Richard's lip quivers; Heidi's eyes are transfixed, trance-like. This is not performance. They believed it then and they believe it still.

Back in 1988, the Johns were hardly your typical ravers—in their mid-thirties, running The Marksman pub in London's Hackney, with a teenage daughter and a baby on the way. Joe Wieczorek remembers encountering them at an early acid house party. 'I got the shock of my life when I walked into this party and I see Heidi and Richard who I knew as fellow publicans up the other end of the road,' Joe tells me in his broad Cockney accent. 'I wasn't expecting publicans to be going to acid parties if you get my drift. It was quite a secret for me and them.' Presumably, he means that a normal publican might regard acid house as competition. But Richard and Heidi weren't normal anythings and, as their experiences in Melbourne would later prove, business came second to pleasure. They were soon swept up in the ecstasy rush at legendary acid house clubs like Clink Street, a former prison on the south bank of the Thames, with Mr C as resident DJ. 'You never heard a vocal in Clink Street,' Richard says. 'It was just purely sound. There was no message in the music, nobody talking or saying subliminal things. Just purely beats. That's what drew people in.'

In the early days, rave broke down class, race and sexual orientation barriers and even football team rivalry.[56] For Joe, a diehard Tottenham Hotspurs fan who'd seen his fair share of violence on the terraces, it was a whole new experience:

> I didn't have to have my back against the wall and I didn't have to have a tool on me. At these parties, I met people I wouldn't normally meet. South London people didn't come

to where we were [in the East End] and we certainly didn't go to where they were and nine out of ten times when you did, you'd end up having murders, you'd have a proper row over there, the two didn't mix.

Throughout 1988, Joe and the Johns spent their Friday evenings driving around the East End of London looking for parties, with mixed success. Joe recalls:

The three of us formed quite a crew ... we'd go out hunting for these places because they were few and far between in the beginning. The longer that went on, the more and more we were going to gaffs where you'd go in there and it'd be a blinding party, you'd pay a fiver and then ten minutes later you're out in the cold because Old Bill's turned up, it'd all be over.

In late 1988 or early 1989, Joe and the Johns decided to hold their own party. They found a warehouse on Vale Road in Seven Sisters, falsified a lease, organised insurance, bought some fire extinguishers and hired security. Everything looked above board but they weren't taking any chances, as Joe explains:

Richard and me went to Bethnal Green fire station. We'd made an appointment to see the fire officer to see whether he could help us with his planning for a private event. The soppy fucker left us in the room. So I just picked up the piece of headed notepaper, put it in my pocket, went back to the office, photocopied it, put our own business name on it and made up a fire certificate! Apparently there's no such thing! But we'd gambled on the cozzers not knowing.

The gamble paid off. On the night of the party, a thousand people turned up, including the local police inspector. Joe showed him around the party and presented him with the paperwork. 'I'm thinking he's going to pull the plug on me,' Joe says. 'And then he puts his hand out and he goes, "Well done son, a very well-run party."' While Joe kept the police at bay, the Johns had been learning how to set up a rave quickly—skills they would later perfect in Melbourne. Richard explains:

> You found a warehouse and everybody from thirteen-year-old kids to people our age, friends and friends of friends, we'd all go in armed with spray cans two hours before the event and spray the thing up to be really colourful ... a sound system would be brought in quick ... you then had to wait for dark until the nightwatchman had gone. There'd be a smoke machine and a strobe. That was it.

A few months later, Richard and Heidi received their visas for Australia. 'By this time we'd started doing things all over the place, we'd been to the south of England, we'd started to get some momentum happening,' Heidi recalls. 'Joe was like, "What are you doing?!"' Under the Club Labrynth banner, Joe went on to run over a hundred illegal raves until one too many confrontations with machete-wielding gangsters finally persuaded him to change tack.[57] But Richard and Heidi had made their minds up. They sensed the mood was changing. 'We knew it was going to crack and that's when we left London,' Heidi says. So they said their farewells to Joe and the villains and football thugs that made up The Marksman's regulars, caught the Tube to Heathrow and boarded an aeroplane to Adelaide. It was the Australian winter of 1989. When they touched down, they thought they'd left their raving days behind them. But Australia had other ideas.

The Pleasure Zone

After a few weeks in Adelaide, Richard and Heidi received a phone call from Nigel Last, an English friend living in Melbourne. He told them about a young man called Mark James who was looking for partners to help him buy out Checkpoint Charlie nightclub on Commercial Road, South Yarra. Mark James was born in Melbourne, but had started his DJ career running dance clubs in Brisbane and the Gold Coast. 'They were really underground,' he tells me. 'We had no alcohol licence. When the police turned up, a buzzer went off at the front door, the bar put the booze away and all the punters threw their drinks in the bin and put soft drinks on the table.' Mark returned to Melbourne in late 1988. It can't have been easy breaking into an established club hierarchy that had changed little since the disco era. Nevertheless, within weeks Mark had sweet-talked his way into gigs at Chasers, the Chevron and IDs Nitespot.

Checkpoint Charlie nightclub, designed with an 'East meets West' brief in mind—the club was named after a famous border crossing in the Berlin Wall—had opened to great fanfare in May 1988.[58] Richard and Heidi helped Mark buy the club out of receivership but the English couple soon regretted their decision. 'It was alright but it wasn't our thing,' Richard tells me. 'It was like taking over another pub really and we'd done that in London.' They must have made an odd partnership: a flashy young wheeler-dealer from Queensland and a pair of thirty-something sixties-throwback Poms. When the Johns walked into Checkpoint, it was like stepping back in time: Melbourne in 1989 felt like London in 1987. 'People say you never had the vibe here in Melbourne,' Richard exclaims. 'Yes you did! You had it fucking blinding here! But not for long.'

For Richard, that vibe began at ZuZus. Tony Patton and Marie Mardon opened Pleasure Zone at ZuZus nightclub on Saturday 17 December 1988. ZuZus was located in a former theatre on the corner of Little Bourke and Exhibition Street in the city (now it's the Rydges Hotel). On entering, one climbed a steep flight of stairs that opened out to an enormous 'Gloria Swanson staircase' overlooking the sunken dancefloor. 'It was the best club in Melbourne,' raver Nimmo Sandilands defiantly declares.

Marie Mardon was friends with Paul Oakenfold. She had hoped to emulate the latter's success with his Spectrum and Land of Oz clubs in London. It was hard work. Some nights, the club struggled to attract more than twenty people. Terrence Ho was one of the faithful. He had moved from Malaysia to Balwyn North in Melbourne's leafy eastern suburbs when he was seven years old. His life changed forever when he watched Steve 'Silk' Hurley's video for 'Jack Your Body' in January 1987: 'To see some video clip of a cartoon and all you hear is "Jack, jack, jack your body", it was crazy! I'd never heard it before.' Terrence quickly realised his love of house music set him apart from his peers:

> I was like the weird kid at school because everybody was into their rock'n'roll, going to the pubs on Fridays and Saturdays with their mates and drinking beer and singing to AC/DC and shit like that. I was more interested in going to nightclubs and listening to 'Move Your Body' by Marshall Jefferson.

One night, Mardon brought out Paul Oakenfold and Danny Rampling to play at ZuZus. 'They were playing some Balearic beats they heard in Ibiza back in the day,' Terrence told the ABC in 2003. 'They only played to fifty people. But those fifty people enjoyed themselves immensely because they were all on acid and stuff, sitting inside bass speakers and going crazy.'[59]

A gay club midweek, ZuZus attracted a mixed crowd on Saturday nights. It's tempting to label those who were there as the original Melbourne old skool: an older crew of people like Ollie Olsen and Mad Rod drawn to the next iteration of abstract electronic music mixing with rave-hardened expats such as Richard and Heidi and schoolkids like Nimmo and Terrence who'd heard dribbles of acid house at Chasers and Chevron and wanted more. Ollie describes the embryonic scene:

It really did have this sense of unity that I think has long kind of disappeared ... like the gay culture, the straight culture, mixing it up together ... everyone was just having a party together, and it felt really celebratory, and it was all new and fresh.[60]

And to hear the freshest acid house cuts, one looked no further than a shy, seventeen-year-old kid with the best record collection in Melbourne.

'An Amazing Ear for Amazing Records'

Inflation basement, Melbourne, 1988. It's late. You've been dancing all night, you're tired and you want to go home. Behind the safety glass in the DJ booth, you vaguely make out a young, lanky figure moving towards the turntables. He carefully places a record on the platter and delicately drops the needle onto the vinyl. The beat of the new track matches the last but there's something unfamiliar that you just can't place. After about a minute, the steady intro gives way to a rousing cacophony of weird and trippy sounds, filling your head with twittering birds, crying babies and growling animals. It's as though an infant has got hold of a sound effects machine and is pushing the buttons at random. You've never heard anything like it before. Your friends are unimpressed and head towards the door. But you're mesmerised. You walk around to the booth and approach the DJ. 'What is this?!' you ask him. He looks at you and smiles nervously. You realise he's just a kid like you. 'It's acid house,' he replies.

'Wow!' You pause. 'What's your name?'

'It's Steve. Steve Robbins.'

When I meet Steve twenty-seven years later, I find a warm, gentle and damaged man. His arms shake and he taps his leg nervously. He's in his mid-forties but doesn't look a day over thirty. Sometimes when he smiles and his eyes light up, I can see that seventeen-year old boy behind the booth. When I tell him he's a legend of the scene, he's clearly surprised and visibly humbled. As we say goodbye, he hands me a CD of his most recent music. 'I wanted to bring more copies so you could give them out to people,' he says. I give him my address so that he can mail them to me. They never arrived.

Steve probably wasn't the first person in Melbourne to play acid house (the DJs at Razor and Mandate are more likely candidates) and he wasn't the best DJ in a technical sense, but his innate ability to find new and interesting music helped shape the Melbourne acid house scene more than anyone else. 'He just had an amazing ear for amazing records,' DJ Brewster B. tells me. 'If you'd go to hear him in the early days you'd go because you knew he'd play something that you'd never heard before or you'd only ever hear him play.' It might be hard nowadays to appreciate why this was so important in the eighties. A techno fan today can be his or her own DJ, spending hours browsing through Spotify or Soundcloud to discover and play new music. But no dance music radio existed then, let alone the internet. You had to go to a club, hope that someone like Steve was playing and then ask for a cassette of the music. 'You'd still be fucked because you didn't know what the records were but you'd just be playing this gold gem,' Brewster tells me. 'You'd never lend the tape to any one, instead you'd tape it for them. So you'd get this generation of tape on tape on tape that was slowly degraded over time.'

Steve started out in the hip hop scene in the mid-eighties, playing in funk clubs from the age of fourteen. In 1986, he asked Jo Palumbo at Central Station Records for a job so he could order the music he wanted to play. Jo hired him to look after hip hop and house. Steve remembers:

> There was really a minimal amount of house music back then, it was only bits and pieces … so you'd only get a couple of new releases a week … without acid house I think house would have taken a lot longer to break into mainstream music. The acid stuff was crazier and completely new whereas house was more mellow and just electronic

versions of older songs. When you heard acid music you'd think, 'You have to be off your head to listen to that!' And that's what it was perfect for.

Steve thinks he first played house music at an underage gig at Inflation in late 1987. On 27 August 1988, Checkpoint Charlie started a 'psychedelic full moon party' called Lunacy. It was one of Melbourne's first acid house parties and Steve's big break into the Melbourne club scene. Writing about the impending launch of Lunacy, *The Age* newspaper appeared to mistake acid house for a revival of sixties psychedelia:

> [Acid house] means grooving to 'Lucy in the Sky with Diamonds' and trying to figure out if Lennon was really talking about his kid's dream.[61]

At least they got the LSD part right. By January 1989, Steve was playing up to six nights a week at clubs like Checkpoint Charlie, Chasers, ZuZus, Chevron and Inflation.[62] It's as though the music was inside him and just had to get out. And when it became too much for one person to handle, he recruited a sidekick for his acid mission—a cocky Calabrian kid called Davide Carbone.

'Adversity in the Face of Conformity'

The son of strict Catholic Italian immigrants, Davide Carbone knows what it's like to grow up as a 'wog' in eighties Melbourne: 'Until the late eighties, Melbourne had historically been divided into wog clubs and gay clubs … the gay clubs had the better music, but if you weren't gay, you weren't going.' By the time he was sixteen, Davide had tired of listening to italo disco with a 'bunch of wogs' and yearned to hear something fresh and new. One day he walked into Central Station Records in the City Square to see what he could find:

Steve [Robbins] was at the counter and I said, 'Mate, I'm trying to get all this house music,' and Steve went, 'I love that house music! I get it all, anything, I get it all.' So I just fell in love with this Steve character.

Davide soon realised his new best friend was something special. 'He was a class above the rest of us. If Steve had been a guy living in America or England, he would have been one of the most successful and popular artists. He just had a natural knack, he had the soul of this electronic music that was happening at the time.'

Acid house's surging popularity shook up Melbourne's clubbing establishment. Davide tells me he encountered opposition from older DJs concerned at losing their jobs:

Back in those days, the amount of people in a club and what they were doing directly related to how you worked as a DJ. There weren't three DJs a night, there were one or two and you had the job for six months so it was really important … and then we'd turn up! We got slapped across the ears, kicked out, nothing major though. They couldn't hit us because we were sixteen.

According to Davide, the hip hop scene felt most threatened. 'Don't think of them as cool hip hop DJs, they weren't, they were typical Aussies in their mid-thirties,' he laughs. 'When you're sixteen you're like, "Who are these old dickheads?"' These 'old dickheads' had worked hard to gain a following for hip hop in Melbourne. But just when they thought their efforts were paying off, acid house came along and stole their crowd.

In 1989, the pair started DJing together at Cadillac Bar at 536 Swanston Street, Carlton. Long since torn down and replaced with shoebox student accommodation, Cadillac Bar began life as Impressions nightclub before receiving an American-themed makeover in the late eighties. Steve thrilled the crowd of trendy schoolkids and in-the-know uni students with his sonic cocktail of house, acid and hip hop. Davide, however, took a while longer to find the right groove, as Steve recalls:

> I remember walking in one time when Davide was starting the night. It was the first time he was on his own and he played a track by Electribe 101 [probably 'Talking With Myself']. It's a really slow song with a sick little acid bit in it but other than that ... you wouldn't dance to it, it was like a listening song. I walk in the door and I could hear everyone standing around talking and [the manager] just goes to me, 'You fucking get up there, you fucking get up there right now. I can't believe that cunt's done that to me!' That was the funniest time!

Fortunately, the pissed-off manager calmed down and gave Davide a second chance. One night while he was playing, Stephen 'The Ghost' Walker approached the booth. The Ghost was the program manager at community radio station 3RRR. He asked Davide what he was playing. 'It's house.' The Ghost asked, 'Do you want your own show on 3RRR?'

'How would I do that?'

'I'll teach you.'

'I don't think anyone wants to hear this music,' Davide told him. The Ghost disagreed. 'Adversity in the face of conformity,' was his cryptic response.

Launched in September 1990, *Rhythmatic* on Wednesday nights helped introduce house music to a wider audience. Steve joined Davide behind the mic. The Ghost had instructed them to be controversial. They didn't disappoint. 'We'd do things like go out and review Sanction [on Tuesday nights at the Chevron nightclub] and bag the shit out of John Course for playing cheesy music,' Davide admits. 'The poor guy, we were just a bunch of dickheads, young kids.' Indeed, some of their on-air antics wouldn't have been out of place in the schoolyard. One time they claimed Mark James's real name was Mark Condom (it's actually Mark Condron). The 3RRR phone lines rang hot with complaints. The Ghost loved it. When they weren't teasing their fellow DJs, Davide kept their listeners up to date with club listings and Steve would do a live on-air mix. Davide remembers when the show started having an impact. 'I'd go to DJ somewhere and hear people playing tapes of *Rhythmatic* in their car ... we kind of had a feeling that something was about to happen.' That something was techno.

Chapter 4

CHILDREN OF ECSTASY

'We were Detroit'

Ripponlea, October 2014. I'm sipping a latte at a trendy café on Glen Eira Road and chatting to Josh Abrahams, one of Australia's most successful dance music producers. A classically trained musician, Josh tells me that techno's non-musicality seduced him:

> I started listening thinking, 'My God, they're using all these minor seconds'. It's a real techno music thing. Basically you've got some DJ who's sampled a whole chord, played the rhythm and then played the next note up … and in music theory, you mostly don't use the minor second. I just fell in love with it.

Josh is clearly excited about this and so I make a mental note to ask Kim to play a minor second on the piano when I get home to better understand what he's saying. Fearful that he may bamboozle me with musical terminology, I carefully steer Josh onto safer ground and ask if he thinks techno in Melbourne during the nineties had a distinct sound. 'We were Detroit', he replies. 'Look, Australia tends to meld everything together but I bet you wouldn't find Sydney people talking about Detroit. The way I remember it, we were always talking about Detroit. We were obsessed with Detroit.'

The root of this obsession is the pervasive myth of Detroit as the birthplace of techno. The story goes like this: Detroit, the once proud 'Motor Town' formerly home to Ford, Chrysler and General Motors, had been immutably transformed after race riots in 1967 killed the auto industry and triggered a 'white flight' to the suburbs, leaving its impoverished black population to languish in the decaying urban core. 'Once commuters cleared out of the downtown in the evening, one could walk for blocks without encountering another person,' Dan Sicko writes of Detroit in the eighties.[1] So, just like Melbourne suburbia today. Detroit is the world's poster boy for urban decay or 'ruin porn', its crumbling buildings and forsaken streets are the stars of Instagram and Tumblr feeds all over the world. Against this dystopian backdrop, three black kids got their hands on some old analogue synth gear and a drum machine. Taking their cues from electro-funk outfit Afrika Bambaataa, George Clinton's Parliament-Funkadelic, and the industrial krautrock of Can, Neu! and Kraftwerk, Juan Atkins, Kevin Saunderson and Derrick May created 'machine music' that eulogised their dying city and worshipped technology as the future.

In 1981, Atkins paired with Richard Davis to form Cybotron. Their 1983 proto-techno release 'Clear' marries electro-funk with sequences and harmonies adapted from Kraftwerk's *Trans-Europe Express*.[2] When May released 'Nude Photo' and 'Strings of Life' in 1987, it became clear that a new sound had emerged. 'If Atkins was the prophet, the one to tap into the unseen and unheard possibilities of electronic music, May was the high priest who brought them about with forceful incantations,' Sicko writes.[3] May referred to techno as 'strictly future music' in contrast to house that he felt was firmly rooted in 70s disco.[4] This 'future music' promised a gateway out of the ghetto.

'Call it Techno'

The Detroit techno narrative presents a wonderful tale of triumph in the face of adversity. Or rather it would, if it were true. In fact, techno owes as much to London's glitzy West End as it does to the downtrodden streets of Detroit. Even the name was an afterthought. In 1988, the UK's *Face Magazine*—at the time one of the world's foremost barometers of cool—arrived in Detroit to interview May, Atkins and Saunderson. May explains what happened next:

> This is the first time that we've ever done interviews. We're being all passionate, throwing our lives on the line for them … and they say: 'You know what, we've got this great story, these really fantastic pictures, we got everything. But guys, we need a name for this music' … Juan stands up and says, 'Call it techno'.[5]

The 'call it techno' story has passed into raving folklore and fans the world over take pride in the name's authentic roots. However, Sicko argues that Virgin Records' Neil Rushton actually invented the name. Hearing Atkins's track 'Techno Music' 'instantly prompted' Rushton to change the name of Virgin's forthcoming Detroit music compilation LP from *The House Sound of Detroit* to *Techno! The New Dance Sound Of Detroit*.[6] However, it seems that both Atkins and Rushton may be guilty of plagiarism. Frankfurt DJ 2XLC had first used the term 'techno' in 1984 to describe 'music created technologically' by New Order, Depeche Mode, Heaven 17, Kraftwerk and others.[7]

Sicko disputes May's claim that techno is 'future music', arguing instead that it has an 'obvious' connection to soul and Motown.[8] Meanwhile, from Kraftwerk in Düsseldorf to Ollie Olsen in Berlin (see Chapter Three) and Charanjit Singh in Mumbai,[9] other artists had also been experimenting with techno-like music during the early eighties. May and Atkins might not even have been the first in Detroit. In 1981, A Number of Names released 'Sharevari' (aka 'Shari Vari'). Nominally an italo disco track, Sicko writes that 'Sharevari' 'introduced the earliest beginnings of techno as its own style and genre'.[10] Similarly, writer Mark Duffett regards 'Shari Vari' as the 'missing link' between disco, Kraftwerk and techno.[11]

Nevertheless, it was the Detroit techno of May, Saunderson and Atkins that gave its name to a genre of music that defined a nascent youth subculture on the other side of the Atlantic. Gradually, house music shifted from its light and fluffy Balearic roots towards a darker, broodier beat that seemed more in keeping with London's dismal grey skies. Record companies and the British music press heavily promoted the 'rags to riches' backstory of Detroit techno because it brought an edgy authenticity to their product. Unfortunately, the truth had gone missing somewhere along the way, as Derrick May explains:

> They are really caught up in this story, this passionate thing of how it happened, 'these black guys, these poor, these poverty stricken guys', which none of us were, mind you. None of us come from poverty stricken homes. We all went to private schools and come from upper middle-class homes.[12]

Those upper middle-class homes were located in Belleville, a commuter suburb some 40 kilometres west of downtown surrounded by forest, lakes and farmland. Not exactly an inner city ghetto. 'We didn't realise we were pawns for a much bigger game,' May says. 'And the bigger game was to develop and nurture a new level of dance music and to make a multibillion-dollar industry out of it.'[13] The Belleville Three, as they became known, didn't realise the extent of their stardom until they started playing in front of 5000 people in England. 'It was crazy to see that many white kids dancing to the music I was playing,' Atkins says. 'I thought this could never happen in the US.'[14] Indeed, besides a few arty middle-class African-Americans, no-one had heard of techno in its supposed hometown. That changed after Saunderson's 'Big Fun' introduced techno to the UK Top Ten in September 1988, but even then Detroiters dismissed techno as yet another marketing fad attempting to mythologise their hometown without giving back to the communities it presumed to represent. They'd seen it all before in the sixties with Motown (short for 'Motor Town'). Once more, white-owned record companies were plundering black music to sell at a profit to white audiences. Melbourne lapped it up.

The Techno We Had to Have

Like Detroit, Melbourne in the eighties was a former manufacturing and industrial city in decline. Its factories and warehouses, once the backbone of a bustling inner city economy, stood empty and unloved. A sharp economic downturn in the early nineties (dubbed 'the recession we had to have' by then Prime Minister Paul Keating) hit Melbourne hard. The state bank collapsed, interest rates topped 18 percent and youth unemployment rose. Young Melburnians, beset with little hope and scant opportunity, may have seen a mirror of their own city in Detroit. Perhaps, techno music's rendering of a similarly decayed and divided metropolis struck a (heavily sampled) chord with another disaffected generation some 10,000 miles to the east.

If their economic and social circumstances were not depressing enough, Detroiters also suffered the ignominy of living in the shadow of their hipper and wealthier neighbours on the other side of Lake Michigan: Chicago, the third largest city in the US and the undisputed capital of the Midwest. With its grand buildings, thriving economy and rich cultural history of gangsters, speakeasies and jazz clubs, it's not hard to see why Chicago was Sinatra's kind of town. Although Chicago gave Detroit artists the dancefloors, radio stations, and lively club scene lacking in their hometown, techno couldn't compete with the Windy City's own electronic dance music revolution in house. The underdog city competing against the big brash metropolis: now here was a story that Melburnians could relate to given their own one-hundred-year inferiority complex at the hands of Sydney.

The English Invasion

In truth, if Melbourne was Detroit then Sydney was more London than Chicago. During the second half of 1988, a mob of English backpackers had turned up and filled the dorms and squats of Kings Cross and Darlinghurst. Having lived through the second summer of love in London, many of them helped launch the Sydney party scene, giving it a distinct English character. 'The rave scene took off [in Sydney], and it was run by an English cartel, basically,' DJ Biz-E told the ABC. 'Some of them were actually Aussies that pretended they were English. They had a really strong grip on it. And they deserved it, man, they brought it here; the Motherland bringing a seed.'[15] Two-hundred years after the First Fleet landed in Botany Bay, the English had invaded Sydney again, this time arriving on flying metal ships loaded with pills, tunes and smiley faces.

Throughout 1989, Sydney promoters RAT, f.u.n. and Sweatbox threw regular dance parties, bringing out American house and hip hop stars like Tone Loc, Kraze and Frankie Knuckles.[16] But by 1990, the English influence was unmistakeable. On 20 January of that year, Unity Productions organised a party called The Beginning, featuring a chill-out room and 'Top London DJs'. The flyer specifies a meeting point, not a party location, and just in case you still didn't get the message, at the bottom it reads, 'This is not just a Rat Party, this is a RAVE'.[17] The Beginning was possibly the first party in Australia to be promoted as a 'rave'. Two months later, Light Productions brought out Balearic pioneer Danny Rampling.[18] Sydney had got right on one, matey.

Scholars Chris Gibson and Rebecca Pagan highlight the role of British backpackers in bringing many of rave's subcultural meanings from the UK, including musical styles, utopian discourses and the subversive use of warehouses.[19] Others emphasise the important role of 'link cultures' and 'link individuals' in establishing the Sydney rave scene, particularly the 'European backpackers' who brought rave culture to Australia.[20] Terrence Ho is characteristically more prosaic: 'There was a whole bunch of English people who came to Australia after the whole '88 thing died out in England because they wanted to continue partying.' Plenty of English backpackers had landed in Melbourne too, but they never had quite the same impact compared to Sydney. It makes sense; if you were English or had lived in England and you liked raving, you went to Sydney where the parties were bigger and it felt more like home. As we'll see, British-style raving would come to Melbourne too but in the early days it was all about techno.

Techno Hour

By 1989, the dedicated Melbourne techno fan could satisfy her cravings five nights a week, beginning with Sanction on Tuesday at the Chevron and ending with one of half a dozen clubs on Saturday, although Inflation with Steve Robbins was the pick of the bunch. In 1988, Grant Harrison had started Xpress at Chasers on the coveted Friday night slot, replacing the club's hip hop night Time Square. He hired the stellar lineup of Steve Robbins, Mark James and Paul Siedle to spin the tunes. 'While rap was on the wane, house music had made an evolutionary leap into the future,' Harrison wrote in 1995.

'The rhythms hardened, the bass deepened and complementing sounds became positively dangerous. Techno had arrived.'[21] In the wee hours of the morning, the club thinned out and the techno faithful climbed out of their dark recesses and slid towards the centre of the dancefloor. 3am was always techno hour somewhere in Melbourne. 'We used to take over Tuesday nights at Sanction at Chevron,' one raver tells me. 'John Course would play his normal stuff till one or two and then he'd start playing stuff like 'What Time Is Love?' [by KLF] and 'Pure' by GTO and we'd just jump on the dancefloor and the normal people who were just drinking and dancing would leave!' Brewster B. says the clubs weren't making any money after 3am because the only people left in the club drank only water. Nightclubs responded by raising the price of bottled water. When that didn't work, they instructed their bouncers to refuse entry to anyone suspected of taking drugs. After 3am, that was just about everyone.

Operation Ecstasy

Nobody knows for sure when ecstasy (aka E, X or eccy) first arrived in Melbourne. My interviewee Marcus says he saw it floating around the gay scene when he landed in 1986. Sean Kelly tells me he first saw it on the dancefloor in 1988. In October of that year, *The Age* reported some students were using the 'designer drug'.[22] I've heard anecdotally that tourists and expats smuggled it in their suitcases when flying in from the UK. 'I had my first [E] when still at Monash Uni, between '86 and '88,' raver Larissa Tittl confesses. 'My boyfriend's friend smuggled some back from the UK … It made me freak out at first … I remember seeing floaty coloured mist coming out of the speakers, and everything glowed.'

On Saturday 3 December 1988, 40 police officers and a sniffer dog raided Checkpoint Charlie nightclub. It was possibly Melbourne's first ecstasy-related raid. And probably the least successful. 'Operation Ecstasy', as the police named it, yielded three arrests for 'hindering police and offensive behaviour'.[23] Officers found a small quantity of ecstasy on the dancefloor but laid no drug-related charges. Nobody had told them that the wildly hedonistic Lunacy parties had switched to Thursday night. Timmy Byrne was DJing:

> I remember all the girls had to go upstairs and all the guys had to go downstairs. They came in the booth, I stopped the music and I had to undo my pants so the police could check I didn't have any drugs. They also searched in my mouth. If they'd come on the Thursday night they might have found something but they found nothing.

Throughout the late eighties and into the nineties, the police hired drug addicts as paid informants and raided countless parties. Davide Carbone tells me the police targeted him for years:

> They mistakenly thought I was the demigod of this whole scene so everywhere I went, they turned up. One night we were playing at a really big party at the Power House … as soon as I came up on stage, the police came in and raided and it was the second or third time they'd raided a place while I was DJing so I put on Eruption's 'All You Bastards' and they lost their mind.

In 1988, ecstasy was expensive, costing around $60 to $80 a pill ($120 to $160 in 2018 dollars), compared to prices of $30 to $40 in the late nineties. It was also unfamiliar. As such, many ravers were unprepared for its effects. Sid Sidney recalls his first time:

> I spent most of the night on the floor and then when the party finished I thought, 'What do I do now? I'm still going.' From what I can remember, I probably only danced for five minutes. Most of the time people were looking after me. I was incoherent. I'd be standing there and someone would

say, 'Somebody look after Sid', and they'd drag me around the dancefloor.

Raver and lighting technician Scott Adcock tells me you had to train yourself to enjoy it: 'You need someone with you who talks you through it and shows you how to experience it rather than you feeling sick and throwing up in a corner, which happened a few times!' But once one had graduated from its uncomfortable initiation, ecstasy promised a completely new experience. Most users feel a heightened sense of empathy and emotional connection to others, a quality often described as being 'loved up'; this makes ecstasy almost unique among recreational drugs. Other positive effects include euphoria, increased energy and self-confidence, decreased inhibition, and feelings of relaxation and wellbeing.[24] Many users report a strong sensation of being 'lost in the moment' with an altered sense of time. A 1997 study on drug use at raves claimed that the ecstasy 'high' usually lasted four to six hours, which goes to show the drugs really were better back in the day.[25]

Ecstasy's side effects include teeth grinding and clenching (bruxism), nausea, hallucinations, dehydration, increased heart rate and erectile dysfunction, the latter a particular frustration of some men who use it as an aphrodisiac. Enhanced intimacy between strangers is wonderful when both parties are similarly intoxicated and awkwardly embarrassing if not. 'There remains a gothic humour to ecstasy usage,' scholar Tara Brabazon writes:

> The bizarre intimacies, the random hugging, the jawbreaker chewing gum and the speed-metal conversations. It has to be a drug with a short shelf life: there are only a limited number of random, hyper-personal disclosures that can be made to complete strangers.[26]

After a drug-free youth, I first took ecstasy at a music festival in England in 2013. I started to come up as I walked across fields that twenty-five years earlier might have hosted the world's first rave parties. When I'm rushing on E, I chain-smoke, chew gum and chatter constantly—three things I never do in 'real life'. Love, warmth and compassion replace my natural wariness of strangers. For a beautiful and unmeasurable period, there is no past or future, only the present moment. The trees have purple auras and people's faces glow in the darkness. My skin tingles whenever anyone touches me. Everyone looks happy. I feel completely safe. And then I see things. What starts out as benign and faintly amusing (for example, I invariably see illegible hieroglyphics written in red ink on the walls—because I'm a writer perhaps?) by the end of the night can transform into something darker: a crack in the wall becomes a crawling centipede while leaves change into green goblins hiding in the trees. Many people enjoy these hallucinations, which incidentally are far more common with LSD than ecstasy. However, as someone who experiences mild visual and aural hallucinations in everyday life, I'm not sure I need to see any more.*

Ecstasy use seldom causes serious illness or death but it can demand a brutal recovery regime. The reality one tried so hard to avoid can be a dark lonely valley when coming down from a weekend long trip to the mountains of euphoria. For habitual users, the comedown can become so unbearable that it's no longer offset by the high. Personally, I find that MDMA demands a five-day recovery, which I think is a little unfair given I've only taken

---

*   This is not as uncommon as you might think. In his book *Hallucinations*, neurologist Oliver Sacks writes 'many cultures regard hallucinations, like dreams as a special, privileged state of consciousness—one that is actively sought through spiritual practices, meditation, drugs or solitude. But in modern Western culture, hallucinations are more often considered to portend madness or something dire happening to the brain—even though the vast majority of hallucinations have no such dark implications (2012, p. xiv).' By way of example, he cites evidence that as many as 10 percent of people have experienced visual or auditory hallucinations under 'normal' circumstances, in other words, excluding such conditions as psychiatric illness, sensory or sleep deprivation and taking psychoactive drugs (p. 57).

the drug a handful of times. Day one (Sunday) is great; I'm still fucked and feeling good. I can't sleep but it's nothing a couple of Temazepam won't cure. Monday is the honeymoon. MDMA lulls me into thinking I've dodged its venom and somehow my magnesium supplement and diet regime has deflected the chemical bullet. But, alas, I wake on day three and invariably feel like shit. My symptoms include nausea, appetite loss, muscle aches, exhaustion, depression, insomnia and anxiety. They don't call it Blue Tuesday for nothing.[27] Day four I call the second honeymoon. All of my symptoms fade and even the anxiety drowns into background noise. And yet there's a strong sense of impending doom—I've been here before. Because Thursday is the killer. My mind cranks up the anxiety dial to extreme and I feel really down. I stay inside if I can. And then, it's all over. MDMA is a wicked temptress—I feel better just as the next weekend is about to begin. While it's a horrible experience, I'm grateful for this painful recovery. I have friends who have taken large quantities of drugs for years and seem to pull up with few ill effects time after time. If this had been me, I'd probably have taken ecstasy every week and I'm not sure that would be a good thing. I certainly never would have finished this book.

'Gurning Like Mad Jackals'

Writer Simon Reynolds claims that all music sounds better on E but house and techno are particularly amazing because 'the sounds seem to caress the listener's skin'.[28] Similarly, researcher Christine Siokou reports that ravers who take ecstasy and other amphetamines can 'literally "feel" the music through their bodies', which enhances their ability to dance.[29] Steve Robbins believes ecstasy is a perfect match for acid house and describes their coincidental emergence in Melbourne as a 'fluke':

> I don't know if ecstasy would have had the same effect if it had come out when hip hop was coming out. You might

have still liked the music but I don't think it would have had that overall thing where everyone was taken in by it.

Let's face it: gangster rap and random hugging don't sit well together. But not everyone welcomed ecstasy's arrival on the dancefloor. 'The problem with ecstasy was that people would (a) not drink and (b) dance to anything,' Sean Kelly tells me. 'When I started DJing, you had to get people to dance. This to me was of no interest. It was just playing beats.' For Sean, the 'getting out of your head' scene of the nineties had replaced the social scene of the eighties. Terrence Ho, on the other hand, was all for getting out of his head but he thinks techno music sounds better on acid, not ecstasy: 'It made different sounds in your head.' LSD remained a popular choice on Melbourne dancefloors throughout the nineties. It's not hard to understand why. Acid was familiar, lasted longer and was three times as cheap, costing around $20 a tab. Many ravers also smoked pot (especially after parties) and inhaled nitrous oxide bulbs for a brief but intense dissociative high.

'When the rave scene happened, it was like punk but it worked,' Ollie Olsen says. 'There were different drugs involved that had a big part to play.' Ecstasy and acid created a different vibe to heroin and alcohol. But even a seasoned partygoer like Ollie found some of the drugs too strong. 'The last time I took acid it was so powerful I was out of it for two days ... that was the strongest LSD since 1975 that one, it was called the Gorbachev. It had a picture of Mikhail Gorbachev on it.'

Combining mind-altering substances with mind-jamming beats fast became a weekly or nightly ritual for a growing cohort of young Melburnians. It's just what you did, as Terrence recalls:

> Every weekend, same club, everyone's on the same fucking amount of drugs, just gurning like mad jackals and letting the music do things for you that it wouldn't have done if you weren't on drugs ... we thought we were all against the

world, we were special because we were on the same mind trip and that's because the drugs really did it for you. You're all going through the same adventure at the same time ... That's what made the whole underground scene for those early years quite special to a lot of people in Melbourne.

The drugs provided an entry point into the scene for those not necessarily drawn to the music, as DJ Natural 1 explains:

Even metalheads and hip-hop-heads would say to me, 'What are you listening to that poofter dance music for?' And then you see them on a pill when they go to their first rave and they go, 'Where's this music been all my life? I love it, it's amazing'.

Ecstasy had become the ultimate free market commodity, its price determined where demand and supply intersects as anyone who's ever tried to score a pill at the end of the night when you're desperate to keep rolling and dealers' stocks are running low will attest. Moreover, suppliers need only pay for distribution because consumers willingly market their product for free. Ecstasy had near-universal appeal. Everyone was taking this new wonder drug, regardless of age, gender or cultural background. 'I remember my mum taking an E once,' Mad Rod says. 'I was like, "Oh my God, my mum's popping an E."'

'Everybody Thought They Could be a Promoter'

Yarraville, August 2014. It's a cold and windy Saturday afternoon, one of those drab Melbourne days where the streetscapes merge into the sky beneath a grey filter. I'm sitting in a small café on Anderson Street with Terrence Ho. My hands wrap around a mug of tea to keep warm. His fingers roll a cigarette. We are the last customers and the waitress is clearly anxious for us to leave, no doubt mildly disturbed at the conversation she's eavesdropping on. I ask my companion to describe the early parties in Melbourne. 'Everybody thought they could be a promoter,' he responds with typical bluntness and a look of contempt. 'They'd go to someone else's party and go, "Oh, I wanna be just like them, I wanna do a party." Eight out of ten of those parties were shit and people lost their cash because they thought they were a promoter and they weren't. So boring man.'

One balmy evening in 1989, Mad Rod was walking home in St Kilda when he saw a flyer for 'A London Acid Party' at the St Kilda Cricket Club. Intrigued, he turned up on Saturday night and found about thirty people hanging out, including a number of old friends from the alternative music and punk scenes. Promoters Patsy and Elizabeth had set up the party underneath the pavilion beneath the stands. 'I can still see this party,' he tells me. 'They had ferns, they'd created a tropical atmosphere, they went to a lot of trouble for the small amount of people who came!'

Davide Carbone tells me people began throwing warehouse parties to create an environment more amenable to drug taking than the increasingly hostile nightclubs:

> It was all about coming and taking ecstasy ... they didn't say it but that's what it was about. These kids from some private school would come to ZuZus and they'd be like, 'I've just had a pill, it's the most amazing thing!' Then they'd hear about rave culture and they'd literally just go off, hire a warehouse, go and find a source for ecstasy (that was fundamentally important) and then, $20 you're in, your pills are cheap, and 200 private schoolkids go to this place.

In 1989, Nimmo Sandilands graduated from Melbourne High, an elite government school akin to a private school but without the hefty fees. He tells me about half the kids in his year were 'into techno'. This Melbourne High techno cabal was highly influential in the early scene. Two of Nimmo's classmates, Thaddeus Lester and Simon Dent, ran parties at Amadeus nightclub attached to the Matthew Flinders hotel in Chadstone. Fashion designer Misha Hollenbach, another classmate, was 'pretty heavily involved in the early scene', while Karl Fitzgerald (aka Swytek) co-founded Earthcore (see Chapter Ten).

As well as the Melbourne High posse, many other early promoters came from solid middle-class backgrounds, although this was by no means exclusively the case. Nevertheless, I can't help drawing a line between these well-heeled techno pioneers and the similarly privileged upbringings of the Belleville Three in Detroit and England's schoolboy entrepreneurs like Eton-educated Tony Colston-Hayter. Does techno have an intrinsic middle-class sensibility that instinctively appeals to arty angsty kids looking to break out from their bourgeois shackles? Scholar Chris Gibson would seem to think so:

> It's a music that's been championed by … an inner-city crowd of people, university students, artists, who see themselves as kind of urbane, bohemian avant-garde. And it's really come out of that sort of social scene in Sydney and probably in Melbourne too, rather than as being an authentic, organic expression of the streets, as it were. If anything, hip hop has been more successful in that regard, here in Australia.[30]

In September 1989, Chasers nightclub organised a warehouse party in South Melbourne called Public Address. DJs Gavin Campbell, Guy Uppiah, John Portelli, Nigel B., Steve Robbins and Davide Carbone played a mix of acid house, disco, hip hop and mainstream dance music. The party featured a fashion parade with costumes from designers David Green, Katherine Hamnett and Bettina Liano. Davide Carbone condemns Public Address as a 'feeble attempt' to replicate the British warehouse party concept. To his mind, the organisers had simply recreated the classy and exclusive nightclub vibe but in a warehouse setting. Rave demanded something grittier and grungier.

A few months later, an architect called Martin approached Davide: 'Obviously he'd read or heard about raves, probably seen it on TV … he was just an outsider, a forty-year-old guy … he was trying to do the whole rave concept.' Martin hired the top floor of the Prince Patrick Hotel in Collingwood and promised Davide a good set if he brought along his crew. 'I played from two until six; there were probably only twenty or thirty people left by that stage but it was such an intense atmosphere,' Davide recalls. Martin called the party Lunatic Fringe. It was yet another nod to the punk scene; there had been a Little Band of the same name. Through late 1989 and early 1990, Lunatic Fringe and similar parties brought together some of the previously disparate groups of techno fans around Melbourne. Suddenly, people listening and dancing to 'weird shit' knew they weren't alone.

Biology

Melbourne, Saturday 10 June 1990. The Power House in Albert Park sends shock waves across the lake, rumbling the foundations of nearby houses. Inside, a few hundred people dance to deep drilling techno that rushes through their blood and makes their bones vibrate with each step they take. A laser cuts through the darkness to reveal glimpses of bare walls and happy faces. Some people write words in the air with sparklers while others hug and chat. A new subculture is taking seed, spreading its branches and entangling everybody with its love and unity. Rave has come to Melbourne.

Punks, rich kids, nightclubs, complete outsiders—it seems everyone had had a go but no-one could get it right. In the end, a pair of longhaired hippies from Hackney had to show them how to rave. For Biology, Richard and Heidi John collaborated with Grant Harrison and Mark James. They had all the essential ingredients: a quality sound system, strobe lighting, high intensity lasers and a dark, dingy shed. Richard and Heidi spent most of the night wandering around the crowd, talking to everyone and making people feel safe, welcome and valued. If people were distressed, Heidi calmed them down. If anything went wrong, Richard stepped in. Mark, on the other hand, focussed only on the music. 'I wasn't a real people person, I was more of a DJ ... I wouldn't even go out into the crowd half the time because I'd been DJing all night and the last thing I wanted to do was walk around talking to people.'

Biology was a triumph, both financially and symbolically. On paper, the organising team seemed a felicitous combination: the Johns had the raving pedigree, Mark supplied the music and Grant brought the crowd. But the party's success masked significant tensions behind the scenes. Mark describes himself as a 'control freak' and the Johns as 'nutters'. For his part, Richard admits he and Mark 'weren't compatible' as business partners. Nevertheless, they put their differences aside to organise a follow-up party at the same venue three months later. Things didn't turn out as planned. 'We did Biology I and that went well, it was legendary,' Mark says. 'And then we did Biology II and we lost lots of money, about twenty or thirty grand.' It's a story that was retold throughout the nineties for Melbourne's rave promoters: incredible highs followed by desperate lows. Kind of appropriate, I think, for a scene built around ecstasy use. Biology II also taught Mark that raving could be hazardous to one's health as well as one's bank balance. The morning after the party, he climbed up a thirty-foot ladder to take down a slide projector:

> Everyone's off their face, there's water and drinks spilled all over the ground and I felt the ladder slide a bit so I turned around and everyone was sat around gurning and I shouted out, 'Someone grab the ladder!' And then ... splat! I broke my arm, wrist, ankle and ribs. Everyone surrounded me going, 'Mark, Mark are you okay?' and I said, 'Yeah, fuck, get back to work,' and then I got up to take down another projector and collapsed. I went home and had a bath and my body just turned purple so I went to hospital and got fixed up.

'Biology was authentic,' Davide Carbone explains. 'By the time it came around, the culture had formed.' Stef agrees. He worked the bar at Biology and many of Richard and Heidi's parties throughout the nineties: 'Biology was a complete eye opener for me because all of a sudden everybody seemed to get it, this thing I had no idea existed'. If we credit Biology with the birth of rave culture in Melbourne, as Stef suggests, then I think we owe that to the Johns. Richard and Heidi knew they had to create a different experience from the nightclub, an environment that immersed people in a time and place they could call their own. Richard clarifies:

> Nightclubs weren't designed for raves ... nightclubs were designed for drinking. The biggest space in the nightclub is the bar and the smallest space is the dancefloor. Whereas at our parties, the biggest space in the place was the dancefloor and we didn't have alcohol.

Steve Robbins agrees that the warehouse party vibe fundamentally differed from a nightclub. 'Clubs were really, really exclusive ... if you walked up as a raver, you'd never get in. The one thing with the raves was you got that instant sense of belonging.'

Given the Johns' influence, Biology naturally bore an undeniable British flavour. They even borrowed the name from back home: Jarvis Sandy had put on the original Biology rave in fields near Watford in June 1989.[31] Richard and Heidi knew how to take what they'd seen work in England and somehow make it look new and fresh in Melbourne. 'People used to say to us, "How did you know this was coming?" and I'd say, "I've come from the future, I've done this",' Heidi tells me. 'And we were, we were from the future.' They didn't need a DeLorean time machine with an in-built flux capacitor to see the future, just the knowledge that Australian cultural trends always lag behind the UK, as Terrence Ho so eloquently explains:

> Anything that happens in England will happen six months or a year down the road here. It slowly filters down. We're the arsehole of the world.

Whether Biology was truly a rave in the British sense is debatable. I'm told that as well as acid house and techno, the DJs played funk, disco and commercial dance. But Richard and Heidi are unequivocal. 'There wasn't anything going on before Biology,' Richard says. 'Biology was the first rave. When we first came to Australia, they were still doing the Bus Stop!'[32]

The Republic of Rave

When the Johns weren't putting on warehouse parties or running nightclubs, they hosted parties at their home in Evans House, a former gold bullion repository built in the Art Moderne style located in the heart of the city at 415 Bourke Street. Although just sixty years old, by 1990 crippling maintenance bills combined with recession-era vacancy rates meant the building lay crumbling and forgotten. But where others smelt slow decay, Richard sniffed opportunity. 'At one point, everything in Melbourne was up for lease … you'd just walk in there and get it.' And so it was with Evans House.

Living on Bourke Street was a very different experience back then. 'There was nowhere to get a bottle of milk,' Heidi exclaims—yes, milk still came in bottles in 1990. 'I used to have to go to Myer or David Jones—that was my closest shop. We had credit at McDonald's! Whoever gets credit at McDonald's?! We would be out sitting on the street waiting for it to open, it was the only place to go.'

Richard and Heidi lived on the first level with sixteen-year-old daughter Driena and infant daughter Jade. Ollie Olsen, Gus Till and Geoff Hales (aka Rip Van Hippy) occupied the third floor. Ollie laughs:

> I called our place the world's most expensive squat … it was a dump. Walls had been smashed down and nothing had been done with them. We were living in rubble really. And then having to pay a lot of rent for the privilege.

In 1989, Ollie had collaborated with INXS frontman Michael Hutchence on the Max Q project, culminating in the release of best-selling album *Max Q*, mixed by New York house music legend Todd Terry. Ollie used the hefty paycheck from Max Q to support his growing immersion in house and techno and to fund an ever-increasing party habit. 'That period was a bit of a blur because there were a lot of drugs involved,' he admits. In September 1990, Ollie, Gus Till and Geoff Hales formed Third Eye. Their first single, 'The Real Thing', layered acid house and synthpop rhythms with trippy Timothy Leary samples. It reached number 76 in the Australian charts. In 1991, journalist Chris Johnston reviewed Third Eye's eponymous debut album for *Rolling Stone Magazine*. Chris loved it but his editor asked him to downgrade the review from five stars. Rock'n'roll wasn't ready to move over for rave just yet.

Third Eye stored their instruments in the old gold safe on the second level. This was also the party floor. Stef worked the bar. One particular night sticks in his mind:

> Because this was before mobile phones, we had this system in place. The bouncers downstairs had a wire that ran up three storeys and I had it hooked up to a set of hubcaps so if the cops came, the bouncers would pull the wire and the hubcaps would crash to the ground and we'd know to put the alcohol away!

It sounds like something out of *The Goonies*. Maybe that's where Stef got his inspiration. For another party, Richard and Heidi bought a blow-up swimming pool, filled it with beanbag beans and rigged up a strobe. As partygoers dived into the pool, the strobe light made the jumping beans appear to freeze in mid-air. 'For the rest of the time they lived there, those fucking beans were all the way down the stairs,' Stef says. 'Once they're free you can't get rid of them. They're probably still there in that stairwell.' I went to have a look in May 2015. Sadly, I didn't find any beans, only corporate offices. Now, the first floor of 415 Bourke Street houses the Malian embassy. Heidi laughed when I told her: 'From the republic of rave to the republic of Mali!'

Total Confusion

Through the latter half of 1990, flyers for warehouse parties began to litter nightclub dancefloors and Chapel Street car parks. Recall how Josh Abrahams fell in love with techno after hearing all those mischievous minor seconds? That party was Kemistri 3 at the Palace nightclub in St Kilda, organised by street music magazine *Inpress* on Melbourne Cup Eve. '[The music] was quite slow to begin with and it was only later in the night that Terrence Ho played this stuff called techno,' Josh recalls. 'It was the first time I heard the word techno. He played 'Total Confusion'.' Josh thinks it might have been the first time anyone in Melbourne had played 'Total Confusion', an undisputed rave classic from A Homeboy, A Hippy and A Funki Dredd.

Terrence almost didn't play at all. On his way down to St Kilda, a policeman apprehended him because of his costume:

> We were going there dressed up as freaks. My girlfriend at that time and her friend were dressed up as twins so they had the same clothes on basically. And I had my full camo garb with Techno Terrorist written on the back of my camo top, black face and a plastic Uzi that shot out ball bearings. I was going to my car and the cop says, 'Right, come with me'.

Terrence's brush with terrorism portended things to come. A few months later, he released a white label with Gus Till and Ollie Olsen called *ISIS Overload*. 'I was the Islamic State. I was ISIS before ISIS was,' he boasts. When he finally arrived at the Palace, Terrence played his set and spent the rest of the night waving his gun around, fucked on drugs and freaking people out. Total Confusion.

The year 1990 closed with Cyber, one of the most notorious parties in Melbourne's raving history. Cyber added yet another colourful chapter to the St Kilda Sea Baths' sordid back pages. Richard and Heidi organised the party with help from, among others, Jeff Jaffers, Andrew Till and Kellie Wilkinson. They billed Cyber as a 'New Year Rave' for 'happy people only'. It was one of the first times in Melbourne the word 'rave' had appeared on a flyer, almost two years after it had first featured in the British partying lexicon. DJ Brewster B. recalls:

> No-one actually called it rave in the early days ... they were called parties ... maybe because of Richard and Heidi and other Brits that were hanging around, they'd seen the second summer of love and they talked about rave but I think it became part of the vernacular in a gradual way.

Cyber is a party that if you weren't there, you wish you had been and if you were there, you probably can't remember. The lineup featured Terrence Ho, Dr Cid, Goa Bro (Fred Disko and Steve Psyko), Garry Hughes and Ollie Olsen. In between wiping the condensation off his records, Terrence spied people fucking in shower cubicles and jumping in the pool at midnight. Earlier in the day, the thermometer had topped 38°C—it was so hot inside that water dripped from the ceiling like rain. When Stef turned up at midnight to run the bar and found punters walking off with bottles of vodka, he decided to get into the swing of it:

> I took way too much acid. After the party I got to Flinders Street station, I looked up at the clock and the dial was squashed into the building and the minute hand was sticking out towards me, like a Dali painting. That was a bit too full on, even for me.

Biology, Kemistri and Cyber represented the first wave of rave in Melbourne—the golden years according to many of the original old skool. 'Those parties had a vibe,' Richard John says. 'It was still underground, it was still only you who knew. That was the first era when you were drawn to it. It wasn't being blasted on every lamp post and radio and being *sold* to people.' As well as regular warehouse parties, two clubs in 1990 provided a weekly underground fix. Razor was one of them. 'Razor had the house music, the openness and the drugs,' Chris Johnston says. 'It was the gateway into the rave and techno scene.' Melbourne's techno promoters 'did their homework' at Razor every Friday night. And then on Saturday evening they crawled out of bed and drove to the Commerce Club.

Chapter 5

PURE RAVERS

Maze at Commerce

Melbourne, March 2017. On a warm autumn morning, I walk into the nondescript chain hotel that now occupies 318–332 Flinders Street in the city. As I loiter in the lobby and peer at framed photos of the building's heyday in the glamorous forties, the concierge approaches me. I tell him that we're standing directly above the infamous Commerce Club. 'This used to be a nightclub?' he exclaims, incredulous. 'Are you sure?' I nod my head. He shakes his. 'We didn't have nightclubs in Melbourne in the eighties and nineties,' he laughs. How little he knows.

In 1913, respected architect Harry Tompkins won a competition to design a new club building and an adjoining 'investment building' (called Commerce House) for the Commercial Travellers Association of Victoria (CTA).[1] The CTA had been established to represent the needs of travelling salesmen in Victoria. Until the construction of the Manchester Unity building in 1932, the neo-baroque CTA Club was Melbourne's tallest building.[2] The CTA installed electrically heated lifts, telephones in every room and one of Australia's first potato-peeling machines.[3] Halfway between a gentlemen's club and an Edwardian-era airport lounge, the club offered meals, drinks and a bed to the commercial traveller as he passed through Melbourne en route to his next sale. In 1959, director Stanley Kramer used the poolroom to shoot scenes for *On the Beach,* a film adaptation of Nevil Shute's post-apocalyptic novel, starring Gregory Peck, Ava Gardner and Fred Astaire.[4]

By the seventies, however, the rise of telephone orders and mail order catalogues meant that the commercial traveller had become obsolete. The CTA club closed its doors in 1976. Faced with a dwindling membership base and rising maintenance costs, the club fell into disrepair. Squatters moved in, lit fires to keep warm, and nearly burnt down the building on more than one occasion.[5] The 'odd dead body' apparently turned up from time to time.[6] During the eighties, in a desperate bid to bring in funds, the CTA leased the upper floors of Commerce House to artists, fashion designers, photographers and writers—anyone prepared to accept squalid conditions in return for cheap rent. There were plenty of takers. Victoria was on the verge of recession. Tenants included the Fashion Design Council of Australia, model train enthusiasts, roleplaying gamers, a conservative party social club and filmmaker Garry Shepherd.[7] The working conditions could be hazardous. Garry recalls how one day a slab of rendered concrete fell from the ceiling onto his neighbour's desk.[8]

Max Poyser, the man behind seventies gay hangout the University Club, opened the Commerce Club in the basement of Commerce House sometime around 1984. Previously a cheese cellar, the basement was dark, dingy and full of hidden nooks and crannies, with its own entrance accessed via a dimly lit narrow alleyway off Flinders Lane. The Commerce Club began life as a series of gay sex rooms during the day and was pretty much the same at night, except with louder music. Mad Rod tells me the venue had an older, seedy vibe: 'Commerce Club before Maze played old music for old people, like a gay RSL club … I'd go there with my friends to eat their pub food and then head upstairs and hang out with some seriously cool people living this very alternative on-the-edge lifestyle.'

In October 1989, twenty-year-old Ian Spicer moved from Sydney to Melbourne with a box of funk records and an ambition to start his own dance club. One night he attended a social event at the Commerce Club and ran into CTA secretary Peter Booth. On hearing about the club's financial difficulties, Ian offered to take over Saturday nights—he'd collect the door and the CTA would take the bar. Peter agreed. It was a bold move. Ian had never run a club before; he was new to Melbourne and knew few people. However, he had one thing in his favour: similar to the Light Car Club (the home of Razor), the CTA possessed one of Victoria's oldest liquor licences, with no restrictions on trading hours or patron numbers so long as management restricted entry to members and guests (limited to two per member). The strict licence conditions and Ian's no advertising policy ensured the club remained exclusive to those in the know. 'It was very underground,' Ian insists. 'If you didn't know where it was, you weren't meant to be there.'

Ian named the club Maze after the American soul band, although other people have told me it was called this because the cheese cellar was shaped like a maze. On opening night, Ian set up his decks and primed the bouncers and bar staff. There was just one problem—his club was so underground no-one knew about it. But that all changed when a cocky Cockney called Rudeboy turned up at the door.

A Rude Awakening

Jason Rudeboy grew up in 'lower middle-class' Chiswick—about twelve miles to the west of the East End ghetto his moniker suggests. Like Richard and Heidi John, he'd seen the second summer of love firsthand in England. 'It was 1988, and ecstasy had just hit,' he says. 'I went to the Trip, which was sort of the breaking point of acid house. It became extremely commercial after that.' His parents bought him a one-way ticket to Australia for his twenty-first birthday. 'I didn't go to university; I was working as a grave digger ... I think my mum wanted to get me out of that.' Rudeboy flew to Brisbane and stayed with his cousins in Beenleigh. He tells me his father was a famous DJ in Brisbane during the sixties ('he was in with the Stones and the Beatles').

By December 1988, Rudeboy had found his way to Melbourne, going to ZuZus and Checkpoint Charlie and meeting people like Ollie Olsen, Richard and Heidi, and Mad Rod. He dealt ecstasy in nightclubs, earning enough money to buy a ticket back to England once his one-year visa had expired. Over the British summer of 1989, he teamed up with travelling free party activists Tonka sound system, hanging out with DJ Choci, DJ Reverse and DJ Harvey. Boasting a free party heritage that dated back to the sixties, Tonka switched onto acid house in the late eighties, throwing parties in London and on Brighton beach.[9] In July 1990, Tonka descended on Glastonbury for the annual music festival and helped forge an alliance between 'New Age' travellers and ravers seeking to defend their right to party in the face of increasing commercialisation and legal action.[10] Matthew Collin writes:

> Heavy acid rhythms pulsed as day broke over the dancers ... phone numbers were swapped, partnerships formed, and two generations of hippies appeared to join hands. When a traveller rode his horse around the dancefloor in the middle of the night, it seemed to herald the beginning of a new era.[11]

But Rudeboy didn't make it as far as Glastonbury:

> It was eight months of going out every single night non-stop ... I was at work one day and I collapsed and they called an

ambulance because they thought I'd had a heart attack or died. The ambulance driver said, 'He's asleep'. I hadn't slept for about a week and a half! I just fell off my chair in the men's room.

In late 1989, Rudeboy bought a bag of records and boarded a plane back to Melbourne. When he arrived, he got a job managing a sex shop in Richmond and went around boasting he was a famous English DJ, which he wasn't. Nevertheless, people believed him and he started getting gigs. Like many DJs, he played around with his name until he found the right groove: I've seen flyers from that period featuring Jason Da Groove, Jason Rudeboy, The Rudeboy and simply Jason.

Rudeboy found out about Maze after one of his friends told him they were looking for a DJ:

> I went down there to see the guy and said, 'I heard you need a DJ'. 'No, who told you that?' Ian replied. 'My friend, Maddie.' 'Well we're not really looking for one', Ian said. I said, 'Your club's empty', which it was at the time. 'I'll fill it, yeah? Then if I fill it, will you give me a job?' Ian paused for a moment. 'Okay.'

The next Saturday night, Rudeboy appeared at the door with a hundred punters queueing behind him. He'd asked everyone he knew to come. Some people even brought their parents. Needless to say, he got the job.

A couple of weeks later, Rudeboy met Terrence Ho at the 2000AD New Year's Eve party at the Film Studio in Waterloo, Sydney. House music pioneer Frankie Knuckles headlined the night in his first Australian appearance. 'We were messed on drugs, dancing away to Frankie Knuckles and we just really connected as people who enjoyed the same kind of stuff', Terrence recalls. But Terrence and Rudeboy shared more than an interest in dance and drugs; both men ardently rejected mainstream society and culture, seeking to conceal their middle-class upbringings behind streetstyle personas. Between them, they boasted an impressive record collection of hard-to-find and rarely heard techno. Terrence had also been in England in 1989, soaking up as much new techno as he could find. 'I remember listening to Doug Lazy 'Let It Roll', Kariya 'Let Me Love You For Tonight' and 'Voodoo Ray' by A Guy Called Gerald,' he says. 'All those types of tracks were the ones that really did it for me.'

After the Sydney party, Terrence gave Rudeboy a lift back to Melbourne. I can just imagine the scene: the 40°C sun glaring through the windscreen, a mixtape blaring from the stereo and a twelve-hour conversation of drugs, sex and techno. In February 1990, Rudeboy brought Terrence into the Commerce Club. Thus began, to quote Ian, the 'golden age' of Maze.

Down the Rabbit Hole

Maze wasn't really a nightclub; it was more like an overgrown house party. It was underground in every sense of the word: unadvertised, located in a basement and playing music you wouldn't hear at Chasers or the Chevron. Terrence explains:

> We played house, acid, everything that was new, really … we did all the 'Voodoo Ray' type stuff, Ron Trent 'Afterlife', underground Chicago stuff, Detroit stuff … There was a period in the nineties when the UK got really into bleep, like Shut Up and Dance, Bleeps International, LFO, all that kind of stuff, we played it all … we broke Network as a label, Nu Groove as a label. No-one else would play it … all the regular DJs in the regular clubs, they wanted to play safe, they just played the normal stuff they played every week. So that's why a lot of people came to our club because we played something different.

I have a mixtape recorded at Maze during 1991, courtesy of Richard Tropea. The track listing is a roll call of underground classics including 'Tricky Disco' by Tricky Disco, 'Do It Believe It' by Joey Negro, 'Indulge' by Neal Howard, 'Somebody New' by MK, 'Dante's Inferno' by Frankie Bones, 'Pure (Energy)' by GTO and Derrick May's 1987 techno standard 'Strings of Life'. Every time I listen, I'm amazed how fresh it sounds.

Raver Sid Sidney never forgot his Maze initiation. 'It was the first time I'd ever been to a club that didn't look like a club … it was just some alleyway, and when you got close to it, all you could hear was bass going through metal.' Every Saturday, the staff packed away the table and chairs, hung a few decorations and transformed the cafeteria into a dancefloor. The DJs set up in the kitchen behind the serving window. There were no set times, which in theory meant people could just get up and play when they liked, but even Ian struggled to prise Rudeboy and Terrence from the decks. 'I think Terrence Ho is probably the true leader [of Melbourne techno],' Maze regular Nimmo Sandilands says. 'He was the one finding strange music. I don't know how he found it but he did.' Meanwhile, Davide Carbone praises Rudeboy for energising the Melbourne scene:

> Whilst he wasn't really playing what they were playing in London and he was a bit of an impostor, he actually had his own thing, which was really authentic and very different to what they were doing in America and what we were doing here.

In the back room, Dr John and Taxi & Kano played rare groove and northern soul beneath a suspended parachute while French barman Stéphane poured cocktails. James 'The Flying Fijian' Greenwood ran the pool tables where he entertained the likes of U2, INXS and Robert Palmer. An East Timorese refugee, known to all as Pumpkin Dave, ran the lights. 'He just turned up one day and started doing the lights,' Rudeboy recalls. 'I thought he was a friend of Terrence. Terrence thought he was a friend of mine. Ian thought I knew him. The guy just walked in off the street.' Just like Rudeboy had done a few weeks before.

Maze capitalised on the Commerce Club's dark laneway entrance. 'And down the rabbit hole you'd go', Nimmo says. Except that when you got to this Wonderland, you bypassed the White Rabbit and the Cheshire Cat and walked straight into the Mad Hatter's E Party. 'Maze was crazy,' says Ollie Olsen. 'It was complete lunacy most of the time. People were completely off their faces.' The archaic liquor licence meant it was one of the last remaining free pour venues in Melbourne. And then there were the drugs. 'We just had lines of stuff, different tablets and things under the turntables and mixers all night long,' Rudeboy recalls. 'People came up all night and gave us things and we didn't really know what we were doing'.

Several of my interviewees describe Maze as one big happy family. Rock dogs and ravers mingled with Rastafarians while S&M fetishists played pool with B-grade celebrities and drag queens. 'There were some real trippers there,' Ian says. 'People on the edge of art.' He recalls two girls dressed in 'Edwardian costumes' spending the night standing in the corner reading fake newspapers. People tell me they felt a sense of freedom, belonging and unity at Maze. 'It wasn't clubs, it was people who understood you,' Davide Carbone claims. 'You'd just take whatever you want to take and hear the music you want to hear … I think Maze was where rave culture was allowed to breathe.'

As well as playing the latest underground cuts from America and Europe, Maze nurtured local techno talent. In 1991, Josh Abrahams brought a cassette to the Commerce Club and asked the DJ to play a track he had just written. 'It had this big build-up and people started going off, dancing and cheering, and I thought, "this is actually working, it's taking off", and then it slowed down and stopped.' He imitates the hiss of a cassette spool getting jammed. 'I only found out years later that the DJ had managed to drop the cassette in the toilet and it was waterlogged!' Maze also featured occasional live acts including Vertigo Hypo (Bryan St James and Narelle Wellington) and Gstaad, a freeform collaboration comprising Rudeboy, singer Baby Lemonade and keyboardist Braden Schlager. Braden recalls:

I was basically grabbing the last track in my head and finding the key it was in and then concocting something that would tie one track with the next. It was really stressful because I was no whizz keyboard player but it was a lot of fun. And sometimes we'd do so well that we'd go on with it and do freeform stuff live. I'd take over the track and Rudeboy would add stuff over the top of it.

Back in the eighties, Braden had played drums and synth with experimental post-punk band Human Backs. His interest in electronic dance music began with Kraftwerk's *The Man-Machine* ('they never cease to blow my mind') and intensified after hearing early techno tracks like 808 State's 'Pacific State'. In 1989, he and friend Miles du Heaume began to chase the perfect techno sound that Kraftwerk had presaged a decade earlier. 'Because we didn't DJ we were writing sets, like an hour-long set, that we could gig,' Braden explains. 'We'd have to write it as one long track. It was really difficult to seam the tracks together back then. Only a few DJs were beat matching.' Braden brought a sampler and a cassette deck into Maze and began playing his sets live. 'The dancefloor doesn't lie … if you empty the dancefloor, you go back to the drawing board.' Playing cassettes was easier and cheaper than pressing vinyl but what he'd gained in convenience he lost in durability. 'The cassettes got re-done and re-done and they would spit out, get stolen or get drinks poured on them.' So, in 1990, he decided to release what he claims was the first dance music record in Australia.

Made in Melbourne

Dance music subverts prior notions of authenticity insofar as the records are original, and live performance is reproduction.[12] DJs, not artists, drive dance music—their favourite records become the dancefloor's most popular tracks. For Australian producers like Braden, getting his record into the hands of a DJ or securing a live gig with a promoter was a costly exercise, as vinyl junkie Nimmo Sandilands explains:

> In England, for example, you could get dubplates and acetates cut quite cheaply, then take your demo to the local clubs, test it out, go back home and refine it … but because of the tyranny of distance in Australia and the small size of the scene, there just wasn't many opportunities for gigs … in Melbourne the first time you got to test it was when you had the finished product that you'd just spent $4000 on.

That 'finished product' came from Richmond Recorders, Melbourne's only vinyl pressing plant. Tim Stobart founded Richmond Recorders in the mid-seventies.[13] The Birthday Party, Paul Kelly, The Go-Betweens and Split Enz all recorded albums there.[14] In the mid-eighties, sharpies icon Lobby Loyde and punk band Painters and Dockers took over the premises and opened a vinyl pressing plant a few doors down on Pearson Street, Cremorne.[15]

Braden tells me Richmond Recorders did a 'reasonable job' with his record. 'I don't think they'd ever done something like that before,' he says. 'They mislabelled it as the wrong speed so a lot of time it came on at 45rpm instead of 33rpm.' He asked his girlfriend to design the artwork and he drew the labels by hand. He called the EP *Schlager on the Moon*:

> I came up with something that seemed to be pretty good although things were moving so quick that by the time I got it onto vinyl I thought, 'Oh God, how old is this?' The key track was called 'Morning'. There were two mixes of that … and then my ridiculous attempt at techno ['Rummage'] on the B-side.

Despite the costs and mistakes, Braden believes the effort was worth it: 'I found it so exciting to actually put it on vinyl … it made sense at the time.'

In Adelaide, Juice Records founder HMC (aka Housemaster C, real name Carmelo Bianchetti) had discovered it was more cost effective to press locally produced music overseas and then sell the records as imported pressings back home.[16] '[Juice] were really clever,' DJ Brewster B. told the ABC:

> [t]hey got their records pressed in Canada, and then they were sold, and the people were going, 'I got this American techno, I got this American house record', thinking it's an American record, because it almost had an American sound to it, and all of a sudden, they're going … Australian producer, lalalalala, 'hang on a minute, that label's Australian?!'[17]

But few producers could afford to cut a record locally or pay the duty on an imported pressing. For many artists, simply getting hold of the right equipment proved the biggest hurdle. 'Black box' analogue synths like the Roland TB-303 and TR-808 didn't come cheap. 'We begged, borrowed or stole as much gear as we could to produce music,' Braden confesses.

I think it's a stretch to honour Braden's ninety-second B-side 'Rummage' as Australia's first techno release. Third Eye's first single 'The Real Thing' could be a stronger contender, although perhaps it has too many lyrics to qualify as techno. Other challengers for the title include HMC's *100% Juice*, reportedly the first Australian-produced 'Detroit techno' record,[18] and *Isis Overload* by Isis Overload (see Chapter Four), both released in 1991. Meanwhile down in Frankston, Andrew Van Dorsselaer (aka Andy Van) and John Course had set up their Vicious Vinyl record label in 1989. Their 1990 release *Witness the Strength* could be yet another candidate if only I could track down a copy to listen to it. Regardless of which came first, one thing's for certain: all these records got a play at Maze.

The Secret Gets Out

In 2003, the ABC identified Maze as Australia's first techno club.[19] Since then, everyone has claimed a piece of it. 'The parallel I make is the Paradise Garage in New York,' Rudeboy states. 'Everybody says they were there, but I didn't see them.' Ouch. Seminal maybe, but Maze seldom filled. Fun came first, profits second. In October 1990, Rudeboy's visa ran out for a second time and he flew back to London. A few weeks later, Mark James and Richard and Heidi approached Ian and offered to buy into the club. Ian felt uncomfortable:

> I really like Mark but we just didn't gel as business partners. He came to me with all these ideas and artworks, like a Maze Christmas cake and Campbell's Soup type pop art and it just didn't work. It wasn't what Maze was about.

But Ian was losing money and so reluctantly, he handed over control of the club to Mark and the Johns. Overnight, the energy of the club changed. 'We used to fill the room with smoke and play nursery rhymes,' Rudeboy says. 'No-one could replicate that.'

On Saturday 2 March 1991, the new owners threw a first birthday party featuring Ollie Olsen and Gary Hughes on decks. Maze was actually eighteen months old but no one was counting. Guests arriving before 1am ate birthday cake and drank complimentary cocktails. It was a lot of fun. But Ian felt uneasy. 'It was our first real promotion,' he tells me. 'We'd never advertised the club before.' Scores of new people began queueing at the door. The secret was out. Maze had lost its underground cachet; it was 'no longer pure'. Mark sacked Ian's bouncers and put girlfriend Gina on the door. Five years later, performing as Gina G, she came eighth in the 1996 Eurovision song contest, representing the UK with 'Ooh Aah … Just A Little Bit'. In September of that year I saw Gina G live, if you can call it that, at Ritzy's nightclub in Nottingham, England. I know, I know, but I was only eighteen.

Ian tells me he never had any trouble with the police during the first year of Maze, which I find astonishing considering there was a police station just fifty metres away on the corner of Flinders Lane and Elizabeth Street. In 1991, Victoria Police closed the Flinders Lane station and divisional command took over responsibility for the area. Within weeks, Commerce Club patrons complained that uniformed officers were stopping and searching them in the laneway as they left the venue. When Ian directed his patrons to leave via the fire exit instead, the police changed tactics. Brewster B. tells me it was common to see plain-clothed police officers at Maze and other parties around that time:

> I saw constables undercover wearing raver clothes but their idea of raver clothes meant they stood out! They looked like they'd dressed to go to a clown concert. They'd just stand around looking at everyone and they weren't dancing.

One time, officers arrived at the club and told Ian they'd received reports of devil worshipping on the premises. Ian took them inside and they stopped beside a giant underwater-themed banner. 'They're looking at King Neptune and one of them bends down and goes, "Yeah, if I look at it upside down then he does kind of look like the devil",' Ian recalls. On another occasion, the police tried to shut the club down because some people had climbed onto the roof of Commerce House and smashed beer bottles onto the ground seven storeys below. Ian managed to convince the officers that the tenants from the upper levels, and not his patrons, were responsible. But he was only prolonging the inevitable. 'They began to follow me around … they would even sit outside my house in their car, it was full on.' By May 1991, it had become too much. Maze shut its doors, closing one of the most colourful chapters in Melbourne's raving history. The CTA limped on for another two decades before finally disbanding in 2014.[20] In Maze's final months, several up-and-coming DJs clamoured for a guest spot. Some were forgettable. Others rocked.

But when Ian invited Richie Rich and Will E Tell to spin some tunes, the Melbourne rave scene changed forever.

Jedi Nights

St Kilda, March 2015. I'm sitting in the office of Richie McNeill, marvelling at his expansive and expensive collection of Star Wars action figures that stare down at me from all angles. In February 1999, Richie declared he'd pay $1000 for a seat at the first screening of the upcoming *Star Wars* movie *Episode I—The Phantom Menace*.[21] (After I saw the film, I felt George Lucas should have paid me $1000 for enduring two hours of Jar Jar Binks). Richie's love of Star Wars is well known in the scene. In 1998, six rival promoters united for the 'War of the Worlds' party, casting themselves as the 'Rebel Alliance' against the 'Evil Empire', the latter a thinly disguised codeword for Richie's Hardware Corporation. As I sit and listen to his rapid speech and watch his eyes twinkle with childlike innocence, I see a nerdy kid trapped behind the mask of a hard-nosed businessman. I can't decide if Richie is Anakin Skywalker or Darth Vader.

Richie grew up in Melbourne's affluent eastern suburbs. He tells me as a teenager in the eighties, he was immersed in many different subcultures:

> I had friends with long hair and flannelette shirts who used to drive around Doncaster on Friday nights punching and getting into fights. I had other friends that went with spray cans, spray painting and listening to hip hop. And I had friends with weird haircuts, black pointy suede shoes and bomber jackets that listened to New Order and The Cure.

In 1987, when Richie was sixteen years old, he was part of a breakdancing troupe that busked at the local shopping centre on Saturday afternoons. His b-boy routines at Doncaster Shoppingtown nurtured three passions that would drive him in adult life: music, dancing and making money. Richie found other aspects of hip hop culture less appealing. He tells me he briefly hung out with a gang of graffiti writers until he tired of 'getting into trouble and running away from skinheads'.

Richie attended Ivanhoe Grammar, a private school in Melbourne's northeast. Saturday night meant the Beehive at the Carron Tavern on Spencer Street or Tok H, a nightclub tucked behind the Trak cinema on Toorak Road. 'Tok H was a known underage haunt,' Richie says. 'A lot of people from Hawthorn-based private schools used to go there.' Tok H occasionally dished up a dancier track by Dead or Alive or New Order or a crossover hit like Technotronic's 'Pump Up The Jam' among its sonic smorgasbord of punk, indie, goth, hip hop and new wave. But it wasn't until Richie heard Steve Robbins drop Phuture's 'We Are Phuture' at Checkpoint Charlie in 1989 that techno left an indelible imprint on his teenage mind:

> It was dark. The smoke was pumping. At the beginning the whistle's going. I was like, 'holy shit what is this?' When the acid came in I was like, 'bloody hell!' People were frothing at the mouth. You couldn't help but get caught up in it. It was nothing that I'd ever heard before. It was so powerful.

Richie celebrated his eighteenth birthday in October 1989. From the perspective of the Melbourne rave scene, it was the perfect time to come of age. For a hard-working and highly motivated kid like Richie, who had just finished school and had time on his hands and few responsibilities, techno presented boundless opportunities. And yet events might have turned out very differently. 'I wanted to be in the Air Force but I didn't get in … I was down to the last couple of hundred but I didn't pass.' Instead, Richie enrolled at Chisholm College (now part of Monash University) to study software engineering. He also got a job as a busboy (aka bussie) at Chasers nightclub. In between restocking the fridge and clearing away the glasses, he scribbled down the names of tracks he liked and befriended DJs Paul Siedle, Steve Robbins and Mark James. On his nights off, Richie used his 'industry' status to jump the queue at Inflation, Chevron and Commerce Club.

Richie tells me the scene went 'bananas' in 1989 and exploded in 1990. Desperate to scale the Razor-wire fence and break into Melbourne's techno compound, Richie asked Ollie Olsen to show him how to use a turntable:

> Ollie was a real inspiration to me. I'd been following his work with Michael Hutchence and all of his earlier industrial exploits … he was so far ahead of his time. He was really into not just the music but also the whole culture, lifestyle, technology and everything. He was out there but incredibly interesting.

But even with Ollie's help, Richie was getting nowhere. DJs clung to their gigs like limpets on a rock. 'Once you got out, you couldn't get back in,' Mark James informs me. 'There's always someone to take your place, to push you to the side.' Ever the entrepreneur, Richie decided to open his own club in late 1990 at a restaurant on Flinders Lane. Marrying his newly acquired software skills with an innate flair for business, Richie built a mailing list database he called his 'Interface Program', printed off 500 address labels, pasted them on envelopes and posted invitations to his opening night. After only a few weeks, the police closed down the club because the venue's liquor licence only permitted a fully seated restaurant, not a nightclub rammed with two hundred tripping teenagers. Around the same time, Richie lost his job at Chasers because the manager thought he was dealing drugs. 'I was a super hyper person, talking a hundred miles an hour, and they thought I was always on drugs—I wasn't—and so I got fired.' With no income and no gigs, things suddenly looked bleak. He had no choice but to return to Dagobah and complete his training. Back in his bedroom, surrounded by his faithful Star Wars figures, Richie perfected his DJing skills and made call after call to his contacts in the industry. His dogged persistence finally paid off when in March 1991, Ian Spicer offered him a set at Maze.

Rubbish to Riches

On the day of the gig, Richie drove to Ollie Olsen's house in St Kilda and asked to borrow some records:

> I told him, 'I'm playing at Commerce tonight,' and he goes, 'I just came back from the UK with these fifteen new records.' I listened to them and borrowed ten of them ... I did a really good set and it just went off.

Buoyed by his success at Maze, Richie launched Illusion at the Star Bar in South Melbourne. He went out in the middle of the night and plastered South Yarra station 'three-high by twenty wide' with 'disgusting looking' purple, white and fluoro green posters.[22] A passing street sweeper saw what he was up to, took down his car registration and reported him to the police. The next day, two constables arrived at his parents' home to arrest him. In court, the magistrate let Richie off after the venue owner took responsibility for the posters. It was a lucky escape. Richie learned his lesson—from now on, he'd go legit.

Richie invited Davide to review Illusion for *Rhythmatic*. At the time, Richie billed himself as Mr Rubbish. 'Don't ask me why it was Mr Rubbish!' he laughed during our interview. I didn't need to. Davide had already told me. One Thursday night Richie attended a Lunacy party at Checkpoint Charlie. According to the bouncer that night (a friend of Davide's), Richie went outside for a walk and came back in with a bag of rubbish. 'He wouldn't come back in unless the bouncer let his mate in,' Davide recalls. 'It turned out Richie was tripping on acid and his mate was the bag of rubbish!

He called it Mr Rubbish for the rest of the night and then for some reason Richie decided to keep calling himself that.' Richie isn't shy in owning up to it. 'It was a horrible night,' he confesses. 'I had a really bad trip.' As for the review, Richie soon wished that he'd never asked. Davide recalls:

> I went [to Illusion] and … I thought it was alright, I thought this kid's playing house and techno … and then for some reason I got on the radio station the next week and I went, 'As for Mr Rubbish, Jesus Christ, I wouldn't have been happy even if he was playing in the toilet, he was rubbish!'

The next day, a devastated Richie rang up Davide. Feeling guilty, Davide took him under his wing. 'As Rudeboy would say, "You created that monster",' Davide laughs during our interview. He tells me that one of his favourite artists at the time was a New York producer working in Chicago called Richie Rich. 'So I said to Richie, "We've got to change your name mate, it can't be Mr Rubbish … your name's Richie, so we're gonna call you Richie Rich".'

Richie Rich scored guest DJ slots at nightclubs throughout 1991 but he remained on the periphery of the scene. 'We were playing at some fucking place in Dandenong and doing guest spots at Jooce in Ringwood.' But at least out there in the depths of Melbourne suburbia, he wasn't alone. For wherever there was Richie Rich, there was Will E Tell.

The Legend of Will E Tell

A highly successful DJ in the nineties, who ran his own record label and toured internationally, Will E Tell (real name Willie Keelan) suddenly disappeared without trace around 2006. Rumours of his present-day whereabouts abound and old skool Facebook threads overflow with 'Where's Willie?' conversations. Some say he's in real estate, others claim he's in India. Wherever he is, one thing's for certain: Willie has turned his back on a scene that made him a star.

Willie ran away from home when he was sixteen, got a job bussing at Chasers and fell in love with techno. 'My mum eventually found me six months later, and I said I would only come home if she bought me two turntables, a mixer, amplifier, and speakers,' he told *groo:vine* in 1999.[23] She obliged. Willie met Richie in Central Station Records on Chapel Street and they became good friends. Like Davide Carbone and Steve Robbins, and Rudeboy and Terrence Ho, Melbourne had forged another techno partnership. 'We'd meet at Central Station on Saturday mornings at 10am, play records all afternoon, pass out, get up, and then I'd get ready to open Chasers and he'd get ready to open Warehouse [a nightclub on Claremont Street, South Yarra],' Richie recalls.

Like Richie, Willie saw the Commerce Club as the gateway into the Melbourne techno scene. He claims he got his first gig at Maze after offering to work for free.[24] Willie called himself Brother Willy or Will E Bear. 'That wasn't going to work,' Ian Spicer tells me. 'We had to find him a new name.' Ian tells me he invented Willie Tell in honour of Ian's dad's favourite piece of music, Rossini's 'William Tell Overture'. Mark James tells it differently:

> I said to Willie one day, 'Everyone calls you Willie, what about Willie Tell?' 'Who's that?' Willie asked. 'He's like a guy, legendary, he was shot at ...' He didn't know who I was talking about but he just liked the name.

On flyers, Willie appeared as Will E Tell. Similarly, Richie became Rich E Rich. Drug dealers must have loved the free advertising.

Many people say that Will E was the finest techno DJ in Melbourne. A 'born DJ', I'm told Will E had the rhythm, the emotion and the mixing skills. Jason Midro became one of Will E's many disciples:

> Will E was the true pioneer ... his skills, his innovation, his creation, his three EQ [equaliser] mixing ... he was so

far ahead of his time and he mastered it so well ... he is the king of the rave scene.²⁵

Will E gained a reputation for playing very hard and very fast music. Regular turntables have a sliding pitch control that allows the DJ to steadily increase or decrease the speed of the platter. The range on a typical turntable, such as the industry standard Technics SL-1200, is +/- 8% of the platter speed. Will E 'turbocharged' his turntables to +/- 16%. Midro recalls the first time he played with his hero:

> I went up to Will E and said, 'Can I play with you?' and he said, 'Do you reckon you can keep up?' I had one record that could go as fast as his! Thank God, he let me take over after that!²⁶

Between 1991 and 2004, Will E estimates he played between 3000 and 4000 gigs.²⁷ Every Sunday morning in Melbourne during the nineties, you'd find Will E behind the decks at 5am, 'the big dude in the big jacket banging out the tunes'.²⁸

In 1996, Will E spent six months touring Europe with German techno producer and perennial Melbourne favourite Oliver Lieb.²⁹ By the early 2000s, he was producing his own music, running his own record label called WetMusik and touring internationally. And then, sometime around 2005, he gave it all up. Richie says:

> I think he got to a point where he just didn't want to travel overseas ... you can't make it from Australia without being over there in Europe working ten months of the year but Will E didn't like the travel so much. And I think musically he was lost.

Ten thousand hours of searing techno had burnt him out. Will E gave everything to his music. It was 110 percent or nothing. 'He gave away something special and I think he regretted it,' Mark James says. In 2006, Midro turned up at Will E's house in McKinnon to buy his turntables and records. Fortunately for the rest of us, Midro asked one of his friends to film the encounter and upload it onto YouTube.[30] The result is a rare and intimate portrait of the one-time superstar. Midro arrives at 9pm to find his idol wearing a suit and watching TV. Will E is affable, if a little uncomfortable. He gives little away. We find out he's married and works in 'real estate and finance'. He talks freely about his DJing past but it's like he's reading from his own biography. 'They were great times,' he says, without a hint of emotion. It's clear he's moved on. 'Is this a sad day for you or do you just want the money?' Midro asks, as he's about to drive away with a van full of Will E's records. The question goes unanswered.

'I'm really disappointed, a lot of us are, because he just walked away from everybody. Everybody. And I don't know how people can do that,' Richie says. He and others have tried to get in touch with Will E but it seems the 'big dude in the big jacket' doesn't want to be found. Midro says the day Will E comes back to DJing will be the 'greatest day for the rave scene'. I'm not sure that day will ever come. Watching Will E sell his records reminds me of the last letter Colonel Kurtz writes to his wife in *Apocalypse Now*, before disappearing up the Nung river into Cambodia: 'Sell the house. Sell the car. Sell the kids. Find someone else. Forget it. I'm never coming back.'[31]

Pure at the Palace

Fifteen years before his vanishing act, you'd find Will E Tell every Friday night playing the back room of the Palace nightclub in St Kilda. The history of the Palace has been one long dance with doom. In 1913, the Phillips brothers opened the Palais de Danse on the St Kilda esplanade, much to the dismay of local councillors and churchmen concerned about the 'temptations of the tango and corruption of public morals'.[32] Two years later, the brothers converted the dance hall into a cinema, thereafter known as the Palais theatre, and built a new Palais de Danse next door. When the Palais theatre burnt down in 1926, locals climbed onto the steel girders of the neighbouring Luna Park fun-fair to watch the blaze.[33] A new Palais theatre was constructed in 1927 in the Art Deco style and remains a popular live music venue today.

During the twenties and thirties, Anne Longmire writes, the Palais de Danse boasted Melbourne's finest dancefloor, which was 'particularly pleasant on a balmy evening, when the doors were opened to the sea and stars beyond'.[34] But then, in 1942, the government requisitioned the dance hall for the war effort, converting it into a post office and storage depot.[35] When it finally re-opened in 1953, the venue never quite recaptured the magic of its 1930s heyday. On 27 December 1968, it was the Palais de Danse's turn to catch fire: '[t]housands of onlookers lined the Lower Esplanade and Marine Parade ... and saw the last great show at the Palais de Danse as its roof appeared to lift off, then collapse in a shower of bricks and glass'.[36] Four years later, the Palais de Dance re-opened as the Palace Entertainment Complex, or the Palace for short.

Mark James opened Pure in the back room of the Palace on 10 May 1991. He partnered with Paul O'Loughlin, known to everyone as Paulie. 'Paulie was an "I have your back" kind of guy,' Mark tells me. 'He knew nothing about music but he came from a publican background so he knew bars.' The back room at the Palace was called the Stardust or the Starwood room; it had a terrazzo dancefloor with a star in the middle that lit up. When Mark took it over, no one had used it for years and the space was full of cobwebs and old junk. It had one key advantage, however: a rear entrance that separated Pure's pilled-up patrons from the moshing rock dogs in the front band room.

Mark started Pure because he was fed up with playing at nightclubs where the crowd stood around, drank and danced to 'dolly music'. He did his homework, advertised the club widely, and brought in Melbourne's top techno DJs—at that time, Steve Robbins and Will E Tell. 'The music was everything we wanted to hear,' Pure regular Sid Sidney tells me. 'None of this Kylie Minogue, none of this hip house, just rave and techno. I was hooked.'

Duncan Plank moved to Melbourne from England in 1991 to play soccer. Every Friday night at Pure, he and his friends stood at the front of the queue:

> We called it the rave train. It was all a 4/4 beat and 120 to 140 beats per minute. It kept you moving. Looking back, the music being played wasn't that hectic compared to how it changed later but it felt hectic at the time.

Duncan's crew called themselves the Purple Forest Posse. While not everyone gave their group a name, the 'crew' became a distinctive emblem of rave culture, as Kim explains:

> You get your own little rave crew and you would go out all the time with them and build up this history of partying together. It was like a little community, it was very special and maybe a bit particular to the rave scene.

For many people, their crew had little meaning outside raving. Intimate friendships would dissolve as soon as the drugs wore off only to re-form at the next party. 'You didn't hook up for coffee on a Wednesday afternoon,' Nimmo Sandilands explains.

Pure attracted a young, loved-up crowd. 'It was pure ravers, none of the old Razor types were there,' Richie Rich says. He reckons he saw 800 to 1000 kids at Pure, although others have told me the club only held 200. Duncan splits the difference. 'We had 500 people in there sweating their tits off,' he says with a characteristically English turn of phrase. Part of the trouble in obtaining accurate patron numbers for Pure is that at any one time about half the crowd was in the car park. Melbourne's mild climate, combined with an Australian love affair with the automobile and the rise of car stereo systems with in-built cassette players, meant ravers could take the party outside. In the Palace car park, people smoked bongs in cars, snorted lines of speed off dashboards and created havoc at nearby St Kilda beach. 'One time someone got paranoid and he thought there were cops everywhere, so he went down to the beach and hid all his drugs in the sand,' Sid Sidney recalls. 'He started coming down, realised there were no cops and so he went back trying to look for it and couldn't find it! So he started telling everyone and then half the party was down there searching around!'

A Scene is Born

'Pure had a definite underground feeling,' Duncan says. 'It felt like we were doing something apart from the norm and we were part of something that no-one else was. It was an unreal place.' Many people agree. Davide Carbone tells me at Pure, ravers could come together in one place, take their drugs, have fun and no one would hassle them:

> I'm loathe to give Mark too much credit. But you give Mark undeniable credit for one thing in starting Pure. That is absolutely, no questions asked, the single most influential club or night. It was the first time it was done properly and it was just magnificent from the get-go.

Richie says Pure 'took the rave scene by the nuts'. If rave was the new religion, then the Palace was the church.

As Pure's congregation expanded, Mark started taking over the main room at the Palace to host larger parties. On 25 September 1991, he brought out Dutch–Belgian techno duo Quadrophonia for an Enjoy party, supported by Will E Tell, Steve Robbins, Richie Rich, Gavin Campbell, John Course and Sydney's Pee Wee Ferris. It was one of the first times a European techno act had played live in Melbourne. Mark's success attracted the attention of the club's owners. 'The bigger I got, the more money they wanted but they didn't realise the bigger I got the more money I had to put into things

… so I said, "Fuck you, I'm leaving!" and they said, "Okay, we'll just get someone else to do what you do", which never happened.'

Pure left the Palace in November 1991, although it would periodically return over the next decade. In the meantime, the main room became one of Melbourne's premier rave venues, hosting international stars like Carl Cox, Laurent Garnier and Frank de Wulf. But the good times couldn't last forever and on 11 July 2007 the Palace succumbed once more to its fiery destiny. Thousands filled the Esplanade and mourned as the nightclub burnt to the ground. Just one month prior, the Victorian State Government had evicted the nightclub's owners following an acrimonious two-year battle.[37] The government wanted to redevelop the site, known as the St Kilda Triangle, and had recently announced a consortium led by the now-defunct global investment firm Babcock & Brown as the winning bidder.[38] The tenants objected, claiming they had thirty-five years left to run on their lease.[39] The police suspected arson and held the venue's infamous alcohol-soaked carpets responsible for fuelling the fire but no-one was ever charged.[40] The morning after the blaze, several ravers went to have a look around. 'It was sad,' Pure regular Robbie Burns recalls. 'That place was like my home.'

Today, all that remains of the Palace nightclub is a flight of concrete steps that lead to nowhere like a stairway to raving heaven. Fitting, perhaps, for a club that invoked such religious fervour in its fans. If one day in the future a progressively minded councillor thinks it apt to commemorate the birthplace of Melbourne rave with a blue plaque, I hope they nail it to a flameproof plinth and erect it somewhere in the centre of that hallowed St Kilda car park.

Chapter 6

TECHNO RENEGADES

Gimps, Whips and Goa Trance

After quitting the Palace, Mark James moved Pure to Dream nightclub at 229 Queensberry Street, Carlton. The music continued but the sparkle had gone. The children of the Palace never really warmed to Pure's new home. 'I didn't like it,' Sid Sidney tells me. 'The venue was small and it wasn't a happy vibe. And it didn't have a car park.' For a start, Dream lay on the wrong side of La Trobe Street. Pure, Maze, Inflation, Biology, ZuZus, Checkpoint Charlie … the Melbourne rave scene had come of age in the city and the inner south. Carlton was a different world. Mad Rod spells it out, with just a hint of hyperbole:

> In Melbourne, the university culture has always been in the north. Many people think university students were doing

something underground and alternative. Sure, they did. However, the irony is that a lot of them only went out whilst they were studying and so they were part-time partyers. Whereas the south didn't have that. I, and many of my peers, we were of the full-time nightclub/party establishment. We didn't go to school. I didn't even go to high school. I went to nightclub school.

In 1992, film director Richard Wolstencroft launched The Hellfire Club at Dream on Sunday nights. Hellfire was one of Australia's first bondage clubs, modelled on similar establishments in New York. 'Whilst downstairs he had people in gimp suits being whipped and naked women and various other things going on, upstairs he hired Ollie Olsen and Andrew Till, and they played Goa trance off DAT tapes from India,' Rudeboy tells me during our interview. 'Some people went for the bondage, but some people went upstairs for the music.' I suggest that maybe some people went for both. 'Quite possibly,' he says. 'It was pretty bizarre there to say the least.' A Rennie Ellis photograph taken at Hellfire in 1992 shows a leather-clad woman standing over a man bent double with his trousers around his ankles, his arms and legs tied with electrical cord and seven clothes pegs clamped to his genitals.[1]

Like Ibiza, Goa in the seventies became a haven for acid-soaked 'freaks and hippie travellers' looking to step off the world and discover the 'ultimate party destination'.[2] Hippies had been throwing parties on Anjuna beach in the north of the former Portuguese colony since the late sixties, but these had been purely acoustic affairs.[3] Then in the mid-seventies, DJs like Goa Gil, Anders Tilman and German Paoli introduced psychedelic rock, jazz funk, Afrobeat and krautrock into the mix.[4] But it took the arrival of Frenchman Fred Disko in 1979 to switch Goa onto an electronic wavelength. Dressed head-to-toe in a sparkling gold costume, Disko mixed the experimental post-punk of Throbbing Gristle with Nitzer Ebb's Electronic Body Music (EBM) and the new wave strains of Joy Division.[5] Many of Goa's original hippie freaks considered Disko's mixes 'too bizarre' and their attempts to stop him playing echoed the folk crowd's reaction to Bob Dylan going electric in 1965.[6] But by 1986, the electronic revolution had been won—largely thanks to Disko and fellow Frenchman Laurent. Laurent used tape cut-up techniques—similar to what Ollie Olsen did with Hugo Klang—to develop a heady mix of new wave, italo disco, EBM, new beat, goth, electro, Hi-NRG, synth-pop and house. He substantially re-edited the tracks he played, removed unwanted vocals, added newsreel soundbites and changed the tempo to suit the crowd's mood, often rendering the original songs unrecognisable. UK DJ Dave Mothersole was there:

> [p]laying for anything up to ten hours at a time [Laurent] would move from dark, hard hypnotic beats during the night, to sweet, uplifting, sun kissed grooves in the morning. From Skinny Puppy and Nitzer Ebb to Koto and Laser Dance; from 100 to 150bpm; from nightmare-ish and scary to blissed out and glorious.[7]

By 1990, Laurent's eclectic creations had earned a name: Goa trance.[8] Some people believed Goa trance (aka Goatrance) pulsed energy waves through their bodies and sent them into trance-like states, hence the name. Unlike the mechanical German trance sound (see Chapter Eight), it's hard to find single tracks that typify Goa trance. 'The Goa trance sound wasn't actually a sound then, it was just different tracks mixed together,' Ollie says. 'It had that feeling of excitement because it was pushing boundaries and doing stuff to your head that wasn't normal. It was truly psychedelic. It wasn't a formula back then, it became a formula later.'

That formula became psytrance, as we'll discover in Chapter Ten. After a police crackdown in 1988, Fred Disko fled Goa for Melbourne, where he formed Goa Bro with Steve Psyko. The pair subsequently collaborated with Ollie as Psyko Disko. Ollie infused the Goa sound into both his studio explorations with Third Eye and his DJ sets at Dream. Ollie, Andrew Till and Dave Thrussell (aka Snog) played twice a week at Hellfire for two years—once in Melbourne and then again at its sister club in Sydney. The trio used to hold 'floor clearing competitions' that rarely yielded a victor: one night Thrussell played Japanese experimental noise group Merzbow for ten minutes and people still danced.[9]

Dark and dingy with a dungeon-like aesthetic, Hellfire wasn't for the fainthearted. And although Pure was held on a different night, Dream nightclub retained its hardcore edge throughout the week. It's as though the walls could not forget (or forgive) what they'd seen and heard each Sunday. Mark James closed Pure in 1992 but Hellfire survived for two more years, becoming a haven for hardcore underground techno DJs like Mad Rod, Liz Millar and Dominic Hogan. In the end, Hellfire became a victim of its own success; 'normals', intrigued by sensational stories about the club on *60 Minutes* and the *7.30 Report*, came to stare at the 'weirdoes' and in doing so scared the latter away.[10]

Dream nightclub foretold one of the first major splits in the scene between a younger, frillier rave crowd and a slightly older, more alternative and—dare I say it—serious, techno fraternity. But that would come later. In the early nineties, a party was a party. Melbourne's raving family danced and dropped together six nights a week and then on the seventh day they rested, rested their blistered feet on the couch and tuned in to 3RRR to hear the voice of rave.

Beat in the Street

Davide Carbone might have been earlier with *Rhythmatic* but when it comes to Melbourne rave radio, Kate Bathgate ruled the airwaves. Kate began working at Central Station Records in 1989. She started her radio career on 3PBS in 1990 before moving across to 3RRR in February 1991. Her show *Beat in the Street* became the Sunday night soundtrack for a generation of Melbourne partygoers. From 10pm to 2am Monday morning, ravers tuned in to hear the latest tracks, guest DJ mixes, interviews with local and international artists and live broadcasts from parties. 'She had the best voice on radio,' raver Aaron Roach tells me. 'When she came on, it would be like, "Ah, Kate!"' Kate regularly gave airplay to local DJs, in many cases helping to launch their careers. 'Kate was a real help to me,' Richie Rich says.

In 1992, Kate invited Mad Rod to join her in the studio. In between giggling fits and tantrums (in 1993, Kate fired Rod after an on-air falling out) the pair found time for a weekly rundown of upcoming parties called 'Mad Rod's Rave Data'. Rod separately maintained the 'Mad Rod phone line' for Central Station, a premium rate number that 'covered everything' including, presumably, illegal raves that he couldn't broadcast on public radio. 'It was me doing a voice recording, you'd listen to this thing for maybe five or six minutes and it would tell you what the fuck is going on,' Rod explains. When Rod left 3RRR, he started his own 'hardcore techno' show on 3PBS called *Tronik Voodoo Exorcism*. In 1993, Kate changed the name of her show to *Tranzmission* and moved it to the coveted Friday night timeslot, warming up Melbourne's ravers for the weekend ahead.

Nigel Slater and Michael Hughes started Kiss FM, originally called kiss 90fm, with the support of nightclub promoters Peter Raff, Eric Pipersberg and Jake Kogakis. Melbourne's first dedicated dance music radio station put out sporadic test broadcasts, typically lasting four to six weeks, between July 1994 and October 1999. The station gained a full licence in 2005. 'When it first started it was very ramshackle and not set up properly,' station manager and former Underground DJ Timmy Byrne tells me. 'At that stage it consisted of two tables, a chair, one microphone and maybe a minidisc recorder. They took the name Kiss from Paul Oakenfold and Danny Rampling's radio show in London.' Kiss FM began above Café Sienna on Chapel Street, South Yarra before moving to Collins Street in the city and later settling on its present Brunswick location.

Techno Threads

Melbourne, February 2015. I've arranged to meet DJ Natural 1 outside the State Library on Swanston Street. He arrives an hour late, breathless and agitated. Natural 1 inhales techno and exhales PLUR. Hearing him speak is like listening to gabber techno—400 words a minute without pause. I like to think his passion for the scene is so strong he can't get his words out quickly enough. I ask him to describe the early nineties raver fashion that found creative expression on the dancefloor. 'Clothing wise, there was never any formalised culture at first … that made it a bit like the hip hop thing as well as the punk thing. There was no "just add water, this is culture."'

Natural 1 says that rave wear encompassed op shop clothing, retro seventies outfits, flared bell-bottomed pants made from denim with curtain panels sewn in, tracksuit pants and crop tops, or English soccer shirts. Some ravers sucked dummies, blew whistles and cuddled soft toys—all trademark features of the London acid house scene. Perhaps the only 'formalised' rave attire in the early days was the footwear:

> Your runners go without saying. Having pimped-out runners, that's a basketball thing, a graffiti artist thing, and then of course this whole culture was about dancing. So you had to have the right kicks, anything Nike of course, and the more air bubble on it the better, or suede Puma Gazelles, the high gloss patent leather chippies or even the Adidas shoes with the red light that ran around the back, although they were rare.

A successful rave outfit matched bright colours with a vivid imagination and a DIY spirit. Many ravers sewed a new costume for each party. More accomplished seamstresses made multiple outfits and sold them to their friends. Style guidelines were loose; you mixed and matched whatever fabric and threads you had lying around—the more creative and colourful, the more you stood out from the older and more serious 'black jacket' crowd. Many ravers waved glow sticks and wore flashing rings and jewellery made from bright plastic colours, known as 'eye candy'.

Fashion designer Bernie Goegan had been making and selling punk-inspired one-off outfits at her Richmond boutique Wrong Shop since the early eighties. Rave brought a new generation of customers, although she often saved her best creations for herself. Natural 1 remembers seeing her wear a top made from fluoro hoops and patchwork quilt faces 'that built up like you were looking at *The Hungry Caterpillar* book'. At Biology, she walked in throwing a ripped-up Yellow Pages into the air as confetti. Ian Spicer remembers her arriving at Maze with a face full of crazy make-up and dragging a pink plastic elephant on the floor behind her.

Heidi John opened Custard Shop in late 1990 on the first floor of their home at 415 Bourke Street. 'It was lots of embroidery and prints,' Heidi says. But a lack of street frontage meant sales were low. 'I don't think anyone ever went there,' Ollie Olsen tells me. 'A couple of people would come in to say hello but that was about it really.' Terrence Ho also caught the fashion bug and discovered that selling clothes paid better than DJing:

> I was making tons of clothing. I was doing up the graphics, getting it printed and then, while there was still a manufacturing industry here in Melbourne, getting some local sweatshop down in Richmond to sew it up. Bang!

Terrence describes his designs as 'drug-related clubwear'— Albert Einstein with a tablet on his tongue and 'E = MDMA' written beneath, or a yin and yang logo with the words 'Better Living Through Chemistry'. In 1990, you could still get away with wearing a shirt with 'E = MDMA' on the front without your mum asking questions. Unless your mum was Heidi John.

In 1988, Darren Till began the hip hop clothing label Renegade in the back room of the Lost Vegas boutique in Greville Street,

Prahran. By 1991, Renegade had branched out into rave wear, specialising in t-shirts and hoodies with pop culture logos, graffiti tags and corporate brand parodies. Darren Till comes from solid underground stock: brother Andrew DJed at Hellfire with Ollie Olsen; sister Diane designed rave flyers; and brother Gus had played in legendary punk band The Ears and collaborated with Ollie on Max Q and Third Eye. Darren cites The Ears and punk rock band JAB as primary influences in his work.[11] He employed graffiti artists to design the clothing, people like Merda who Natural 1 lauds as one of the 'king graf writers' in Melbourne, if not the world. For Merda, crossing over from spraying walls to spraying t-shirts made perfect sense:

> [i]t was a great personal statement ... back then, if you were going out clubbing you'd print a design before you went; usually my tag, Merda. It was about making it and seeing it printed.[12]

Renegade clothing became tremendously popular in nineties Melbourne, ironically becoming the type of brand its earlier t-shirts had subverted. 'Literally you'd go to a rave and everyone would be wearing a Renegade rave outfit, boys and girls,' Natural 1 complains. 'I thought this isn't the counterculture that rave's about and so I decided I was never going to own a bit of Renegade gear ever.' However, most ravers disagreed. By the mid-nineties, Greville and Chapel Streets in Prahran and the Sportsgirl Centre on Collins Street had become hubs for rave and hip hop inspired streetwear.

'We Couldn't Get the Music We Wanted'

Back in 1990, Jill Klein kept a few crates of techno out the back of her Greville Street boutique Rich clothing. Despite the intrinsic pleasures of crate-digging at shops like Rich, in 1990 there was still only one place in Melbourne where DJs could buy enough records to sustain a three-hour set: Central Station Records. DJs like Steve Robbins at the city store and Miss Krystal Pussy Cha Cha (real name Kristina Prpa) in the Chapel Street shop imported new house and techno from the US, the UK and Europe. 'Central Station got a track in like 'Passion' [by Gat Décor] and then everyone had 'Passion', everybody was playing 'Passion',' Nimmo Sandilands recalls. 'It was kind of alright because it was a good track but it was very hard to find something different from 'Passion' that week.' DJs could ask Central Station to order in lesser-known records they'd read about in *mixmag* or *DJmag* but it was risky. Some tracks could not be sourced and those that could took up to six weeks to arrive and brought no guarantee of quality. 'We'd do blind orders,' Nimmo says (I wonder if 'deaf orders' may be more appropriate). 'You'd get them and listen to them. There would be thirty records and twenty-eight of them were complete shit.' In today's era of digital downloading, buying twenty-eight dud tracks on Beatport or iTunes might cost you $70 (although with the ability to preview music beforehand, the chances of making an unwanted purchase lessen considerably). Back then, however, when a single vinyl record might cost up to $20, you could easily lose over $500.

In late 1990, Davide Carbone established a mail order service called Rhythm Records with newfound protégé Richie Rich in the front room of a friend's house in Hawthorn East. 'Central Station has started to dry up a little bit because they're buying in bulk now,' Davide explains. 'It was still a great source of music but they didn't buy the underground stuff.' Or maybe they did, but Jo Palumbo kept it under the counter. Every week for a few months until a spat between its co-owners forced its closure, Davide called his contact at London record store City Sounds to arrange a new shipment of house and techno.

In December 1991, Rudeboy and Terrence Ho opened Octave Records on the corner of Greville and Izett streets in Prahran. They felt that Central Station had shifted too far towards the 'commercial vocally, housy thing'.¹³ 'We had a rapport with Central Station ... but our orders weren't coming through, and we couldn't get the music we wanted,' Rudeboy says. So they bought two crates of records from a contact in Detroit and hired a room upstairs in David Heeney's It Inc. complex. Octave imported American, British and German underground labels and sold rave clothing, including some of Terrence's designs.

Over time, Prahran became a hive of dance music record stores. Along with stalwarts Octave and Central Station, by the late nineties customers could choose from DMC Records (techno), Euphemism (techno), Soundboy (breaks/drum n bass), Obese Records (hip hop), Rhythm and Soul (commercial) and One Stop DJ (trance). But the market was reaching saturation point. 'There's only so many records you can sell to only so many people,' Rudeboy replies when I ask why Octave finally shut in 2001. 'I think that stuffed us. And GST fucked us as well, you know.'

In 1991, shortly after Rhythm Records had folded, Mark James introduced Richie Rich to Colin Daniels and Scott Murphy one night at Pure. Colin and Scott ran Mushroom Distribution Services (MDS), an offshoot of Michael Gudinski's Mushroom Records. Richie immediately asked them for a job. 'They just thought I was this crazy, young DJ partying too hard and thought I'd be loose and useless, so the first job I got with them was packing boxes in the warehouse,' he recalled in a 2014 interview.¹⁴ When Colin left to attend the New Music Seminar in New York, Richie stayed up all night placing orders with overseas distributors and managed to break the company's sales record. On his return, Colin hired Richie as his assistant. When Colin moved to London to run Mushroom's UK operation, Richie took charge of Mushroom's dance music division.

Richie tells me his single most useful source at MDS wasn't a distributor, a trade magazine or even a DJ but a New York journalist called Miss Moneypenny:¹⁵

Before *DJmag* even started [in 1991], there was this news information sheet that would come through on a fax machine you could subscribe to. Not many people knew about it, it was called *Brand X* and this was worldwide one of the most important media that labels and DJs got into … it was one page of news and then one page of the *Brand X* top fifty … If it was good quality it would end up on *Brand X*. I'd order everything in the top fifty, it was all the cool shit. How she was onto it, I don't know.

Every Tuesday morning, Miss Moneypenny's tipsheet waited patiently for Richie on the MDS fax machine. As well as underground US labels like Experimental, Strictly Rhythm and Nervous, *Brand X* broke R&S from Belgium, Rising High from the UK and major artists like Underground Resistance and Moby, all of which Richie subsequently bought and distributed in Australia. *Brand X* gave Richie an exclusive window into the future, much like the *Gray's Sporting Almanac* that Biff Tannen used to build his Trump-like billionaire empire in *Back to the Future Part II*. MDS soon became the largest distributor of dance music in Australia, breaking major new acts like Aphex Twin, Leftfield and Underworld. Richie estimates MDS controlled 70 percent of the Australian market, with Colossal and Shock accounting for most of the rest. The company started its own specialty dance music label called Dancenet and manufactured singles locally, hoping to score a Top 40 hit. With his record bag crammed full of cutting-edge techno, Richie's status in the scene began to rise.

Mark and Emmy

On 27 July 1991, Emmy Boudry hired Richie to play at Quadrant in a 'socialist warehouse on A'Beckett Street'—probably the Socialist Alliance/Green Left headquarters at 14 Anthony Street. Emmy and boyfriend Mark Hogan arrived in Melbourne in 1991 after fleeing the crumbling London rave scene. 'Melbourne was fresh and innocent,' she says. 'It wasn't tainted like it was over there. Everyone was honest. It was so small and we loved that. It had a community feel to it.' Mark had organised raves in London because, he says, he couldn't just partake in it, he needed to be a big part of it.[16] To avoid any ambiguity about their mission statement, Mark and Emmy labelled their Melbourne promotion company Right On One Productions.

Melbourne's ravers clamoured for Mark and Emmy's unique brand of English rave sensibility coupled with a lo-fi aesthetic. When I met her in 2015, Emmy gave me two photographs taken at Quadrant. The first shows four people dancing in what looks like an office, complete with dropped ceiling, fluoro strip lighting and a hand-painted banner at the back that reads 'The time has come to go out of your mind'. The second photo shows Mark and co-organiser Charm (aka Daniel Wittenberg) smiling nervously for the camera while Ollie Olsen, eyes wide and mouth agape, aims 'jazz hands' towards the lens.

A'Beckett Street is an urban no man's land. The CBD proper lies one block to the south, with its gleaming glass office towers; one block north brings you to Queen Victoria Market and the seedy Irish pubs and backpacker hostels of Victoria Street. In 1991, Richie lived in an apartment in nearby Jeffcott Street. 'That whole area was a bit of a ghost town with lots of factories,' he says. 'It was semi-industrial, mainly clothing factories and wholesalers. There weren't any shops and very few apartments.' Sounds like the ideal location for a noisy rave—and yet somehow the police still found out. Richie remembers what happened:

> [i]t's three or four in the morning, Mark's disappeared and Ollie jumps on to DJ and then all of a sudden, these cops come up the stairs. The cops shut this thing down and then one of them asks me, 'Who's running this event?' and I'm like, 'I don't know'. I think they just got some statements

from people and were happy to realise that whoever was running it had left. They had some details from the sound and lighting companies that [Mark] had booked. So they just waited until we all left and locked up and then took it up with him later I think.

Emmy's recollection differs from Richie's. She tells me the police arrested Mark, locked him in the toilet and demanded to know where the drugs were:

> I was banging on the door going, 'Let him out! You can't do this!' and they were harassing him going, 'Where's the drugs?' They're looking in the toilet and eventually they let him out.

Clearly unfazed by their run-in with the cops, Mark and Emmy organised a second Quadrant in March 1992 on Smith Street, Collingwood (no-one can remember the name of the venue—it must have been a good party). This time, the pair paid a visual artist to paint 3D projections on the wall. 'We gave people 3D glasses as they came in,' Emmy says. 'I went to the cinema where they were showing *A Nightmare on Elm Street* in 3D and I got given heaps of glasses for free.' I'm hoping the film didn't inspire the artwork for the party; seeing a three-dimensional Freddy Krueger on acid gives new meaning to a bad trip. Through 1992 and 1993, Mark and Emmy put on dozens of parties at various locations across the city, including the Banana Alley Vaults on Flinders Street and the Polly Woodside, a three-masted iron-hulled barque permanently moored on the south bank of the Yarra. 'It was called Floatation,' Richie says. 'It was in the little function room at the back of the boat. It was legal in the sense that they paid the owner rent but I don't think the owners really knew what was going on in there.'

Richie tells me the Right On One parties were great fun and the music rocked. But they were far from polished productions:

[t]he makeshift sound system would blow up and turn itself off for ten minutes and I'd be standing there with 300 people screaming at me but I couldn't do anything because the amps had overheated and they just needed to cool down. [Mark and Emmy] did things on the cheap. They were cutting corners because they were just out to have a good time, they didn't think much about the production side. It was let's get a sound system, draw some artwork, photocopy flyers, give them out and do a party.

Mark and Emmy turned a tidy profit from their raving enterprises. They often hired the venues for free on the condition that the owners received the bar takings. 'He'd then spend $500 on the sound system, $500 for two decks, two subs and a mid-high, charge $20 a head and get 500 people in there,' Richie tells me. 'He was making a killing!' Meanwhile, Richie picked up a measly $100 for a night's work in noisy, smoky and often hazardous conditions. It wasn't even enough to buy ten new records. Working for other people was a mug's game. From now on, he'd do the hiring.

Hardware

The south bank of the Yarra River, New Year's Day 1992, 8am. You're dancing on the footpath, watching the river sparkle in the sunlight like a carpet of diamonds floating on the water. Even the ghastly Gas and Fuel Buildings opposite look beautiful in this light. In the rowing shed behind you, the DJ brings in a new track. As the first few bars of Orbital's 'Belfast' chime in, everyone cheers and hugs. It's the record you've all been waiting for. For the next eight minutes and ten seconds, time seems to stand still. This is your moment.

Hardware was Richie's moment:

> I got in before everyone else. I knew Richard and Heidi and everyone else were going to try and do a party and I thought, 'fuck 'em!' I had me, Will E and Hess who were

the three most popular DJs back then. It sold out and it was awesome!

Richie booked the Mercantile Rowing Club, printed full-colour flyers and littered hundreds of lampposts and walls with posters. He also scored a crucial guest DJ spot on Kate Bathgate's *Beat in the Street* the week before. Hardware trounced the competition. Steve Robbins had organised a Lunatic Fringe party at the Carron Tavern with Davide Carbone, Rudeboy and Terrence Ho. 'We flopped and he took off like a rocket,' Steve says. 'Everyone was at his party … we were convinced ours would be a success but we had a hundred and he had a thousand.' Richie remembers Rudeboy coming down to Hardware in the morning, standing on a subwoofer with his sunglasses on and pumping his hands in the air. It was a symbolic moment. After two hard years of trying, Richie had finally broken into Melbourne's techno hierarchy.

'I did it for me and Will E and Hess because we were getting underpaid,' Richie says. 'I started paying $400 to $500 a shift which back then was a lot of money. And I was paying everyone on the night. Everyone would come to the office and get paid before they left.' Gone were the days of chasing promoters for money days or weeks after the event. Richie brought a business mindset to the dance music industry that distinguished him from his competitors. As friend Nimmo Sandilands informs me:

> From day one he started an Excel spreadsheet … four weeks out from his next party he knew how many people had bought tickets, and he was able to set up graphs and stuff like that. He'd be able to tell you whether he was going to make money in six months' time whereas Heidi and no one else would ever report that way.

Richie's father, Kevin McNeill, worked as CEO for Try Youth and Community Services, a charity for disadvantaged youth. Kevin suggested Richie run Hardware as a Try Youth fundraiser. In return for forfeiting his profits, Kevin provided his son with financial assistance, operational support and business training. Flying under the Try Youth banner also helped Richie obtain the necessary permits and approvals and gave him access to venues that might have been out of bounds for other promoters. But there was a catch. His parties had to be all ages and alcohol free. 'No-one really drank anything anyway,' Richie laughs with a mischievous glint in his eye.

Hardware was a family affair, as Richie explains:

> My parents used to enjoy working at the shows, they were really interested in meeting young people. Mum used to complain about the music so she put earplugs in while she was counting the money. Dad used to wander around and have a look—he loved it, especially all the colourful clothing. My sister worked there too.

Richie acknowledges the debt he owes his parents but tells me their support would have meant little if he hadn't worked hard. 'Some people say I'm spoilt because my dad gave me money to do it, but actually I worked my arse off, standing on the corner in the rain handing out flyers and putting up posters at two in the morning.' Back then, being a promoter meant you had to go out and walk the streets. As opposed to nowadays where we sit in front of a MacBook, create an event on Facebook and then gently sigh when only a quarter of the people who RSVP'd actually turn up on the night.

For Hardware 2, Richie needed a new venue because someone had put a hole in the roof of the Mercantile Rowing Club toilets causing about $400 worth of damage. This time, his mum came to the rescue. She worked for a philanthropic trust that had previously awarded grants to the Power House in Albert Park. The manager was only too willing to return a favour. On 27 June 1992, the Power House walls rattled once more to the sound of thumping techno beats, two years after Biology had written the venue into Melbourne's raving history. 'When I think back to those days, I remember the innocence and the people and the renegade-ness of it all,' Richie tells me. He hung hand-painted banners from death-trap scissor lifts, rigged together makeshift DJ consoles and pushed mattresses against windows to stem the sound. It was all very DIY.

Richie followed up with Hardware 3 on 23 September in a two-storey warehouse (long since converted into trendy apartments) in Coromandel Place in the city. 'It was a cracking party, up with the best,' Nimmo recalls. Hardware 3 featured a 'purelight' full-colour computer-controlled laser brought down from Sydney and, as always, Richie and Will E banging out the tunes. Richie booked out the Melbourne Showgrounds in Flemington for Hardware 4. 'You could go all night back then because there weren't houses around it.' In 1994, Richie opened Hardware Records in a converted terrace house on Chatham Street, Prahran. 'The shop had a real contact with the street, and all the DJs were coming through and we were selling all the tickets for the shows … it was the real heart and soul beat of the city rave wise.'

BlastOff Sound System

A couple of weeks before Hardware 1, Terrence Ho donned a suit and walked into a real estate agent's office in North Melbourne. He'd found a warehouse in a Kensington backstreet and told the agent he wanted to hire it to film a music video. 'It was a thousand bucks for the weekend, no problem,' Terrence says. 'All we did was set up a portable camera stand with a dodgy VHS camera Portapak in one corner and that was it; that was our music video filming.' While Terrence arranged the warehouse, Rudeboy bought a bootload of booze 'on tick', meaning he could return any unsold liquor to the supplier after the party. He knew he'd never get a licence for a warehouse rave and so borrowed an idea he'd seen at underground gay parties:

What you'd do is you'd give away some rubbish gift, let's say a giant teddy bear, and you would raffle it. A ticket was four bucks a ticket, and you got a free drink with every ticket. You didn't need a licence, because you're not selling booze, you're giving it away.

Rules are there to be broken. ESP: The Sleeper Awakes on Saturday 14 December 1991 was a three-way collaboration between Terrence, Rudeboy and Andrew Till. They called themselves BlastOff Sound System. The Kensington warehouse had a two-level scaffolding tower. The DJs played on the lower tier while Baby Lemonade sang live from the upper level. 'It wasn't like $10,000 of lighting, it was just a couple of hundred bucks' worth of a spot, a strobe, a smoke machine and maybe a pissy little laser, that was it,' Terrence recalls. 'This was before the whole $10k laser system blah blah blah advertised on flyers. Back then it was all about the music.' Rudeboy recalls a neighbouring taxi driver arriving home around midnight to discover his windows rattling:

> 'What's going on here?' he asked. We didn't want him to call the police so I immediately stuck a beer in his hand, gave him a hotdog and said, 'Oh, we're filming something for a movie, it's a party. You can drink as much as you want at our bar for free'. He went, 'Brilliant'. At the end of the night he comes up to me and goes, 'Are you going to have another one next week?'

On Saturday 8 February 1992, Blastoff put on Nexus at the Riverside Inn, featuring guest DJ Richie Rich and Terrence playing for the first time as DJ H2O. Formerly the Sir Henry Barkly Hotel, the Riverside Inn on the corner of Punt Road and Harcourt Parade in Cremorne had been continuously occupied as a hotel since at least 1843 and had once boasted a skittle alley and a boathouse.[17] But by 1992, the Tudor Revival style hotel, complete with conical turret, was rundown and unloved. It's little wonder: the construction of the Monash Freeway during the sixties added an on-ramp at Harcourt

Parade, cutting off the hotel from the river and transforming what had once been an idyllic waterside retreat into an urban dystopia. In the early nineties, dying venues like the Riverside Inn and the nearby Bridge Road Club welcomed whatever they could to balance the books: that generally meant bands, bikies and raves. When the Riverside Inn burnt down in 1999, its charred remains made way for a gigantic advertising billboard and a car park. How appropriate.

A Temporary Autonomous Zone?

In 1991, Hakim Bey (real name Peter Lamborn Wilson) coined the term 'temporary autonomous zone' (TAZ) to define a 'guerrilla operation which liberates an area (of land, of time, of imagination) and then dissolves itself elsewhere/elsewhen before the state can crush it'.[18] 'Left-anarchist' thinkers have repeatedly co-opted the TAZ to characterise raves.[19] By constantly moving and hiding in 'the cracks of contemporary society',[20] ravers not only evade detection by the authorities but they also *subvert* conventional capitalist notions of land ownership and property rights. The anarchist urban planner in me loves the idea of the proletariat disrupting the territoriality of power and freeing the city from the insidious tide of privatisation and state control. But is this really how it happened?

I think what Richard and Heidi and Joe Wieczorek did in deserted warehouses in London's East End came close to realising Hakim Bey's ideal. It's a trend that continues today, albeit with a twenty-first century twist. Promoters in the 'London squat rave scene' find venues by searching 'To Let' listings on the internet, and then advertise their parties through social media. 'When you're looking for something that isn't being provided, it's only natural that it comes from a slightly illegal source,' host Clive Martin said in a 2016 VICE Media documentary. 'There's that edge of danger [that] makes it a lot more fun.'[21] Nimmo Sandilands tells me the Sydney rave scene of the late eighties followed a similar pattern:

They'd just drive around and look for an empty warehouse and smash into it. They'd destroy the place because it had carpet and stuff in the offices. They'd let it get ruined.

In Melbourne in the nineties, Rudeboy practiced what he'd seen in England and Sydney: 'We started doing illegal raves, where we broke into places and had a generator and did them for free.' The parties featured rebellious names like Eat the Rich and Class War, but whether these names reflected a deeper political ideology or were merely marketing gimmicks is uncertain. Nevertheless, it was hard-edged, no-frills raving at its finest. 'We did a thing called the Bring a Torch party because we didn't have any lighting or electricity,' Rudeboy tells me. 'The generator would only run the sound system. On the flyer, it was, "Bring a torch, because there's no fucking lights".' The parties may have been illegal but the organisers still cleaned up after themselves. After all, this wasn't Sydney:

> We brought brooms out at the end while everyone was still off their heads at nine in the morning and we went, 'Right, sweep up'. If we trash it, then they're going to get onto us. If it's been broken into but it's all nice and clean, the guy's not really going to give a shit.

Others also tapped into the free party vibe. Raver Adrian Cartwright recalls a free party under the Westgate Bridge, a favoured location in the nineties:

> [it] was really cool with all these sculptures and people with firesticks … but then as the light started coming up we realised we were in what looked like a toxic waste dump [*laughs*] … we thought this is awful, let's get out of here and jumped in the car before we could see too much.

This free party tradition lives on today. From time to time, Facebook makes me aware of illegal parties in Melbourne, such

1: *Banner*. Credit: Voodoo. Courtesy of Phil Woodman.
2: *Time*. Credit: Voodoo. Courtesy of Phil Woodman.

3

4

3: *Escher girl*. Credit: Voodoo. Courtesy of Phil Woodman.
4: *Tribal trip*. Credit: Voodoo. Courtesy of Phil Woodman.

5: Untitled. Credit: Sioux Dollman. Courtesy of Natural 1.

6 & 7: Collage of M.U.D. parties at Westgate Sports & Entertainment Centre, Altona c. 1998/99.
Credit: M.U.D./ Various Artists. Courtesy of Hydi John.

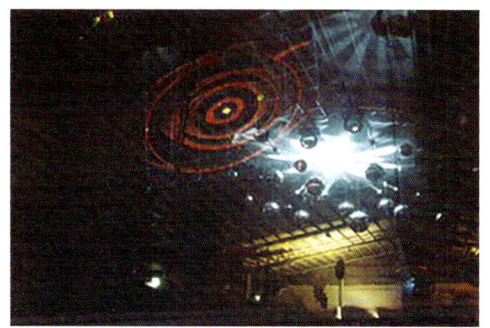

8: Ravers at Global Village. Credit: Hydi John.

9: Ravers at Global Village. Credit: Hydi John.

10

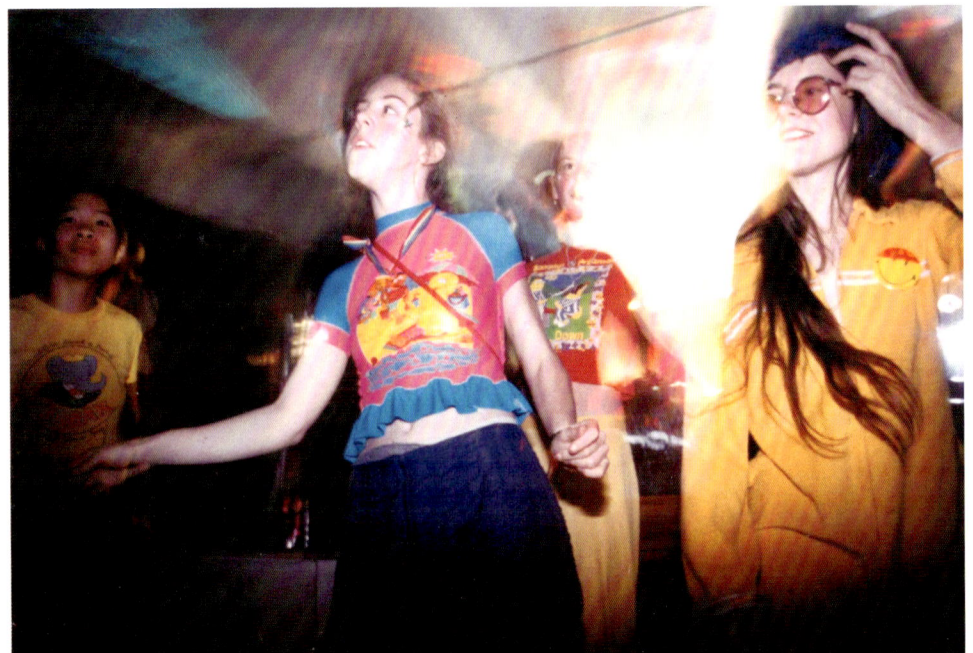

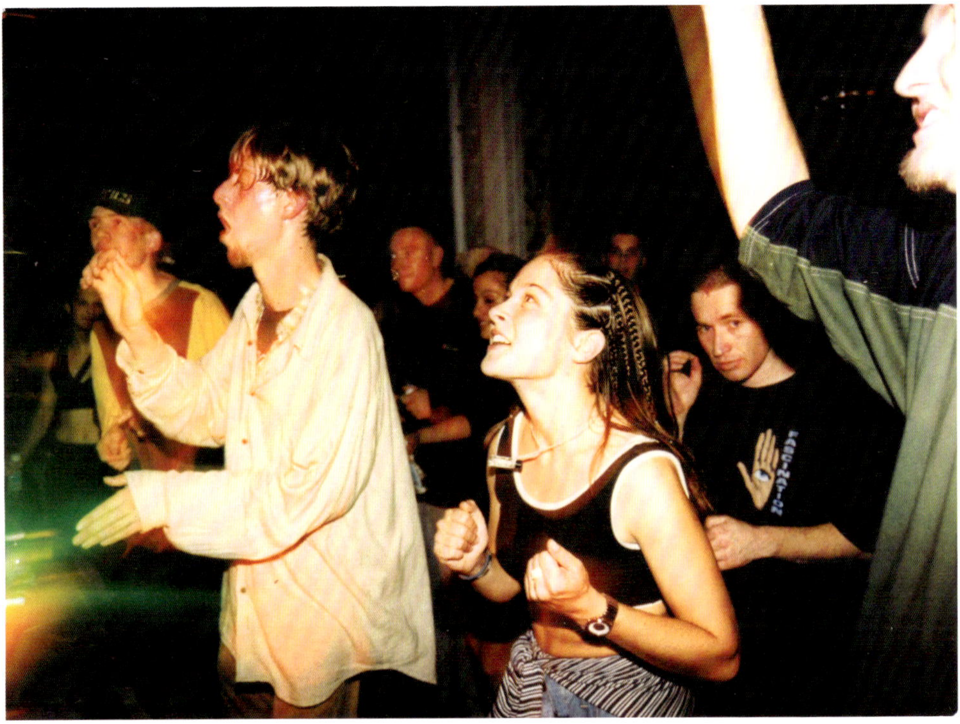

11

10 & 11: Ravers at Global Village. Credit: Hydi John.

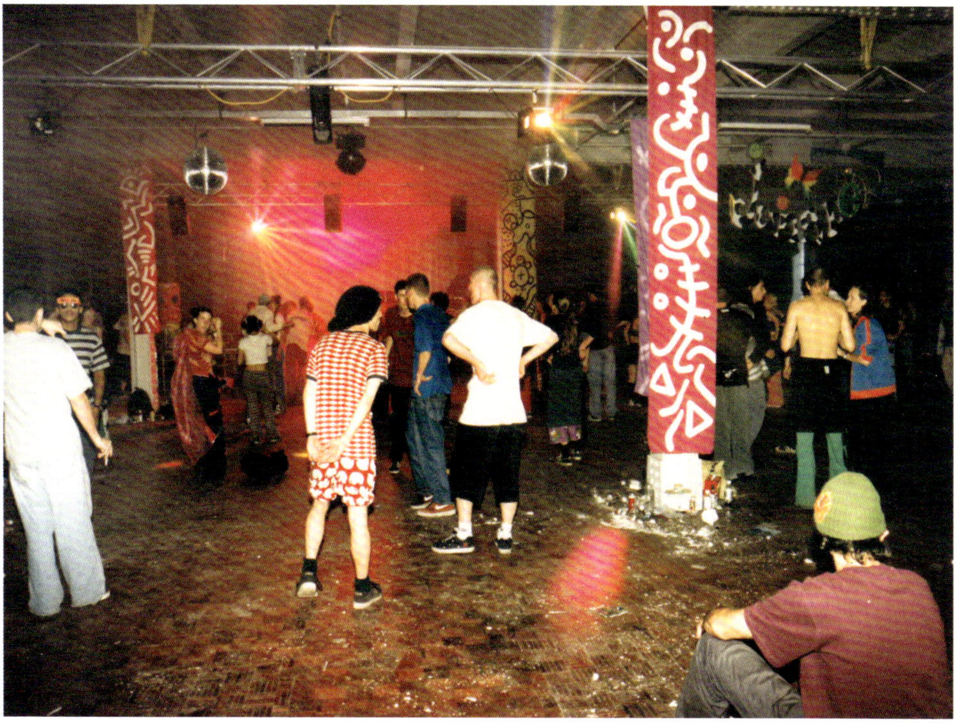

12

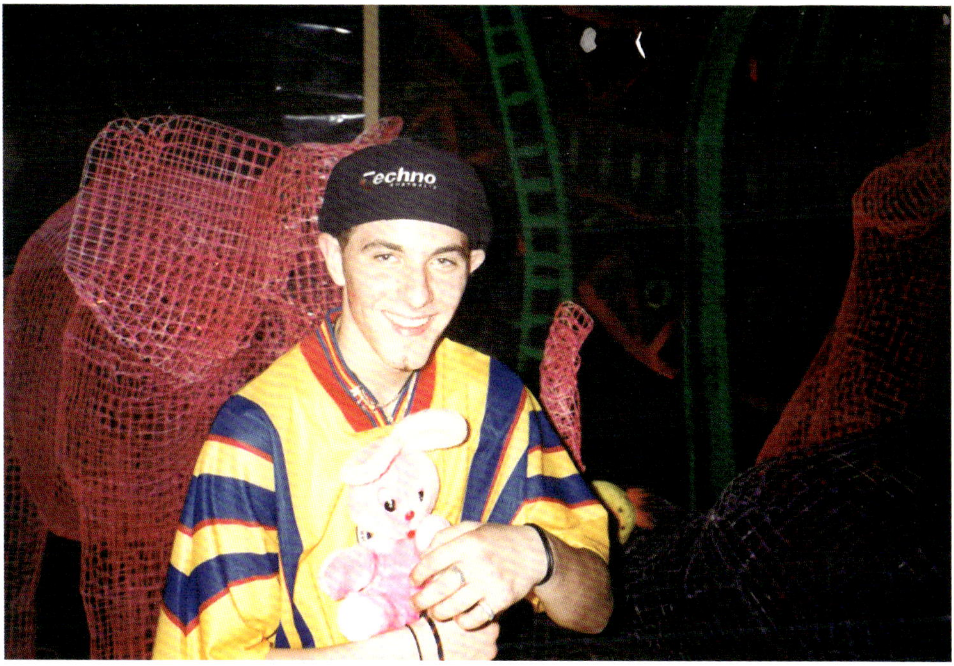

13

12: Ravers at Global Village. Credit: Hydi John.
Note the talcum powder on the floor near the base of the pillar.

13: Global Village jungle room c. 1996. Credit: Olivia Geselle.

14: Raver at Global Village. Credit: Hydi John.

15: Shelley Harris (left) and friend at home before Genesis party, 1995. Credit: Natural 1.

16

17

16: Beck Hill, Nicole Maguire, Kylie Brown, front centre Renee Dirckze. Palace, St Kilda c. 1998. Credit: Beck Hill.

17: Lu Diamond (3rd from right) and friends, Belfast 4, Palace Entertainment Complex, St Kilda, Oct 1998. Credit: Lu Diamond.

18

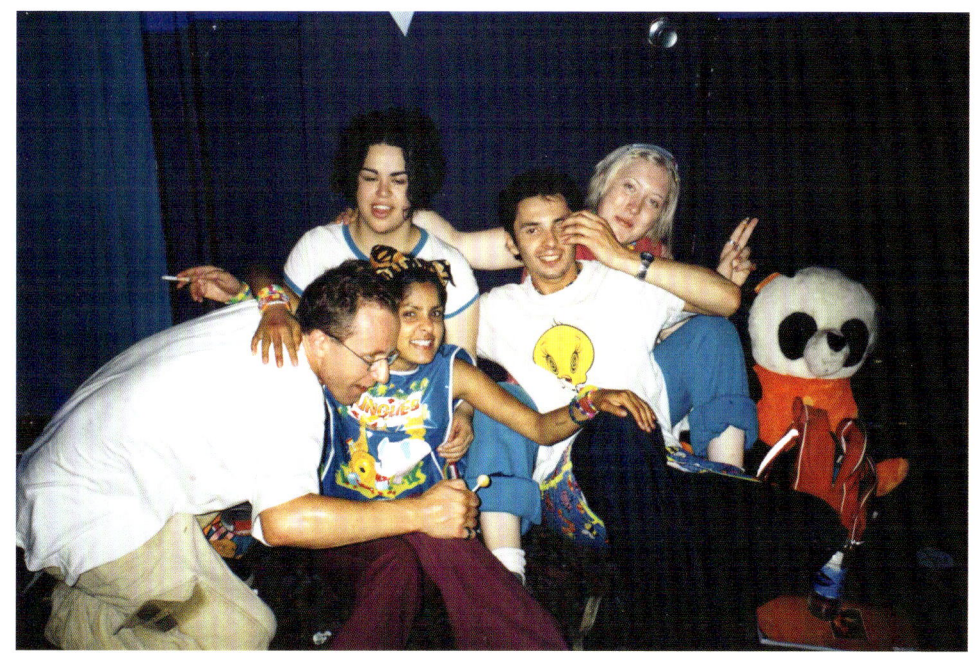

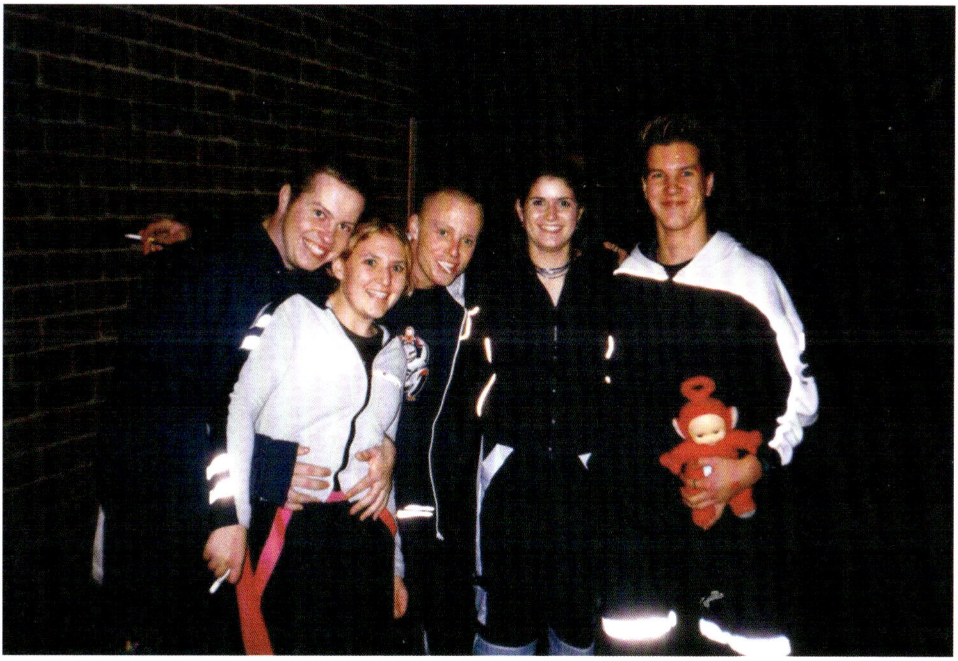

19

18: Kim McClelland (front right) and friends, @mosphere, 2000. Credit: Kim McClelland.

19: Mick Smith (centre) and friends, unknown party, c. 1999. Credit: Mick Smith.

20: Fraser Nairn (left) and friends, Technosis, 1999. Credit: Fraser Nairn.

21: Merowyn at @mosphere, 2000. Credit: Kim McClelland.

22 & 23: Cookie Monster rave, Plaster Funhouse, Westmeadows, 2000. Credit: Kim McClelland.

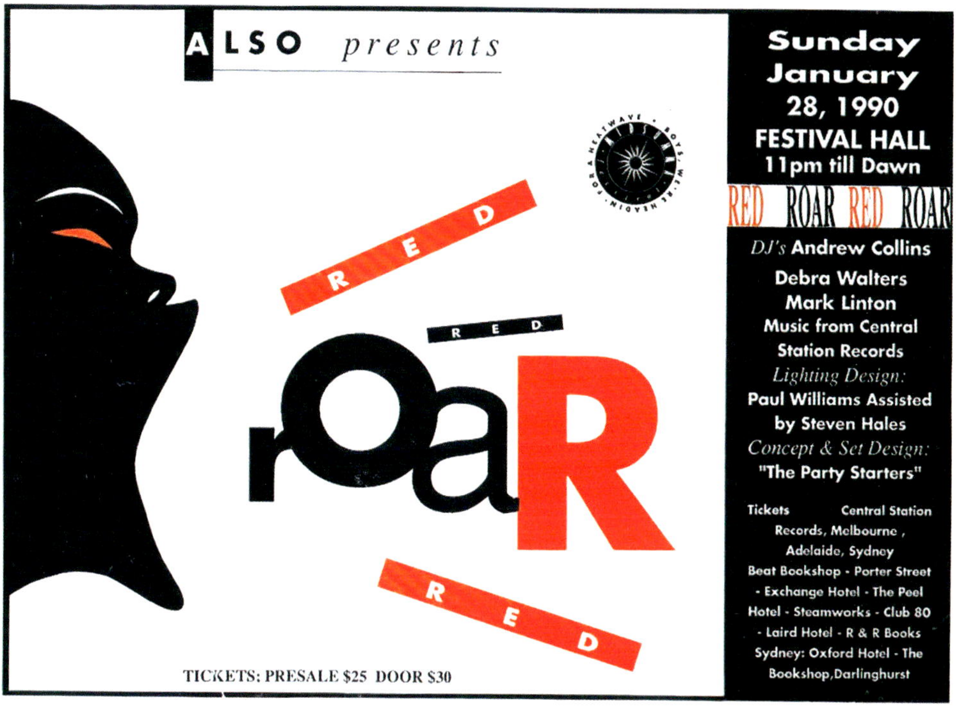

24

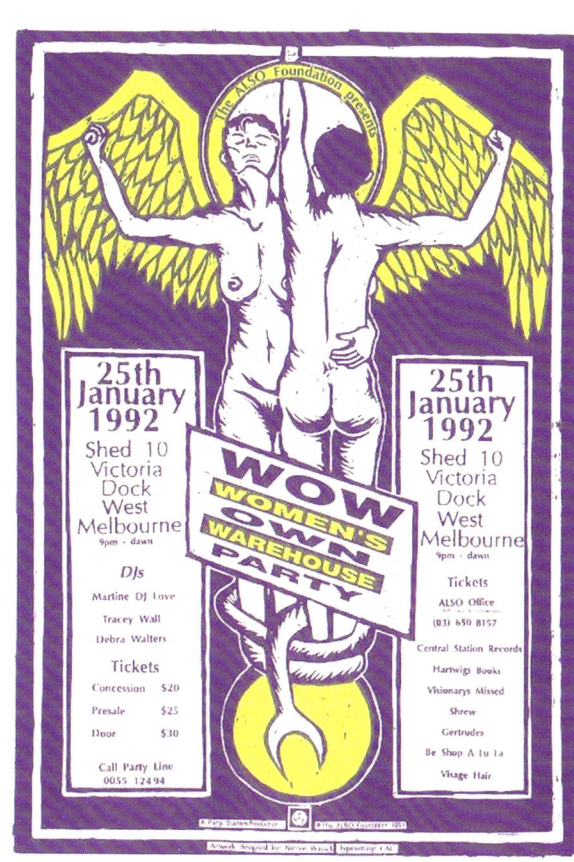

24: Flyer for Red Roar (Red Raw), 28 Jan 1990. Credit: ALSO Foundation. Courtesy of ALGA.

25: Flyer for Women's Own Warehouse Party, 25 Jan 1992. Credit: ALSO Foundation. Courtesy of ALGA.

25

26

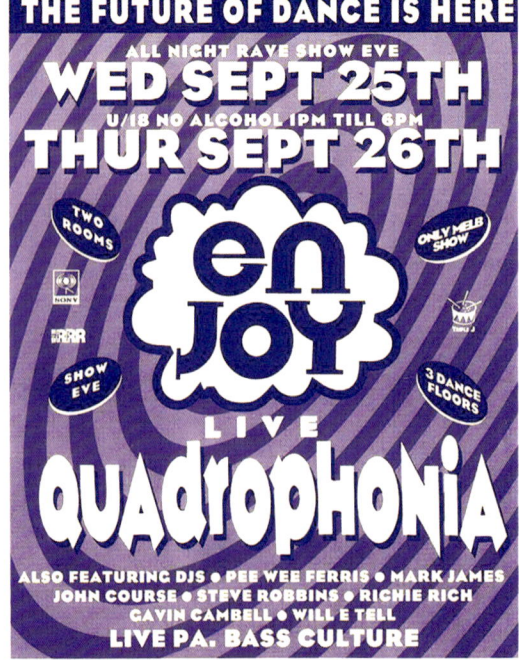

27

26: Flyer for Lunacy party, 20 Jul 1989. Credit: Unknown. Courtesy of Steve Robbins.

27: Flyer for enjoy, 25 Sep 1991. Credit: Mark James.

28: Flyer for Biology, 10 Jun 1990. Credit: Mark James. Courtesy of Nimmo Sandilands.

29: Flyer for Maze 1st birthday party, 2 Mar 1991. Credit: Ian Spicer, Andrew Till, Diane Till.

30

31

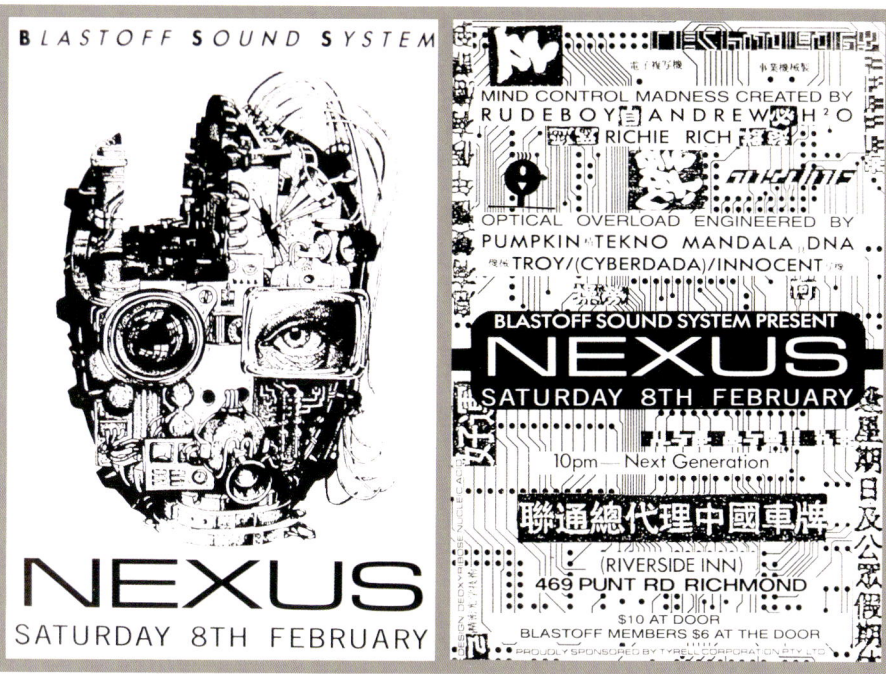

30: Flyer for Nexus, 8 Feb 1992. Credit: Andrew Till. Courtesy of Adem Jaffers.

31: Flyer for Harmony, 15 Aug 1993. Credit: Unknown. Courtesy of Adem Jaffers.

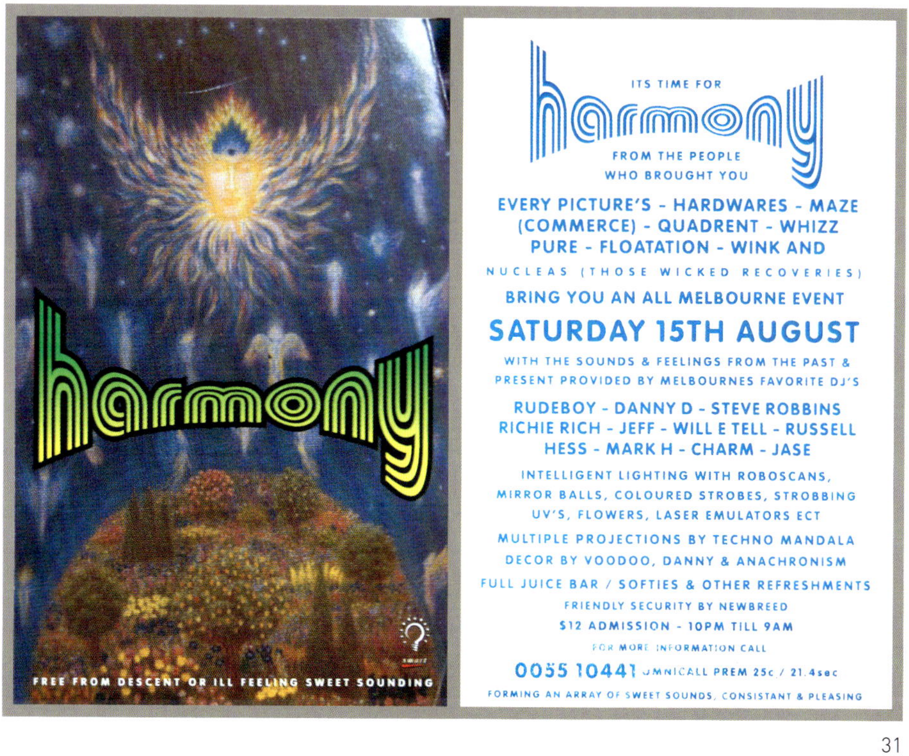

32: Flyer for Hardware, 31 Dec 1991. Credit: Hardware Corporation. Courtesy of Nimmo Sandilands.
33: Flyer for Hardware 3, 23 Sep 1992. Credit: Hardware Corporation. Courtesy of Nimmo Sandilands.

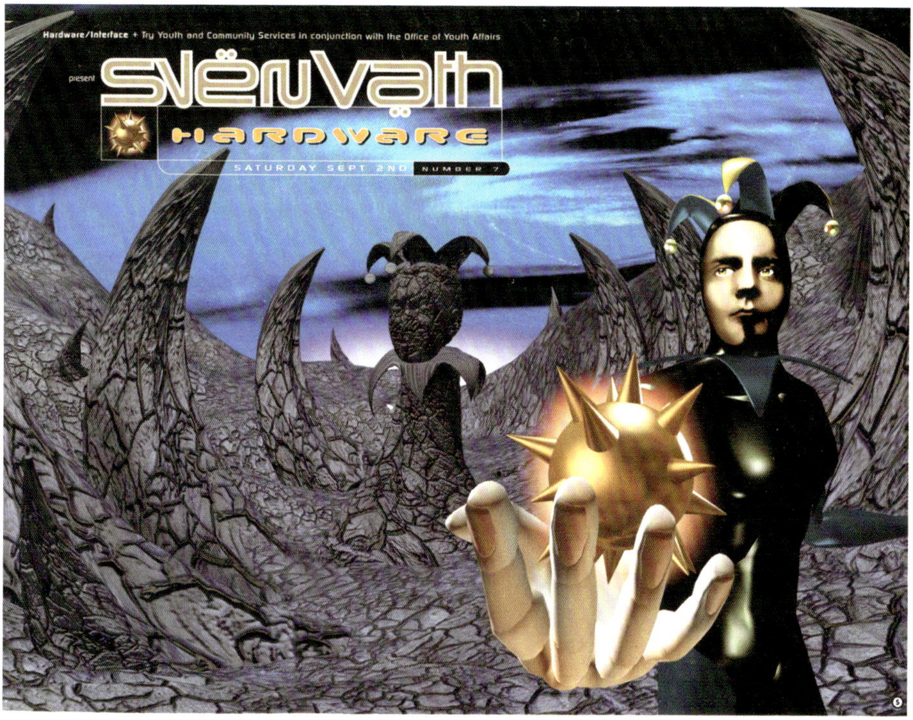

34

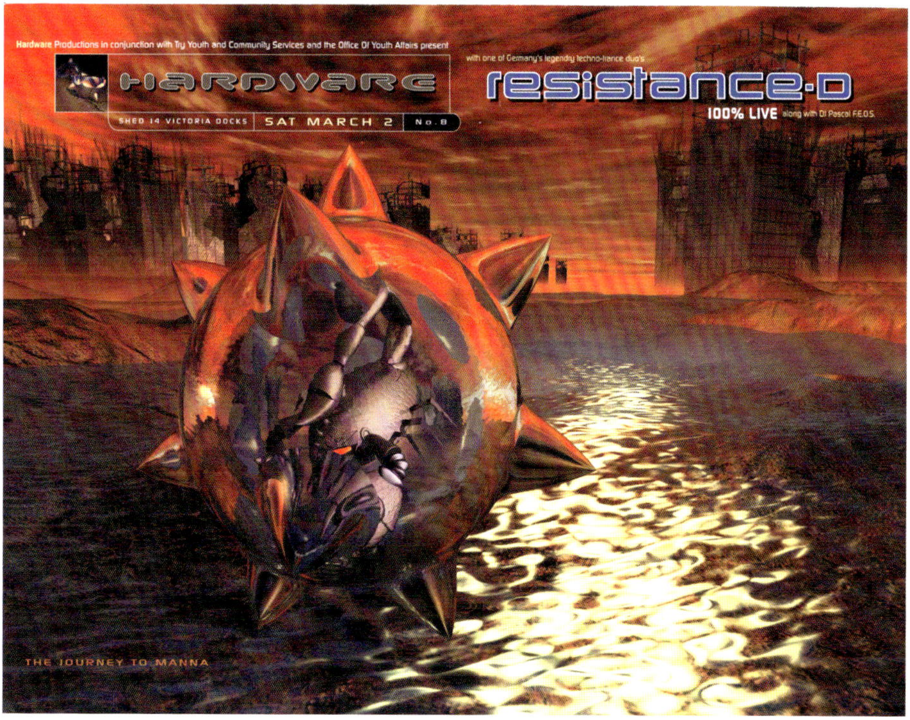

35

34: Flyer for Hardware 7, Shed 14, 2 Sep 95. Credit: Hardware Corporation.

35: Flyer for Hardware 8, Shed 14, 2 Mar 96. Credit: Hardware Corporation.

36: Flyer for Every Picture Tells A Story, 7 Mar 1992. Credit: The Shelter Foundation. Courtesy of Adem Jaffers.

37: Flyer for Every Picture Tells A Story 3, 20 Jun 1992. Credit: The Shelter Foundation. Courtesy of Adem Jaffers.

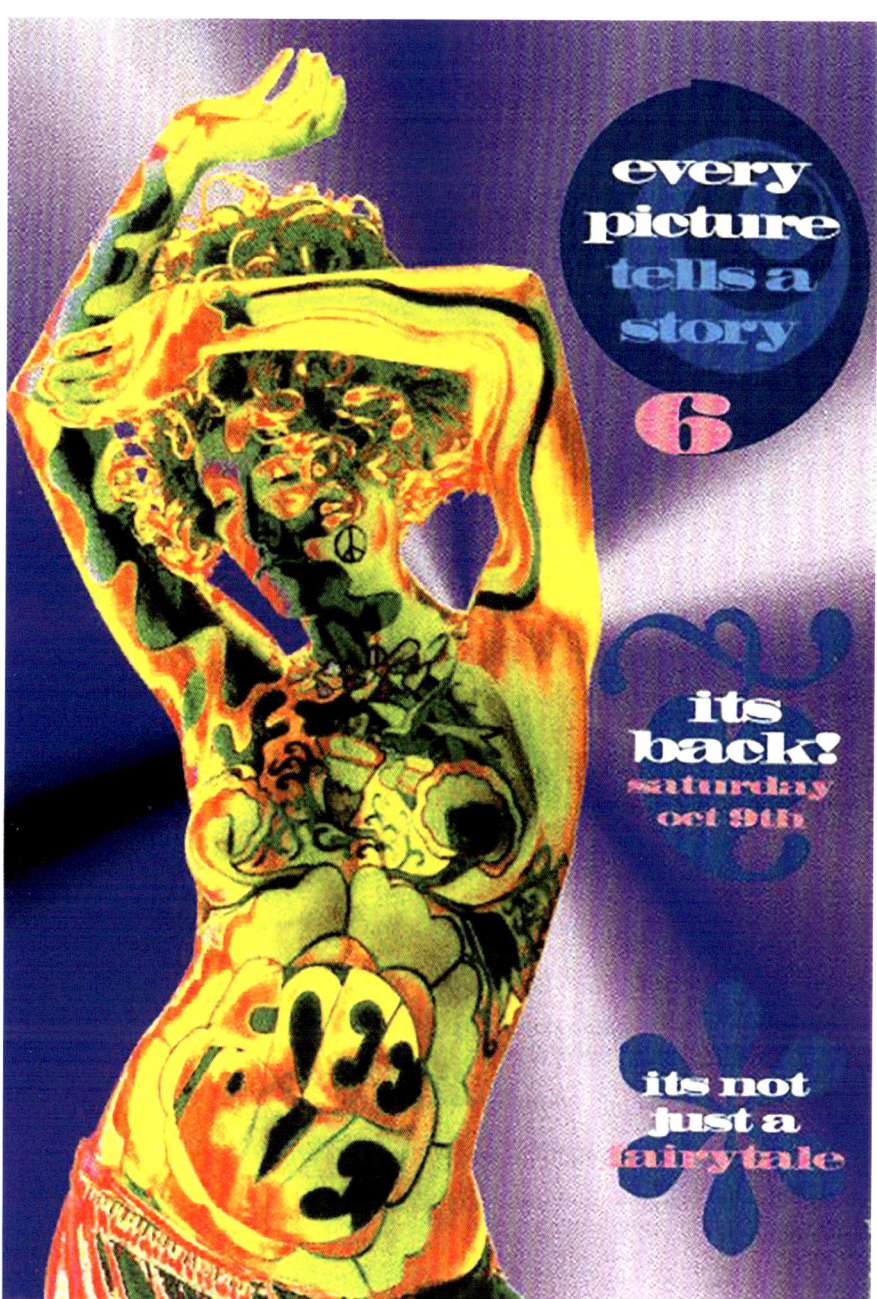

38: Flyer for Every Picture Tells A Story 6, 9 Oct 1993. Credit: The Shelter Foundation.

39: Flyer for Pleazure, NYE 1994. Credit: The Shelter Foundation. Courtesy of Adem Jaffers.

40: Flyer for Psychic Harmony, 21 Oct 1995. Credit: Troy Innocent. Courtesy of Adem Jaffers.

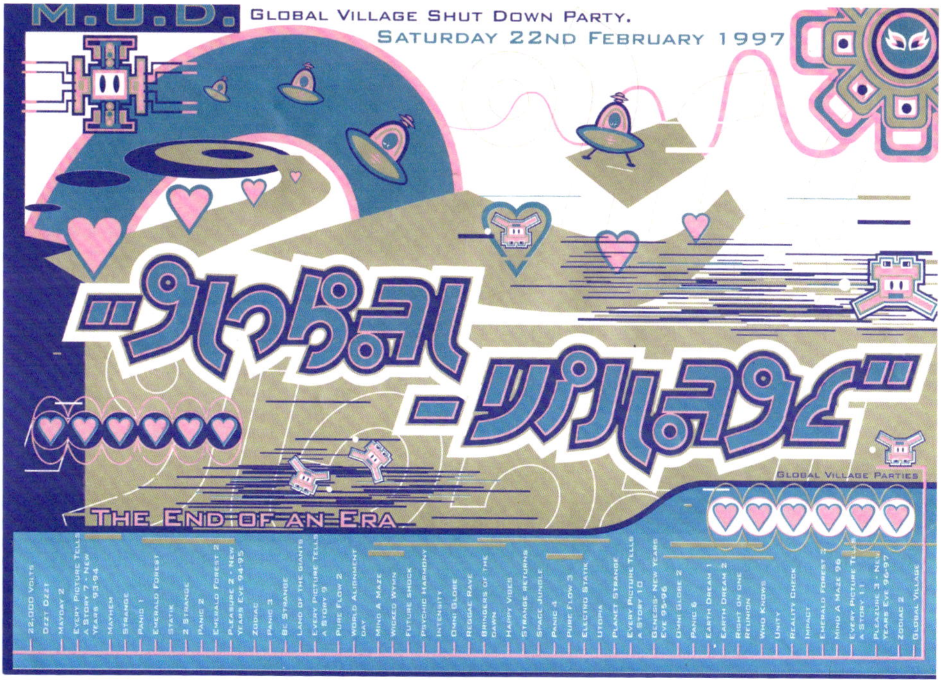

41: Flyer for Global Village Shut Down party, 22 Feb 1997. Credit: The Shelter Foundation. Courtesy of Hydi John.

42: Flyer for Every Picture Tells A Story 17, 20 Mar 1999. Credit: The Shelter Foundation. Courtesy of Natural 1.

43: Flyer for Every Picture Tells A Story 18, 24 Jul 1999. Credit: The Shelter Foundation. Courtesy of Natural 1.

44: Flyer for Madasss 2, 17 Oct 1998. Credit: Under the Floor Productions. Courtesy of Lani G.

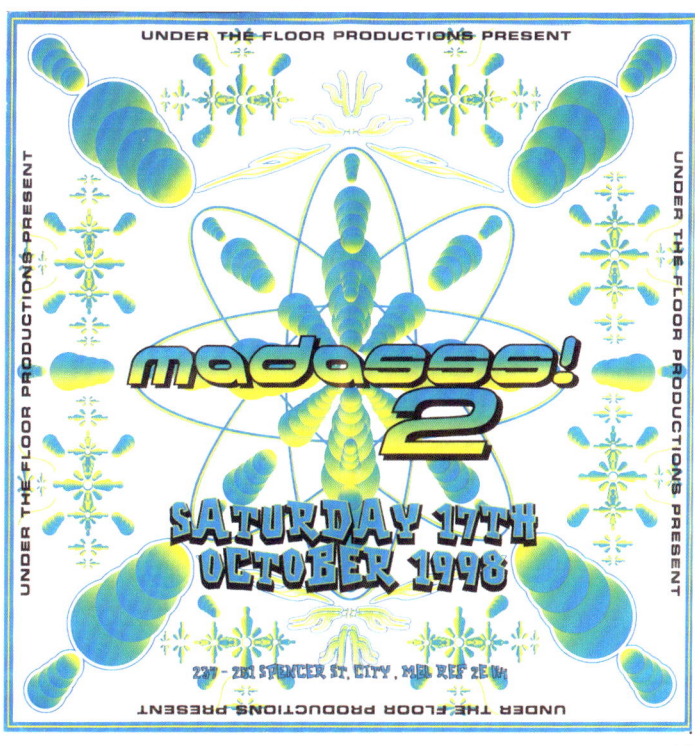

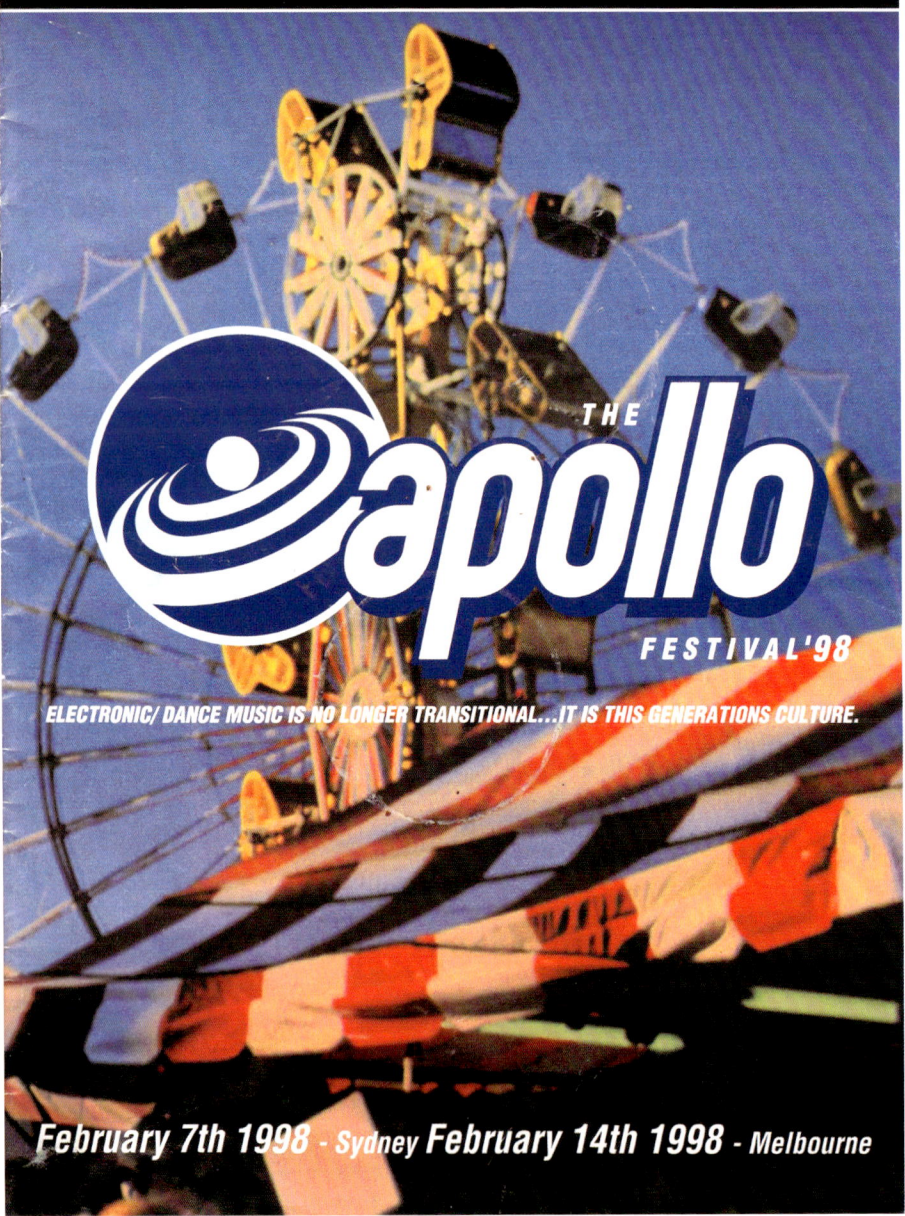

45: Flyer for Apollo festival, 14 Feb 1998. Credit: Hardware Corporation/ Gemmco/ Michael Coppel. Courtesy of Steve Robbins.

46: Flyer for Club Filter, date unknown. Credit: Singtoh Roddajun-Dogon. Courtesy of Rod.

47

48

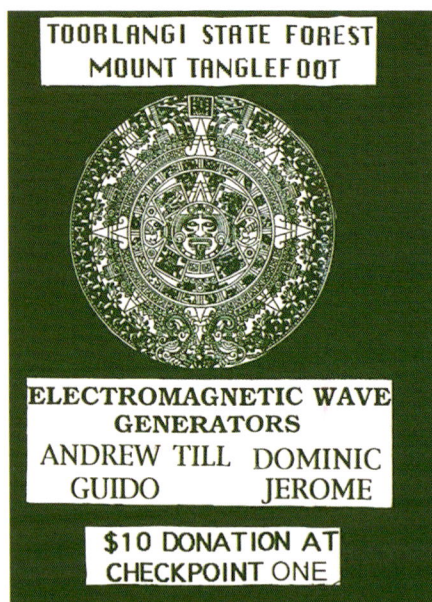

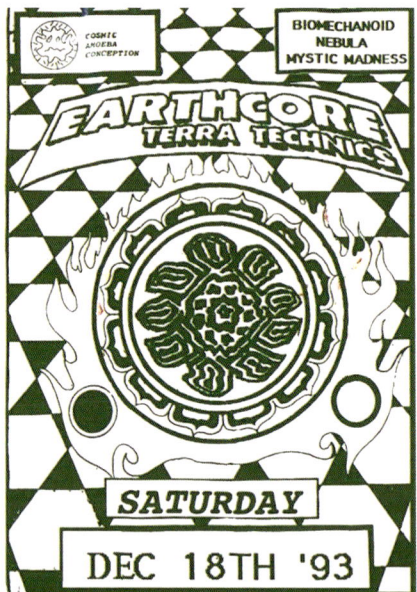

47: Flyer for first Earthcore, 18 Dec 1993. Credit: Spiro Boursine.

48: Flyer for Earthcore 6 Feb 1999. Credit: Earthcore. Courtesy of Natural 1.

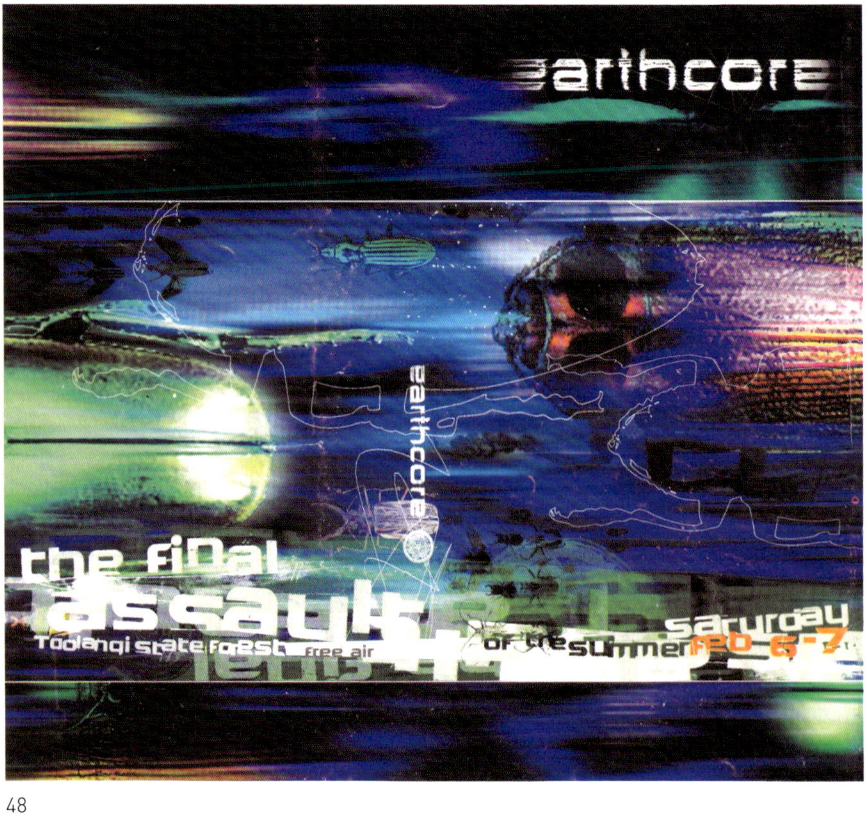

49

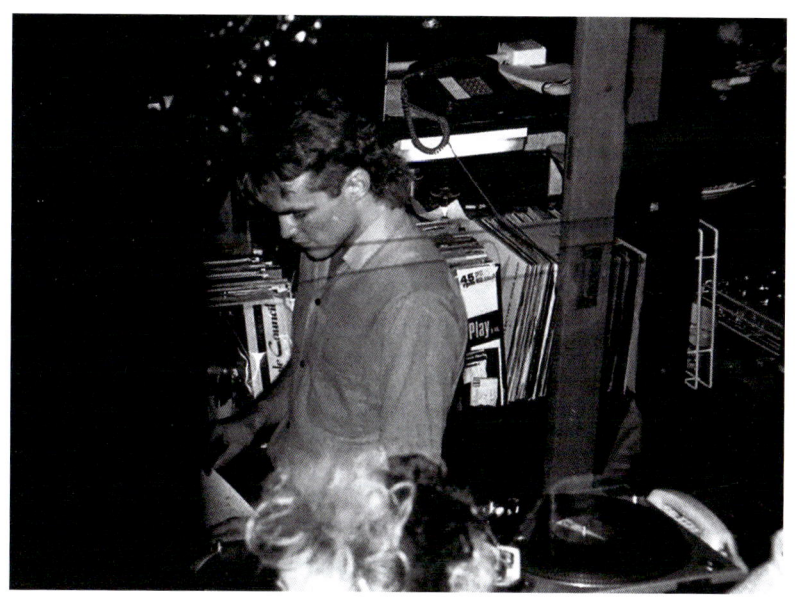

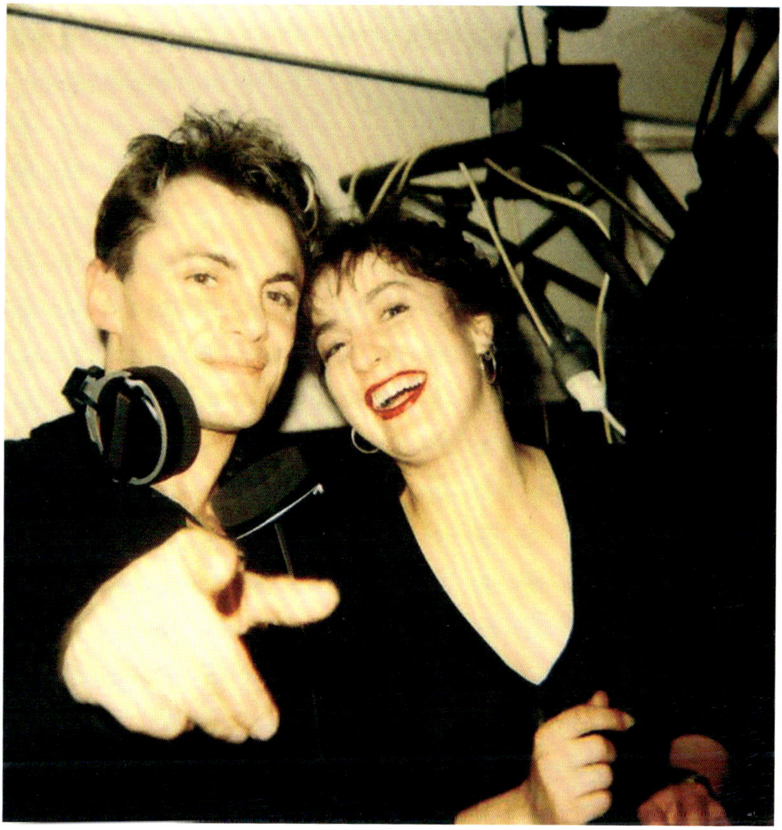

50

49: Gavin Campbell Djing at Underground, 1985. Credit: Gavin Campbell.

50: Gavin Campbell and Kate Seeley at Razor, 1990. Credit: Gavin Campbell.

51

52

51: Steve Robbins at Inflation basement c. 1990. Credit: Davide Carbone.
52: Heidi and Richard John, c. 1990. Credit: Susan M. King.

53: Rudeboy and Davide Carbone at Maze, c. 1991. Credit: Davide Carbone.
54: Steve Robbins and Terrence Ho at Maze, c. 1991. Credit: Davide Carbone.

55

56

55: Mark James at Xpress, Chasers. c. 1991. Credit: Mark James.

56: Ravers Kirsten, Jodie and Nadine at Pure, Palace Entertainment Complex, St Kilda, c. 1991. Credit: Davide Carbone.

57

58

57: Amanda Collier, Will E Tell, Richie Rich, Nadine, Davide Carbone, c. 1990. Credit: Richie McNeill.
58: Ollie Olsen, Mark Hogan and Charm at Quadrant, 1991. Credit: Emmy Boudry.

59

60

59: Nick Gill (2nd from right) at Quadrant rave, Antony St warehouse, CBD, 1991. Credit: Emmy Boudry.
60: Quadrant 2, Collingwood, 1992. Credit: Emmy Boudry.

61: Jason Midro and Emmy Boudry at Street Rave 12, Fitzroy, Oct 1999. Credit: Emmy Boudry.
62: Street Rave 11, St Kilda, Feb 1999. Credit: Emmy Boudry.

63 & 64: Ravers outside Global Village, early morning. Credit: Hydi John.

63

64

65

66

65: Kim McClelland (left) and friend, outside Westgate Sport & Entertainment Centre, Altona North, Every Picture Tells A Story, 24 Jul 1999. Credit: Kim McClelland.

66: Westgate Sport & Entertainment Centre, Altona North. Credit: Hydi John.

67

68

67: Every Picture Tells A Story, Bertie St warehouse, Port Melbourne c. 1999/2000. Credit: Hydi John.
68: Car Park rave outside Leslie St warehouse, Brunswick c.1997. Credit: Olivia Geselle.

69: Mick Smith (2nd from right) at Hardware 15, Shed 14, The Docks, 10 Jul 1999. Credit: Mick Smith.

70: Shufflers at Pleazure, Fennell St warehouse, Port Melbourne, Jun 1999. Credit: Mick Smith.

71

72

71: FSOM (L-R Steve Robbins, Josh Abrahams, Davide Carbone), 1996. Credit: Andrea Jerzyna.
72: Sonic Animation supporting Chemical Brothers, Metro, 2000. Credit: Fraser Nairn.

73

74

73: Lani G, Madasss 3, Feb 1999. Credit: Lani Greer.
74: Rudeboy and Mad Rod at Filter. Credit: Jane Alway.

75

76

75: Cookie Monster rave, Plaster Funhouse, Westmeadows, 2000. Credit: Kim McClelland.
76: Trade featuring Paul van Dyk, The Docks, June 2000. Credit: Fraser Nairn.

77

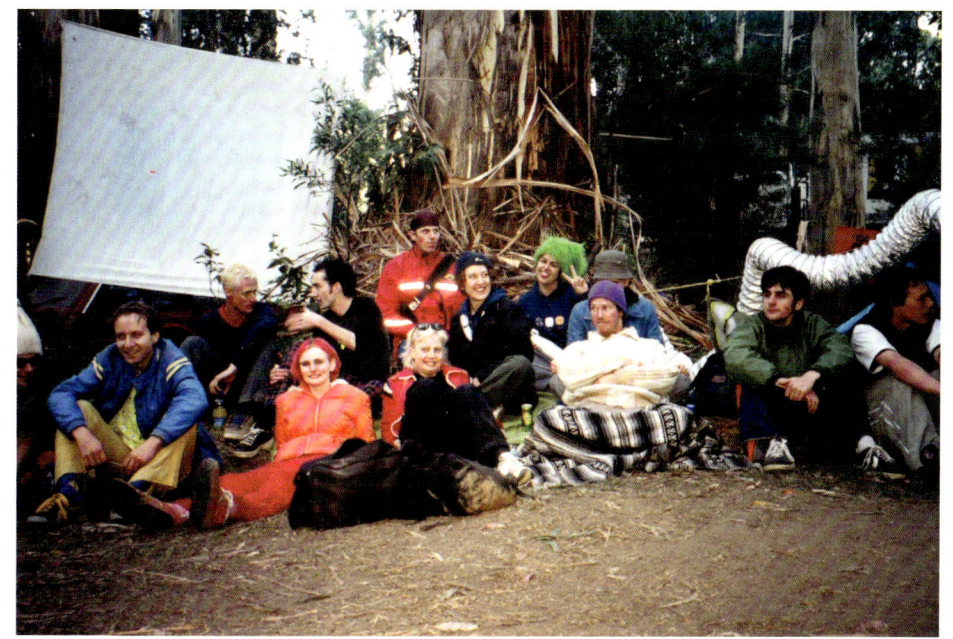

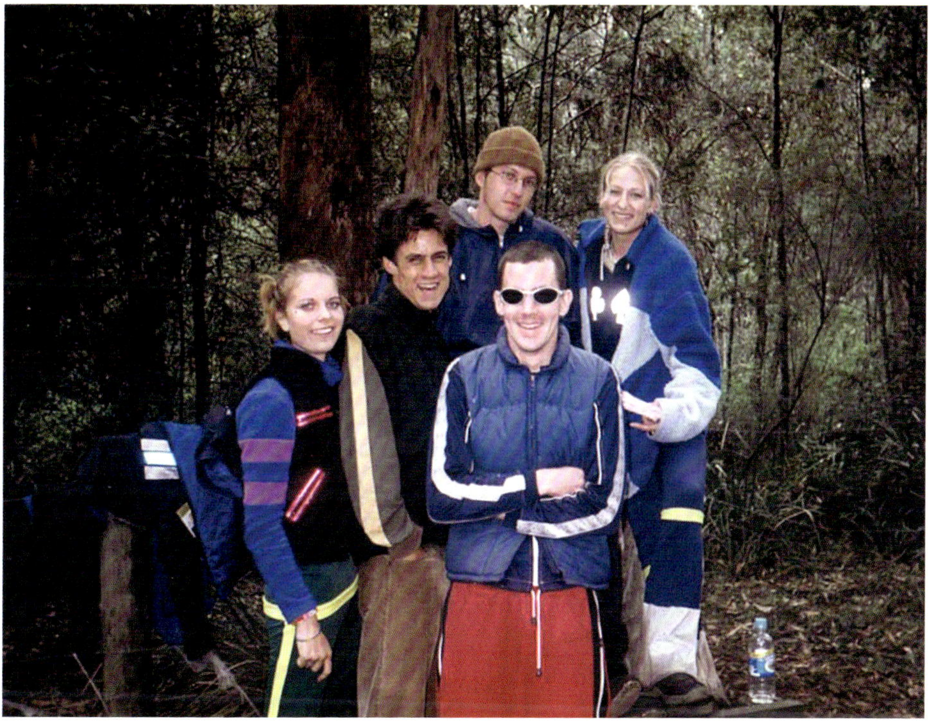

78

77: Earthcore, Mountain Bay, NYE 1999. Credit: Kim McClelland.

78: Lu Diamond (far right) and friends, Earthcore, Toolangi State Forest, Feb 1999. Credit: Lu Diamond.

79: DJ Brewster B., 1997. Credit: Brewster B.

80: Natural 1 wearing 'body mechanic' jumpsuit, Feb 2018. Credit: Paul Fleckney.

as the ones that periodically occupy the hideously rundown Bradmills warehouse in Yarraville. Overwhelmingly, however, rave in Melbourne was quasi-legal rather than outright unlawful. Richard and Heidi exemplified this more restrained approach. They organised insurance, hired portaloos, signed leases and maintained cordial relations with the police. Having grey hair helped. 'We used to tell the police, "You're talking to forty-year-old people who just want to dance all night,"' Richard explains. 'We're not kids, we're adults.' The Johns also employed the 'making a film' ruse to hire warehouses but I think it's naïve to assume agents were always oblivious to such tactics. A severe recession in the early nineties caused industrial property prices to dip and more than 20 percent of commercial space in the Melbourne CBD lay empty.[22] 'Agents were happy to have any sort of cash coming in, so we'd offer them $1000 for the warehouse for the weekend, cash under the counter, no questions asked,' Garry Shepherd told the ABC in 2003.[23]

Another common police-avoidance tactic copied from England was to print a telephone number on the flyer instead of the party address. On the night, punters rang the number (usually starting with the premium rate dialling code 0055) to hear a pre-recorded message that included details of the rave's location or the venue for the pre-party where the location would be disclosed. I query the effectiveness of these 0055 raves—surely a police officer in possession of the flyer could simply dial the number and discover the venue? Davide Carbone dismisses the 0055 fad as an attempt by some promoters to make their parties appear 'cool and authentic'.

'Melbourne didn't even really need raves,' Nimmo claims. 'I mean, in England the clubs closed at one or two. In Melbourne, they closed at seven. You could go out all night in Melbourne whereas in England the club would close and you'd still be pilling off your head so you'd need somewhere else to go.' Sure, people took drugs, illegally flyposted walls and lied to real estate agents (who hasn't?), but raves were hardly 'guerrilla operations'. They didn't need to be—

Melbourne's promoters had other tricks up their sleeves. 'We hated using the same venue twice,' DJ Natural 1 says. 'Every promoter would try to have a new venue for almost every party. That's what made it fun and exciting.' In the nineties, almost nowhere was safe from the glowstick and sneakers brigade. My non-exhaustive survey of Melbourne rave venues includes leisure centres, swimming pools, cricket stadiums, go-kart tracks, a flower market, town halls, piers, rowing clubs, textile factories, shops, city parks, film studios, disused grain siloes, children's play centres and an old abattoir complete with holding pens.[24] 'I liked the pop-up aspect of it,' producer Josh Abrahams says, borrowing a twenty-first century word to describe a nineties phenomenon:

> You'd get a couple of JBL speakers, not so big but still incredibly loud, an amp and a DJ rig and that's it. You could set up anywhere, in an abandoned office building, a warehouse or wherever … some of them were just amazing, they'd transform this warehouse into a magic wonderland in the middle of some industrial park … [but] when they were bad, they were a bit tragic, you had this vast space with hardly anyone in it.

Perhaps the closest we ever got to Melbourne achieving the left-anarchist's wet dream was the spontaneous car park rave that sprung up outside clubs and parties throughout the nineties, often as a result of image-conscious nightclub bouncers denying entry to sweaty ravers dressed in t-shirts and jeans. 'We'd have our own little party outside off in our own little tripping land,' Nimmo tells me. 'It would be like thirty little ravers running around being idiots outside in the streets and in the car park.' Unplanned, unpoliced and unlicensed, ravers treaded the asphalt long into the morning.

Street Rave

Moorabbin, March 2015. I'm sitting with Emmy Boudry in her garden on a warm autumn afternoon, listening to her stories, flicking through a photo album and swatting half-heartedly at a wasp that won't leave us alone. 'Street rave gave ordinary people a chance to view rave culture,' she says. 'People got to experience the culture firsthand who wouldn't normally see it except for the negative, distorted view from the media, i.e., dingy warehouse, everyone's on drugs. Instead they saw the proper version of it.' I ask what she means by 'proper'. She replies without hesitation: 'A street full of ravers in broad daylight, loud and proud going, "We're here, we're loving it, this is it".'

In 1991, Mark and Emmy shared a dilapidated Edwardian terrace on Moor Street, Fitzroy with four housemates. I imagine their living conditions as somewhere between *Dogs in Space* and *The Young Ones*, perhaps with less blood and more bass. After one too many house parties, Emmy proposed to take the party out onto the street. She secured the support of her housemates and friends across the road and then put it to her neighbours. Amazingly, the whole street signed up. Clearly, the latte-sipping gentrifiers had yet to colonise this well located if somewhat decrepit pocket of inner city Melbourne. Emmy presented her petition to the Fitzroy City Council and the officers granted her permission to close off the street. I can't believe this would happen now. Street closures aren't unprecedented in Melbourne, but for a rave?

Emmy set up a DJ rig in her front garden and hung a strobe in the upstairs bedroom. 'We put flyers out at all the raves and about fifty people came down … we had Will E Tell and Hess and I think Richie Rich might have played. Mark played. Charm played. That was Street Rave 1 in a residential street.' The following year, Emmy successfully lobbied the organisers of the Melbourne Fringe Festival to bring street rave into their program. Initially occupying just one block of Brunswick Street, by the end of the decade, the rave stretched from Alexandra Parade to Johnston Street, a distance of 500 metres. 'Street rave thrived on the honest energy of ravers celebrating being a raver in full daylight,' Emmy says:

> We had old people rocking out to techno and children watching the ravers … everyone's happy, everyone's smiling, there's never any violence. The only thing was sometimes people got too excited and tried to dance on the shop rooves so we'd have to turn off the music and get the DJs to ask them to come down.

In 1999, Mark and Emmy began a second street rave as part of the St Kilda Festival. They cordoned off Cavell Street, sandwiched between Luna Park and the Palais theatre. As the crowds swelled under the palm trees, the rave spilled out onto The Esplanade and stopped the traffic.

Harmony

In the early days, the scene basked in a spirit of cooperation and unity. DJ Brewster B. tells me promoters wouldn't usually put on a party on the same night as a competitor:

> Between 1990 and 1993, there was very little animosity within the scene. You didn't have any harshness. Sure, there was always a little conflict here and there but the general vibe was everyone just got along. There was a harmony, a oneness.

This oneness reached its zenith on Saturday 15 August 1992. The 'Sydney cartel', so the story goes, wanted to throw a party in Melbourne on the same night as Richard and Heidi. Mark James, Mark and Emmy and Richie Rich—at that time Melbourne's biggest promoters—united with the Johns to put on Harmony at Footscray's

TVU Warehouse. 'We all joined forces to show these Sydney promoters they couldn't come to Melbourne and do a rave on our turf,' Emmy tells me. Harmony featured the cream of the city's DJing talent: Richie Rich, Will E Tell, Steve Robbins, Hess, Rudeboy, Danny D, Jeff Tyler, Mark Hogan, Russell Hancorne [aka Mystic Force] and Jayse Knipe. Who would go anywhere else? The Sydney crew got the message, packed up and went home. But they didn't forget. Years later, Richard John tried to hire Homebush stadium for a New Year's Eve party and arranged to meet a promoter he knew at Sydney's Central station:

> I called up my contact and within half an hour eight of them came down the station and threatened and verbally abused me: 'Who the fuck are you? You fucking Melbourne promoters. Coming up here, hiring Homebush to do New Year's'. And I said, 'No, I want to do it with you guys, I want us to work together'. But they weren't interested, they wanted to beat the shit out of me.

The Docks

For a hundred years, Victoria Dock served as Melbourne's primary port connecting the city to London, Liverpool and the world. But by 1980 the harbour's greatest advantage—a location immediately to the west of the CBD—had become its downfall. Bigger cargo ships too wide for the harbour's narrow channel and increasing containerisation in the shipping industry led the government to construct a series of new docks downstream of the Bolte Bridge.[25] Divorced from its original purpose, Victoria Dock became a post-industrial wasteland cut off from the city by Spencer Street railway station and Footscray Road.[26] From a future development perspective, architectural critic Kim Dovey called it 'the greatest waterfront opportunity Melbourne would ever see'.[27] In the meantime, Melbourne's ravers transformed the isolated warehouses and sheds into their secret playground, a place to 'go off' without fear of complaining neighbours.

The ALSO Foundation first realised the party potential of the docks in 1987 when they put on Raw Hide 5 on Australia Day Eve at Jupp's warehouse on the corner of Dudley and Sudholz streets.[28] ALSO returned to Victoria Dock in January 1991 when they booked Shed 10 for Women's Own Warehouse (WOW) and Red Raw over the Australia Day weekend. At the far end of a small pier, jutting out into the middle of the harbour and almost invisible from the road, Shed 10 was the perfect venue for an all-night party. For Australia Day 1993 ALSO hired Shed 10 and neighbouring Shed 9. With WOW scheduled for Friday and Red Raw on Sunday, it left the Saturday night slot free for anyone who wanted to throw a last-minute dance party. Naturally, they approached the best in the business: Richie Rich and Richard John. Rave had come to the docks.

Richie and the Johns took advantage of ALSO's cutting-edge production rig, which included a full-colour laser and eight computer-controlled moving Intellabeam lights, like those used for rock concerts. Richard and Heidi brought in Gary Hughes from Adelaide and Ming D from Sydney while Richie Rich, Will E Tell and Jase Knipe represented the Hardware contingent. The week before, Richie spruiked the party on *Beat in the Street*, promising a night of 'hard trance' and 'classic' tunes.[29]

In 1994, ALSO's Tracey Wall invited Richie to sign a joint five-year lease for Shed 14, a vast warehouse opposite Shed 9 on Central Pier. The shed wasn't generally available to commercial operators but ALSO and Hardware Corporation claimed an exemption thanks to their not-for-profit status. 'ALSO wanted to get a permanent lease of the venue to stop other people from coming in,' Richie admits. In return for five-year exclusive use rights, Hardware and ALSO promised to improve the venue. 'We put in three-phase power and running water, fixed up the toilets and emergency lighting and mended all the locks,' Richie says. 'Then we started running

Hardware shows there from Hardware 5 onwards. Hardware 5 was August 1994 with Laurent Garnier.'

Between 1994 and 1999, Richie put on fourteen Hardwares and dozens of other parties at Shed 14 featuring international DJs like CJ Bolland, Jeff Mills, Adam Beyer and Richie Hawtin. In 1998, Mark James took control of Sheds 2 and 4 at the tip of North Wharf Road for his Future parties. Richard John, however, wasn't so lucky. 'Do you think we could hire the docks?' he says angrily. 'Oh no. We were blacklisted. The owner would never let us rent those sheds.' I ask why not. 'Everyone used to ask the same question,' Heidi replies. 'Because we weren't allowed there.' I didn't push it but I wonder if it's because the Johns, with their long hair and tie-dyed t-shirts, didn't look 'corporate' enough.

Walking through Docklands today is a bit like an ant crawling through an IKEA showroom—a befuddling maze of criss-crossing streets with temptations to spend on every corner. Docklands' architects seemed to suffer from a crisis of colour, as though painting a chessboard or Mondrian's golden rectangles onto a façade could make up for the precinct's inherent blandness. In the nineties, the area was similarly hard to navigate but with far fewer painted glass boxes. For many people, the docks experience began when they boarded a shuttle bus at Spencer Street station, winding through the deserted backstreets down to the waterfront. In Tom Griffin's 2005 novel *Playgrounds: A Portrait of Rave Culture,* narrator Lucas describes the journey back to Spencer Street from Sheds 2 and 4:

> The bus took us through what looks like a war zone. The Docklands is a mess of development, with signs of construction all around, roads closed off and temporary signs flashing yellow neon at you about road closures and different routes to take.[30]

Meanwhile, with his hands on Shed 14, Richie subverted the erstwhile mantra of 'new party, new venue'. It also meant he could sever the fraying thread that tied him to the Johns. Richard and Heidi had given him some of his first gigs. They had put on parties together. He'd even dated their eldest daughter Driena. But now it was time to go it alone. As for the Johns, they didn't need Richie or his shed. Four kilometres to the west on the banks of the Maribyrnong River, they were busy transforming the warehouse rave into an artform.

Chapter 7

GLOBAL VILLAGERS

Every Picture Tells a Story

In 1991, Richard and Heidi John formed Melbourne Underground Development (M.U.D.) with Phil 'Voodoo' Woodman, Sue (aka Sioux) Dollman and a rotating band of artists, musicians and hangers-on. M.U.D.'s *Artistic Manifesto* urges followers to quit the material 'rat race' and dance together to an 'infinite primal driving beat'.[1] It sounds almost cultish and in some respect, I think that's what the Johns tried to achieve. 'Some people don't understand it and end up not staying [whereas] for others this is what they've been searching for all their lives,' the *Manifesto* reads.[2] Like hipsters to a Northcote food truck, M.U.D. drew in thousands of disciples month after month. Their favourite party was Every Picture Tells a Story.

In January 1992, Richard approached a planning officer at the City of Melbourne to probe the council's position on warehouse parties:

> 'You're not going to have one of these rave parties, are you?' and I said, 'No, not at all'. 'Look Richard,' he said, 'I'll give you two tips. Don't ask permission, just do it. And when the Council come and say, "You can't do this", you've got something to argue with because if you've been doing it for a year and a half you can say, "Well, there's been no complaints". But if you go and ask to do something they'll come up with all these reasons for why you can't do it.' 'Great,' I said. 'And what's your second tip?' 'If I was you,' the officer said, 'I'd just go out of the city a bit, just out of sight.' It was him who told us to go west.

Every Picture Tells a Story was born on Saturday 7 March 1992 at the Pack and Stack warehouse in Footscray. Down by the wharves, on a dead-end road and 300 metres from the nearest house, it was the ideal venue for a noisy rave. Every Picture brought together DJs from three cities: Sydney's Joe 90 and George Vegas; Melbourne's own Richie Rich, Will E Tell, Rudeboy, H2O, Kate Bathgate and Liz Millar; and Gary Hughes and HMC from Adelaide. '[Our DJs] weren't as raw and underground as half of the Adelaide DJs I can name,' Natural 1 tells me. 'Their general culture embraced the true raw and hardest people and put them on centre stage.'

Richie Rich's fruitful partnership with Try Youth for his Hardware parties had not escaped Richard and Heidi's attention. After a short-lived collaboration with ALSO for Every Picture 1, they established the Shelter Foundation for 'underprivileged children', as Heidi explains:

> That's what Every Picture was all about ... kids from the street could come in, no matter what their issues were, and work with professionals on something that gave them an opportunity to pull themself up and extend themselves. They could work in lighting, in multimedia or in sound.

Richard and Heidi subsequently signed up to the Victorian Government's FReeZA program, an initiative providing young people between the ages of twelve and twenty-five with the opportunity to attend affordable and accessible music and cultural events. 'We were the first people to do the FReeZA program because we had experience in these parties and we were based in the western suburbs,' Heidi says. Entrenched disadvantage looms large in Melbourne's west. In the nineties, Footscray and neighbouring Braybrook had two of the highest unemployment rates in the state.[3] Sadly, little has changed in the last two decades.

Richard and Heidi copied the Every Picture Tells a Story name from one of Joe Wieczorek's Labrynth parties in London. That wasn't all. 'All the graphics and stuff were basically stolen from Club Labrynth,' Nimmo Sandilands says. 'They must have just gone through their old flyer collection.' The flyer for Every Picture 1 replicated an earlier Labrynth design, right down to the font, background image and supersized first letter 'e' in 'every'—a not-so-subtle product placement for ecstasy beloved by promoters in the early nineties. Richard and Heidi took their musical cues from London too, bringing out Labrynth DJs Adrian Age, Sarah HB, jungle pioneers Rat Pack and drum'n'bass maestro, Kenny Ken. Hardcore had come to Melbourne.

Hardcore, You Know the Score

English journalist Simon Reynolds calls hardcore (aka hardkore or 'ardkore) the second wave of rave.[4] For a generation of British youth (myself included), hardcore *is* rave. Breaking the reliance on US imports, hardcore ushered in a new and distinctly English flavour of electronic dance music. Defining hardcore in musical terms is difficult given it means different things to different people at different times. It could be Unique 3's bone-crunching '7 A.M.' and 'Weight for the Bass' and the bleep and bass of LFO's 'LFO' and 'Aftermath' by Nightmares on Wax. Or it's the 'techno-as-heavy metal' of Joey

Beltram's 'Mentasm' and 'Energy Flash' and the 'industrial-tinged techno' of Belgian New Beat tracks like CJ Bolland's 'Horsepower' and T99's 'Anasthasia'. Finally, it's the ripped-off riffs of 'Raving I'm Raving' by Shut Up and Dance and the 'toytown tekno' of sampled children's TV shows overlaid with blatant drug references—The Prodigy's 'Charly' and 'Ebeneezer Goode' by The Shamen top this list.[5] If there's a common element, it's the break beat, once the bedrock of hip hop looped and sped up for the nineties' techno generation.

Reynolds writes that hardcore married drug-fuelled hedonism with underclass fury arising from twelve years of Thatcher rule. "Ardkore seethes with a RAGE TO LIVE, to cram all the intensity absent from a week of drudgery into a few hours of fervour,' he writes.[6] In reality, this meant getting fucked on drugs and dancing like a nutter to mental music, the harder and faster the better. At 150 to 180 bpm, hardcore makes acid house and Detroit techno seem sedate. It's strictly dancing music; no one ever plays 'Mentasm' at a dinner party.

True to rave tradition, hardcore began as a DIY music scene: artists recorded tracks in home studios, pressed up white-label 12-inch singles and sold them directly to dance music record stores.[7] Despite frequent appearances in the UK Top 40 charts, British record companies and the mainstream media overlooked the homegrown sound to begin with until it became too loud to ignore. Journalists who dared venture into this underworld seldom escaped unscathed. In 1993, a *mixmag* writer filed the following report from Joe Wieczorek's Club Labrynth:

> [t]he breakbeats seem to be getting faster, the faces bonier and uglier, the eyes expanding like they're about to explode … I'm alone in hardcore hell, being jostled by skinny lads who are jogging on the spot. Everywhere I look I see The Scream. The phrase 'loved up' could never apply to these hardcore gurning children. The grinning ones look like mass murderers; the aggressive dancers resemble skinhead

thugs and the ones with vacant stares look like the scary schizophrenics you meet in shopping centres. Somebody grabs my arm and I actually scream.[8]

As the nineties progressed, hardcore evolved into derivative forms like jungle and drum'n'bass. Jungle celebrated dance music's African-American roots and won over a black urban crowd who had distanced themselves from the earlier acid house scene. 'When it first came over [to England], a lot of people thought house music was poof's music, white people's music, and a lot of black people wouldn't go to raves', Kenny Ken told Matthew Collin.[9] Richard John says it was a 'natural progression' from reggae to jungle and drum'n'bass. 'If it was new music, we'd play it,' he explains. 'We were the Melbourne Underground Development, developing the Melbourne underground. It was fresh and on the edge. It wasn't following a format of the music industry; it was following its own industry.' His friendship with Joe Wieczorek jemmied open a window to a scene that had lain largely hidden from Melbourne's raving fraternity.

In Melbourne, not everyone could handle the bone-rattling bass, violent vocals and darker-than-night attitude that hardcore demanded. Duncan Plank had been raised on a diet of uplifting Chicago house: 'I didn't like breakbeat, period … I didn't want to keep following the underground just for the sake of it being underground.' Davide Carbone concedes the breakbeat sound wasn't 'über-popular' to begin with, although he lauds the Every Picture parties for putting it under the same roof as Detroit techno, acid house and Euro trance. And while I've heard stories of ravers—men, of course—competing with each other to see who could swallow the most pills in one night (a lifetime on a disability pension the result of one such misadventure), the feverish and self-destructive hardcore sensibility never seemed to infect the whole scene, as it had in England in 1991. Perhaps Australians didn't have as much to get angry about. The weather's better, for one thing. And our prime ministers don't tend to hang around long enough to bring about the kind of rage-filled desperation Margaret Thatcher inspired in her subjects.

Global Village

For Every Pictures 2, 3, 4 and 5, M.U.D. used the TVU warehouse on the corner of Wingfield and Maribyrnong Streets in Footscray.[10] 'Deep in a dirty dungeon the argon laser cut thru the crowd like a hot knife thru butter', H2O recalls.[11] Today only the north wall of the 'dirty dungeon' remains: a developer demolished the warehouse in 2010 to make way for high-end apartments boasting fine views of the Maribyrnong River and the city skyline. For Every Picture 6 on Saturday 9 October 1993, M.U.D. took over a disused warehouse in Brunswick. After an eleven-month hiatus, it was clear from the flyer that something had changed at M.U.D. mission control. The oversized 'e' for ecstasy was gone, replaced by a topless woman decorated in psychedelic colours, peace symbols and the words 'free love' daubed on her belly. Richard and Heidi's earlier parties had reimagined the gritty rawness of the late eighties London acid house scene; now, it seemed, the English pair had regressed further in time to their 'flower power' childhoods. Heidi had been twelve years old during the first summer of love in 1967, Richard a year or two older. Under their spiritual guidance, M.U.D. awakened rave's hippie roots and nurtured a New Age philosophy of tribalism and transcendence.

Back in 1991, Phil Voodoo had attended a warehouse party in the former Docklands Cotton Mills, next door to Pack and Stack. The party was called 22,000 Volts, named after the electrical substation humming away in the back courtyard. A small crew of artists occupied the warehouse. When they moved out, Voodoo took on the lease. He called it the Strange warehouse and moved in with partner Sioux Dollman and a bunch of artist friends. Voodoo told the ABC: '[i]t was our own little world … we never had to leave there, it was great. Just made parties, and that was our life.'[12]

Stef lived at Strange for two years with Voodoo's brother Dan Woodman, D-REK and Brent Kells. 'At some stage there was eight of us', he says. 'We had people not leave after parties sometimes.' The accommodation was far from salubrious; Brent lived in a cubby above the kitchen and Stef slept next door to the transformer room:

> It was freezing cold! We had a potbelly stove but we had no chimney so we couldn't actually light it because the whole place would smoke out. Food was difficult too. There were really no cooking facilities so we'd go down to the little Vietnamese lady next door and buy her *bánh mì*.

People literally starved for their art at Strange. When Stef left in 1996 on the verge of a nervous breakdown, his six-foot frame weighed only fifty-six kilograms.

Strange worked well as an artist's studio but was too small for rave parties. Thankfully, providence lent a hand. 'We had been there a couple of months when one day an emergency exit door that shared our internal staircase had been left open and it led into this amazing huge warehouse space with parquetry flooring perfect for a dancefloor,' Voodoo recalls. 'This became Global Village.'

Vietnamese businessman Henry Tru held the lease for the Cotton Mills complex. Between 1975 and 1982, the Fraser government accepted tens of thousands of Vietnamese refugees following the end of the Vietnam War. Henry was one of the many hundreds who chose to settle in Footscray. Similar to reactions over the southern European migrants who arrived after World War II, many Melburnians eyed their new neighbours with suspicion and contempt. As late as 1986, Inflation nightclub refused to admit Vietnamese patrons.[13] Six years later, Geoffrey Wright's movie *Romper Stomper* portrayed the violent tensions between the Footscray Vietnamese community and a gang of neo-Nazi skinheads.

Global Village was located in the former Global Warehouse on the corner of Maribyrnong and Parker streets. Henry retained the ground floor of Global Village for a 'Vietnamese market', selling second-hand goods and *phở* while M.U.D. used the first floor for their parties. With 6000 square metres to play with, they no longer had to find a new venue each time, as Voodoo explains:

> We had a number of moveable sound panel walls and so for every party we would create different rooms and different entrances so that when people came in they would get lost in this wonderful, mysterious, secret place.

With over a dozen roller doors, fire escapes and back entrances to choose from, just finding your way in was part of the fun. From 1993 to 1997, Global Village hosted over a hundred parties, including four Every Pictures, three Emerald Forests and six Panics, the latter the first large scale jungle parties in Melbourne. 'Rave had no home in Melbourne until Richie got Shed 14 and the M.U.D. crew took over Global Village,' Natural 1 says. When Voodoo gave me a tour of Global Village in July 2015, he explained why it made such an effective rave venue. 'It's a unique building with giant steel pillars, a solid concrete roof and thick brick walls,' he said as we walked up and down the original staircase and tiptoed across the hallowed parquetry flooring. 'This meant we could go to town on the sound system with no fear of complaints. It was rave heaven.'

Child's Play

Richard and Heidi's youngest daughter Jade spent much of her early childhood at Global Village. 'I learnt to ride a bike in the driveway out the front,' she tells me. 'It was a second-hand pink one. I bought it from the Vietnamese market.' Jade loved watching the artists at work but her fondest memories are of the parties:

> The biggest parties used to be on a full moon. We all stood up on the first or second level while the security was getting prepped and the sound checks were going on and we'd stare

at this giant moon emerging over the city. That was always the start to the night. And then after that I'd be told, 'Jade, get away, go and make yourself busy'.

In 2018 the idea of a six-year-old girl wandering around an all-night techno party in a dingy, drug-fuelled warehouse is laughable. In Queensland you can be arrested if you let your child walk to school alone.[14] Admittedly, Jade's parentage made her an extreme case but in the nineties you'd often find children as young as twelve at parties like Every Picture. Being an unlicensed event meant anyone could attend—including people from the other end of the age spectrum. 'Kids used to bring their parents,' Richard says. 'They loved it. We had parents that we told, "you've gotta leave now unless you're buying a ticket". An hour and a half later they're still there!'

Jade tapped into the euphoria that enveloped the Global Village dancefloor:

> I wasn't taking drugs obviously but I still got the same feeling as everyone else did and I've never had that same feeling from any other party. There were never any problems. There was never any situation where I felt unsafe or uncomfortable. Everyone really loved what he or she was there for.

A typical night for Jade meant wandering from room to room, falling asleep in one of the live-in artist's bedrooms and then getting up around 4am to find the dancefloor again. For her parents, the evening pulsed to a more hectic rhythm. 'They'd be under extreme pressure rushing around doing a thousand things but at the end of the night you'd always find dad doing his classic little boogie dance at the back of the dancefloor,' she laughs. 'And mum would be somewhere not far away.' Not even pregnancy could keep Heidi at home—she tells me she was still dancing at seven months. And yes, infant Joshua came to the parties too: with a cuddly toy under his arm and a dummy in his mouth, I'm sure he fitted right in. '[Rave] was let's revert and go back to a childlike period when the world was good and we were happy and we didn't have any cares in the world,' Natural 1 states. Global Village was Melbourne's largest kindergarten. Ravers sucked dummies, dragged teddy bears, carried children's backpacks and wore cartoon characters on their clothes.

Voodoo Magic and Mutoid Madness

'Global Village was loved so much because it was a complete escape from reality,' Voodoo tells me. Voodoo started out as a break-dancer and graffiti artist in the hip hop scene before crossing over to the rave scene in the late eighties. In February 2015, I met him in a Northcote café where he showed me samples of his work. The pieces are brightly coloured and highly imaginative, drawing from a wide range of influences, including Japanese manga, Hindu deities, Star Trek and Sonic the Hedgehog. One of my favourite banners shows three luminescent dancing stick figures that look like they've just walked off a Keith Haring mural, surrounded by talking snakes and pink-petalled flowers with yellow smiley faces. I asked Voodoo where he got his inspiration. 'Psychedelics,' he replied with a gleam in his eye. Although Richard John insists that the decor at his parties created an environment where one didn't *need* drugs or alcohol to have a good time, several ravers have told me that Voodoo's artwork took on a new life when viewed through acid-tinted spectacles.

The alternative world that was Global Village took more than a few waves of Voodoo's magic wand. Every party had its own theme, the preparation for which took weeks and involved dozens of people painting, welding and hammering in the Strange warehouse next door. 'A whole group of artists got together for who knows how long to prepare every single prop, which was different for every single party,' Jade says. 'Many of the artists had homes to go to but they were here 24/7 working around the clock to get it perfect.' For a party to celebrate the Mayan New Year, they hung 150 five-metre-high fluorescent banners. 'Fluro [sic] is to techno what spray cans are to hip hop', Voodoo told *Techno Renegade* in 1998. 'The fluro, when combined with black light UV lighting illuminates with its own light source and in colours similar to your mind's eye.'[15] For Emerald Forest in 1994, M.U.D. covered every room from floor to ceiling with paintings. Every picture told a story. Meanwhile, Pleazure on New Year's Eve 1996 featured a *Lord of the Rings* themed 'happy herbs' marketplace. 'You even got to the point where up in this room on the second floor they had a beach theme and they had to get tonnes of sand up here,' Jade tells me. 'I don't know how they did it! There were no lifts or anything. But they wouldn't leave any room undecorated.'

Writer Graham St John casts Global Village as an 'alternative arts precinct' with 'relatively unhindered artistic freedoms'.[16] The experimental eighties had hatched a brood of talented artists, designers and graf writers, squatting and hanging out in Melbourne's disused factories and condemned office buildings. M.U.D. delivered an outlet for their combined creative genius. 'All the arty-farty people sided with them because they were being more creative than I was,' Mark James admits. 'And they had a bigger budget I guess.' M.U.D. set a standard for artistic expression that was rarely surpassed. 'Richie had great music and a good sound system but there was no decor,' Stef claims. 'There was one big fucking laser and some lights whereas what we were doing was to set up things to fuck people up.'

When I heard about this commitment to overflowing creativity, I wondered if it was worth it. The artists exhibited their work for one night only and earned barely enough to feed themselves. By the late nineties, however, it seemed their hard work had paid off. Melbourne's warehouse rave scene had become known nationally and internationally for its arts content. 'The problem with Melbourne is that it looks outside for its uniqueness but its uniqueness is internal,' Heidi says. That internal uniqueness delivered magical wonderlands saturated with escapist fantasies and artistic flair. My wife Kim says:

> [i]t was an intensely creative space … the parties always showcased stunning decor. They were highly planned

events but in a way, they were highly unstructured when we got there and I really liked that—the lack of order, lack of structure and yet everything held together really well. It was organised anarchy.

Talk of 'organised anarchy' brings us to Robin Cooke. A graduate of the early eighties London squat party scene, Robin formed Mutoid Waste Company (MWC) with fellow artist Joe Rush in 1985. On Saturday mornings, Robin and Joe dressed in 'mad outfits' and drove up and down the Portobello Road Market in 'mutated cars', including a burnt-out Bedford coach known as the 'Skull Bus'.[17] Fusing hippie idealism with punk-inspired anarchy, MWC began throwing free parties in vacant London warehouses.[18] Robin and Joe spent days building massive sculptures from car parts that they would set fire to on the night of the party.[19]

Robin brought MWC to Melbourne in 1991 after the English rave dream crumbled. That year, he organised a Mutoid party at St Kilda's Esplanade Hotel (aka the Espy) and then an Earthdream party at the Weston Milling grain silos (aka 'Love Mills') on Munster Terrace, North Melbourne.[20] The Mutoid crew swirled ultraviolet paint through four inches of water on the dancefloor, converted the toilet into a 'Skull Throne' and shot projections onto the silos.[21] Robin partnered with a number of different Melbourne crews, including M.U.D. Ahead of each party at Global Village, he and Voodoo climbed into Voodoo's truck and drove down to Reverse Garbage, a local junkyard. Heidi says:

> We were their best customers! I remember being in Global one day and this guy's come in all week to do the electrics in the place—the place was buggered on electrics. The rubbish starts arriving and it's literally piles of rubbish getting bigger and bigger and he goes, 'What's happening?' and I said, 'It's just the artwork arriving. We're having an art exhibition'. Throughout the week, he watched the rubbish transform

into the most amazing art and at the end he said, 'I cannot believe what I've just witnessed'.

Robin's creations in Melbourne are legendary: cars on fire, spinning DNA rings and 10-metre-high animals crafted from brass pipe and rebar. For one Global Village party, he suspended a Saab from the ceiling and it swayed from side to side, crashing into the roof while people danced below. 'We jumped in this thing and we started swinging it back and forth,' raver Adrian Cartwright tells me. 'There were about twenty of us in it. We probably weren't supposed to be there but we had a ball that night!' Heidi remembers cleaning up later and finding someone asleep in the car.

As well as providing a psychedelic canvas for painters and sculptors, the rave scene offered creative opportunities for graffiti artists, graphic artists and lighting designers. One night in 1991, Scott Adcock (aka Beam Me Up Scotty) discovered the lighting guy at Pure 'off his chops' lying in a corner. 'I climbed up on the bass bins and I was basically on the DJ podium … on one side was the DJ and on the other side was a lighting console. I just sat there and started fiddling with the lights.' Scott had some prior training from having worked in the film industry but he soon found that artistic flair mattered more than technical knowhow:

> It all became about working with the DJ, not through anything they were telling me to do, it was purely instinctive, but in terms of how it makes me feel. Using the strobe and the smoke, building it all up, it was just like running an orchestra. I was conducting the lights to bring on more sensations.

Lights, music and art have been essential ingredients of live performance for thousands of years. Then the nineties delivered a fourth medium into the mix: video.

Last Night a VJ Saved My Life

Thornbury, July 2015. I've tracked down Adem Jaffers, a pioneering video jockey (VJ) in the Melbourne rave scene. He's sitting on my couch, sipping a cup of green tea and flooding me with technical jargon. I learn that VJing is a continuum that stretches from simply playing one music video after another ('very primitive, but that's a mix!') to live mixing of animation on top of background graphics in time to the music. I ask him when he first saw VJing of the latter kind at raves. 'I don't know,' he replies. 'I know that brother Jeff played videos at Checkpoint Charlie in 1988 but he didn't VJ per se. And there were plenty of video artists around, they just hadn't made it into the rave scene by then. Maybe I was the first.'

To clarify, 'brother Jeff' is not a monk with a taste for techno (now there's a crossover genre I'd like to see) but Jeff Jaffers, Adem's older brother. A good friend of Ollie Olsen and Gus Till, Jeff produced the video for Max Q's 1989 hit 'Monday Night by Satellite'. 'If you look at that film clip, you'll see fractal mandelbrots and colour cycling,' Adem says. 'Where Michael Hutchence is floating, there's this pulsating textiled coloured computer graphic image behind it. It was truly psychedelic stuff. From that moment, I was hooked.' The animations for 'Monday Night by Satellite' may look primitive by today's standards but they were leading edge in 1989. After seeing Jeff's work and UK psychedelic music videos like 'Stakker Humanoid', Adem knew it was time to hack.

Australia boasts a rich legacy of audiovisual experimentation. Adelaide-based artist Josef Stanislav Ostoja-Kotkowski explored the concept of Visual Music in the fifties: he fed musical inputs into a modified television to produce abstract images on the screen.[22] Two decades later, composer Warren Burt, working at the La Trobe University music department in Melbourne, integrated an EMS Spectre video synthesiser with a Serge modular audio synthesiser to make 'formative video synthesis works'.[23] However, most audovisual artists could not afford the kind of equipment that Burt had at his disposal. Instead, invoking the DIY ethos, they repurposed existing technologies and extended their use beyond their intended application—just like the Chicago acid house pioneers had done with the Roland TB-303. Adem cites the example of 'old skool circuit bender' John Hansen who hacked the TV video game *Pong* to build his own video synth. Then, Sydney band Severed Heads started using the Amiga computer to synchronise electronic music with computer-generated imagery.[24] The VJ was born.

Adem's VJ journey began with a single Amiga computer and a program called Deluxe Paint. Used by the likes of Disney and Hanna-Barbera, Deluxe Paint supported automated colour cycling (a technique whereby colours are rapidly changed to create the impression of animation) and a symmetry tool that displays symmetrical graphics through multiple planes. Watch any rave animation from the nineties and you'll likely see both these trippy functions in abundance. Many VJs favoured the Amiga because it plugged straight into the back of a VHS player. 'It was the ultimate VJ tool,' Adem says. 'You didn't need expensive technology to convert it. You'd just bang it straight in and press record. I started recording tapes at home, pause the videotape, play another animation, record, pause. It was a sort of crash editing.'

In early 1991, brother Jeff produced two longform extended music videos, called *Meltdown I* and *Meltdown II*, from unused material he had dumped to tape while editing Third Eye's singles 'The Real Thing' and 'Pray'. 'As far as I know, these were the first Australian cyberdelic videos that encompassed music and trippy graphics,' Adem claims. He defines cyberdelic as 'the cyber punk tekno acid art culture/movement/ aesthetic emerging at the time'. Adem sought to replicate what Jeff had done with *Meltdown*, but live at a rave. He didn't have access to the kind of video editing technology available to his film director brother: while fine for the bedroom, 'pause, play, record' wouldn't work in a live environment. There was only one option left. He'd have to build it himself.

In 1991, Adem embarked on a decade-long 'DIY garage project' to construct the ultimate VJ rave console. His rig comprised two pods he named R2D1 and R2D2—that Star Wars theme again. Each pod contained four Amiga computers, a VHS player and about a kilometre of cabling. Prior to a gig, he'd create multi-layered background animation loops and record them onto videotape. On the night, he triggered the various loops at different playback speeds in sync with the music. He then used Deluxe Paint to create real-time freeform visual layers on top of the loops:

> I might have the bassline going and then I could paint the piano riffs that floated over the top and blend them to make it look like a robotic tempo change ... it was a very unconventional way of VJing, it was unique in its own way. And only I knew how to use it.

Cyberthon

In 1990, Adem contributed to a documentary called *Cyberdelia*, featuring interviews with key artists in the emerging 'tekno cyber' scene. When producer Liam O'Hara made the broadcast master, he found that some of the edits had come through as black. Liam told Adem who then had an idea:

> I said to him, 'Let's just play out the segments live and we'll crash-edit them, hit play and mix over to that interview and throw it out to air live.' Liam agreed. But then I thought why not also show a seminal example of each artist's work? So, when Jeff Jaffers was on, it was the *Meltdown* videos, when Cyber Dada came on, it was from their manifesto *Digitise the World*, when Third Eye came on it was from their 'Real Thing' film clip ... Once we finished that, we started mish-mashing the tapes all together live on-air to background music and then when we ran out of material we just started grabbing tapes off the shelves and mixing it in.

What should have been a thirty-minute segment on the community access TV station RMITV turned into a three-hour freeform audiovisual experiment. It was cyber-anarchy. Out of the six or so people who tuned in to Channel 31 to watch it, one happened to be Steve Middleton from VJ outfit Don't Shoot the Messenger. A few months later, Steve invited Adem to make another broadcast. 'So I thought, let's do a cyberthon,' Adem says. 'It was a daggy name in hindsight. But that's what we did. And this time it was a twenty-four-hour event.' *Cyberthon* screened in December 1991 and featured four-hour VJ sets from Cyber Dada, Jeff Jaffers, Adem Jaffers and Don't Shoot the Messenger. Ollie Olsen DJed and Acid Deathbed performed live. Although the artists outnumbered the viewers, *Cyberthon* fused an enduring bond between video and music in the scene. 'It was a very rave style of doing things,' Adem says. 'Everyone came together and jammed.'

In March 1992, Richard and Heidi invited Adem to manage the chill-out room at the first Every Picture party. He brought in Cyber Dada and Don't Shoot the Messenger. Troy Innocent and Dale Nason had formed Cyber Dada in 1989 while studying art at Swinburne University. Adem credits their 'cut and paste computer art' as a formative influence in his work.[25] Cyber Dada's 1990 manifesto *Digitise the World* was a celebration of cyberdelia that presaged the coming digital age and the rise of cyberspace. In the nineties, Cyber Dada became known for a 'noisy multi-form aesthetic' that blended performance and installation.[26] Adem lauds Don't Shoot the Messenger as the 'Amiga gurus' of Melbourne. 'The stuff they were doing, they were light years ahead,' he says. 'Whatever I learnt about Amiga technology was through those guys.' Steve Middleton and partner Attilio Gangemi embraced a similar DIY 'cyberpunk' ethic to Adem, hacking together their VJ setup from retrofitted old technology. The Messengers carved out a niche in the chill-out room at raves in Melbourne, across Australia and internationally. 'You'd go to one of their shows and they'd be sitting there on their cushions like Arabic sultans or Pashtuns with their peace pipes,' Adem says. 'That was all part of the visual aesthetic.'

'A Real Community of People'

Writing about the English rave scene, Simon Reynolds asks, '[Is] it possible to base a culture around sensations rather than truths, fascinations rather than meaning?'[27] I don't doubt that for some people, rave was primarily a sensory experience mediated by drugs, art, video and music. But, as DJ Brewster B. explains, many ravers felt like they were part of something bigger:

> I was in the middle of the dancefloor and I suddenly realised, 'These are my peeps'. I'd looked for these people and I didn't know they existed. I'm looking around and I'm seeing all these smiling faces and everybody's on the one wavelength. And it's at that point I realised this is where I belong.

Much has been written (including earlier in this book) about ecstasy bringing people together. But one didn't *need* drugs to feel a sense of belonging at a nineties rave. Kim partied with and without e's and every time her experience of the crowd was the same. 'It was like a real community of people, everybody was so accepting, so loving and we shared similar lifestyles and philosophies. I loved that,' she says. 'There was no pressure to do anything or not do anything while you were there.'

In 1999, Christine Siokou surveyed 500 Melbourne ravers and seventy DJs for a Melbourne University research project. She found that many people reported a sense of unity at raves based on group dancing, drug taking, a feeling of safety and above all a shared appreciation of the music:

> [T]hrough the experience of dancing to electronic music at a rave, 'the vibe' or collective identity is formed among the crowd ... [and] ... this is exemplified when a classic or anthem song is played.[28]

Heidi observed it time and time again at Global Village. 'We're human beings. We like to share our feelings with each other ... if you're all focussed on the same direction, it's phenomenal.' It's no wonder people compare dancing at an all-night rave to a tribal experience, casting the DJ as the shaman or witch doctor. However, this sense of unity tends to last only as long as the rave or until the drugs wear off, whichever is sooner.[29] The vibe is ephemeral—you cannot take it with you when you leave. You leave your raver persona behind in the warehouse, ready to pick it up again the following weekend. That said, a chance encounter with a techno brother or sister on the outside could briefly reanimate the rave child within. Once, a guy approached Kim on the street and asked her for 50 cents to buy a Slurpee. She gave him the money and then they stared at each other. 'We both went, "I know you!" and we worked out that we knew each other from this and that rave,' she tells me. 'Those kinds of connections were really special.'

Siokou found that raves allowed people to express their 'authentic' self, perhaps for the first time, in contrast to the 'inauthentic' identity they presented to the real world.[30] Indeed, many people concealed their nocturnal life from employers and parents because of negative media perceptions about rave.[31] 'You didn't tell people you went to rave parties because of the stigma of being a drug taker or because your boss would think you're taking a sickie every Monday because you got high all weekend and you're coming down like a ton of bricks,' Natural 1 tells me.

Raves attracted a diverse crowd, partly because 'alternative' people received a warmer welcome than they did at mainstream pubs and clubs and also because techno music appealed to minority groups like homosexual men and Southeast Asian youth. But there's more to this story. 'I always used to say the invisible word above Global Village was "Respect",' Heidi says. Parties at venues like Global Village offered a refuge to socially awkward kids, people who came from tough family backgrounds, and the nerds and 'smarts' who didn't fit in at school. 'It was a real cross-section of Generation X trying to have as much of a good time as possible in this dark and doomy period of man's existence,' DJ Mark Hogan says.[32] What disco had done for New York's black and gay communities in the seventies, rave did for Melbourne's disaffected youth in the nineties.

'That really epitomised what that culture was for us,' raver Aaron Roach says. 'It felt like all the people who'd had concerns in their lives, all the people who felt isolated, they all had somewhere to go and all they wanted to do was have a good time.' Aaron fell in love with techno when his uncle lent him a mixtape in 1989. By 1991, he was regularly calling up Kate Bathgate on *Beat in the Street* to request his favourite records. Then in 1993, his parents moved to Gippsland. 'Two and a half hours out of Melbourne, it was very difficult to find dance music ... everyone was into drinking, playing pool and listening to Pantera ... it just wasn't me.' When Aaron returned to Melbourne five years later, his sister and her boyfriend kindly offered to accompany him to his first rave, a Hardware party at the Palace:

> I didn't take anything, we were there the whole night till close, everyone's happy and I was like, 'This is where I belong'. Because of my agoraphobia, I was so worried about something happening, thinking everyone's after me and then all of a sudden I'm surrounded by these people who ask, 'Are you having a good night? What have you had?' and people would come up and offer me water or they'd give me a hug and I went, 'What the hell is this?'

Goodbye to the Meat Market

Ritzy's nightclub, Norwich, England, 1996. The room is spinning and I can't walk straight. I'm dressed in regulation nightclub attire—a blue long-sleeved shirt, tailored trousers and black leather shoes. I sit down next to a blonde-haired girl and awkwardly strike up a conversation. Before I even catch her name, her boyfriend appears and punches me in the face. I'm so drunk I don't even feel the pain. I walk to the bathroom, look in the mirror and see blood coursing down my cheek. After washing my face, I retreat to the bar and drink another pint while my eardrums strain under the relentless beat of commercial 'choons'. Two more hours and this will all be over.

Hatred of the nightclubbing experience transcends gender, race and geography. For many, the discomfort begins outside. King Street, Melbourne's most famous nightclub strip, was a dangerous place during the nineties. Responding to a spate of stabbings on the street, in 1995 the state government proposed mandatory metal detector screening for weapons, on-the-spot fines and heftier penalties for nightclub operators serving underage patrons.[33] 'You have knife fights, people brawling,' Senior Sergeant Danny Walsh said at the time. '[I]t's almost like you walk in the door, the bell rings and it's time for a fight.'[34]

Those who dodged the punches and made it past the elitist door policy walked into a lion's den teeming with sexual predators and macho thugs. Inside this 'drunken cattle market', a mainstream crowd fixated on the social and sexual aspects of going out, paying little attention to musical or aesthetic concerns.[35] 'I only went clubbing twice and I hated everything about it,' Kim says. 'The music, the aesthetics, the pick-up vibe and the cliqueyness. Everyone just stood around and danced in a circle. It was weird.' It's little wonder that when many people first walked into a rave, they exhaled a sigh of relief, as Josh Abrahams recalls:

> To discover a scene that was loose runners, loose jeans and a cool t-shirt [where] you could go and sit down next to anyone and go, 'Having a good night?' 'Yeah, me too, seeya', and there's no intimation of pick up or sleaze ... for me, that was just heaven.

Many people who had grown up with rules, rigid norms of social behaviour and strict dress codes found attending raves liberating and exhilarating. 'Nobody could tell you what you could and couldn't do, I loved that,' Kim says. On the other hand, even the word 'club' invokes an air of exclusivity that reeks of membership and privilege.

For many women, raving offered their first experience of unaccompanied and unsupervised nocturnal entertainment. Free from the handbags and high-heels pick-up culture, women could dress and dance how they liked without fear of harassment or sexual objectification. 'We wanted to create the environment where you could dance without someone putting their hand up your skirt or something horrible like that,' Heidi explains. To achieve this, rave promoters stocked their fridges with Red Bull instead of beer, implemented inclusive and non-discriminatory door policies, and hired friendly but firm security staff to weed out patrons with the wrong vibe but not the wrong clothes. Health and safety was also a paramount concern. 'We learnt from what had happened in Sydney with Happy Valley etc.,[36] and so we always had the St Johns first aid crew at every gig to make sure people were safe if something happened,' Voodoo tells me. At many parties, Ravesafe staff provided advice on safe sex and drug taking and handed out condoms, earplugs and water.[37] Provided by ravers for ravers, RaveSafe even offered pill testing. I asked Aaron Roach if Ravesafe still existed today. 'No!' he laughed. 'They would *not* be allowed to go to a party anymore!'

Siting the rave as a refuge from macho culture is a popular narrative, but not one to which everyone subscribes. Many men found ecstasy had similar aphrodisiac qualities to alcohol. 'E for me was more of a physical, touchy-feely, trying to get into your pants kind of thing,' H2O admits. 'That's what it was built for, wasn't it?' he asks, alluding to ecstasy's urban myth status as a marriage counselling drug. Anecdotally, several men and women have told me they frequently hooked up at raves, although this was seldom their prime motivation for attending. And ecstasy did little to disrupt the 'corporate boardroom' style gender imbalance behind the decks.

Women on Deck

Thornbury, May 2015. Lani G (real name Lani Greer) has given up her Sunday morning, left her three kids at home with their father and driven 40 kilometres across town to chat with me. I thank her for making the effort. 'No,' she replies. She's honoured and humbled that I want to talk to her. I offer her a cup of tea. She gives me a homebaked orange cake. Tall with long dark tresses and bright blue eyes, Lani mixes worldly confidence with childlike fascination. She left school at seventeen and started going out in the gay scene in Melbourne. 'That's how I got into the scene, through the gay clubs,' she tells me. 'All the gay clubs and rave clubs were intermingled; it was all one big scene.' A quarter of a century later, Lani still works as a DJ and promoter. 'Raving pretty much saved my life.' Tears begin to trickle down her cheeks. 'It gave me a creative outlet and a place in the world and I'll be forever in debt to everyone who ever helped me out over it.'

Electronic music intrinsically appeals to a subset of young males because it allows them to demonstrate their masculinity through control and mastery of technology.[38] Maybe this explains why during the nineties a cohort of twenty or thirty male DJs dominated the Melbourne scene. For example, Kiss 90FM's seventh test broadcast in May 1996 featured five times as many male presenters as female.[39] And while Mark James did organise a female DJ only party at Chasers in 1994, calling the event 'Girls On Top' did little to disrupt the patriarchy.

I asked Lani what inspired her to break into this watertight boys' club. 'I went to a M.U.D. party and I saw Cara Caama playing,' she replied. 'She was playing all these amazing tracks and I was sold. I caught the bug really bad.' Cara Caama took up DJing in 1993 after seeing Cosmic Baby at the Palace. 'He was playing 'Visions of Sheeba' [sic] and I was like, "oh my God I love this song, oh my God look at him, oh my God I want to do it"', Cara told *groo:vine* in 1998.[40] Heidi John has been a long-time supporter of female DJ and she invited

Cara to play at Global Village. Cara paid it back, championing the cause of aspiring female DJs on her radio show. 'There are a lot of girl DJs out there,' she told *groo:vine*. 'It's just that a lot of them are scared.'[41]

Lani admits she was scared too. But she didn't let it stop her. In 1994, she started working as Richie Rich's personal assistant, enrolled in a DMC DJing course and paid Jason Midro $30 a week to teach her how to mix. 'Midro never really liked me,' she says. 'I'd ask him for gigs and he'd go, "I'm a cunt, Lani. I'm not gonna give you anything!"' Richie also wouldn't hire her to begin with. Her first gig came courtesy of an 'underground art world' figure called Justin who had hired the Leslie Street warehouse in Brunswick, a basketball court-sized, soundproof space tucked away down a dead-end street. 'No-one came, I don't remember there being one person there!' Lani recalls. 'This guy Berserker played. He was full on hardcore. And then there's me in my first gig!'

In the early days Lani played happy hardcore, gabber ('happy hardcore without the happy,' according to Josh Abrahams) and something she calls machinegun Goa. I ask her to explain. 'There was a track called 'Mig 31' by Mig 31 ... it's really good Goa trance but it's got this underlying bassline that's just about 2000 bpm so it's like a constant drone but it's just beautiful.' Lani didn't beatmix to begin with because she, like many others, felt Goa trance didn't warrant it. Not to mention that matching beats at 2000 bpm is like trying to time your roulette throw so the ball lands on red fourteen every time. 'I was very lucky just to do the cross-fade thing and for it to be all angelic and not terrible ... but then when I got into techno I got right into beat matching and scratching.'

Lani tells me the 'boys' respected her DJing aspirations and were always willing to help. Nevertheless, she owes much of her early career success to the techno sisterhood. In 1995, Emmy Boudry invited Lani to play Street Rave. 'I knew it was hard for female DJs so I always tried to give them a chance and support them,' Emmy says. Lani, Cara Caama and upcoming DJ Kate S played regularly at Emmy's parties. Lani says most promoters didn't discriminate on gender but there were exceptions. In 1998, she told *Techno Renegade* about a frustrating encounter with production company Aurora: '[t]hey're like: chick DJ yeah fuck you, sure were [sic] going to hire you.'[42]

In 1996, Lani began organising her own parties with sister Kylie Greer and boyfriend Warren Hunt. For Karmagenics 1 and 2, they hired a warehouse at the rear of 27 Johnston Street, Fitzroy. 'They were really underground,' Lani says. 'We'd only get forty people, if that. We were selling fifty cent cups of cordial. It was really quite innocent.' Lani started the Madasss! parties in 1998. For Madasss! 2 she hired the Wilson car park next to Spencer Street station. Promoter Frank Venuto gave her the idea—he'd been running his Green Ant parties in city centre car parks since 1997:

> He obviously saw something in me and let me do my parties with Wilson. He gave me my first step into scouting out venues just by taking me with him when he would do stuff. And Wilson were so lovely to trust us and give us a chance. We had no experience of running big events. But they gave us a shot.

For Madasss! 3, Lani asked Care Parking if she could book their car park at 113 Batman Street, West Melbourne for an 'art exhibition with music'. I find it amazing that as late as 1998 people were still falling for this ruse—hadn't they heard about rave on the news by now? 'I swear this guy was in La La land,' Lani says. 'He was about sixty, he was like, "yep, yep, whatever, $700, okay".' 113 Batman Street was Lani's favourite venue:

> There was heaps of black space. You'd need 6000 people to fill that space. You've got the indoor area and then there's the outdoor area, which is a quadrangle, like an outdoor car park. So we used that as the second room and the main room was inside.

In keeping with the Melbourne tradition, Lani tells me she tried to use a new location each time because that's what excited the punters. She lists the right venue as one of her six ingredients to running the perfect warehouse party—the others are sound, lineup, art, drugs and safety. 'You couldn't have a derelict warehouse that was falling down,' she explains. 'You had to make sure there were fire escapes and you had the right security in the right places. People tried to break in and they could hurt themselves trying to do that.' Lani never played at Global Village but the venue cleaves to her heart. 'I go to Global Village and I just sit there and cry because it had such an effect on me … that's what raving does to people. I love Melbourne so much.'

Shutdown

Everyone knew Global Village couldn't last forever. But few were prepared for its untimely demise. 'One day we went down there and there were security guards on site with dogs and guns,' Richard says. 'All the doors were closed and we couldn't get in.' Henry could no longer afford the rent and the site's owners had decided to sell up. Not content with barricading the doors, the guards had also smashed up the artwork they'd found inside. Lesser mortals might have simply walked away but not M.U.D.. 'True to renegade form we just moved the final party outdoors and into the car park,' Voodoo says.

The flyer for the Global Village Shut Down party on Saturday 22 February 1997 promised to 'focus the combined energy of all past events into the sacred stomping ground of Global Village, offering everybody the opportunity to "go off" one last time'. They might have been locked out of their techno temple but M.U.D. still knew how to preach. They booked twenty-one DJs to play across three stages. Putting rivalries aside, the Hardware trio of Richie Rich, Will E Tell and Jeff Tyler joined the Global Village regulars. Ten-year-old Jade watched the night unfold perched on top of a hot tin roof:

The car park was full of people, unbelievably full. The police came in and Jason Midro was playing, it was his sunrise set. I still remember it as clear as day. The cops were saying, 'Where's Richard John? Where's Richard John?' and Dad's standing up on the stage going, 'Turn it off! Turn the fucking music off!' So they stopped the music but the people wouldn't stop. Everyone was dancing, it didn't matter if there was music or not. The police couldn't stop it because people wouldn't stop. That feeling was amazing.

The Shut Down party couldn't be shut down. The police couldn't risk trying to disperse 2000 rushing ravers through a 3 metre wide archway. So, they stood and watched while people hugged, cried and kissed the ground. During our Global Village tour in July 2015, I asked Voodoo how he felt to be back at the scene of so much joy and creativity. 'It's hard to feel anything because it looks so different,' he replied but his eyes told another story. For him and thousands of others, Global Village was their home. 'Some of the best parties in the southern hemisphere probably happened in there,' Robin Cooke claimed.[43] I only wish I'd been there to see it.

'When I was in Global Village, I used to have to bunk the trains to get to work because we had no money,' Richard says. 'All our parties were financed by ourselves, there was no money from lighting companies or record companies and no sponsorship.' And then there were the legal costs. The council repeatedly took the Johns to court for holding parties without a permit, forcing Henry to make alterations, install new staircases and pay for consultants' reports. 'The Footscray council have a thick file on me,' Heidi says. 'If you go in there and mention Every Picture Tells a Story, they won't let you out again!' Instead of investing in shares, property or a comfortable lifestyle, Richard and Heidi poured their money into raving, where the returns were emotional and spiritual rather than financial. They did it for the love—and they weren't alone, as Richard explains:

I'd say three-quarters of the crew and the artists, they worked their arses off because they loved it like we did and they never got a penny out of it. People would go, 'Great party!' and I'd go, 'Oh yeah, we had beans on toast that night'. We were there until 6pm Sunday night picking cigarette butts up out in the street so we could do it the next time.

Even on the few occasions they threw parties elsewhere, M.U.D. still managed to walk away with nothing. 'We did an Every Picture in Byron Bay,' Richard tells me. 'We rocked up and they gave us eggs and chickens and we needed money for petrol!'

After the Shut Down party, M.U.D. migrated to the Westgate Sports and Entertainment Centre in Altona North, 15 kilometres west of the CBD. By day a sports hall with suburban kids playing soccer and tennis, at night it became a Dionysian den filled with psychedelic art and scrap metal sculptures. Ravers scaled the rock-climbing wall and swam in the pool. Video footage of an Every Picture party at the Westgate in 1998 shows fire twirlers, a spinning car and thousands of tired, sweaty ravers dancing to Will E Tell and Jason Midro as the morning sun streams through the skylights.[44] For Every Picture 17 at Altona, M.U.D. chose an Atlantis Rising theme, including divers in fish tanks, girls dressed as mermaids, a twenty-foot tall King Neptune and the city of Atlantis rising behind the stage as the night wore on.[45] 'The Westgate was a challenge because at 8am on Sunday it became a sports centre again so we had to finish and clean up by then,' Voodoo tells me. 'Often I would start setting up on the Friday night and then continue all day Saturday and I wouldn't be out of there until 5pm on Sunday.'

On the morning of Sunday 5 November 2000, Richard and Heidi put their brooms away for what seemed like the last time. It was an auspicious date. Four-hundred years earlier, Guy Fawkes had attempted to blow up the Houses of Parliament in London. The Johns had exploded the Melbourne rave scene but it was time to move on. Richard says:

Everything had become more expensive … the security started going up, the lighting cost goes up, the venues go up … the DJs wanted more and more money. It was greed, greed, greed … we were losing money.

It also became harder to find warehouse spaces, secure the right permits and take out insurance. 'It had turned into a business—exactly what we were against from the start,' Voodoo says. Mark James is surprised they lasted so long. 'You still have to stick to a budget … they were getting 6000 to 8000 people at their parties but they needed 16,000 to break even.' For ten years the Johns put their raving days behind them but like a flea-bitten dog the itch wouldn't go away. In 2010, they returned for Every Picture Tells a Story: Frequency Shift at Shed 4 in the Docklands. It was a big mistake. 'There were a few thousand people there but not enough to pay for what the thing cost,' Richard tells me in January 2015. 'Ouch. We're still fucking suffering.' The frequency had shifted but Richard and Heidi had forgotten to turn the dial.

Chapter 8

MELBOURNE SHUFFLERS

Stompers

South Yarra, April 2016. I'm sitting on Natural 1's black, leather couch on the twenty-third floor of an executive apartment building. Packing boxes, racks of neatly ordered CDs and a stash of *Techno Renegade* magazines surround me. In the corner of the room I spy Dan Sicko's book *Techno Rebels* glaring at me, as if to say, 'You better get this story right Paul or I'm coming after you.' I'm here for two reasons. The first is to collect a box of 'rave treasures'—assorted photographs, flyers, magazines and techno paraphernalia that my host has carefully assembled over the last six months. The second is to learn the true story of the Melbourne Shuffle.

Natural 1 is Melbourne's original techno rebel. The son of a Polish Holocaust survivor, the spirit of resistance flows through his veins. Starting out as a graffiti writer in the hip hop scene—a habit that's hard to give up judging by the box of spray cans in his hallway—Natural 1 immersed himself in techno during the nineties, first as a punter and later as a DJ. In 2015, I saw him turn up to an 'old skool party' dressed in a pair of goggles and a white jumpsuit with RA sprayed on the back:

> I was paying homage to house music, which is the body mechanic, so I wore an all-in-one jumpsuit. Because I was a graffiti artist, I'd aircraft spray a suit. That's the whole fighter thing too, the revolution for change thing. And the goggles represent the New York b-boy who used to wear goggles to the block party or have them on his shoulder.

Ra is one of Natural 1's many aliases. The name symbolises rave's union of ancient mysticism and science fiction futurism, representing in this case the Egyptian sun god Ra and the Rebel Alliance—Luke Skywalker's comrades who fight against the Galactic Empire in Star Wars.

Natural 1 is the best shuffler I know. Watching him dance is a joy to behold. When he DJed in Wales in 2009, several people went to the gig just to watch his dance moves. He says that before shufflers Melbourne had stompers:

> The stomp was heavy, high leg lifts with the feet slamming down. You might work in quadrants, so a full swing or a quadrant stomp to the left and a quadrant stomp to the right, a quadrant stomp to the back left and then a quadrant stomp to the back right. And then through these four quadrants, you might make circular patterns, half-circular patterns or three-quarter patterns as well. Arm movements may or may not have gone with it—that wasn't as important with the stomp.

'Stomp' as synonym for a dance with a heavy, rhythmic step dates from the early twentieth century jazz era but what Natural 1 describes above probably owes more to eighties hip hop. He points to music videos from rapper K-YZE and Onyx ('bald shaven black guys playing really hardcore militant rap music') that show stomp-like dance moves:

> You can even look at the girl who dances during the opening credits of *Do The Right Thing* [a Spike Lee movie, released 1989]—she's dancing with her titties out and just a jacket on but her legs are stomping.

The stomp also borrows from new jack swing and the running man, a hip hop 'bounce groove' popularised by Janet Jackson and MC Hammer in the late eighties, where a dancer walks or run on the spot with her foot coming down firmly on each step. The running man remains a cornerstone of the Melbourne shuffle.

'External influences like b-boy, breakdancing, rap, Michael Jackson, MC Hammer etc. made boys want to dance [and] enjoy dancing freely,' raver Kane Goldsworthy told me on Facebook. I think he means that despite (or because of) John Travolta's example in *Saturday Night Fever*, shy straight boys in the disco era didn't venture onto the dancefloor alone, but instead clung to the safety of the bar-rail or waited for a slow song to ask a girl to dance. House music and hip hop changed all that. The rise of unpartnered dance steps like the running man, the moonwalk and jacking (see Chapter Three) gave young men the freedom and confidence to find their own dance. Dancing can assist vulnerable and troubled young people, particularly boys, to express their feelings, strengthen their self-image and heal trauma.[1]

Sharpies and Skinheads

But I think there are other reasons why the stomp appealed to young men. Stomping one's foot down hard on the ground is an aggressive macho gesture. Long before its association with hip hop and techno, stomping in Melbourne meant kicking in someone's head while the victim lay helpless on the floor. This kind of stomping was a popular pastime for the sharpies, a youth subculture in sixties and seventies Melbourne. Often to be found in 'migrant-heavy neighbourhoods', the well-tailored sharpie wore pinstripe, herringbone or checked Flag pants with 22-inch bottoms, a knitted top known as a 'conny', and a pair of chisel toe shoes with a stacked heel.[2] Sharpies invaded local high school dances and fought pitched battles against crews from neighbouring suburbs.

By the late seventies, the sharpie had traded in his chisel toes for a pair of steel-capped Doc Marten boots. People nicknamed the boots romper stompers after the children's toy of the same name. Over time, the phrase also came to mean the skinheads who wore them, as in the 1992 film *Romper Stomper* (see Chapter Seven). Natural 1 explains:

> Stomping was already in our vernacular. It was built around kicking heads. It was a violent, aggressive thing. Stomping suited us because it was hardcore and Melbourne people are very hardcore, no matter what subculture we get into … when we adopt a subculture from overseas, we get it pre-packaged either from America or England or a bit of both. But once we adopt it, these subcultures often live longer than they do in the countries where they started. And this is the unique thing about Melbourne in that we might not be that good at inventing our own subcultures but the ones we love, we hold on to and we get very hardcore about them.

In the late eighties, underage clubs like Time at Metro or Def at Chasers brought these different subcultures together. 'Here in Melbourne we had skinheads, [graffiti] writers, rudeboys, breakdancers and ravers all going out to these underage things at once,' Natural 1 says. 'So all these dance styles were cross-pollinating. Some people would form allegiances while others would get bashed up.' It sounds brutal, yet gang violence was thriving in Melbourne at that time and not just at the movies. Down in the southeastern suburbs, Noble Park's 3174 gang waged war against rival street gang the MC3 from neighbouring Dandenong. It was all very South Central—right down to the red and blue bandanas worn by opposing sides. 'It was a tamer version than Los Angeles,' Natural 1 says. 'We didn't have drive-by shootings but there were certain murders where people were rolled up in carpet, there were lots of stabbings and lots of fights.'

When techno arrived, it took stomping to another level. 'Acid house is tough beats, man!' Natural 1 says. 'They cane the 808 and 909! So, with techno you've already got a militant beat, a breakbeat, which means sonically we're here to kick heads but also when we dance we're here to kick heads.' I asked him to show me and he gave an impromptu routine in his lounge room:

> It was hard militant on the 2 and the 4 beat. The main beat hit hardest, that's where your foot would stomp down. The offbeat, or the 1 and the 3 beat in between, is where'd you have the time to lift your leg up to stomp it into the next position, or your arm would do something to accentuate that part.

Northern Soul

Meanwhile in England, stomping meant something else entirely. DJ Ian 'Frank' Dewhirst recounts a visit to the Pier in Cleethorpes in 1976: '[i]t's four in the morning. And all you can hear is STOMP! Multiplied times a thousand'.[3] What Dewhirst heard was northern soul, a scene that captivated the imagination of white working-class youths across northern Britain during the seventies. Londoner Dave Godin coined the term 'northern soul' to describe the fanatical appreciation for soul music he observed at Manchester's Twisted

Wheel nightclub in 1970.[4] DJs and fans obsessively tracked down unsuccessful records and B-sides from the sixties Motown era. Posters and flyers advertised not only the DJs but also the rare and unheard tracks that punters would hear on the night. '[It's a] genre built from failures,' Brewster and Broughton write. 'If a track sounded like it had been recorded in a garden shed in Detroit, then so much the better.'[5]

By the mid-seventies, the northern soul scene had splintered into two factions: a Blackpool Mecca crowd flirting with early disco and the Wigan Casino faithful, fixated on the 'pure' northern sound.[6] Ian Levine, Mecca's resident DJ, recalls what happened when he brought the two groups together:

> It was like two football crowds ... [it] didn't work. At that time we were playing all this modern disco stuff ... [and] ... they were playing anything with a stomping beat. All of these Wiganites with their singlets and baggy pants were shouting, 'fuck off! Get off! Play some stompers!'[7]

In many ways, northern soul was a prototype for rave. A white male-dominated scene driven by a fanatical love for rare and little-heard black music coming out of Detroit: this could be 1991, not 1971. At the Wigan Casino, speed-fuelled soul boys and girls danced all night on sprung wooden floors in 'highly gymnastic', unchoreographed and unpartnered routines.[8] The scene embraced freedom of expression, room to move and an emphasis on footwork— all three central tenets of the Melbourne stomping code in the late eighties. Northern soul also gave us breakdancing and wide baggy trousers 'big enough to accommodate a family of four' so dancers could drop, backflip and spin across the dancefloor.[9] Two decades later, the raver's beloved phat pants were designed along similar principles, although typically adorned with ultraviolet fluoro or fur.

PBS announcer Vince Peach attended his first all-nighter in Wigan in 1965 and had formerly DJed at the Twisted Wheel.[10] In

1982, he started a northern soul scene in Melbourne.[11] I've been unable to find any direct connection between the northern soul and rave scenes in Melbourne but it seems likely that more than a few kids crossed over, bringing with them their dance moves, baggy trousers and amphetamines.

The Surfer Stomp

But stomping wasn't all hard-edged hip hop, speed-fuelled dancing and skinhead violence. It had a softer side too. In the early sixties, when they weren't getting their heads stomped on by sharpies, surfies danced the surfer stomp, which combined jazz and tap moves with a rebellious attitude. While still paying respect to its Californian roots, a uniquely Australian surfer stomp developed out of the Wild Colonial Club in Lorne on Victoria's Great Ocean Road and on Sydney's surf beaches.[12] The dance became so popular that some councils closed their church halls to stompers for fear of the buildings falling down.[13] It sounds faintly ridiculous now, but my dad tells me that British dance halls banned the Dave Clark Five's 1964 hit 'Bits and Pieces' because people were stamping their way through the floorboards as they danced.

The Encyclopaedia of Surfing condemns the surfer stomp as an 'artless but irresistible foot-stomping dance … performed to up-tempo 2/4 rock-and-roll numbers'.[14] More than thirty 'Stomp-titled singles' were released in Australia in 1963 and 1964, including 'Everyone Let's Stomp' by Jay Justin and Little Pattie's 'He's My Blond-Headed Stompy Wompy Real Gone Surfer Boy'.[15] The dance involves multiple bent-knee leg raises, foot flexing, pelvic shifts with one foot shuffling on the floor and the other in the air, a basic t-step (both feet momentarily together at the heels, toes apart) and a one-footed double stomp on the ground with the other leg raised.[16] As with other variants of the stomp, arm and upper body movements were less important than the footwork.

Fast-forward a quarter of a century and it's as though the children of the sixties' stompers had trained their parents' dance moves to a techno beat. Sure, they are dancing to a different rhythm but the footwork is similar and both work best on a sprung wooden floor. I suggest to Natural 1 that perhaps we can draw a thread from one stomp to the other. His eyes glow with excitement. 'There's a whole lineage there but it had to travel to England where rave gets invented and then it comes back to us … but subversively they were influenced by us! There's an unspoken, almost spiritual, circle going on here.' I like to think so too.

A Voodoo artwork from the late eighties shows a green and blue snake spouting the words, 'Act real crazy stupid insane!' in between three stick figures dancing the stomp. Brightly coloured and thrashing around like out-of-control puppets, the stompers must have been quite a sight to the champagne-sipping nightclub set that danced with their feet planted firmly on the ground. DJ Brewster B. says that stomper became a derogatory term:

> I remember at places like Chasers if you wore certain clothes or you looked a certain way or you danced a certain way, people would go, 'Those stompers! Taking up all the dancefloor. I'm trying to make my moves on my chick!' They didn't like us because we made them look bad.

'He's Fucking Shuffling!'

And then, at some point, the stomp became the shuffle. I ask Natural 1 how the name came about. Big mistake. 'Look, Australians are really nuts and bolts people,' he insists. 'We're not like you English—you have five spoons before you even get past the entrée!' I squirm in my seat. 'We're not simple but we're very direct and to the point. We look. What are they doing? He's shuffling across the floor. He's shuffling! We don't try and put some fancy name on it. He's fucking shuffling! That's what he's doing. End of story. Don't sugar-coat it. Next.' It's impossible not to love this guy.

Everyone, it seems, wants to claim the Melbourne shuffle for him or herself. In the 2005 *Melbourne Shuffler* documentary, Richie Rich says he started the dance at Maze in 1990.[17] When we met in 2015, I asked him to tell me more:

> Most people were just doing this sort of acid house thing with their hands in the air, gloves on, blowing whistles and shouting 'Acieeed!' Some people were stomping. Ollie [Olsen] was shaking his long hair around like he was a zombie, Terry Ho also had a weird dance thing going on, you know everyone was dancing differently ... and then I'd go a little bit crazy and I started doing this super-fast footwork and spins ... we started shuffling and then there were ten or fifteen of us and then it just got bigger and bigger and bigger.

Richie formed a shuffling 'troupe' with Mel Burns, Raelene Kwashook, Nimmo Sandilands, Sid Sidney and Driena John, Richard and Heidi's daughter. They refined their moves at clubs like Chasers and the Chevron and performed at fashion parades and product launches. Richie tells me he learnt to shuffle after watching an English guy called Andrew:

> He came down to Melbourne from Sydney and he was doing this weird shuffling footwork. It wasn't really from the stomp. Apparently they were doing this sort of thing in the UK, which is how this guy knew about it. I just copied him.

Although others have told me similar stories about 'English backpackers' they saw shuffling at clubs like Maze, the lack of detail makes this story sound apocryphal to me. Anonymous Andrew marches into Melbourne's underground like a Pied Piper leading all the children astray with his shuffling finesse. Hmmm, I wonder. There *were* people shuffling in England in the late eighties. They just happened to be poor, black and living in Manchester—hardly the type to jump on an aeroplane to Australia for a gap year before university.

The Manchester Shuffle

Manchester DJ Greg Wilson laments how the standard house music narrative whitewashes decades of black culture:

> [i]f you told many of those [in] the scene today that it was mainly black kids in the UK who first embraced the music, they'd no doubt look at you incredulously, for everybody knows that Ibiza '87 was year zero, as this is how the story has, and continues to be told—the true origins in the relatively grim cities of the North and Midlands buried deep beneath the sun-drenched romance of the White Isle.[18]

Wilson argues that black kids in Birmingham, Nottingham, Sheffield, Leeds and above all Manchester tuned into house long before the London acid house boom.[19] For Exhibit A, he tables a YouTube clip of black youths dancing to house music at the 8411 Community Centre in Moss Side, Manchester on 27 September 1986.[20] In eighties England, Moss Side was a byword for urban deprivation and crime, up there with London's Brixton and Toxteth in Liverpool. My cousin lived in nearby Hulme in the early nineties. When I visited him, I expected to see burnt-out cars, drive-by shootings and drug dealing on street corners à la *Crimewatch UK*. Alas, I didn't even hear a police siren wailing in the distance.

When I first watched the Moss Side clip, I felt like a Victorian explorer discovering a new tribe. In September 1986, Darryl Pandy's 'Love Can't Turn Around' had only just hit the UK charts and house megahits 'Move Your Body' and 'Jack Your Body' were still months away. And yet here was DJ Mike Shaft spinning a treasure trove of early underground house music, including 'Tonight (Love Will Make It Right)', a little-known 1985 club release from Hanson & Davis and Adonis's 'No Way Back', put out on Trax in 1986. Meanwhile out on the dancefloor, young black men and women t-step and shuffle their feet. Later in the clip, dance troupe Foot Patrol perform a routine that comprises breakdancing, jumping, sideways kicking and plenty of shuffling. Wilson claims these 'prototype foot shufflers' had adapted jazz-fusion footwork to house music rhythms.[21] Ravers who have seen the video tell me Foot Patrol's pared-back shuffling wouldn't have looked out of place on a Melbourne dancefloor in the nineties. 'That minimal shuffling is exactly what you used to see at the end of the night when everyone has spaghetti legs and is too fucked to move,' Kim says.

A mile up the road at seminal Manchester club the Haçienda, the Moss Side shufflers steadily took over the dancefloor through 1987 and 1988. A 'young kid from Moss Side' had introduced Haçienda DJ Mike Pickering to house music after handing him a copy of 'No Way Back'.[22] Pickering had formerly been a DJ on the northern soul circuit, as had Mike Shaft and fellow house music pioneer Colin Curtis.[23] House rapidly gained a foothold at the Haçienda thanks to Pickering and fellow resident Hewan Clarke, a graduate of the early eighties jazz-funk scene. When the foot shufflers weren't dancing, they were busy making their own music in their bedrooms. In 1988, Piccadilly Radio DJ Stu Allan played a tape on his Sunday night show given to him by 'a guy called Gerald from Hulme'.[24] Gerald Simpson, aka A Guy Called Gerald, followed up with 'Voodoo Ray', an instant and enduring classic of the techno genre.

For a short time, the Haçienda was a foot shuffler's paradise, offering room to move, freedom of expression and homegrown house music. But when 'e'd up white kids' riding the Balearic wave of the second summer of love took over the club in July 1988, Wilson says the shufflers were forced to cede their 'precious dancing space' to the dayglow masses:

[t]he dance of the [acid house] ravers wasn't about footwork, but arm and hip movements, the feet pretty much rooted to the same spot, which was never going to satisfy the

physicality of those who'd graduated from the school of Fusion, where the feet did the talking, and cutting shapes didn't mean 'big box little box' type moves.[25]

A preference for flowing footwork over 'hands-in-the-air standing room only' dancing is where I think the Melbourne and Manchester scenes collide. But whenever I ask Melbourne ravers where they think the Shuffle came from, they invariably point to The Prodigy, a London band that formed five years *after* the Moss Side clip. Natural 1 remembers seeing The Prodigy dancer Leeroy Thornhill performing shuffle-type moves in the music videos for 'Charly' and 'Everybody in the Place', both released in late 1991. Melbourne DJ Simon Slieker makes a similar claim: 'I remember Leeroy … dancing in [some] of their film clips just with this out-of-control style, his legs are just rubber and gliding across the floor'.[26] Leeroy credits James Brown as an influence and makes no mention of the Manchester scene.[27] Meanwhile, Wikipedia claims (without citations, I might add) that Rosie Perez's dancing in the opening credits of *Do the Right Thing* inspired Leeroy's dancing style.[28] This is the same dance routine that Natural 1 says influenced the stomp. If you think we're going around in circles, you're right! When it comes to the Melbourne shuffle, everyone has his or her own story.

Baby Steps

St Kilda, July 2014. I'm standing on a busy street corner on a cold winter's day waiting for Robbie Burns. He arrives late and seems wary and impatient. Forsaking the warmth of a nearby café, he leads me on a sprint-paced walking tour of St Kilda's raving heritage, which terminates at the site of the former Palace nightclub. As I shiver and curse under my breath for not bringing a coat, he points to where Pure used to be. 'I was one of the first Melbourne shufflers,' he declares with dogged pride. "The shuffle started in the Zoo Crew and we started shuffling at the back of the Palace just for fun … at the time people were cutting shapes but nobody was doing what I call the proper shuffle, which is going from left to right and doing it in time.'

St Kilda born and bred, Robbie attended Pure religiously every Friday night, wearing 'crazy beanies' and outfits sewn by his mum. He called himself Mr Frog because he liked to hop and bounce across the dancefloor. Other members of his Zoo Crew included Panda Bear, Monkey and Giraffe. I didn't ask him how they got *their* names. Robbie insists the Shuffle began at Pure:

> I've read in different places that people like Richie and his crew are trying to claim they invented it in 1989 but I think that's bullshit. Nobody was shuffling then ... because in order to shuffle, you need a wet floor. People might have been saying they were shuffling, but they weren't really doing it until the time of guys actually physically running to the toilets with water bottles and dropping down water on the floor to give us more lubrication.

Nightclubs promptly banned water on the floor, so the sliders, as they were known, sprinkled talcum powder instead. 'Most clubs were lacquered or carpeted and a sticky floor with soft drink cordial poured on it was the worst environment for a rave,' the ever-reliable Natural 1 informs me. 'The talcum powder got invented because people wanted to glide and swoosh [and] for some people hard jarring movements like the stomp hurt their feet.' But Melbourne ravers didn't 'invent' the talcum powder. Back in England in the seventies, any self-respecting dancer at the Wigan Casino brought along an Adidas or Gola sports bag stuffed with 45s, amphetamines, a change of clothes and talcum powder to 'dust the dancefloor'.[29] Northern soul boy Jonathan Woodliffe recalls 'a mountain of steam ... and the smell of Brut talcum powder' when he arrived at the Pier in Cleethorpes for a dance in 1976.[30]

Brut, with its aura of seventies string vest machismo, wouldn't work for a scene built on peace and love. In nineties Melbourne, a 200 millilitre bottle of Johnson & Johnson baby powder became the must-have accessory for ravers, along with Chupa Chups, cigarettes and a gram bag of pills. 'You've already got dummies in your mouth and you're dressing like little kids already,' Natural 1 says. 'Baby powder was just hand in hand with that stuff. Plus, the reference to drugs, it looked like you had an ounce of coke on you in a bottle. It was fucking funny!' Nightclubs grudgingly tolerated the trails of white footprints running from the dancefloor to the bar and toilets. But the talcum powder mystified visitors from overseas. 'You walk into a nightclub and usually the smell of stale beer and cigarettes wakes you up,' UK producer Lab-4 told the *Melbourne Shuffler* crew. 'But you walk into clubs in Melbourne and you go … [sniffs] Babies? Babies? What the fuck is going on?'[31]

Natural 1 tells me that, with or without talcum powder, ravers slowly started adding shuffle-type moves to their dance routines:

> You'd look at other dancers and try to either add on or learn from their moves, not so much copy but adapt them to your flow. It's the same in graffiti as well: I like those extensions or letter forms, I'm going to incorporate that and make it in my style. And the key point is: 'in my style'. There was no one-size-fits-all dance.

As the tempo increased, dancers amplified their moves to match the intensity of harder drums and deeper basslines. Not everyone took it seriously at first. Duncan Plank recalls looking on with bemusement as people slid across the floor on one foot. 'It looked very awkward, as though they didn't quite know what to do … we used to say, "Watch out, there's a slider coming", and pretend to get out of the way.'

As shuffling became more popular and the moves more expansive, many dancers found they lacked the room to fully express themselves and sought out more suitable venues. Like the church halls and community centres favoured by stompers of old, Melbourne's warehouses and waterfront sheds had wooden floorboards or polished concrete floors with ample room to swivel and slide. 'Unlike today, people had the room to dance,' Voodoo explains to me during our Global Village tour. 'Nowadays, all the clubs are so crammed, you can't move.' I nod furiously, thinking back to a 2014 John Digweed gig at the Prince Bandroom where I felt like I was wearing a straitjacket with my shoes glued to the floor. I couldn't even raise my hand in the air to point my index finger towards the DJ booth or make big box, little box shapes in front of my chest (that's how we dance in England). Baby powder, baggy trousers and the warehouse—Melbourne needed just one more ingredient to bring the shuffle to life.

'This Thing Called Trance'

Yarraville, August 2014. My interview with H2O is about to finish. He's got plenty left to say but the café is closing and he has to move his car to avoid a parking ticket. 'Another thing that changed the whole scene for me is this thing called trance, mate,' he exclaims and pulls a face like he's bitten into an aspirin instead of swallowing it. 'It's fucking rubbish. It's this German shit that came out around '92 that everyone in Melbourne embraced. I think that changed the scene. Before then it was about American techno, it was about American house music. And then all of a sudden ...' He ferociously mimics a few bars of a fast bleepy trance track, kind of like Darude's 'Sandstorm' in double time. 'It's this piano driven Cosmic Baby shit ... that's the shit that a few DJs in Melbourne made popular and they made it into the anthem or the sound of the Melbourne rave scene.'

Melbourne techno evolved in three stages: acid house and Detroit techno from 1988 to 1990, a brief flirtation with hardcore in 1991 and 1992 and then the supremacy of trance from 1993 onwards. Although hardcore departed from the 'pure' Detroit sound, it still maintained a 'machine-music' techno sensibility. Trance, however, borrowed more from Beethoven than the Belleville Three. 'That's not underground, that's just shit,' H2O insists. 'It's a production line of music. You're not using anything different, you're just doing some keys on a keyboard in proper piano chords or whatever and putting a 4/4 beat onto it. That's not techno.'

Trance encompasses a minefield of genres ranging from chakra-aligning meditation music to gushing orchestral symphonies layered over big basslines. In contrast to Detroit techno, trance is generally more melodic and often has ambient, spiritual or classical music overtones. Trance adds a kick drum on every downbeat and makes liberal use of arpeggios, minor keys and chord progressions. A classic trance tune will build, peak and drop, often multiple times. See, for example, one of my favourite trance tracks 'Wizards of the Sonic' by Westbam v Red Jerry (Matt Darey remix), which has a classic drop at 5:04 that brings back the bass and melody after a thirty-second build-up.

It's possible to trace techno's roots through a century of American black music via hip hop, disco, funk, soul and R&B back to the spiritual music of the Deep South. As James Baldwin reminds us, American black music begins on the auction block.[32] Trance, on the other hand, came out of the European mansions of slave traders' descendants, where producers blended nineteenth-century classical music with seventies progressive rock and echoes of Eurodisco. Trance and techno share a common ancestor in the 'motorik', a style of monotonous percussion found in Kraftwerk's albums from *Autobahn* to *The Man-Machine* and perhaps given ultimate expression as the sound of 'train wheels hitting the connections between the rails' in 'Trans-Europe Express'.[33] But despite their reputation as the 'ultimate white band', Kraftwerk fused their European avant-garde harmonies with black American funky rhythms.[34] Nineties trance producers loved the harmonies but forgot about the funk. For many people, trance represents yet another stage in the whitewashing of black music, a process that began with jazz in the 1920s and continued through soul, disco, hip hop and house.

Trance Mission

English writer Simon Reynolds claims that Europe was awash with German trance by late 1992.[35] Australia picked up the sound almost immediately without the usual twelve-month time lag. 'Here's a bit of trance for you,' Kate Bathgate announced on a January 1993 edition of *Beat in the Street*. Later that year, trance had become so popular that Kate changed the name of her show to *Tranzmission*. The arrival of international DJs catalysed the Melbourne scene's infatuation with trance. Nuremberg's Cosmic Baby (real name Harald Blüchel) first played Melbourne on 22 September 1993 and again on 24 April 1994, both times in the main room of the Palace, traditionally a rock concert venue. Ahead of his first Melbourne appearance, Cosmic Baby did an interview with Kate on *Tranzmission*. 'I was classically educated on piano and then I listened to Kraftwerk for [the] first time in my life and I was so impressed and electrified that I really wanted to have drum machines as well,' he says in his Teutonic monotone.[36] Cosmic Baby's classical training shines through on pieces like 'Treptow' and 'Fantasia', which have all the tension and romance of a Rachmaninov piano concerto albeit with faster percussion. He cites composers Philip Glass, Laurie Anderson and Tangerine Dream's Klaus Schulze as formative influences. Casting himself as a trance pioneer, Cosmic Baby tells Kate it took a while for the new sound to catch on in Europe:

> [t]he people here, they wanted to get hardcore only and it took very long to put this music in but now it's wonderful. The techno music, you don't need that much equipment ... you need only good ideas, a drum machine, two good synthesisers and then you can play.[37]

Similar to Cosmic Baby, Frankfurt's Sven Väth enjoys a huge Melbourne following. He played at the back of the Palace in 1994 and returned a year later for the Hardware 7 morning set at Shed 14. Raver Sid Sidney remembers watching Sven put on a record and then walk off to mingle with the crowd:

> He played a song for twenty minutes and the vibe was just getting lower and lower and he builds it down so everyone is standing around and relaxed and then he just builds it up in one track and everyone was going mental. By that time, it was ten in the morning, it was daylight, the light was coming through the cracks in the warehouse and I had no energy left, my legs were just mush but I was still having a good time.

Sven Väth and Cosmic Baby would probably top a poll of Melbourne ravers' favourite artists in the '90s, much to H2O's disdain. 'Cosmic Baby in another life would have been some Hi-NRG disco producer or he would be some Eurovision song contest winner with some shitty song like 'Perfect Day',' he rants. H2O has an ally in Simon Reynolds, a self-confessed hardcore fan who lambasted Sven's 1992 album *Accident in Paradise* as 'all arpeggiated synth-wank and piano trills as frou-frou as Enya'.[38] But Melbourne loved its trance. 'The peak of Melbourne's rave sound was definitely the Cosmic Baby, Paul van Dyk, Sven Väth stuff,' Duncan Plank tells me. 'The German trance thing was Melbourne, a hundred percent. At that time in '93, '94, it was going full steam and it felt very at home in Melbourne.' It was a similar view from overseas. Club Labrynth's Joe Wieczorek observed that the Melbourne sound was more 'trancey techno' than the breakbeat-driven London scene.

Trance pushed Europe's axis of techno steadily eastwards. In 1991, it had centred on Belgium and England. By 1993, the frontline lay somewhere between Frankfurt and Berlin. At MDS, Richie Rich imported heavily from both cities, stacking Melbourne's record shelves with the latest cuts from labels Harthouse, Eye-Q, MFS and Superstition Records and artists like Sven Väth, Kid Paul, Marmion, Jam & Spoon and Paul van Dyk. Armed with the latest German releases, Richie flooded Melbourne's dancefloors with wave after wave of Teutonic trance.

Richie told me he liked to play the 'emotional uplifting trippy sort of voyage stuff'. I suspect that by 'trippy voyage' he means a journey through time and space as opposed to a psychedelic trip, since trance cleansed techno of its more nefarious connotations. 'A lot of the music was too serious and lacked the 'e rave' flavour from previous years,' raver Seth Taylor says. Producers did away with stolen samples and blatant ecstasy references to create safe and fluffy electronic dance music for kids who worked hard and did what they were told. Kids like me. Growing up around people who visibly shook whenever they saw a person of colour (a biannual occurrence in the Tory heartland of rural Norfolk), black music was never going to be in my bones. Whiter-than-white trance, on the other hand, reverberated through my body like I had knocked my funny bone.

Nimmo Sandilands tells me he didn't know anyone who didn't like trance in the nineties: 'We were very serious about it although if I'd seen people my age now looking at us when we were twenty-year-olds, I'm sure they would have called it cheesy, stupid music.' Trance is the chardonnay of the Melbourne rave scene; no-one admits to liking it now, but back then it was everyone's guilty pleasure.

'We Used our Legs and Arms'

Whereas hip hop and hardcore demanded heavy stomping leg movements, trance was softer and more flowing. 'Melbourne was unique, we used our legs *and* arms', Natural 1 says:

> The foot was going up and down in the air to the 2 and 4 and the arms did the 1 and 3 to get the gliding motion. It was floaty, frilly movements as you moved from side to side

and it changed particularly because of trance music. This frillier, fluffier, softer and more melodic music made you dance differently. And all the piano riffs, wailing black diva voices and oscillated arpeggios used in trance—that's what softened it as well. Especially the oscillations that made you float and move up and down and move your arms and legs like that.

Josh Abrahams disagrees. He condemns trance as 'marching music' with 'nothing for the hips'. While this may be true of straight-up 'doof doof' tracks like 'Sandstorm', I think what Natural 1 says makes sense when applied to fluffier and more melodic trance tunes like 'Wizards of the Sonic' or Lost Tribe's 'Gamemaster'. Whenever I hear these songs, all my limbs can't help but move.

Their elegant footwork had already distanced the shufflers from the acid house 'hands-in-the-air' crew. Now, their trance-induced flowing arms took the dance one step further, breaking away from earlier variants like the Stomp and the Manchester foot shuffle.* To be clear, I'm not suggesting that Melbourne's raving fraternity spontaneously invented a new dance style the moment they heard their first chord progression. Instead, ravers evolved their dancing styles organically over time. It all depended on the music, as Natural 1 explains:

> The wailing parts made you want to float and then the hard rave synth or breakbeat would come back in and make you want to stomp again. The music governs how people's bodies move. Rhythm and the groove and the general beat tempo create the framework for the body to move and then the melody or the vocal part where you can dance more

---

* This distinction also helps to separate the 'old skool' shuffle (as described here) to the 'new skool' shuffle which is more footwork-focussed with less emphasis on gliding and bouncing arm movements.

freely and isn't as time-clocked as a bassline or a drum tempo or rhythm is, that's where the frilly floaty part of the shuffle evolved as well.

By the late nineties, Melbourne's ravers had taken the t-step and the running man from the stomp, added a foot shuffle, dusted their dancefloors with talcum powder and tuned their bodies to the sound of trance. American hip hop, jazz-fusion, new jack swing and surfie culture; British northern soul and the Manchester house music scene; Melbourne's own skinheads and sharpies—the Melbourne shuffle insatiably swallowed up local and overseas influences and melded them to form a new style. I think it's ironic that the shuffle's best claim to uniqueness stems from the scene's love of German trance music—ironic because the infatuation with trance is something many Melbourne ravers would rather forget. Richie is right to claim a hand in starting the shuffle but I think perhaps his passion for playing trance music at raves did more to change the way people danced in Melbourne than his moves in front of the booth.

Black Box Bandits

As the trance express gathered steam, local artists hopped on board. In 1993, Melbourne techno trio FSOM released their breakthrough EP *Beyond* on Candyline records. The key track was 'Welcome', an old skool trance classic with a catchy housey piano riff. FSOM stands for Future Sound of Melbourne; band members Josh Abrahams, Davide Carbone and Steve Robbins took the name from English electronic group Future Sound of London.

After his raving epiphany at Kemistri 3 in November 1990, classically trained Josh struggled to make sense of techno:

> I'd been listening to XTC and Frank Zappa, who are so brilliant, their lyrics are so clever, they're so dense musically and conceptually—and techno is the opposite: it's one thing,

it's one or two notes, it's endless changing energy levels of one idea. So I had to understand what the point of that was.

Josh used an Ensoniq EPS sampler to compose his first techno tracks but getting hold of the right records to sample from proved challenging. One morning after hearing a track he later identified as 'Future' by Mr Monday, he walked into Central Station Records. 'I tried to sing it to the guy behind the counter who was incredibly snooty and unfriendly in a "Who the fuck are you to talk to me?" kind of thing.' A friend had suggested Davide could help and gave him Davide's number. Josh called Davide and asked if he would record some of his music in return for cash:

> Davide replied in true Calabrian style, 'Forget the money, I'll do you a favour now, you can do me a favour sometime'. So he recorded a whole bunch of records onto digital audio tape, I got to study them, and then a few weeks later the phone rang, it was Davide and he said, 'So that favour we talked about …' but I'd forgotten about our deal and I said, 'Huh, what favour?' and he goes, 'Well I'm working with this kid, this young DJ, Steve Robbins, who's been getting some ideas down. I heard you've got a studio, I'd love to get him in to work with you on this track'.

Steve had been busy teaching himself to program the TB-303 bass synthesiser and TR-808 drum machine. 'I thought I would suss this shit out', he tells me. 'I kept trying but for the first couple of months I wasn't really getting anywhere, it was getting annoying. And then one night it just clicked all of a sudden.' He started mixing 303 and 808 loops into his DJ sets at Pure:

> I hooked up my two little machines when I was playing records and started doing it. No-one would really know. Sometimes I'd play the whole song and other times I'd do things like stop the kick drum, build it up and then drop the

drums back in. I just did it off the cuff the first time, it wasn't like I had rehearsed it ... when I realised that everyone was still going off when I was playing my own songs I thought I've got something here so I may as well try and make the most of it.

When I heard this story, I told Steve he reminds me of Larry Levan. He nodded his head. 'When I saw *Maestro* [a 2003 documentary about Levan], I had this instant connection with it because it was exactly like what we had gone through, trying to get people into the music,' he says.

Josh condemns FSOM's early releases *Melodia* and *Wear 'n' Tear* as 'weak' and sample-driven. By 1993, his musicality and Steve's technical wizardry had combined to produce a highly marketable sound. At gigs, FSOM alternated between playing their studio tracks off cassette and jamming live, as Josh explains:

> We'd have a huge rack with maybe three drum machines, a couple of 303s, a bass one and a lead one, maybe a synth hooked up to one of them and a mixing desk with an echo unit ... I used to joke it's like shooting fish in a barrel. You start off with maybe the bassline 303, you put on the hi-hats, turn off the hi-hat and then drop in the kick drum and people went berserk. [The crowd] loved any musical event happening, it was quite easy to work well.

Steve and Davide were well known in the scene but Josh felt like an intruder, often having to argue his way into parties because the bouncers didn't believe he was part of the band. Switching between his everyday and raver personas sometimes required rapid transformations worthy of Clark Kent:

> At several New Year's Eves, I'd have a New Year's Eve gig with the wedding band I was playing bass in, this oldies music, it was almost like playing on the Titanic, and then

about 1.30am, I'd be in the car, tearing off my dinner suit, changing into my jeans and t-shirt on my way to the docks to get on stage to play live with FSOM at 2.30 m.

Sunny Arias and Dark Stab Samples

In 1996, FSOM took home Best Dance Release at the 10th ARIA Music Awards for their CD *Chapter One*. It cemented their reputation as Melbourne's number one techno act and squeezed Sydney arch-rivals Itch-E and Scratch-E into second place. 'We were competitive with Sydney,' Josh tells me:

> Sydney was all piano, sung vocals and light beats, representative of their weather, sunny and light ... if you take Itch-E and Scratch-E, it was bouncy light stuff whereas we had 909s, 303s [and] dark stab samples ... the Itch-E and Scratch-E stuff was pop songs essentially, no way would we ever put vocals in our tracks, we were purists.

Earlier that year, the UK's dance music bible *mixmag* had praised *Chapter One* for its 'pure and polished' breaks, 'tight, electronic grooves' and 'trademark Melbourne 303'.[39] Melbourne's dominance of Australian dance music was complete. 'We had the bigger and better parties and the bigger and better scene,' Natural 1 claims:

> Melbourne was the king and leading it in all the genres of dance music, fashion, lighting, lasers, DJs, international artists and venues. I mean checkmate across the board ... The scene started reaching more of a critical mass in '93 and by '95, '96 ... That was when a lot of clubbers started going to raves and Kiss FM was getting really big with their billboards all over Melbourne.

After the ARIA, FSOM played live gigs at home and overseas for a couple more years but its members itched to move on to other projects. 'I think it really did fall apart musically here around '93, '94 ... it had gone bad German,' Davide says, conveniently ignoring his own contribution to Melbourne's trance canon with 'Welcome'. In 1998, he relocated to England to pursue a new musical direction in drum'n'bass. Josh moved to Sydney and became a successful dance music producer. His credits include 'Addicted to Bass' (with Amiel Daemion) and the chart-topping single 'Everyone's Free (To Wear Sunscreen)', a track co-produced with film director Baz Luhrmann. Dark stab samples gradually gave way to vocals. 'It's been a really long, slow journey back but I'm now rediscovering the human voice,' Josh told *Techno Renegade* in 1998. 'If you add the human voice you make the music more approachable no matter how distorted or crunched up the beats might be. It gives the music more of an emotional connection.'[40]

While Davide and Josh built successful careers overseas and interstate, Steve stayed home, seldom venturing beyond the Melbourne underground that has been his refuge for the last thirty years. When I caught up with him in 2015, he handed me a copy of his latest CD. Full of slick acid and grumbling basslines, *Beatfreaks* is dark, bleak and magnificent. 'Steve was notorious for not turning up, he only turned up at our studio bookings about half the time,' Josh remembers. He continues:

> But it was worth all the frustration because Steve was brilliant. He was so picky and precise with every detail of the track, to the point where we could spend a whole day just working on the high-hat sound and pattern, so that when we finally finished the track it was so pure and exact. And people responded to that level of detail, they loved it.

Davide agrees: 'Sure it had a lot to do with Josh and I, but FSOM was really about Steve.'

Sonic Animators

In 1994, Adrian Cartwright attended his first rave, a Frank de Wulf gig at the Palace:

> I had no idea how to dress, there was a whole group of us going and they said, 'Wear whatever you're comfortable with', and so I thought, well I can't really wear sneakers so I put my Docs on and walked into this mind-blowing experience … I just got blown away, there was a new dimension of dancing which I had never really experienced before … it felt so comfortable, there was no violence anywhere, no-one giving anyone dirty looks, everyone was there to have a really good time … it brought something out in me that felt sort of tribal … I was really infected by it.

British-born Adrian played in an indie band called Scarlet Garden with Canadian expat Rupert Keiller. After his raving epiphany, Adrian put his faithful drums to one side and started learning how to use a keyboard and sequencer. A few weeks later, Adrian and Rupert walked into a clothing store on Chapel Street where they got chatting to Steve Bertschik, an old skool shuffler and DJ from the early days of Melbourne rave. Steve had just bought an Atari running Cubase software. 'He was interested in writing electronic music so we agreed to get together,' Rupert says. 'We hit it off pretty well and started going to raves together and started to write more music. Adrian was also influenced quite heavily by 808 State and was experimenting with producing electronic music.' Calling themselves Sonic Animation (aka sonicanimation), the trio released their self-funded debut EP *Time Is An Illusion* in 1995.

Initially, Sonic Animation emulated what they heard played at raves. They recorded big trance tunes in the vein of Marmion's 'Schöneberg' and 'Two Full Moons And A Trout' by Union Jack. In 1995, they signed to Richie Rich's trance label Azwan Transmissions.

'We were following what everyone else was doing,' Rupert said in 1999. 'It's pretty much what every band does until eventually they develop their own sound which is identifiable.'[41] Gradually their music evolved to absorb the big beat sound of The Prodigy, The Chemical Brothers and Fatboy Slim as well as trip hop, progressive house and increasingly more eclectic influences. 'We're into old jazz and blues as well as Underworld and Massive Attack,' Adrian said in 1999. 'It's nice to draw [in] all different styles and having a go at putting it in an electronic format.'[42] Their audiences loved it. In 1999, they headlined the Big Day Out festival while their EP *Theophilus Thistler* appeared at number eighteen on Triple J's Hottest 100 poll. The following year, they supported The Chemical Brothers at Metro. They had come a long way from their first gig when they had to mime to a backing track because they lacked the technology to perform live. 'I don't think it would have happened without Steve and his contacts,' Rupert says. 'It was fantastic to play so many big shows so early in our career.'

From Melbourne to the World

In 2000, Sonic Animation scored a guest programmer slot on *rage*, the ABC's late-night music video show. During the episode, Rupert used the term 'Melbourne Shuffle' to describe the style of dancing he'd observed at raves. Rupert may have introduced the term to the mainstream media but he didn't invent it. In November 1998, *groo:vine* magazine exhorted ravers to wear flat shoes when dancing to prevent injury:

> [t]he Melbourne 'foot thing' has been going on at raves for a long time. I think you know what I mean when I say that … you know the Melbourne 'shuffle' that everyone perfects at home before leaving for a rave. Well, this type of dancing, or exercise, can cause heavy damage to the feet and lower legs.[43]

I've not been able to find an earlier mention of the Melbourne Shuffle in print, however, I'm told that people had been using the term on the dancefloor since at least the mid-nineties.

In 1999, Kim bumped into a friend who had just returned from Detroit. Someone had identified she was from Melbourne because of her dance style. 'When I was partying back then I didn't really think of that being something that defined Melbourne but of course now I look back on it and I realise it was totally unique,' Kim says. By 2002, *The Age* acknowledged that the shuffle had become recognisable in 'international dance circles' although the newspaper unkindly characterised the dance as a 'cross between the chicken dance and a foot-stomping robot'.[44] The release of the *Melbourne Shuffler* documentary in 2005 further enhanced the dance's popularity.

Fast-forward to 2018 and the dance continues to evolve and grow. Its inclusion in the music video for LMFAO's 2011 megahit 'Party Rock Anthem' won over a new generation of fans. Internet servers are crammed with terabytes of data inviting browsers to learn the dance steps and read the history of the Shuffle.[45] Type in 'Melbourne Shuffle' on YouTube and the top-ranking result has over 39 million views. 'Suddenly we saw a whole load of videos, some with Italian kids in car parks or Filipino or Singaporean kids in their bedrooms,' Natural 1 says. 'They'd never even been to a club, they'd never seen what the shuffle is. And then suddenly everyone's giving tutorial videos on it and I thought that was quite silly.' The tutorials generally focus on the t-step and the running man at the expense of the more fluid and floaty leg and arm motions that typified the nineties Melbourne shuffle.

But the shuffle was never meant as a one-size-fits-all dance. Old skool ravers learnt the basics and mixed in moves and add-ons copied from their peers to develop their own unique style. Watch any two old skool Melbourne shufflers and they won't dance the same way. 'This whole Melbourne shuffle thing is very strange,' Duncan Plank tells me. 'It seems to have got a lot faster and a lot more involved.' Raver Desiree Laz agrees. 'It became competitive,' she says. '[It was] everyone seeing who could dance the fastest with the "coolest" moves.' The shuffle has changed from 'dance any way you like' to 'dancing well'.[46] Several interviewees in the *Melbourne Shuffler* documentary are careful to badge themselves as rockers as opposed to shufflers. 'Shuffling is more of a specific way of dancing whereas rocking is just letting everything out and having a lot of fun,' Steve, a self-styled rocker, explains.[47]

I think the story of the shuffle neatly illustrates how youth subcultures evolve. They begin 'on the street', so to speak, and are given expression through niche micromedia like fanzines, alternative radio shows and the street press. As the trend gains popularity, the mainstream media picks it up, commoditises it and sells the new 'product' to an uninformed yet eager audience. With the Melbourne shuffle, an expression of individual style has been reduced to a set of prescriptive steps. It's no wonder that many Melbourne old skoolers disown the dance they helped create, hiding behind Facebook groups with names like *STOMPERS!!! (The Original Pre Melbourne Shufflers)* and instructing authors who want to write about their scene: 'less shuffle, more techno'.

Chapter 9

GATECRASHERS

The Tasty Raid

Tasty nightclub, Melbourne, Sunday 7 August 1994. It's 2am and Lani G is shuffling across the dancefloor dressed in full raver gear. Suddenly the lights come on, the music stops and a male voice barks, 'Freeze! Hands in the air!' Some people drop gram bags on the ground while others throw things at the barman who deftly puts them in the bin, unobserved. The police line up the men against the wall and strip-search them on the spot, aggressively pulling their pants down and bending them over. A female officer escorts Lani into the manager's office, closes the door and orders her to strip down to her bra and undies. The cop thrusts a plastic bag containing white powder in Lani's face and asks, 'Is this yours?!' Terrified, Lani shakes her head and turns away. The officer lifts up Lani's bra and slides her fingers inside her undies. She finds nothing. The physical sensation of being groped lasts just a few seconds but the feelings of shame and terror will linger for years.

After Razor folded in 1992, Gavin Campbell started Tasty at his new underground venue Temple Bar and Nightclub in the old Masonic Hall on Flinders Street. As well as his own club nights, Gavin hosted other underground promoters' events including Richie Rich's and Jayse Knipe's Friday night rave club Sektor 3. 'Richie doesn't realise how significant Sektor 3 was,' Gavin says. 'Maze was one thing but it was very trippy, very out there, whereas Sektor 3 was the start of the weekend. It had a very young crowd. He was educating the next generation of ravegoers.' Temple struggled financially at first. Then just as the club was starting to make money, Gavin arrived one Monday morning to clean up and found he couldn't get in. 'There was a trend happening at the time whereby buildings were being turned into apartments,' he says. 'They called it Postcode 3000. People were interested in our building because there was talk that the Gas and Fuel building opposite was going to come down.' Temple was housed in the old Masonic Club on the corner of Hosier Lane and Flinders Street. Bulldozing the seventeen-storey Gas and Fuel towers would clear a million-dollar sightline to the Yarra River. A 1993 study found the Masonic Club building unworthy of inclusion on the heritage register, paving the way for its redevelopment.[1]

Gavin failed to secure an injunction against the eviction. Not wanting to lose the momentum he'd built up, he moved Tasty to the Commerce Club. 'We were pretty much allowed to do what we wanted,' Gavin admits. The 'chains and leather' vibe of Temple gave way to drug-fuelled hedonism at Commerce. 'The big walk-in safe was almost a part of the club,' Gavin says. 'It's where all the money was kept but it's also where all the coke was snorted. It was full on. It was just weird that when they raided the club they found no drugs in it!'

Actually, there was nothing weird about it. Gavin later confessed to me that a queer police officer had tipped him off prior to the raid. On the night, police found over 100 'deal bags' discarded on the floor, but only a few contained LSD, ecstasy or amphetamines.[2] Officers charged just eight of the 463 patrons with drug, alcohol and public order offences. *The Age* picked up the story on Tuesday and followed up with a front-page report two days later and a call for an independent inquiry. State premier Jeff Kennett weighed in on Wednesday, criticising the heavy-handed police tactics and labelling the raid as 'extreme ... remarkable and disturbing'.[3] On Friday, the right-leaning *Herald Sun* finally entered the fray. It labelled Kennett's response as 'disgusting' and ran a full-page yes/no debate about the raid on page fifteen.[4] Former deputy police commissioner Paul Delianis argued that while strip searches can be 'embarrassing, humiliating and intrusive' they can also produce 'excellent results for police'.[5] Further, he suggested the 'homosexual lobby' was trying to intimidate the police.

Government and public opinion sided with the victims, helped in part by vocal complaints from high-profile victims like future deputy Lord Mayor Gary Singer and fashion designer Peter Alexander.[6] 'They got the wrong gay people with very rich families,' Davide Carbone drily noted when I asked him about it. In November 1994, the Victorian Ombudsman handed down a damning report following its investigation into the Tasty affair. While it upheld the legality of strip-searching and uncovered no concrete evidence of abusive language or rough handling by police, the Ombudsman criticised the operation's planning, particularly the ratio of two female officers to 130 female patrons. It deemed the decision to search all 463 patrons as unreasonable and one that caused considerable distress to a large number of innocent people. It also failed to find adequate evidence to justify the operation in the first place and expressed concern that police may have embellished the search warrant. The Ombudsman concluded that the raid was not motivated by homophobia but the police had discriminated against the club because it was a gay club.⁷ I'm not sure I understand the difference.

The police had codenamed the raid 'Operation Maze', supposedly because of a series of chipboard cubicles in the basement advertised as the 'Grope Maze'.⁸ However, between November 1990 and April 1991 when Maze was operating at the Commerce Club, police received seven reports of suspected drug trafficking but took no action at that time. In contrast, it took a single and undocumented anonymous tipoff in March 1994 to trigger the Tasty raid.⁹

The Ombudsman saddled Victoria Police with a good behaviour bond and recommended new guidelines to deal with similar situations in the future. Yet senior police command took no disciplinary action against individual officers. Many of the victims didn't get off so lightly. 'They treated me like absolute crap,' Lani G tells me. 'I was really scared of cops after that, for the next ten years. If I ever saw a cop I'd just shake and have a panic attack.' Gary Singer subsequently led a class action against the police, which awarded damages of up to $10,000 to victims, including Lani:

> I was on a tram on Brunswick Street and my friend Josie was on the street and she saw me on the tram and shouted, 'Lani! Payout from Tasty raid! You've got to call the lawyers!'

Lani used the money to fund her first warehouse parties. With the benefit of hindsight, Gavin views the Tasty raid as a blessing in disguise. 'It almost needed to be busted up,' he laughs. 'It was out of control.'

Nightclub Nemesis

On 5 August 1994, two days before the Tasty raid, LGBT newspaper *Melbourne Star Observer* claimed that 'Night Club Owners' wanted to close down Tasty.¹⁰ The Victorian Ombudsman investigated the claim and was particularly concerned about the role of the Westend

Forum, an alliance of nightclub owners, Melbourne City Council and Victoria Police that had been established in June 1990 to address violence concerns in the area bounded by Spencer, Flinders, Queen and Latrobe Streets.[11] The Forum's members included George Frantzeskos, brother to Sam, part-owner of Inflation and Metro, and president of the Nightclub Owners Association (NOA).[12] Sam had helped set up the NOA after the 1987 Metro raid (see Chapter One). 'Because we were so big and threatening it seemed the authorities were out to get us,' Sam says. 'We hoped the Association would give us some clout to fight back.'

The Ombudsman found no evidence that nightclub owners had unduly influenced the police's decision to raid Tasty.[13] However, H2O tells me the NOA had tried to shut down Maze in 1991. 'They were just freaked out because this club could go to 9am in the morning and attract so many people and nobody went to their clubs on a Saturday,' he says. 'They were losing trade.' Richie Rich informs me the NOA also tried to close down some of his parties. So I asked Sam about these claims and to my surprise he nodded his head. The rave scene was taking people away from the clubs, he told me:

> This became a threat to the Nightclub Owners Association and we went after them. We tried to close them down ... we had an eight and a half million-dollar investment [Metro nightclub] and it was under serious threat and so we did everything we could legally do to try and chase those buggers off.

Sam felt aggrieved that while he and other nightclub owners had to spend 'millions' on fire sprinklers and the like to comply with onerous safety regulations, rave promoters could get away without taking such measures. But Richie disagrees. 'Compliance was always going to cost more money for them because if you want to do it 365 days a year and you want to have millions of people going through your doors, then it's got to be stricter than someone that just has

10,000 or 20,000 people come through his doors five times a year.'

The NOA successfully lobbied the government to bring in the Responsible Serving of Alcohol program and mandatory criminal record checks for security guards, both of which hit the rave scene hard. 'When they brought those laws in, we lost a lot of good security guys who we really trusted but maybe had a little bit of a shady past or a misspent youth,' Rudeboy says. However, there was a fatal flaw in the NOA's tactics, as Sam explains:

> By a stroke of genius or just sheer luck, Richie and Mark [James] went into Shed 14 and that venue complied … now they were allowed to sell liquor. Well, in hindsight we were fucking idiots, we should have just let things be and let the authorities close them down in time but No! We let them really hurt us! Because as soon as they could sell the liquor, they were making a lot more money.

By the mid-nineties, many nightclub owners realised that rave was the future. The NOA adopted a less combative stance, much to the relief of larger promoters like Richie and Mark, although their incursion into raving territory frightened some smaller operators, such as one anonymous promoter quoted in 1998:

> [T]he nightclub association's never been that interested in seeing raves develop, but now that they're getting to the stage where they know they can't ignore it they're jumping on the bandwagon themselves … [the nightclubs] have got the heavies, they've got … the money … I mean it's just a matter of squeezing.[14]

Rave on Trial

The sheds and sports halls created a physical barrier between the rave and the outside world, but the drugs delivered the emotional escape from the stress and tedium of real life. Being lost in the moment at eight in the morning when you'd normally be waking up is a feeling that's difficult to surpass. But then at some point you emerge into the cold, grey morning and shudder when you realise the party's over. The reality you tried so hard to avoid can be a dark lonely valley when you're coming down from a forty-eight-hour trip to the mountains of euphoria. For some, it was a journey from which they never recovered.

'You'd hear about people getting too into it, falling into a drug hole,' Josh Abrahams says. 'You could see it sometimes, over the years, people looking less and less healthy, they'd look really ugly. No sleep, week-long benders, sunken eyes and shit skin, just really not taking care of themselves.' Melbourne's raving folklore abounds with sad stories of suicides, overdoses and car accidents. In 1991, Duncan Plank found his best friend hanging from a tree in the back garden of their sharehouse in Prahran. 'The funeral was full of ravers, friends and acquaintances,' Duncan recalls. 'We played three tracks at the service—'Everybody's Free' by Rozalla, 'All Together Now' by The Farm, and the real reminder tune—'Belfast' by Orbital.' Already established as a Melbourne rave scene anthem, 'Belfast' now took on an even greater poignancy.

Most people believed that ecstasy posed a threat only to long-term, excessive users. That all changed on Sunday 22 October 1995. At around 1am, Sydney teenager Anna Wood swallowed an ecstasy tablet before entering the Phoenician club in Ultimo to attend an Apache rave party. By dawn, she was vomiting and feeling unwell. Her friends escorted her from the club and drove to one of their houses where her condition continued to deteriorate. By the time somebody finally called an ambulance, it was too late. Anna died three days later. Although the exact cause of her death was never unequivocally established, it's generally accepted that Anna died from complications resulting from taking a single ecstasy tablet.[15] It was only the second time she had tried it.

Anna's death shattered the scene, especially in Sydney, a city still reeling from a violent confrontation between ravers and police in Sydney Park six months prior. The *Daily Telegraph* ran front-page reports on Anna's death for nearly two weeks.[16] Moral panic erupted. Rave and ecstasy became the 'new folk devils' of youth subculture.[17] Before Anna Wood, the Sydney press had viewed rave parties with curiosity and fascination, often downplaying the drug-taking element.[18] Almost overnight, the media switched to demonising rave as a deviant and dangerous youth pastime and condemning rave spaces as subversive sites lying beyond the mainstream.[19] Newspapers exploited pretty Anna's schoolgirl face and comfortable background to induce panic in middle-class parents about the perils of drugs. Their hysterical coverage contrasted with the response to an earlier ecstasy death in 1991. The *Sydney Morning Herald* dismissed that victim, 'Amanda', as a 'street kid from the wrong side of town' and the 'type of girl who [experimented] with drugs'.[20]

Dressing fifteen-year-old Anna as a wholesome child stolen from us by malevolent forces, the media pursued a range of scapegoats, including the Phoenician Club and the shadowy drug dealer figure that 'peddles death to children'[21]—conveniently forgetting that Anna bought the pill that killed her *outside* the club and from someone she knew. The NSW government imposed tighter regulations on rave operators and tried to push patrons towards commercially oriented and licensed dance parties, ironically like the one that Anna had attended.[22] Their anti-rave agenda borrowed from precedents overseas. In 1994, the English parliament had passed the Criminal Justice and Public Order Act or the CJA for short. The CJA permitted police to arrest gatherings of twenty or more people where amplified music was played at night and the 'music includes sounds wholly or predominantly characterised by the emission of a succession of repetitive beats'.[23]

In 1996, scores of Australian teenagers returned home from school to find a paperback with Anna's face on the cover sitting by their bed. I think I can sum up *Anna's Story* in four words: say no to drugs. Or, to be precise: say no to rave. Author Bronwyn Donaghy seems to have little time for the aesthetic aspects of raving:

> [t]echno music relies heavily on a repetitive thudding beat. It is raucous, continuous, monotonous and loud. Some numbers have limited lyrics and these, too, are repeated over and over and over, with no discernible change in key … illuminated by green, red and purple strobes, crowds of people writhed and jerked to the grating techno beat … there wasn't much room to move but it didn't matter. This sort of dancing required no fancy foot movement, there were no steps to learn.[24]

Similar to the tabloids, Donaghy emphasises Anna's innocence. She places the 'smiling golden girl' in school uniform on the front cover, and tells us twice that Anna died a virgin.[25] In the foreword, David Bennett portrays Anna as a 'marvellous young person, cruelly snatched from life in her nubile prime'.[26] Personally, I find this fixation on Anna's innocence disturbing and disrespectful to the victim. To me, the tragedy of Anna's story is that if it wasn't for the negative social stigma surrounding ecstasy use, Anna's friends would probably have sought help sooner and possibly saved her life. Donaghy unwittingly reveals the absurdity of this situation when Anna's mother Angela angrily asks Anna's friends what her daughter has taken and they tell her that someone must have spiked her drink at the go-kart track.[27] Why is drinking alcohol, an activity that kills over 5000 people annually, socially more acceptable than taking a drug that causes around a dozen deaths a year?[28]

'The Deadly Agony of Ecstasy'

On the Sunday after her death, the front page of Melbourne's *Herald Sun* displayed a photograph of five-year-old Anna Wood wearing a swimsuit. The tabloid's sympathy for Anna jars with their disrespect for the hundreds of gay and lesbian victims of the Tasty raid fourteen months earlier. In the same edition, the newspaper ran a two-page exposé titled 'The deadly agony of ecstasy' on the dangers of Melbourne's own rave scene:

> [c]hildren as young as 15 have easy access to alcohol and designer drugs such as ecstasy at illegal rave parties held regularly in Melbourne … The parties operate without council or alcohol permits and patrons are alerted by broadcasts on alternative radio stations to telephone a number to find out where they are held.[29]

The article and accompanying editorial warned parents of the 'new teenage phenomenon known as rave parties', seemingly ignorant that people had been attending raves in Melbourne for at least six years.[30] In fact, the newspaper presented a maze of misinformation, suggesting that under-18s could buy alcohol at raves (unlikely), venues were overcrowded (generally not) and bouncers turned away anyone 'who doesn't look sufficiently reggae' (seriously?)[31] However, it did manage to get a couple of crucial details right. A Hardware flyer appears on page five and the reporters identify a 'disused second-storey warehouse in Footscray'—clearly Global Village—as a major rave venue. A subsequent news story identified Mark James as one of Melbourne's leading rave promoters. 'They said I'd kill the whole fucking city with what I was doing,' Mark recalls. 'That's when reporters would follow me, jump my fence, yelling, "you're Mark James, that Dancing to Death guy".' The secret was finally out.

Aaron Roach recalls how the media's perception of raves changed in Melbourne after Anna Wood's death:

> In the early days, the media was very curious. And then there was passive acceptance. But after things like Anna Wood, it started to become more and more victimised to the point where they felt that raves shouldn't happen. The

media created a dodgy perception of raves in that they're all bad and they're only good for drugs. To be honest, when I heard about Anna Wood at that time, I didn't want to take anything because I was worried I would die.

Sarah Thornton writes that while mass media approval is often the 'kiss of death' for youth subcultures, media *disapproval* can actually legitimise them as authentic underground scenes, 'breath[ing] longevity into what would have been the most ephemeral of fads'.[32] Once the initial panic had subsided, a faint aura of danger and mystique began to envelop the Melbourne scene, ensuring its continued growth in size and prestige. For years the scene had remained exclusive to those in the know. Now, the whole city had got right on one.

'The Drugs Had to Be Coming From Somewhere'

Big promoters and nightclub bosses weren't the only people to profit from the nineties rave explosion. 'It was always obvious that there was some sort of underbelly,' Josh Abrahams tells me. 'The drugs had to be coming from somewhere.' There's a quaint innocence to ecstasy's emergence on the dancefloor in the late eighties. One DJ told me the owner of the club where he worked paid him to drive to Sydney and come back with 'a boot full of eccies'. Several people have told me that bussies regularly dealt drugs at nightclubs. Some DJs also sold drugs, as Mark James recalls:

> I would see people coming up to the DJ console and I'd go, 'Fuck, you're getting a lot of requests tonight, aren't you?' Then he'd pull out a matchbox and go, 'I'm only down to two e's, I've sold thirty e's tonight'.

Joe Fitzgerald (aka Little Joe) began dealing at thirteen. One night, the all-ages nightclub where he worked hosted a rave. He walked into the office and saw an old skateboarding pal from

Elwood pulling rolls of banknotes out of his pockets and stuffing them into envelopes. He bragged that selling ecstasy to ravers was easy work. The cash excited Joe but the dealer's status left the greatest impression. Joe believed that dealing would make him cool. It was a shy schoolkids's dream. He started selling speed he got 'on tick' before earning enough to deal ecstasy and LSD. 'I was high on the thrill of sourcing stuff and cultivating these relationships,' he says. 'They'd trust me to take their dollars and come back when I had the stuff. I had to trust others to do the same.' He worked several nights a week, sneaking out of bed when his parents were asleep and returning before dawn.

In 1995, researcher John Fitzgerald (no relation to Joe) observed dealers going to a nightclub on Friday afternoons to take orders for the weekend. Anything the bouncers picked up on the night by frisking punters they would later use or resell.[33] 'The sense I got was that promoters wanted dealers in the house,' Joe says. Security staff knew what he was up to and would often tell him to hide if police arrived. Joe says 'big dealers' in the scene didn't conform to any stereotype. He remembers 'a couple of pretty single women who looked like butter wouldn't melt in their mouths', two ex-skinheads who lived in a house with bulletproof windows, a VCE student at a prestigious private school, and three or four drug addicts who ripped off other dealers and frequently got bashed for it.

Joe tells me that rave felt like a 'big drug amnesty'. He dealt out of a bum bag (it was the nineties after all) and sold to anyone who asked. For four years, he felt invincible, hiding behind his youthful, cherubic looks. Then, when he was seventeen, the police raided the family home. On bail and facing the possibility of adult jail, he realised he wasn't quite the gangster he imagined. Moreover, his legal problems were the least of it. Dealing had funded a burgeoning drug habit. Joe spent the next fifteen years trying to get clean. 'Rave culture normalised drug taking,' he tells me. 'I was already predisposed to drug abuse because of my upbringing but an early start in the world of rave and the connections I made poured petrol on a smouldering fire.'

Few people ever considered the true price of their weekly journey on the MDMA express. Natural 1 shares the somewhat naïve perspective of many ravers towards their chemical companions:

> Our revolution was a silent peaceful one. Even though a lot of people used drugs, no dealers had guns in our scene here in Melbourne, there was no real heavy shit going on. And when it did, it was left at the door.

In 2008, the TV series *Underbelly* finally exposed a 'generation's denial of the criminal elements behind ecstasy's fetishised status'.[34] It's hard to reconcile Natural 1's halcyon view with the 'brutal economies of drug production and distribution' in nineties Melbourne that triggered a vicious gangland war leaving dozens dead, destroyed a police force's reputation and ensured that almost all the pills washing around the city's dancefloors had passed through some very filthy and bloodstained hands.[35]

Joe tells me the 'heavies' crossed over into the rave scene around 1992. At a Showgrounds party, he watched a dealer shove a gun into a rival's mouth. While small-time dealers like Joe spent their Saturday nights hanging out in waterfront sheds and industrial parks, Melbourne's druglords preferred the glamour of South Yarra to snort coke and buy off pretty young things with their wads of ill-gotten cash. Half-brothers Jason and Mark Moran had exclusive run of Dome nightclub at the Chevron where the bouncers barred entry to rival gangs.[36] The Morans had been trafficking ecstasy from the wharves of West Melbourne into the nightclubs of Chapel Street since the late eighties. As demand intensified, the brothers found it cheaper to cook their own product from precursor chemicals like pseudoephedrine bought from wholesalers or corrupt cops.[37] Fuelled by the growing party scene, the illegal pill market had become 'obscenely lucrative'.[38]

Carl Williams had been manufacturing industrial quantities of ecstasy and speed with drug trafficker Tony Mokbel since the mid-nineties. One dealer recalls shifting 40,000 of Mokbel's pills in six weeks.[39] In 1997, Williams flooded Melbourne's dancefloors with cheap 'ecstasy' tablets made from speed, ketamine and glucose. Stamped UFO and FUBU, they sold for as little as $20 on the street.[40] In October 1999, Williams offered to introduce the Morans to a large-scale precursor supplier. The trio met at the Barrington Crescent Reserve in Gladstone Park.[41] What should have been a simple business deal quickly turned nasty. The Morans accused Williams of undercutting his rivals and swindling them out of $400,000. As tempers flared, Jason pulled out his .22 Derringer and shot Williams in the stomach. It triggered a decade-long gangland war that claimed thirty-six lives including both Moran brothers and Williams, the latter bashed to death in Barwon Prison in 2010 with the stem of an exercise bike.[42] Williams's biographer Adam Shand describes his subject as a 'product of the state's failed "war on drugs" … aided and abetted by corrupt police'.[43] One can't help but wonder if all this would have occurred if ecstasy had been legalised. For sure, the death count would have been lower but then would we have found *Underbelly* such gripping viewing?

Legitimised Deviants

Once the preserve of gay men and ethnic minorities, by the late nineties, dance music had overrun a rock'n'roll town. Dance music website inthemix.com.au celebrated the late nineties Melbourne scene as one of the 'most notorious warehouse parties of all time'.[44] On New Year's Eve 1997, an estimated 10,000 people turned up to a Hardware party at Shed 14.[45] Earlier that year, Sasha and John Digweed headlined a Future party on the same night as Richard Maher's Where the Wild Things Are (featuring Jeff Mills): both events attracted over 3000 patrons.[46] 'I recall having discussions with major music industry people who couldn't understand why bands at the Espy struggled to pull in a few hundred people when the docks were regularly packed with 5000 each weekend,' raver Andrew Ong writes on Facebook. While other cities were clamping down and moving on, Melbourne's parties just got bigger and bigger. Natural 1 says:

> It kept going here because we didn't have an Anna Wood ... people would come from overseas and laugh, 'What, you've still got a rave scene here and warehouse parties? What happened to you guys, are you in a time capsule?' ... if somebody had died, there would have been a clampdown.

Instead of shutting down the parties, the Victorian government invited Mark James and Richie Rich to help draft a set of guidelines based on the *1997 NSW Code of Practice for Dance Parties*. The *NSW Code* imposed a range of harm minimisation measures on party organisers, including free tap water, prohibiting re-entry of patrons to curb drug dealing and providing needle disposal instructions for staff.[47] Many ravers applauded these and other safety measures but expressed concern the *Code* would penalise smaller operators who couldn't afford to comply.[48]

For the big promoters, however, going 'legit' made good business sense. Tacit government backing extended the scene's longevity and afforded some protection against criminal gangs and unscrupulous operators. Richie explains:

> We were able to continue to do raves in these city fringe locations and do them regularly because the government supported us. The Liberal Kennett government felt that the Docklands were a cultural hub because the gays were doing their thing and that made Melbourne a nightlife entertainment capital.

Conservative Premier Jeff Kennett may seem an unlikely rave hero. However, he was merely following an international trend whereby 'creative city' narratives made popular in the nineties inspired governments to unlock the economic benefits of 'creativity' through promoting 'local culture' in city marketing campaigns.[49] Melbourne's thriving warehouse dance party scene became a point of difference from other cities competing for precious global status.

But perhaps government lent unspoken support to the rave scene for altogether more sinister reasons. The *NSW Code* and the Victorian guidelines (finally published in 2004 as the *Code of Practice for Running Safer Dance Parties*) signalled a shift in approach from zero tolerance to 'control and contain'. Scholars Chris Gibson and Rebecca Pagan argue that government policies sought to incorporate rave events within society as 'legitimised space[s] for subversive activities'.[50] Containing errant youth within tightly policed venues keeps them off the street and out of sight. Want to deter skaters from your leafy park? Rip up the ledges, level the concrete and lay some 'textured pavement'. Keen to stop writers tagging your walls? Simply transform your graffitied laneways into street art tourist destinations. Fed up with ravers breaking into warehouses and waking the neighbours? Herd them into clean, comfortable, licensed techno theme parks. 'The rave as temporary autonomous zone has become the club as pleasure-prison, a detention camp for youth,' Simon Reynolds laments.[51] A detention camp where the inmate pays for his own incarceration? Let's not give the Australian government ideas.

Many commentators have tried to pinpoint when the scene changed, that pivotal moment when, in the words of Richard John, people were no longer drawn to it but were being sold to. Researchers Christine Siokou and David Moore claim the rave scene morphed into a 'semi-commercial alternative music scene' after 1992.[52] Graham St John notes that by 1995 the 'dance/techno' brand attracted a wide market and earned big profits.[53] In a 2003 interview, Richie explained how things had come a long way since the days of dodgy sound systems and foam mattresses blocking fire escapes:

It's a lot more professionally run now ... there's a lot more money you have to spend on proper infrastructure set up. When you're running an event for fifteen thousand versus three hundred people you've got four or five hundred staff to worry about and all sorts of liability issues ... and a lot more permit approval stuff that needs to go through different Council and Government channels, so it's a lot more work as well.[54]

The music was changing too. 'When I was young and going out in the gay scene, the music was fucking amazing,' Mad Rod tells me. 'It was stuff you wouldn't hear on *Countdown* or *Top of the Pops*. It was underground. And then I don't know what happened but it all became commercialised.' In any music scene, commercialisation is inevitable. Ten years ago, even David Guetta was cool.[55] My research reveals a simple formula to calculate exactly when the music became commercial. You need to take the date you started going out and then add five years. For Mad Rod, it was all over by 1984. For me, 2000. What about you?

'I'm guilty that I understood at a very early stage that cheese sells,' Metro's Sam Frantzeskos confesses. Many DJs and producers were caught in a similar bind. Mark James began his production career with the best of intentions. In 1992, he and Carl Cox put out 'Eternal' by Eternal on Vicious Vinyl—five minutes of pure headbleeding underground techno including a Freddy Kruger sample from *Nightmare on Elm Street 4: The Dream Master*. But Mark soon learnt that underground doesn't pay the rent:

Commercial is a funny word ... everything's commercial at the end of the day. It starts off underground, it goes a little bit trendy, then it goes poppy, it goes backwards and it ends up in the suburbs.

Mark followed up Eternal with Bass Culture, an openly commercial venture featuring girlfriend Gina Gardiner (aka Gina

G of future Eurovision fame) on vocals. 'I'd made the underground and techno music commercial by that point, a commercial sound, commercial clubs were playing it ... the world had picked up on it.'

Rave, a one-time subversive and exclusive subculture, had become co-opted into the mainstream via commercialisation and 'legitimised deviance'—or so the popular narrative goes.[56] But let's not forget that rave has always had a capitalist edge due to the huge profits available—recall how Britain's acid house entrepreneurs had tapped into the Thatcherite 'greed is good' mantra of the late eighties. And for all the resistance rhetoric, many Melbourne ravers had clearly worshipped 'commodity consumption culture' from the start, as shown by their love of expensive import records, designer shoes and clothes.[57] Local street press publications *Listen Up*, *Techno Renegade* and *groo:vine* always featured plenty of dancefloor fashion, event flyers and 12-inch reviews. A 'symbiotic relationship' developed between rave promoters who used well-known brands to lend their parties credibility and companies who used rave culture as the target market for their product.[58] Promoters like Richard John and Mad Rod resisted the lure of corporate sponsorship because they felt it tainted the scene's underground soul. Not so Richie—he believed sponsors 'enhanced' his events.[59] But no amount of sponsorship could ever match the lucrative potential of the dance music industry's killer app.

The New Rock Stars

Mark James tells me that when international DJs first arrived they might have been big names overseas but in Australia 'they were faceless, they were just a song'. For Carl Cox, that song was 'I Want You Forever', his 'World Wide Smash Hit!' according to the flyer for his first Melbourne gig at the back of the Palace on Australia Day 1992. In the early nineties, Sydney promoters brought out international dance music acts like Cox, The Prodigy and The Shamen on the back of UK chart single success and then on-sold them to Melbourne promoters. But Richie knew Melbourne ravers weren't as tuned in to the English rave flavour as their Sydney cousins and decided to turn things around:

> I was looking at Richie Hawtin and Claude Young and then CJ Bolland and the German guys, Oliver Lieb, Sven Väth, Laurent Garnier. I started touring less of the English acts and more of the European and Detroit acts ... these guys were my heroes musically. I just wanted to meet the guys— that's how it started ... and those DJs were coming here through a Melbourne company, they were being shown around the country having a great tour and their best show was in Melbourne.

Claude Young (aka DJ2120) was one of the first Detroit DJs to come to Melbourne. He played Amnesia on Sunday 7 June 1992 in the former Elwood cinema on Ormond Road. Claude DJed out of the old projection room. It was his first overseas trip, something organiser Oliver Goldsmith discovered to his cost when the Detroit DJ clocked up a $2000 phone bill while staying at his house. Claude's set at Amnesia was almost drowned out by ardent fan Will E Tell's frequent 'wait for it!' voiceovers. If that wasn't bad enough, neighbours complained about the noise and the sound was turned down to 'barely louder than a home stereo', according to Nimmo Sandilands. Thankfully, the promoters had the sense to provide a host of other attractions to keep punters amused, including a flying fox, a giant blow-up castle (that promptly deflated) and a spa bath. In retrospect, the last of these might not have been such a great idea at a rave. '[The] spa bath [contained] way too many things you don't want to think about,' Toby Borrow writes on Facebook. Eww.

Three months later, Underground Resistance (UR) played Whiz at the Mansion. UR is the Detroit darling of the Melbourne scene: a militantly subversive collective who reject the commercialisation of techno and maintain a fierce independence from record company control. The nucleus of UR is a collaboration between ex-session musician Mike Banks and industrial DJ Jeff Mills.[60] UR sought to return Detroit techno to its black roots, sensing that the 'African American component of techno music was under siege'.[61] The group brought a militaristic edge to both their music and appearance; Natural 1 tells me they often wore 'full subversive camo gear' on stage. 'No-one was prepared for the way UR orchestrated their music, their band, or their business,' Dan Sicko writes in *Techno Rebels*. 'UR's low visibility created a mystery in the minds of its fans and foes—one much larger than it could have created on its own.'[62] Their mystery (and therefore their marketability) was as strong in Melbourne as anywhere. The city's love affair with Detroit only grew stronger as the nineties rolled on. Richard Maher brought out Derrick May in 1994, followed by fellow Detroit favourites Stacey Pullen and Carl Craig. 'A lot of people tried to jump on the bandwagon by that stage,' Maher said in a 2017 interview. 'Like if you brought out a good Detroit artist, you could just about guarantee you were going to get about 2000 people to come to a show.'[63] As well as Detroit, Melbourne looked to Europe's techno capital Berlin for inspiration. Love Parade started as a small street party in central Berlin with the motto 'Friede, Freude, Eierkuchen'—Peace, Joy, Pancakes.[64] Founder Dr Motte first brought Love Parade to Melbourne in 1994. After Love Parade '96 at Festival Hall, a few hundred ravers paraded down the streets to a recovery party in Flagstaff Gardens. 'That recovery went down in history as one of the greatest moments ever,' Seth Taylor tells me. 'I think about 500 ravers were there. It was awesome.'

Belgian DJ CJ Bolland headlined Hardware 11 on Saturday 30 August 1997 at Shed 14. When I caught up with him in April 2015, CJ told me that whenever he walked into a venue in Melbourne, he felt like he was in Berlin:

> The people were very into their music. Pretty much anyone in the crowd knew pretty much any record you were playing

because they were so into it themselves [and] buying all the music in the record stores every week as well. They were very savvy. It was always very comfortable playing there because you never felt out of sorts, you never felt as though you were miscast in any way.

DJ Brewster B. claims that the punters' appreciation and knowledge of the music placed Melbourne on the 'global techno map' for European and American DJs. They might be unknown in their home country, but Melbourne treated international visitors like rock stars. The guests paid it back with accolades like 'world class' and 'techno city'.[65] Carl Cox loved Melbourne so much he moved here.

'We toured the shit out of everybody,' Josh Abrahams recalls. Natural 1 regards the Melburnian obsession with international artists as another chapter in Australia's long history of cultural cringe. 'We look to overseas for our inspiration [because] we don't think we're good enough,' he says. 'And then if you do get good enough, we'll bag you for it and you're forced to go overseas where you get the appreciation, the love and the paycheck.' I agree, but I think there's more to it. In an underground music scene, records earn 'prestige and authority' over time (the older the better) or distance (the farther the better).[66] Ollie Olsen knew this and put it to the test when he created a fake band called Shaolin Wooden Men:

> People would go, 'This is really cool music, where did you get it from?' And I told them it was from Hong Kong. People would appreciate the music if I lied about it but it was actually me!

Promoters capitalised on the searing demand for overseas artists. Securing a high-profile international headliner meant they could charge as much as $130 for a single night. The arrival of global clubbing brands Cream and Gatecrasher symbolised a new techno-colonialism, transplanting a foreign product onto Melbourne soil with little respect for the local context. The parties could have been anywhere. Simon Digby graduated from house party DJ to partner in Hardware Corporation. 'When you do the figures at the end of the day, party budgets, it really does make a difference,' he told the ABC in 2003:

> You can pay a super-DJ what seems like a silly amount of money—thirty, forty, fifty thousand dollars. You can still make your money back. Whereas, if you take down the other scale and you're paying maybe five hundred bucks for a local guy who deserves more, you might not make your money back because the market just isn't gonna go.[67]

Things have come a long way since Mark James brought out Carl Cox in 1992 for '£1000 and a dodgy flight'. 'People would have an e and they'd be standing on the dancefloor, feel the rush, hear a good song and it was hands in the air,' Mark tells me. 'It didn't matter who the DJ was back then.' These days, the DJ *is* the party. Check out any dance party poster today and you'll find the DJ listing takes up more than half the space, many with [UK], [NZ] or [SYD] after their names to add the cachet of distance. Lineups for some events run into hundreds of performers. 'The cult of the DJ began to rear its ugly head because of the increasing accessibility of dance music,' Mad Rod says. 'Dance music is the new rock'n'roll.'

The cult of the DJ turned dancers towards the booth, like a devout congregation listening to a sermon. As promoters packed venues tighter to maximise profits, people stamped on the spot and raised their hands or pumped fists in the air, like soldiers at a Nuremberg rally. The view from the booth of a thousand adoring acolytes merely served to fortify the DJ's already overinflated ego, as DJ Brewster B. explains:

> All of a sudden I'm the conductor, I'm the instigator and now we're going on my journey because I'm in control ... I can understand why pop stars get so egomaniaced up when everybody in the crowd is at your fingertips when you're

on stage and there have been moments like that when I was working as a DJ … it's just exhilarating. It's addictive. It's like a drug.

As their bank balances ballooned, DJs took control of the scene, demanding the best set times and turning themselves into parodies of all they had once despised. Melbourne producer Ito saw Sven Väth play in 1993 and then again in the late nineties:

[He was] dissing rock'n'roll … saying, 'techno is so much more, so much more, because we've gotten rid of all this show biz pap', and I thought, 'yeah, that's right!' And I thought later, 'rubbish! It's just changed face; now it's called Sven Väth. You're the show biz pap! Nonsense! You're just Elvis in another pair of pants with a funky hairdo. Please!'[68]

Apollo 98

In 1997, Richie Rich asked Big Day Out (BDO) festival organisers Ken West and Vivian Lees if he could run the Boiler Room, a dedicated dance music stage that had recently been added to the festival's lineup:

It was always a Sydney-based line up and it never worked in Melbourne … I was travelling around Australia, I knew which DJs would be good for each territory and I said you've got to tailor it more for each city so let's get CJ Bolland and these other DJs in. In the end they said no and I went, 'Fuck it, we'll do our own thing'. And so I went and did Apollo.

Richie partnered with rock concert promoter Michael Coppel and electronic music promoters Terry Thompson and Jerome Jolson to put on Australia's first dance music festival. Named in honour of the Greek god of music and the first spacecraft to land on the moon, the Apollo festival hit Sydney on 7 February 1998 and

Melbourne a week later on Valentine's Day. Local live acts FSOM, Sonic Animation, Viridian, Honeysmack and Voiteck supported headliners Jeff Mills, Basement Jaxx, Jimmy Somerville, Jeremy Healy, DJ Sneak, BBE, Ultra Nate, Frankie Knuckles and Daft Punk. The Melbourne edition spread out over five stages across the length of Sheds 16 and 17 in Victoria Dock (where Newquay Promenade is now).

Boasting a stellar lineup, affordable tickets and a gap in the market left by a temporary BDO hiatus, Apollo should have succeeded. Instead, the festival flopped. 'It was just ahead of its time, it was just a year too early,' Richie conceded.[69] Acts like Basement Jaxx and Daft Punk were breaking out overseas but hadn't quite reached Australia. In the end, it was more Apollo 13 than Apollo 11. Aiming for the moon, they'd run out of oxygen in the stratosphere.

At least Richie still had Shed 14. But in January 1999, he learnt that Future Entertainment had double-booked the venue for the Labour Day long weekend. His agent called an emergency meeting between Richie and Future's Mark James and Jason Ayoubi:

> I was like, 'Well this is my date—I've done it for the past six years'. And [the agents] said, 'Well if you both look in your contracts, because of the imminent development coming there's a clause in there that with six weeks' notice we can cancel the contract—so we're going to cancel unless you two can work it out'.[70]

Work it out they did. Born out of panicked necessity, the resultant festival called Two Tribes became the glittering triumph that Apollo should have been. Buoyed by his success, Richie saw the upcoming Millennium Eve as an opportunity to crush the competition. Future had partnered with Michael Gudinski's Agent Mad for the last two New Year's Eves, bringing out Carl Cox and then Oliver Lieb for Halcyon Knights at the Royal Exhibition Building in Carlton. 'Mark had been getting a shit deal so I said, "Why don't you come over and do fifty-fifty with me in Sheds two and four?"' Richie recalls. Mark couldn't refuse.

Millennium Millions

Welcome 2000 on New Year's Eve 1999 at Sheds 2 and 4 was the largest dance party yet in Melbourne and one of the biggest Millennium Eve parties in the world. Mark recalls:

> Gatecrasher fucked up because it pissed down with rain ... Creamfields on New Year's Eve—no-one went. People in the UK stayed home because of the myths about the Y2K bug going to shut down everything! People all over the world got really worried about that except in Australia—we don't give a fuck, we just wanna go out and party.

Richie reckons 20,000 people came. Mark says double that. The combined might of Hardware and Future pulled in CJ Bolland, Jeff Mills, Leftfield, Derrick Carter, Paul Daley and Adam Freeland to headline the event. With tickets selling at $130 apiece, Mark and Richie had struck gold. Meanwhile over at the Exhibition Buildings, the third iteration of Halcyon Nights failed to ignite. 'I know that was the beginning of the end for Agent Mad, when Future left them off the New Year's Eve thing,' Richie said. 'They lost a lot of money that Welcome 2000 year, we killed it at Docklands.'[71] The party didn't stop when the sun came up on the new millennium. Thousands of diehard ravers stumbled down Flinders Street to the Royal Botanic Gardens for Summadayze, Future's open-air daytime dance festival. Mark remembers it well:

> That was one of the highlights of my career, standing there at Summadayze the next day. I was really shagged because I'd worked five days straight setting up at the Docks and then going straight from the Docks to the Myer Music Bowl, being there at six in the morning all the way through. But

standing there towards the end, because I always played the closing set in those days, it was the most amazing feeling. And that was the last closing set I ever played.

In just nine years, the Melbourne rave scene had evolved from two hundred ravers diving into the pool at the St Kilda Sea Baths to tens of thousands dancing their way around the Melbourne waterfront. Meanwhile Richie Rich, still ten months shy of his thirtieth birthday, had graduated from backroom DJ to techno millionaire.

After another successful Two Tribes in 2000 and riding high on the Millennium wave, Richie's company Totem/ Hardware partnered with Future again for Welcome 2001. 'We thought we'd definitely drop from 20,000 to maybe 10,000 but it went to like 6000 and all that money we made the year before we lost,' Richie says. He had to sell his jetskis and remortgage his house to pay his debts. 'My mum and dad were about to have a heart attack,' he remembers. 'They were like, "What have you done? You've just lost everything". And I was like, "It's okay mum, I'll work it out"'.

It didn't take Richie long to float back to the top of Australia's dance music hierarchy. From 2002 to 2006, Two Tribes was Australia's most popular dance music festival.[72] Richie dissolved the partnership in 2006 because he felt the music had become too commercial.[73] With Richie gone, Future rebadged Two Tribes as Future Music Festival. Not to be outdone, Richie partnered with OneLove's Peter Raff, Frank Cotela and Dror Erez to launch Stereosonic on Saturday 1 December 2007 in a day format:

> As day events, they became more appealing to a wider audience—people that were like thirty or thirty-five and used to go to clubs in the '80s and '90s started coming to these things again because they were like 12pm to 10pm. Rave culture attracted a crowd that would party pretty hard. The day events toned it down a little bit ... you could be home by midnight and go to work on Monday.[74]

In 2011, Stereosonic attracted 240,000 people across five cities.[75] Two years later, American electronic music giants SFX purchased Stereosonic's parent company Totem OneLove for $75 million.[76] 'I don't have to work again, really,' Richie announced in 2014. 'Who knows? Its early days and I am reconnecting with the music I love and family, and I am enjoying it.'[77]

As its organisers sought to make their event globally competitive with US and European festivals, Stereosonic pushed Australia's axis of dance music culture ever northwards. 'The local has been left behind, overcome by the commercialisation of the transnational mega-festival that can be easily transported piece-by-piece between geographically dispersed cities and re-assembled in mirror image,' Ed Montano writes.[78] He describes Stereosonic as a 'cloned festival' and reports a sense of déjà vu when he visited the Melbourne and Brisbane legs after starting in Sydney: 'Same stage names, artists, sets and branding'.[79] Richie's earlier insistence on tailoring the festival experience to the local market seems to have fallen by the wayside.

Personally, I feel the music festival has become a trope for our globalised times: breadth over depth, quantity over quality and conformity over diversity. I take little pleasure from queueing for an hour to buy a warm, overpriced UDL or dancing 100 metres back from the stage in a midden of plastic cups, broken thongs and chewing gum. It would seem that H2O agrees:

> I don't have 30,000 close friends. I will never have 30,000 close friends. So why the fuck would I hang out in the park with 30,000 people dancing to stupid music that I don't like? I'd rather have a dingy warehouse with 800 people, laser in your eyes burning the irises out of your head. Sweet, that's me. Sweaty, no roof, whatever. But that's the underground. Not GateCrapper, not fucking Summadayze. All those things that came in the mid nineties? Shit. As soon as they started calling raves festivals, fuck off mate, there's no such thing.

Even Mark James acknowledges that festivals 'dragged the coolness out of the scene' as people stopped living for the weekend and saved their cash for the big one. DJ Brewster B. agrees: 'Stereosonic, Summadayze, to me those things aren't raves, they're just big parties with loads of muzzas'.

Chapter 10

TWO TRIBES

Old Skool, New Skool

Commercialisation had brought a new, younger crowd to the door. Many old skool ravers labelled these intruders 'teenie boppers', 'beefcakes' and 'dirty clubbers', the latter a dig at the nightclubbing crowd who many felt didn't belong at raves.[1] However, the most hated new arrivals were the 'muzzas', defined as:

> heavily muscled young men, commonly of Southern European or Middle Eastern background, who use cocaine and steroids, wear tight clothing, have gelled spiky hair, are obsessed with cars, have 'no class', dance in an overly aggressive way and hold extremely sexist views.[2]

The poster boy for this reviled crew of rave-wreckers is the pumped-up shirtless stud dancing in front of the Portaloos at

Stereosonic or Summadayze (aka Steroidsonic and Muzzadayze). The word 'muzza' may derive from 'muscular' on account of the muzza's presumed fondness for working out in the gym, or from 'Mario', a twenty-first century synonym for 'young male wog'. However, some people have suggested to me the word stems from Murray Road, an east-west arterial road that crosses Preston and Coburg in the muzza's heartland of the northern suburbs. Murray Road is a short distance from 'Bell Street Maccas', the McDonalds restaurant on the corner of St Georges Road and Bell Street in Preston reputed to be the muzza's spiritual home.

While primarily a 'Mediterranean' stereotype, some people extend the muzza label to encompass other ethnic backgrounds, including South East Asian and Indian. Muzza should not be confused with muzzer, the latter a derisive term for Muslims—although some muzzas are also Muslims. Usage of the term tends to be strongest with female ravers, perhaps because of the muzza's reputation for sexually predatory behaviour.[3] According to raving folklore, the muzza begins his Saturday evening cruising up and down Chapel Street in his souped-up VL Turbo before loading up on speed and coke, partying at Dome or Mansion nightclub, and ending the night trying to pick up underage 'Marias' or 'Muzza chicks' at 'Muscle Mary's' (aka Virgin Mary's—a recovery club on Commercial Road). When dancing, muzzas supposedly punch the air, roll their hands and keep their feet still.[4] 'Learn to shuffle or you can become a sweaty muzza cokehead. You've got two choices,' Brent, the self-styled 'coolest guy in the world', tells us in the *Melbourne Shuffler* documentary.[5]

Where does this antipathy come from? Unfortunately, in some cases I think it amounts to closet racism and classism. Old skool ravers seldom invoked ethnicity to define their own identity but explicitly drew on ethnic differences to distinguish themselves from muzzas, even though they sometimes come from similar ethnic backgrounds.[6] In 2015, I posted a photo on my Facebook page of partygoers exiting one of German trance-meister Paul van Dyk's gigs at the Docks on a cold June morning. 'You can tell by the dude with his top off that it was van Dyk,' one user quipped. van Dyk plays hard trance, reputedly the muzza's favourite genre. The 'dude' in question is dark-skinned and toned. The muzza is also often characterised as crass and unsophisticated, which sounds to me like bourgeois-speak for working-class. Recall that techno, like punk, developed as a middle-class scene, favoured by university-educated, inner city types.

But I think there's more to this story. Scholar Sarah Thornton uses the term 'subcultural capital' to measure an individual's status within a subculture.[7] Markers of status can be visible, such as well-assembled record collections, or invisible, such as being 'in the know'.[8] Crucially, the longer one has belonged to a scene, the more subcultural capital or 'bragging rights'[9] one accumulates, simply because they happened to be in the right place at the right time. The enduring claim of the nineties raver is that he or she was part of something authentic and underground that has long since disappeared, an 'idealised and now defunct golden era'.[10] 'There was definitely the feeling of being part of something that no-one else was,' Duncan Plank says. 'We belonged to this special group of people who liked this different music which wasn't played on normal radio. We were so far beyond them.' This authentic identity relied on a perceived separation from the mainstream 'other'. But as the lines blurred in the late nineties, old skool ravers desperately sought to distance themselves from the newcomers. A 2006 study found that old skool ravers believed younger 'mainstream' partygoers were replacing the authentic rave focus of dance music, clothes and PLUR with a new narrative based around alcohol, picking up and excessive drug taking.[11] Kim says:

> [t]he scene was very sacred and only a few people knew about it which kept it very pure ... but as soon as the cat got out the bag, you got all these fucking idiots that now thought rave was cool ... I'll never forget the time we went to Brown

Alley in the city and there's some guy on the dancefloor with a bag of coke just holding up the bag and going like this [*she mimes someone greedily snorting coke through his nostril*]. It was a really nasty in-your-face arrogant attitude. You can't have that and have a unified rave scene.

Genre also became a weapon in the battle between old and new skool. Chris Brookman reports that old skool ravers in Sydney dismissed the musical tastes of new skool ravers as 'underdeveloped' and 'cheesy'.[12] Conversely, old skoolers characterise their own tastes as more developed, diverse and intelligent.[13] '[O]ld skool ravers manage to project a desire for continued exclusivity of rave culture; that is if [a] certain genre's music [is] more difficult to appreciate then it will effectively exclude people who are unable to appreciate those genres,' Brookman writes.[14] In Melbourne, divisions emerged between 'difficult' old skool genres like acid house and Detroit techno and more 'accessible' new skool styles such as hard trance.

In the end, it's all relative. No matter how old skool you think you are, someone will always claim it was better before you got there. DJ Brewster B. tries to set the record straight:

> A lot of the older crew were going, 'We're old skool, you're new skool, you don't know anything' … well my response to them was if you're going to call them new skool then where did *you* learn that stuff from? People gave their time to you, held your hand, showed you where the dancefloor was, made sure you didn't go to the dodgy drug dealer—you should be paying it forward. But a lot of people didn't see it that way.

The underground is like the grains of sand in an egg timer. It gradually drains away to nothing and then you flip it over and start again. 'I'm sure you've had everyone say, "Oh, it's not what it used to be",' Aaron Roach says during our interview in 2015. I nod. He continues:

It's not. It's an evolution. What we got to experience was the birth of it, so to speak, and then there would be people older than me who would say, 'We witnessed the birth of it', and then before them it was Mantronix and Afrika Bambaataa and Kraftwerk saw the birth of it …

In the meantime, rave has become a dirty word. Conveniently forgetting that it was the muzza's parents' love of disco that gave birth to dance music in Melbourne, the old skool has surrendered rave to the next generation and developed a collective amnesia that it ever danced to Paul van Dyk.

Genre Overload

'It was just called techno then,' Robbie Burns says of the late eighties scene. 'There was no jungle, drum'n'bass, trance … it was just techno music.' DJ H2O relates a similar story. 'We didn't have any names for it, there were no genres,' he says. 'It was just music that went fast and music that went slow.' But by 1994, techno in Melbourne had already dissolved into at least twelve competing styles: house, deep house, progressive house, gabber, hardcore, jungle, breakbeat, trance, deep trance, acid, hard acid, ambient, and tribal trance.[15] Textbook management theory teaches us that companies can increase revenue in two ways: sell cheaper or differentiate the product. As CD burning technology, file-sharing services like Napster and a thriving DIY production industry eroded their traditional sales channels, record companies pursued an aggressive product differentiation strategy based around celebrity DJs and an ever-expanding suite of genres. This process of genrefication began in England, as Detroit techno pioneer Derrick May explains:

> The English have to have a name for every goddamn thing … and it's always got to have some sort of marketability behind it. I know it's a business but God leap! I mean here we are still trying to retitle and rehash old music with new

titles and new genres ... I mean, what is it now? I don't even know what it is any more, it's always something new, it's always some stupid ass name for music.[16]

It's tempting to dismiss May as out of touch in an Abe Simpson 'I used to be with it but then they changed what *it* was' kind of way.[17] But I think he's onto something. As of 2018, Wikipedia lists over 200 genres of electronic dance music, half of which I've never heard of.[18] Record companies matched genres to specific demographic segments or customer value sets, much like the car industry has done since the sixties. Paradoxically, this explosion of new genres delivered a *less* diverse dancefloor experience. Instead of offering a sonic smorgasbord of different styles, many nightclubs pumped out a steady stream of same-tempo records all night long. They were pigeonholed along genre lines: Savage at the Palladin for house; NRG clubs Hard Kandy with Scott Alert and Jason Midro's Bass Station for hard trance; Monkey at the Palace on Sunday nights for progressive house and US house; tech house with DJs Jeff Tyler and Scott Finemore at Mansion's Phreakin; and minimal techno with Will E Tell and his WetMusik crew at Brown Alley and Storey Hall.

New genres like minimal techno, tech house and progressive house signalled a shift towards 'intelligent' dance music designed as much for the listener as the dancer. 'I'm not even going to justify the progressive house scene that for me was as boring as watching the grass grow,' old skool raver Seth Taylor tells me. 'The likes of Sasha and [John] Digweed and all that cak was a waste of time, but it did have a massive impact on growing the scene in Melbourne.' Writer Simon Reynolds savages progressive house as featureless and long. 'Sasha and Digweed ration out three climaxes per nine-hour set,' he quips.[19] Personally, I think of progressive house as trance's older brother. He still likes to party but has to get up the next morning to go to work and pay the mortgage.

'Music started becoming more about how cool it was,' Aaron Roach tells me. '[But] at the same time, I felt it alienated a lot of punters from going to clubs because they're not playing that kind of funky music any more.' I suggest to Aaron that it sounds very different to a rave party. He nods. 'People at a rave are hanging on every beat, they're waiting for the drop in the record, it was great, it was wonderful.' Rave had lost some of its anger and its thrill. Yet the hangover was only just beginning.

Booze and Bad Drugs

Exiled from the dancefloor for the first half of the decade, by 1996 alcohol was making a comeback. That year, Richie Rich parted ways with his dad and Try Youth, raised the age limit to eighteen and started selling liquor at his Hardware parties. 'I mean we were all getting older. I wanted to drink … if you don't serve alcohol … you end up with a room full of druggies and that's it.' As the nightclubs had discovered in the late eighties, a 'room full of druggies' won't cover your costs. Brewers sought to entice pill-popping ravers back to liquor with sugary alcopops and RTDs (Ready to Drink). By 1999, alcohol had become so pervasive in the scene that *Tekno Renegade* magazine, erstwhile defender of the underground, ran an advertisement for the Bacardi-based alcopop Cubano.[20] Emmy Boudry's choice of corporate sponsors for Street Rave 1999 reveals the changing face of rave in the late nineties. Red Bull and Chupa Chups represent an older crowd still fixated on all-night dancing and ecstasy, while Musashi sports supplements and Stolichnaya vodka herald the influx of younger partygoers with different tastes.

Many ravers lamented alcohol's return to the dancefloor. Adrian Cartwright felt it attracted the wrong crowd:

> [d]evious, scary people would come in and they would hang around at the back. They had this feeling that a lot of ravers were easy targets to pick up. They would get drunk and then start harassing some of the girls or try and pick fights with people. That was something that was really sad.

As alcohol marketers seduced ravers with sexy brand names and vaunted product benefits to give consumers the illusion of choice, Melbourne's druglords took heed. Joe Fitzgerald tells me there were three main types of ecstasy in the early nineties: 'speedy' Purple Speckles, 'lovey dovey' White Doves and 'smacky' Wholemeals. By the late nineties, however, ecstasy as a brand name had become too restrictive. Now, dealers sold 'pills'. The novel *Playgrounds: A Portrait of Rave Culture* follows a crew of Melbourne ravers over New Year's Eve 1998 and New Year's Day 1999. Between them, they ingest a dozen different types of pill, each with its own name, colour, logo, shape, intended effects and price point. At the top of the scale, $80 buys a Triangle White Dove: 'you just tingle all over ... can't fucking move'. Hormones or Sex Pills are 'pure ecstasy' and cost $45. While for those on a budget, the choice includes Gypsies, Pink Suns, Yellow Clouds, White Skies, DLs and MDMA caps.[21]

By the early 2000s, ecstasy use among youth had become 'normalised' in rave and club settings.[22] But the vibe was shifting. 'I started to notice a change in use and quantities,' raver Desiree Laz tells me. 'The drugs seemed to be the prime experience, [not] the rave. People were taking everything together and shooting up trips and e's! The drugs got dirty.' Whereas in the past, ravers had taken drugs primarily to enhance and prolong their experience of the music, people and atmosphere, now it seemed some users went to parties only to 'get wasted'.[23] At the same time, long-term users reported that drug purity and strength had peaked in the early nineties before dealers started cutting 'old skool ecstasy' with adulterants and cheaper substitutes like speed, MDA and LSD.[24] H2O observed it firsthand: '[ecstasy] became cheaper but the quality certainly dropped off if everybody started listening to that trance crap', he jokes.

'I think we had our first overdose from a bad ecstasy tablet at Hardware 7 or something like that,' Richie recalls. 'Then all of a sudden GHB comes along and you're getting eight or ten in one night.' Gamma-Hydroxybutyric acid (GHB), commonly known as GBH (Grievous Bodily Harm) or G, invaded Melbourne's dancefloors in the late nineties. Dangerous enough on its own, mixing it with alcohol can render it lethal. Ecstasy appeared tame, quaint even, compared to GHB and other hard drugs like ketamine (K), ice and heroin.

Richie blames ice and GHB for killing the vibe. After eight people overdosed at a Two Tribes party in the early 2000s, he had to ask Melbourne football hero Jim Stynes to vouch for him in front of the police commissioner and a rampaging media pack. The experience shook Richie and he now openly speaks out against drugs in the scene:

> There is almost no vibe amongst these festivals any more because the drugs they are taking are just unsociable … that's why I don't like going to events any more and it was a contributing reason to why I left after we sold the company … I could have stayed there five years, got paid really well and had a good time [but] the crowds and their knowledge of music … their passion is just not the same [and] the drugs they are taking are destructive and shit.

Fistfights and Machetes

DJs have always been fiercely competitive, scratching off the titles of records or refusing to announce song names on the radio so they could claim exclusive ownership of a track. But as the big money rolled in, the rivalries became increasingly hostile. 'The scene turned nasty when the corporations started,' Richard John tells me. I ask him to explain. 'The Hardware Corporation! Fancy calling it a corporation? Fucking hell! It was the very thing we all went against and then he [Richie] calls it that. And they were a corporation and they were nasty. They wanted it all.' But it seems the Johns gave as good as they got. After one of many verbal spars with Mark James, Heidi walked up to him at Dream nightclub and punched him in the face.

In the early days, organisers wouldn't throw a party on the same night as another promoter. By the late nineties, that rule no longer applied. DJs became pawns in an escalating war. After Hardware and Future split, Mark James forbade 'his DJs' from working for Richie. Meanwhile, Agent Mad's Melanie Dimattina lured boyfriend Will E Tell from Hardware. 'This is a friend of mine of about five or six years, we grew up together in the scene as DJs and I thought that was wrong,' Richie says. 'She should have valued the fact that he and I were friends before that.'

The bitterness and enmity culminated in the poster wars. Many promoters found illegal flyposting gave them far greater exposure than using a traditional advertising business like Rock Posters. 'Everyone, whether they were into parties or not, would feel like the city was coming alive because for four or six weeks beforehand the posters would start appearing, sometimes for four or five parties at once,' Natural 1 says. Promoters paid 'poster boys' like him up to $2 a poster:

> [o]n a 14,000-poster campaign, we were making good coin for a month's work, cash in hand ... we took a graf mindset of designating different areas and getting up along the train lines whereas a lot of the other promoters didn't have that mindset. We were hardcore and quite prepared to break the law because we all used to be graf writers and paint trains ... we started doing the whole Western Ring Road and freeways. It had never been thought of before.

Natural 1 adhered to a strict code of ethics borrowed from his graffiti background. 'If we get it first, don't cap us or go over us because that's disrespectful,' he says. 'Instead, respect us because we got up early, we got smarter and we got there first.' But respect was hard to find in the late nineties scene. Rival gangs ripped down posters and put up their own. There were violent 'beatdowns' and some poster boys narrowly escaped with their lives:

> [This promoter] lived on Brunswick Street. He came out about six in the morning and he literally came up to where our jeep was, we were about to do a turn, and he macheted through the top of the tarp and just missed Richard Maher's head as we were driving off.

Richie also remembers being chased by 'idiots with machetes' in the early morning. When it comes to rave, clearly the sword is mightier than the pen.

On the Move

In Sydney, the rave scene fragmented along sociospatial lines—happy hardcore in the working-class outer west, doof in the trendy inner west, house in the gay-friendly eastern suburbs, and 'commercial' techno on the affluent north shore.[25] By contrast, in Melbourne the scene converged upon the city centre with spokes radiating out to Docklands and Footscray in the west, Fitzroy, Collingwood and Brunswick to the north and South Yarra, Prahran and St Kilda to the south. The geography of rave in Melbourne is no accident. The city's monocentric and radial urban form makes cross-town travel difficult and renders central locations the most accessible and attractive. 'Everything happens in the same five or ten square kilometres of the city, so it doesn't matter where you live, if it's Werribee, Box Hill or Frankston, you've always got to come into the city,' raver Robbie Burns explains. Scholar Kate Shaw has mapped the changing locations of 'indie' cultural activities in Melbourne from 1991 to 2009. Her data show how live music and arts venues have become increasingly clustered in the city centre, suggesting that the 'desire for centrality and easy access to audiences is evidently as important as rent'.[26]

Nevertheless, rental pressures intensified in the nineties as an increasing concentration of highly paid service jobs in the CBD made inner city living more attractive to those with medium and high incomes. In 1992, Melbourne City Council launched Postcode 3000 in a bid to revitalise the city centre and transform Melbourne into a twenty-four-hour globally competitive metropolis. The Council tore down rickety steel awnings, relaxed height limits and paved the laneways with bluestone. Under-capitalised sites became high-rise residential towers while architects repurposed industrial buildings and warehouses as luxury apartments.[27] During this time, many venues disappeared, redeveloped as apartments (TVU, Mansion, Metro, Chevron), hotels (Commerce Club, ZuZus) or offices (Global Village). Lani G recalls when the developers moved in to 'her' precinct of West Melbourne: '[a]ll these big trucks moving in, they're knocking shit down, they're redeveloping stuff … you could just tell by driving down the street it was over.' Down at the docks, even the combined might of Hardware and Future couldn't defeat the inexorable force of gentrification, as Richie explains:

> In late January of 2001 we got the letter from the Docklands Authority saying the lease [for Shed 14] is now no longer available and we are exercising your thirty-day termination clause because we are going to start with new developers. Mark was in Thailand and Jason Ayoubi was on his honeymoon and I was like, 'Fuck'.

Facades were sometimes saved but developers took a wrecking ball to the social and cultural heritage embedded within. If cultural heritage is the 'sum of our past creativities', as scholar Charles Landry maintains, then three decades of dance music history amounted to very little in the eyes of city councillors and planners.[28] The few venues that survived fell prey to rising noise complaints as wealthy residents moved in. 'They couldn't use the Power House in Albert Park any more because the sound got better,' Nimmo Sandilands says. 'We put on one party, and the sound travelled across the lake and nearly rocked the houses on the other side of South Melbourne off their foundations.'

For a brief time, the rave scene defied the law of centrality, gradually pushing outwards as intrepid promoters explored new urban territory away from the threat of complaining neighbours. Mad Rod remembers scouting for sites in West Footscray. 'It was basically old market gardens and huge warehouses … it was just so isolated,' he says. M.U.D. pushed out further, hosting Every Picture parties in Altona and then Laverton North, some 20 kilometres west of the CBD. Others discovered hidden nooks tucked away in industrially zoned areas close to the city centre, such as the sliver of abandoned warehouses and old textile factories sandwiched between Sydney Road and the Upfield train line in Brunswick and the Bertie Street precinct in Port Melbourne. Voodoo tells me he threw some 'sick' parties at the Bertie Street warehouse, right next to the Westgate freeway. 'We had moved back into old skool style for these gigs—fake address, 0055 numbers etc., to avoid any troubles … we had massive sound rigs outside pumping all night.' Hardware jumped the city limits altogether, booking out Kryal Kastle near Ballarat for Hardware Universe on New Year's Eve 1998. 'Even though it was a really tacky looking castle, the fact that it was somewhere different and it was outside … just made it a little more fun,' Adrian Cartwright recalls. Many ravers remember Kryal fondly for DJ Pat Lindsay's impromptu beat boxing when the power cut out.

By the 2000s, however, Melbourne's warehouse party scene was fading fast. 'That shift from all-night raves to that festival explosion happened when city development drove those all-night venues away … and [government] restrictions made it harder and harder to do things all night,' Richie says.[29] The scene had little choice but to retreat to the safety of the CBD where its historical function as a business district afforded some protection against noise complaints. The city centre's diversity of building types, sizes, ages and uses also provided a ready supply of highly adaptable and relatively affordable spaces.[30] Not to mention, of course, that licensed CBD nightclubs are far easier for authorities to monitor and control than a windswept warehouse somewhere in the wilds of the western suburbs.

Rave.com

Unsurprisingly for a movement that worships futurism and technology, the rave scene embraced the internet from the outset. *Cyberthon III* in June 1992 included a bulletin board system (BBS) to allow users to log in and upload graphics that could then be broadcast as part of the transmission. BBSs were a precursor to the world wide web. 'Someone said to me later that what we were doing was like Facebook on TV,' Adem Jaffers tells me. 'I didn't think of it like this at the time but it was a form of social media … the TV medium was like a timeline, it was forever pumping crap out.' Yep, that sounds like Facebook, I think to myself, as I glance at my Newsfeed and see a goat dressed as a duck sitting in a supermarket trolley. In November 1994, RMITV broadcast *Cyberthon IV* over the internet to universities around the world. 'It was a bit like YouTube, it was designed for delivering lectures—I mean NASA picked it up!' Adem recalls. 'We also broadcast on CU-SeeMe, which was the first Skype-type technology on dial-up. The picture was thumbnail size!'

By the mid-nineties, many raves featured computer terminals with internet access, a boon for nerdy kids at a time when only three per cent of Australians had an internet subscription.[31] At Psychic Harmony at Dream nightclub, punters could log on and chat to people overseas using internet relay chat technology. A shadowy figure known as Prof helped set up the network. Ollie Olsen recalls his shock at discovering Prof's true identity years later:

> A friend of mine on Facebook said, 'Hey, isn't it funny what happened to Prof?' I said, 'What do you mean?' He said, 'That's Julian Assange, man.'[32]

A decade before WikiLeaks, you'd find twenty-five-year old Assange running cables and writing code in a dingy Carlton nightclub. Like so many other outcasts, the brilliant yet troubled young man had sought refuge in the darkest corners of the Melbourne underground.

By 1999, the internet had moved to the centre of rave culture, providing a 'noticeboard of clues to the location of future events', a space to share event photos and an 'uncensored outlet' for ravers to voice their concerns about the scene.[33] In Melbourne, the website www.raves.com.au, (aka raves dot com or RDC) nurtured a loyal online community. Ravers no longer had to go to a warehouse party to find likeminded people or listen to new music; all they needed was a computer with an internet connection. Lani G recalls a conversation with an editor from *Beat* magazine in the early 2000s: 'She's like, "The rave scene's dead". I said, "Well it's alive and well in my lounge room"'. The world wide web had compressed the dancefloor into a binary stream of zeros and ones.

The internet democratised the scene, opening up rave to new audiences who previously might have been excluded. But connectedness came at a price. Speak to anyone who raved in the nineties and they'll tell you about the intimate moments they still cherish today: a random hug with a stranger, a deep and meaningful conversation with a new friend or a feeling of oneness with the whole crowd. Kim recalls a Darn Tootin' party at the Docks:

> There was this massive big sliding door at one end and as the sun was coming up at five or six in the morning, someone got a chainsaw and cut off this door and then about twenty people got on the end and pushed the door open and the whole room went ballistic as the sun poured through.

The internet can never replicate experiences like this. In fact, the ubiquity of smartphones and social media renders such intimacy almost impossible nowadays. During my interview with Mad Rod, he grabs my iPhone off the table. 'If I was to do a gig now, I would make a rule that you cannot bring these inside, you've got to leave them at home, too bad, you're not coming in,' he declares. I raise a wry smile. We both know it would never work. American teenagers send an average of 120 to 200 electronic messages a day.[34] My own observations at the University of Melbourne suggest this is a low estimate for Australian youth. Go to a warehouse party these days and selfie photos will be up on Facebook the next day. The cult of 'I' triumphs over everything, even the cult of the DJ. Rave, like religion, requires us to give up some part of ourselves to something bigger. But first we need to look up from our screens.

Music to Make You Melt

I could, and perhaps should, end the book here. But if my readers will permit me (and if John Fowles fans can forgive the plagiarism), I'd like to submit an alternative ending. Undergrounds evolve continuously. As one falls prey to the media, the marketers and the internet, another rises to fill its place. 'Rave' became persona non-grata in the underground lexicon and 'techno' reeked of commercialism. So people started saying 'tekno' instead. Tekno sought to strip away rave's commercial packaging and rediscover its authentic roots in experimental electronic music, psychedelic spirituality and grassroots resistance. When *Techno Renegade* magazine rebranded to *Tekno Renegade* in December 1998, it was evident the zeitgeist had shifted.

But the underground tekno revolution had begun much earlier than that. In 1993, at least one club successfully resisted the German trance invasion. Club Filter at Lounge paired techno renegades Rudeboy and Mad Rod with an alternative music crowd seeking to escape kandy ravers and Cosmic Baby's chord progressions. Rod recalls:

You'd have friends of ours in their forties who were from

the old rock'n'roll punk movement still going out because basically they're not interested in anything normal … we'd have university students who were really 'out there', old skool people from the ages of thirty-five up to sixty, techno enthusiasts whoever they were, and also a lot of the gay scene would come here too but not the cliques … and even the ravers who used to come were more of the hardcore ones, not the ones who want to go out on the weekend only.

Rod and Rudeboy played 'extreme' music ranging from acid techno to experimental electronica and 'trans-sexual hardcore'. 'I wanted to make people melt,' Rod says. Filter also featured guest DJs and regular live acts including drag queens and 'electro poets'. Rod calls Filter a 'techno social club':

> I found that most people I spoke to were shunned people … they'd come to me and say, 'I need to talk to you, I'm going to kill myself', 'I need to talk to you because I think I'm gay' or 'I need to talk to you because I've got no money' … I was like the techno social worker … the music was actually secondary.

Rod and Rudeboy tried to provide a safe haven for drug addicts, the mentally ill and kids from broken homes. Kids like Prime Suspect. Growing up in an affluent middle-class family, Prime Suspect's father's death from cancer left his mother bitter and impoverished.[35] By year 10, he found computers better company than his relatives and retreated into cyberspace where he met fellow hackers Trax and Mendax (aka Julian Assange).[36] The trio used RMIT's computers as a launchpad for cyber-attacks on Australian and overseas networks. But then on 29 October 1991, the Australian Federal Police raided Prime Suspect's home.[37] The trauma from the raid triggered a hopeless cycle of dope, ecstasy, speed and rave. Prime Suspect spent his weekends at warehouse parties and Wednesday nights at Club Filter:

He didn't consider himself addicted to drugs, but the drugs had certainly replaced his addiction to hacking ... dancing to techno-music released him. Dancing to it on drugs cleared his mind completely, made him feel possessed by the music ... he liked to go to techno-night at The Lounge, a city club, where people danced by themselves, or in small, loose groups of four or five. Everyone watched the video screen which provided an endless stream of ever-changing, colourful computer-generated geometric shapes pulsing to the beat.[38]

Rod and Rudeboy ran Filter for the love. The club was never a successful commercial venture. 'I remember once we had one of the biggest nights ever and we made a dollar profit and we put the dollar coin on the table and gasped,' Rod recalls. Underground didn't pay the rent. Nevertheless, when the club closed its doors in June 2003, it held the record for Australia's longest running techno night.

Psychic Harmonies and Devil Fish

By 1993, Ollie Olsen was setting a new course into the depths of the Melbourne underground. Third Eye's second release *Ancient Future* broke with the sung vocals and synthpop rhythms of Ollie's eighties oeuvre and augured a new Goa-inspired direction for his music:

> [t]he reason electronic music was invented in my mind was to attain all those sounds, frequencies and scales that you couldn't get from traditional instruments ... and it is those undiscovered frequencies that are leading the charge back into [Goa] trance music.[39]

Clearly unable to pick up Ollie's 'undiscovered frequencies', his record company Regular Records refused to release *Ancient Future* and sacked him from the label.[40] So Ollie started his own label with Andrew Till and Bruce Butler. 'There wasn't much going on because no-one had actually made that jump, especially in releasing the more leftfield kind of music,' Ollie told *Tekno Renegade*. 'So Psy Harmonics started out as a techno label ... to fill the void for artists wanting to produce interesting music.'[41]

Psy Harmonics supported some of Melbourne's best-loved underground artists including Lumukanda (Dominic Hogan), Mystic Force, Psyko Disko, Rip Van Hippy, the wonderfully named Antediluvian Rocking Horse and Steve Law's Zen Paradox project. Zen Paradox's debut album *Eternal Brainwave* (released in 1993) featured a modification to the Roland TB-303 called the Devil Fish.[42] Developed by Melburnian Robin Whittle, the Devil Fish added more knobs and buttons to the 303 to extend the range of sounds that could be produced.[43] Richie Rich recalls driving out international artists like Richie Hawtin and Hardfloor to Whittle's house in Thornbury:

> They'd heard about this legendary Australian guy who had made these modifications and I'd say, 'Yeah, I know the guy, he's done my 303, I'll take you out to meet him right away'.

Psy Harmonics pushed the Goa trance sound in Australia and influenced the burgeoning scene overseas. In 1994, Goatrance became a marketable genre in the UK when Paul Oakenfold played a Goa mix on Radio 1 after Ollie introduced him to the new sound.[44] Meanwhile, Ray Castle built links between the Australian and Japanese scenes, primarily through his collaboration with techno artist Masayuki Kurihara. 'Masaray has a spiritual quality to it and it also has what I would call a real Goa feeling about it,' Castle said in 1995.[45] At MDS, Richie exported Psy Harmonics to the US, Europe and Asia. His efforts led to Australian artists appearing in UK publications *DJ Mag* and *Mixmag* and licensing deals in Germany and Belgium.[46] Back in Melbourne, the Psy Harmonics crew frequently ran the chillout room at raves. Journalist Chris Johnston recalls seeing Ollie and company DJing cross-legged behind a long low table covered in fruit and candles 'like a Renaissance painting'.

Scholar Graham St John lauds Psy Harmonics as an 'enduring platform for genre-defying electronic psychedelia'.[47] He's careful not to use the label psytrance, a portmanteau for psychedelic trance that he claims didn't emerge until the late nineties.[48] Ollie similarly distances himself from what nowadays is a global phenomenon. '[Psy Harmonics] had nothing to do with psytrance, the label was actually short for Psychic Harmonics,' he tells me. 'I think someone took that name from our label. But it should have been called psychic trance, not psychedelic trance.' Ollie tells me his early work with Psy Harmonics excited him because the music pushed boundaries and 'did stuff to your head that wasn't normal'. However, over time he felt the music had become formulaic and repetitive, exactly the reverse of what Psy Harmonics had set out to achieve. After a brief flirtation with drum'n'bass, he made his exit from the techno scene in the late nineties:

> I thought there are so many types of music to make and for me it wasn't exciting me any more. I had gone through various stages and tried different things and just didn't see the point any more because musically if you did something too out of bounds people just didn't get it. It's the kind of music I guess will be appreciated in years to come.

While vinyl remained the preferred medium for DJs, home listeners preferred the convenience of the CD, which by the mid-nineties had replaced the audiocassette in popularity. Andrez Bergen believed good techno should work on the dancefloor and in the lounge room. Speaking about his 1998 CD album *Pop Tart*, released under the moniker Little Nobody, he says he wanted to make 'an interesting listening experience' as well as satisfying his DJ impulse to 'make parts of it up-tempo as well'.[49] Andrez boasts impressive qualifications when it comes to Melbourne techno. After writing his university thesis on seventies industrial music, he contributed to and later edited Zebra, the dance section of *In Press* magazine.[50] In 1995, Andrez started If? Records with Brian Huber and Mateusz Sikora. Their first release, *Zeitgeist — Spirit Ov Thee Times,* was a compilation CD of underground Melbourne techno artists. The CD included a Thomas P Heckmann remix of FSOM's 'Welcome', 'chillout grooves' by Sonic Voyagers and TR-Storm and 'hardcore acid grinders' from Voiteck, Pura and Soulenoid.[51] Subsequent *Zeitgeist* compilations in 1996 and 1997 featured the cream of Melbourne's techno talent, including Artificial (Nicole Skeltys), Black Lung (David Thrussell, formerly of Snog) and Honeysmack (David Haberfield). But running an independent label in Australia was hard work. 'We were maybe averaging 200 to 300 unit sales for each album', Andrez told the ABC. 'So, generally, we made a loss on each release. It's a labour of love.'[52]

Filter, Psy Harmonics and If? represented a new breed of artists and promoters in Melbourne clamouring to regain the underground. For some people, however, the city still hung under a cloak of commercialism. It was time to go bush.

The Bush Doof

In 1992, Sydney techno collective Non Bossy Posse shared a two-storey Victorian terrace in Erskineville, a few hundred metres from Sydney Park. Annoyed by the relentless beat pounding through the walls, their German neighbour Helga banged on the door and yelled, 'What is this Doof Doof Doof all night long? … this is not music'.[53] Locating Helga's outburst as the birth of doof is a much-loved fable in Australian techno—although it might not be true. DOOF is also the name of a major psytrance festival and record company in Israel that seems to have emerged independently.[54]

In Australia, 'doof' has several meanings: it is perhaps best known as an onomatopoeic style of music, introduced to the world as 'Australia's slang term for techno' on the back of the Doof Wagon that featured in the 2015 action movie *Mad Max: Fury Road*.[55] Doof also refers to a 'rave underculture' whose participants shun passive consumption of mainstream club culture and seek to escape from the 'encroaching forces of state, capital and cliché'.[56] In this book, however, I generally use doof to mean a not-for-profit DIY event, often held outdoors, where people dance all night to electronic music.[57]

Graham St John reports that 'feral hippy' doofs held on moon cycles and solstices have been operating in northern NSW since 1992.[58] Some people have told me they attended outdoor parties (also known back then as bush raves or forest festivals) held on family farms or in state forests in the Melbourne hinterland around the same time. These early bush doofs were low budget affairs— raver Robbie Burns remembers traipsing around a forest with a photocopied map to find 'dudes with a sound system' and no running water. While the bush doof has roots in the UK sound system and free party culture (see Chapter Three), the Australian scene took on a distinctly local character. This was partly from necessity—a dusty rust-red paddock enclosed behind a shotgun-protected electric fence lacks the carefree ambience of a lush, verdant meadow in the 'right-to-roam' rolling hills of Hampshire. Eucalypt forests in national and state parks provided a safer and greener environment.

In May 1993, Spiro Boursine threw his eighteenth birthday party in a disused quarry at Mount Tanglewood in the Toolangi State Forest, two hours' northeast of Melbourne. He called the party Mystic Madness and booked Zen Paradox to play live.[59] Spiro had previously run the Nebula and Biomechanoid parties in Melbourne but this was his first foray into the bush. He returned to Mount Tanglewood on Saturday 18 December 1993, but this time he printed up hundreds of green and white flyers and hired 'electromagnetic wave generators' Dominic Hogan and Andrew Till. The party was called Earthcore. Between 1993 and 1998, Earthcore invited ravers and doofers to explore a range of Victorian bush locations, including Echuca, Lake Eildon and Mount Disappointment. 'I went to one of the first ones out at Mount Franklin, which is an extinct volcano, and you can drive up the side of this hill into the old crater and we had a party there,' Scott Adcock tells me. Just as ravers looked forward to a new secret warehouse location for each party, Earthcore patrons from far and wide relished the sense of adventure that came with exploring a new site. 'At the last party we did at Heathcote last New Year's Eve, about half of the number plates were from NSW,' Earthcore co-founder Karl Fitzgerald claimed in 1998. 'I think half of it comes down to the fact that it's a test of your survival skills … It's like a grown-up version of your school excursion.'[60] Kim vividly remembers her first Earthcore. 'We got there, it was already night time and it was incredible to see the whole festival lit up with lights.'

By the summer of 1998 and 1999, Melburnians could choose from at least half a dozen bush doof parties, including Alien Nation, Bosh, Psycorroboree, Transelements and Green Ant's Rainbow Serpent Festival. Frank Venuto, Krusty (real name Eugene Gaffney) and Sugar (real name Felix Hamer) formed Green Ant in 1997. After running warehouse parties and their own record label in Melbourne, they transplanted their transcendental flavour of psychedelic trance into the pristine bushland of the Wombat State Forest in January 1998. Rainbow Serpent remains the longest running continuous outdoor electronic music festival in Australia.[61]

Bush doofs typically have a psychedelic aura and psytrance is usually played. But doofs are more than just music and mushrooms. Many parties tried to foster a deep ecological, cultural and spiritual connection with the land itself. In 1997, Spiro told *Techno Renegade* that after each Earthcore, the organisers picked up a year's worth of camper's rubbish, leaving the sites cleaner than they were before.[62] Some promoters went further, leveraging their events to support 'green' political causes such as opposing old-growth logging or protesting against freeway expansion.[63] Psytrance DJ Alex Lambert writes that bush doofs are 'laced with the rhetoric of peace and love, New Age idealism, eco-spirituality and shaman magic'.[64] None of this is new, of course. In fact, Lambert's words could have come straight out of the M.U.D. manifesto. But whereas the Global Village faithful had worshipped at the holy altar of rave inside their three-storey brick temple, doofers found communion under the stars through primitive stomping beats and psychedelically altered states of consciousness.

Other people sought to integrate an Indigenous narrative into doof, paying homage to the land's original inhabitants, whom two centuries of white oppression had displaced and marginalised. Tribal drumming and the didgeridoo found their way into psytrance and painted Aboriginal faces with Uluru backdrops appeared on CD covers.[65] Graham St John reports that psyculture exhibits a 'typical deference ... towards Indigenous custodians who would be regularly evoked as ritual and cultural authorities'.[66] Connecting with the land and the native peoples it had once housed allowed doofers to tap into a primal beat, as Krusty explains:

> The island continent of Australia has had an intimate relationship to dance with the indigenous people of the land stomping on the earth for over 60,000 years. My understanding is that this geomantic practice set up a resonant frequency across the continent which is still active today, and thus offers a totally unique opportunity for the modern trance-dance-entheogen experience—or as we call them now, 'bush doofs'.[67]

But despite all the lip service paid to elders past and present, doof was still a whitefella's game. For example, Rainbow Serpent referenced the Indigenous creator spirit in name but the organisers didn't invite participation from traditional owners until 2007, nine years after the festival began.[68] Moreover, the festival's scheduling on the Australia Day weekend, a public holiday that celebrates European occupation, could be considered culturally insensitive.

The bush doof has become one of the most enduring expressions of the nineties underground rave scene. Telling its story is beyond the scope of this book and others have achieved this admirably elsewhere.[69] But as with all popular movements, commercialism is just one big paycheck away. What had begun in 1993 with a $10 donation and four DJs playing from the back of a ute, had by 1997 transformed into three events over three months attracting thousands of partygoers paying $26 a time. That year's Earthcore lineup featured local talent Andrew Till, Swytek, Artificial, Cara Caama and Antedeluvian Rocking Horse and guests from Sydney, Byron Bay and Israel. For New Year's Eve 2000, the Earthcore crew held a week-long festival in Lindenow, three hours to the east of Melbourne. On seeing the flyer, Graham St John realised something had changed:

> Earthcore's key summer event ... would be divided into four 'primal element zones': earth, air, fire and water. It didn't take a particularly astute observer to note that this cultural production ... is designed principally to accumulate the fifth element: $.[70]

Yet again, the mighty dollar had drilled through the foundations and caved in the underground. '[Y]ou can't live in the past,' Spiro insisted in a 2003 interview. 'Other things come into place that counteract that loss of intimacy ... we play a wider range of music now.'[71] While Earthcore was busy entertaining a new crowd, Melbourne's dreadlocked army had two choices: pack up their kombis, fold away their rainbow flags and truck off to Byron Bay; or take their bongos to the street.

Reclaiming the Street

In the late nineties, crews of highly politicised ravers united with environmental and social justice activists to campaign for nuclear disarmament, clean energy and anti-globalisation. Techno had become the folk music of the nineties and the beat resonated to the sound of grassroots democracy.

Underground subcultures are natural breeding grounds for direct action. An alliance of punk bands and 'anarchist squatters' based around Newtown in Sydney had been politically active since the eighties. Calling themselves the Jellyheads Collective, they tried to close down the Sydney stock exchange in 1988 and blockaded the Aidex international arms fair in Adelaide in 1991.[72] Despite reluctance from some hardcore punks who mistrusted techno's capacity to further their political aims, the Jellyheads gradually switched on to the electronic rhythms seeping in from Goa, Koh Phangan and England in the early nineties.[73] In 1993, they renamed themselves Vibe Tribe in honour of their heroes, UK free party roving activists, Spiral Tribe. They began throwing all-night free parties at Sydney Park, passing round a bucket to raise money for a range of political causes.[74] Their non-violent resistance came to an abrupt end at the Freequency party in April 1995 when police with batons, riot shields and dogs charged the 'offensive dancefloor' at 2am, arresting nine and putting two ravers in hospital.[75]

'Dancing all night on all manner of substances is an active resistance, is an active rebellion in itself,' Graham St John writes. 'The freedom from the nuclear family, TV, the dominant social mores [and] the parent culture that such environments contextualise is really important.'[76] Natural 1 agrees. He tells me rave was 'anti-branding, anti-eighties greed, anti-corporate culture, anti-all culture'. Melbourne never quite gained the level of activist momentum achieved in Sydney but the southern capital's post-rave tekno tribes were nonetheless 'fashionably committed' to pleasure and politics.[77] In June 1998, Robbie Burns helped Krusty put on the Yellowcake rave at Monash University's Caulfield campus, campaigning against the imminent construction of the Jabiluka uranium mine in Kakadu National Park:

> We were basically doing it for free, we did all the organising for free, we got the venue for free, all the DJs played for free ... and all the cash that came across the counter in ticket sales was 100 percent deposited in Aboriginals' bank accounts so that they could buy supplies to protest ... I deliberately got one DJ from each scene and then we met them to make sure that no-one else was going to organise parties that weekend so we had a free weekend.

That same year, mobile sound systems invaded Melbourne's streets as Reclaim the Streets (RTS) paired militant urban planning with window-shaking beats. Challenging the physically destructive and socially divisive power of the automobile, RTS is an unrehearsed 'guerrilla' street festival that explores what a world without cars might look like.[78] The first Melbourne event on 28 March 1998 closed off Victoria and Lygon Streets and ended with a 'free community doof' in Flagstaff Gardens.[79] For the 1999 edition, participants assembled in Carlton Gardens and stopped traffic through the city before heading to a 'secret destination' with 'hard arse electronic sounds' from Krusty, Sugar, Jason Midro, Psyburbia and Cara Caama.[80] Techno-fuelled resistance peaked in Melbourne in September 2000 when ravers joined forces with anti-capitalist protestors to blockade Crown Casino during a World Economic Forum meeting. Despite frequent police intimidation, the protestors maintained a carnival atmosphere for three days. They hung banners, daubed graffiti on the barricades, held aloft giant puppets and hauled around a mobile sound system painted to look like a drum of nuclear waste.[81]

Many ravers, however, shied away from the political side of rave. 'I was never sucked into that kind of change the world thing and I don't think most people were, either,' Nimmo Sandilands says. 'We were too middle-class for that.' One young pair of DJs, however, were determined to keep channelling the 'radical potential' of techno.

Teriyaki Anarki Saki

On 23 May 1996, DJ Slack and Dee Dee launched Teriyaki Anarki Saki at Sadie's Bar, a former Japanese restaurant in Coverlid Place in the city. The club's website explains the story behind the name:

> The Japanese restaurant and our very naïve but well-meaning fascination with Japanese culture in general, were the catalyst for such an unlikely brand. But the Anarki … well that's a more personal thing and it no doubt stems from our fierce determination to party hard our own way.[82]

DJ Slack and Dee Dee arrived in Melbourne in 1995 after immersing themselves in a range of underground techno cultures across Australia and overseas. In Melbourne, they drew inspiration from recently arrived Sydney and Byron Bay artists and the 'hand built, risky, improvised' DIY warehouse party aesthetic embodied by crews like Imagineering, Ozone and Vibe Tribe.[83] Dee Dee had played with Vibe Tribe in Sydney and was on the decks spinning an 'Irish jig, doof track' when NSW police violently gatecrashed the Freequency party in Sydney Park.[84]

Teriyaki on Thursdays added a third night to the underground tekno calendar, slotted between Filter on Wednesdays and Global Warming, a Sunday night club at Little Reata (now Boney) on Little Collins Street. Between 1996 and 1998, Teriyaki moved five times—to Fitzroy, Thornbury and then Collingwood, before returning to the CBD for a brief stint at the Velvet Lounge followed by a three-year residency at the Hi-Fi Bar on Swanston Street. The Fitzroy venue sat above an accessories store on Brunswick Street. Two decades earlier, the Little Bands had thrashed and clanged with impunity in a shopfront a few hundred metres away. Now, twenty years of gentrification meant a mere creaking floorboard would raise the neighbours' ire. The club received 'hundreds' of noise complaints.[85]

Davide Carbone, Adam '8bit' Fischer, Chris Coe, Julian Culpan (aka Mute Freak) and Simon Slieker joined residents Dee Dee and

Steve Robbins on the decks. The scores of guests included Will E Tell, Voiteck, Honeysmack, Rudeboy, H2O, Andrez, Richie Rich, Steve Law and internationals Luke Slater, Claude Young and Thomas Schumacher. Over time, Teriyaki expanded their initial acid techno focus to embrace a broad range of classic and emerging techno styles and cutting-edge DJ techniques. DJ H2O commends the Teriyaki crew for playing a 'grungy techno sound' at a time when Melbourne rave generally meant piano anthems and hands in the air. Dee Dee and DJ Slack gave air to established artists and 'new school' DJs alike. Slovenian hard minimal one week, Japanese techno the next—with Teriyaki you never quite knew what to expect.

From its Fitzroy incarnation, Teriyaki integrated performance art into its lineup. Exploding birthday cakes, umbilical cord sex change operations or a young woman pulling freshly made toast out of her head—the club scoured the city for the most bizarre performers and put them centre stage. Visual artists also contributed their creativity and expertise. 'It was a new level of decor and perhaps only crews like "Every Picture" in their halcyon Global Village days would have gone to more effort to commission underground art for a dance party in Melbourne,' DJ Slack writes of a 1999 party at the Hi-Fi.[86]

Whether it was hauling bass bins onto the streets or redefining the parameters of art to sidestep mainstream club culture, the tekno revolution offered avenues of protest for those looking to subvert the system. But the most enduring source of resistance came from the relative safety of the suburban bedroom.

Anyone Could Make Music

Marshall Jefferson claims that house 'let the non-musician know that he could make music'.[87] The tools of electronic music offered creative opportunities to people who didn't know a crotchet from a quaver. 'Most of the guys I came across weren't trained musically and it was that naivety, that lack of knowledge about which notes are meant to sound right together, that created the techno sound and the house sound', Josh Abrahams says. A techno producer, he argues, only needs to learn how to sample a chord and play a few basic notes on a keyboard. Trance requires slightly more musical knowledge: enough to hold one chord and slide the fingers across to the next one. If you played too slowly, it didn't matter, you simply used a sequencer to speed it up. For kids too frightened to get up on stage and play guitar, techno gave them a less daunting entry into the world of music.

In 1994, Aaron Roach started writing music using Scream Tracker, a music tracker that translated the keys on a standard QWERTY keyboard into notes (for example Q might be C, W would be D etc.). A committed technophile, by 1995 Aaron was collaborating with American producers over the internet:

> They'd send parts over and I'd work on it and send it back to them for further production. But sharing files was just ridiculous! We're talking 14.4 kilobits per second modems—I'd upload to an FTP site and it would take forty-five minutes for a 3-megabit file.

Aaron couldn't afford a pair of decks so he used MP3 digital audio workshop software to emulate the turntable experience, allowing him to cut up and mix different tracks together: 'you could pitch bend, there'd be sliders on the side of each deck and if you were lucky you would have a split cue on your headphones so you could listen to the cue and listen to the live/master.'

By 1999, producers could download free mixing and sampling technology from shareware internet sites.[88] Meanwhile, the internet delivered a cheaper way for artists to distribute their music than going through the traditional channels. Scholar Chris Gibson described the computerisation of musical production as 'wonderfully democratic':

> [i]f you think about the kinds of technologies that were required to produce music in the '60s or '70s, to get a recording of decent quality enough that you'd be able to

commercially distribute it, you're talking about literally millions of dollars' worth of equipment in recording desks [and] in the machinery to be able to press recordings; you do all of that within a computer now.[89]

But freedom from the capitalist machine offered no guarantee of commercial success. 'It's all very good and well to sit in a studio and make music, but to then be able to market it and get it manufactured and get it distributed yourself, as an independent, is a really difficult thing to do, especially from Australia', Adelaide producer Cinnaman told the ABC in 2003.[90] Even the lucky few who secured record deals with MDS or Shock received no promise of financial return.[91] Unable to access 'real-world' distribution networks, some producers released their music for free. But free music only led to a seemingly exponential increase in material and convinced a generation of listeners they no longer needed to pay for music.[92] New technology also did little to empower women in the scene. In 2003, only 5 percent of Melbourne's techno producers were female.[93]

Yet despite their struggles, Melbourne's artists in the nineties built a legacy of techno that continues to feed a healthy and world-renowned local scene. 'I think it laid the foundation for what we have now and it created a soundtrack for the kids growing up whose older brothers and sisters were listening to this stuff', Kiss FM's Timmy Byrne says. Today, Melbourne producers like Will Sparks are at the forefront of the global techno industry. In 2013, Ministry of Sound picked up on the emerging 'Melbourne Sound', releasing a *Melbourne Bangers* compilation. They followed up in 2014 with *Melbourne Bounce Sessions,* which sought to 'elasticize your ears with the sound of the Melbourne underground'.[94] This new take on the Melbourne scene caught Timmy by surprise:

> Here I am amongst it all and it's one of these things that just popped up out of nowhere … What is Melbourne Bounce? It's sort of morphed into EDM. The Dutch sound. Dutch

became electro. But then again, Dutch ... there's been several waves of that. I remember in the early nineties, it was all Dutch house but it wasn't Dutch like it is now. And the italo stuff in the early eighties—that was called electro.

Timmy's words prove that the only certainty in dance music is the constant recycling of the past. Listen to any Top 40 dance track now and the chances are you'll hear the ghost of nineties techno rippling through the mangled vocals and cheesy piano chords. Writing about the contemporary American EDM scene, Simon Reynolds claims that 'the riffs and vamps, the pulses and pounding beats ... could have been beamed straight from Gatecrasher or Love Parade circa 1999'.[95] Such reckless appropriation from the past incenses Mad Rod:

> EDM usually has been regurgitated from amazing original electronic dance music and now sounds like awful shit—what the fuck?! A lot of this EDM stuff I've seen, especially overseas, has got no individualism at all, it's McDonald's music for the masses. It's fucking hideous. It's like junk food, it's junk music!

'The EDM resurrection isn't so much déjà vu but a rebranding coup', Reynolds writes. 'EDM is what was previously called electronica (in 1997) and techno (in 1991) ... What is different is the overall sound ... [it's like] Monster Energy drink for the ears.'[96]

A Special and Unique Time

Lounge, Melbourne, August 2014. Mad Rod has spent the last two hours telling me about his life in the Melbourne rave scene during the nineties. I ask him what he feels when he thinks back to that time. 'I think how lucky we were back then [and] what a beautiful time it was,' he says. 'It's like how old grannies used to talk about the thirties and I can now understand and relate to that because it really isn't beautiful anymore.' I suggest that perhaps he's feeling nostalgic. 'Yes, that's the word', he replies. 'Nostalgia. I'm so glad I have those beautiful memories.'

Rod's feelings are shared by almost anyone I speak to who raved during the nineties. 'I wish I could be stuck in that forever,' Steve Robbins says. 'It was the best time of my life.' Kim agrees. 'It was a very special and unique time,' she says. 'Why can't it still be the same? Where did it all go and why did it disappear?' And yet, in 2018, parties like Electric Gardens and Rainbow Serpent soak up tens of thousands a year, while illegally occupied warehouses in Port Melbourne and Yarraville vibrate to the thump of underground techno. 'Melbourne still loves to dance,' Robbie Burns says. 'I walk through the city and I see a lot of kids wearing Techno Shuffle gear … everything's got to have a dash of fluoro on it.' Cheap flyers plastered to Brunswick lampposts scream 'Techno Rave!' and warehouse party invites regularly arrive in my Facebook Newsfeed. Organisers billed one such party as a 'dodgy rave from the 90s':

> For this type of event we wanted to keep the element of rawness that underground abandoned warehouse raves were known for back in the day. You used to find out about the location just hours before and no other details, and this would be part of the adventure.[97]

Maybe the rave scene didn't disappear. Perhaps we all just got older. 'Definitely not,' Kim insists. 'Melbourne has moved on. You can't have a gritty rave scene with this squeaky clean, latte-sipping, cocktail-guzzling, coke-snorting group of people.' Davide Carbone agrees. 'Melbourne's way too popular to be cool now and too affluent to be funky.'

We all have a tendency to romanticise the past, to think that life was better, simpler and more elegant when we were younger. But perhaps, in the case of nineties rave, it really was. Instead of simply importing an off-the-shelf subculture lock stock and two smoking bass bins from London, Melbourne's raving community blended a searing passion for music, dancing and art with a deep respect for an underground scene built on seventies punk and eighties gay dance party culture. For all its subversive undertones, the scene had a childlike innocence that I think has been lost forever. People weren't afraid to go out, take risks, meet new people and have fun because they knew they'd feel at home in a likeminded community.

A quarter of a century later, nineties ravers share a fondness for fun times, lifelong friendships and a gratitude for having been in the right place at the right time. In rave, they found a level of self-awareness and a deep respect for the world that has stayed with them. Nineties rave also struck a balance between safety and freedom, something I feel we have lost sight of now, where young people's bids for autonomous fun are thwarted by lockout laws, licence freezes and over-zealous authorities. Writing about the Sydney pub and club lockout laws in 2016, businessman Matt Barrie states, '[a] special little person has decided that there is a certain time at night when we are all allowed to go out, and there is a certain time that we are allowed into an establishment and a certain time that we are all supposed to be tucked into bed.'[98] With the rise of the daytime festival format, that time is forever getting earlier.

In 2013, 15,000 young people turned up to an impromptu all-night New Year's Eve dance party at Edinburgh Gardens, a park in Melbourne's inner north. The following year, Yarra City Council paid $250,000 to erect fencing and hire security guards to prevent a repeat occurrence. Letting the event happen and then paying for the clean up would have cost just $30,000.[99] It seems the authorities today are afraid of young people having unstructured and unsupervised fun. They've clearly forgotten that dance music emerged as the soundtrack to a generation of young people fleeing decades of oppression. 'The rave scene was driven by youth angst,' Heidi John reminds us. 'Look at today, people are pushed so far against the wall now. It's ripe for a re-emergence.' I hope so. This time, I'll be standing at the front of the queue.

Acknowledgments

This book would never have come about without the warmth, love and support of the Melbourne raving community. A massive shout to Brewster B. for opening the door to the scene and putting me in touch with so many generous individuals eager to have their story told. Huge props to Natural 1 who has kept the faith since the beginning and whose gentle prods and kicks got me moving when my wheels were spinning. My warmest appreciation to the hundreds of ravers who have expressed their support via my website (www.technoshuffle.com.au) and Facebook page (www.facebook.com/technoshuffleAU).

Thanks to all those who granted interviews and shared their memories for this book: Aaron Roach, Adem Jaffers, Adrian Cartwright, Andrew Peter Collins, Braden Schlager, CJ Bolland, Davide Carbone, Duncan Plank, Emmy Boudry, Gavin Campbell, Grant Harrison, Heidi John, Ian Spicer, Jade John, Jason Rudeboy, Joe Fitzgerald, Joe Wiezcorek, Josh Abrahams, Lani Greer, Marcus, Mark James, Nimmo Sandilands, Ollie Olsen, Phil Voodoo Woodman, Richard John, Richie McNeill, Robbie Burns, Rupert Keiller, Sam Frantzeskos, Scott Adcock, Sean Kelly, Sid Sidney,

Singtoh-Roddajun Dogon, Stef, Steve Robbins, Terrence Ho and Timmy Byrne.

Special thanks to the many ravers, DJs, party people and others who contributed stories, commentary and/ or illustrations: Andrea Jerzyna, Andrew Ong, Andrew Till, Beck Hill, Chris Gill, Chris Hatzis, Chris Johnston, Cyclone Wehner, Damian Stephens, Damon Weetman, David, Desiree Laz, Eddy Sarafian, Fraser Nairn, Jandy Rainbow, Janee Alway, Jason Platts, Jules Galloway, Kane Goldsworthy, Katie Lou, Lucas Hipkins, Lucien Fender, Lu Diamond, Matt Newton, Merowyn Hampton, Michael McLean, Michelle Chrimes, Mick Smith, Olivia Geselle, Peter Sayers, RA Feutz, Richard Maher, Richard Tropea, Robert O'Farrell, Ryan Anderson, Seth Taylor, Sioux Dollman, Spiro Boursine, Steven Niewinski, Steven Winstanley, Susan M. King, Toby Borrow and Vanessa Neil. My sincere apologies to anyone I've forgotten.

A huge shout to Nick Henderson and the Australian Lesbian and Gay Archives for helping me sift through the ALSO archives. Thanks to the University of Melbourne for keeping me in gainful employment, allowing me the freedom to pursue this project *and* pay the rent.

My special thanks to Nat McGlone and David Nichols for helpful feedback on earlier drafts. Full props to Larissa Tittl for her superstar services as editor and 'agent'. Thank you David Tenenbaum and the team at Melbourne Books for seeing my vision and taking a chance on a dance music book in a rock'n'roll city. A big thanks to Iryna Byelyayeva for her scrupulous edit and thoughtful suggestions. Any errors in this edition are all mine.

My raving journey began after friends James Hill and Leon Easter and my brother Neil Fleckney turned me on to the music in 1995. Much love and thanks - it's been too long between drinks.

Finally, endless love and gratitude to my wife Kim McClelland – raver, contributor, reviewer and moral support. I couldn't have done it without you.

Interviews Conducted

Aaron Roach, Melbourne, 16 August 2014
Adem Jaffers, Melbourne, 14 July 2015
Adrian Cartwright, by phone, 13 July 2014
Andrew Peter Collins, by phone, 16 September 2015
Braden Schlager, by phone, 17 February 2015
Brewster B., Melbourne, 29 November 2015
CJ Bolland, by phone, 27 April 2015
Davide Carbone, Melbourne, 10 December 2014; 24 January 2015
Duncan Plank, by phone, 17 January 2015
Emmy Boudry, Melbourne, 8 March 2015
Gavin Campbell, Melbourne, 20 October 2015
Grant Harrison, by phone, 25 February 2015
Heidi & Richard John, Melbourne, 18 January 2015
Ian Spicer, by phone, 6 October 2014; 8 July 2015; 2 February 2015
Jade John, Melbourne, 1 March 2015
Jason Rudeboy, by phone, 21 September 2014
Joe Fitzgerald, by phone, 13 July 2016; Melbourne, 26 January 2017
Joe Wieczorek, by phone, 4 February 2015

Josh Abrahams, Melbourne, 10 October 2014
Kim McClelland, Melbourne, 7 July 2014
Lani G, Melbourne, 31 May 2015
Marcus, Melbourne, 3 August 2015
Mark James, by phone, 19 October 2014
Natural 1, Melbourne, 23 February 2015; 16 March 2015; 13 April 2016
Nimmo Sandilands, Melbourne, 11 October 2014
Ollie Olsen, Melbourne, 28 January 2015
Phil 'Voodoo' Woodman, Melbourne, 17 February 2015
Richie McNeill, Melbourne, 16 March 2015
Robbie Burns, Melbourne, 10 July 2014
Rupert Keiller, by email, 12 February 2016
Sam Frantzeskos, Melbourne, 2 March 2015
Scott Adcock, Melbourne, 18 October 2014
Sean Kelly, Melbourne, 27 February 2015
Sid Sidney, Melbourne, 20 September 2014
Singtoh-Roddajun Dogon, Melbourne, 8 August 2014; 18 December 2014
Stef, Melbourne, 11 November 2015
Steve Robbins, Melbourne, 24 January 2015
Terrence Ho, Melbourne, 23 August 2014
Timmy Byrne, Melbourne, 19 February 2015

Sources Consulted

Adams, Rob. *Transforming Cities.* Presentation given to University of Melbourne, August 2010.

Aitken, Stuart. 'Charanjit Singh on How He Invented Acid House ... by Mistake'. *The Guardian.* 10 May 2011.

'also: celebrating 30 years'. *The Star.* 10 June 2010. Retrieved from http://en.calameo.com/read/000199795be45c099d351.

Andrews, Ian & Blades, John. 'The Lost Decade: Post-Punk Experimental and Industrial Electronic Music'. In G. Priest (ed.), *Experimental Music: Audio Explorations in Australia.* Sydney: UNSW Press, 2009, pp. 36–56.

Andrez. 'Big Beat Diatribe'. *Techno Renegade*, Vol. 2, No. 3, November 1988, p. 11.

Andrez. 'Masaray Psy-Harmonics'. *Listen Up*, 1995, p. 23.

Australian Broadcasting Corporation. *The Stomp, a 1960s Dance Craze*, 2015. Retrieved from http://splash.abc.net.au/home#!/media/522277/the-stomp-a-1960s-dance-craze.

Ayto, John. *Twentieth Century Words.* Oxford: Oxford University Press, 1999.

Baldwin, James. 'Of the Sorrow Songs: The Cross of Redemption'. In R. Kenan (ed.), *James Baldwin: The Cross of Redemption (Uncollected Writings)* New York: Vintage Books (original work published 1979), 2010, pp. 145–153)

Barrie, Matt. *Would the Last Person in Sydney Please Turn the Lights Out?* 3 February 2016. Retrieved from https://www.linkedin.com/pulse/would-last-person-sydney-please-turn-lights-out-matt-barrie.

Bathgate, Kate. Interview with Cosmic Baby for *Tranzmission* radio show on 3RRR. August 1993. Retrieved 9 June 2016 from https://www.mixcloud.com/richardtropea/tape-20-recording-of-kate-bathgates-tranzmission-radio-show-on-3rrr-cosmic-baby-special/.

Behlendorf, Brian. *The Official alt.rave FAQ*, 1994. Retrieved 30 December 2014, from http://hyperreal.org/raves/altraveFAQ.html.

[Ben Pitcher's Industry Insider]. Melbourne Music City, Music Victoria, Richmond Recorders, Industry Insider [Video file], 3 November 2013. Retrieved 7 October 2016 from https://www.youtube.com/watch?v=ldeVXxDT1W0.

Berstan, Roseanne. 'A music odyssey deep in the forest'. *The Age*, 29 November 2003. Retrieved 28 April 2017 from http://www.theage.com.au/articles/2003/11/28/1069825990550.html.

Boudry, Emmy. (Producer). Untitled documentary on the Melbourne rave scene, 1995. [VHS cassette lent to author].

Boudry, Emmy. 'Ollie Olsen'. *Techno Renegade*, Vol. 2, No. 1, January 1998, p. 8.

Brabazon, Tara. 'Dancing Through the Revolution: The Political and Social Meaning of the Rave'. *Youth Studies Australia*, Vol. 21, No. 1, 2002, pp. 19–24.

Brewster, Bill & Broughton, Frank. *Last Night a DJ Saved My Life*. London: Headline, 1999.

Bridges, Elizabeth. 'Love Parade GmbH vs. Ladyfest: Electronic Music as a Mode of Feminist Expression in Contemporary German Culture'. *Women in German Yearbook*, Vol. 21, 2005, pp. 215-240.

Brocker, Carsten. 'Kraftwerk: Technology and Composition' (M.Patterson, Trans.). In S. Albiez & D. Pattie (eds.), *Kraftwerk: Music Non-stop*. New York and London: Continuum, 2011, pp. 214–230.

Brookman, Chris. *'Forever Young': Consumption and Evolving Neo-tribes in the Sydney Rave Scene*. Bachelor of Science undergraduate thesis, 2001, University of Sydney, Sydney.

Brown, Simon. 'Mad Max: Fury Road's War drumming Doof Wagon Doesn't Represent Doof, Says Documentary Maker', 2015. Retrieved 28 Apr 2017 from http://www.abc.net.au/news/2015-05-19/etymology-of-mad-max-fury-road-doof-wagon/6478782.

Button, James. 'Culture Clubs'. *The Age*, May 16 1986, pp. 36–37.

Carroll, John. 'You Wanna Twist? Or Maybe you Wanna Stomp?' (nd). Retrieved 14 Sep 2016 from http://www.socandance.org.au/pages/stompandtwist.html.

Cataldi Verrina, Francesco. *The History of Italo Disco: Italian Dominance on the Dance Culture of 80's* [English version]. Kriterius, 2015.

Chamberlain, Patrick. 'Sven Väth was watching football on his iPhone while DJing at Awakenings', June 29 2016. Retrieved 5 Jan 2018 from https://pulseradio.net/articles/2016/06/sven-vath-was-watching-football-match-on-his-iphone-while-djing-his-awakenings-set.

Childs, Kevin. '7 Draft Men Get Their Freedom'. *The Age*, December 7 1972, p. 3.

Cohen, Tobi. 'Rude Mechanical Guy'. *Tekno Renegade Magazine*, Issue 12, August 1999, p. 10.

Coles, Stephen, Knispel, David & Knispel, Michael [Directors]. *Melbourne Shuffler* [documentary film]. Melbourne: Underground Epidemic Productions, 2005.

Collin, Matthew. *Altered State: The Story of Ecstasy Culture and Acid House*. London and New York: Serpent's Tail, 1997.

Connellan, Greg & Delianis, Paul. 'Stripping People's Dignity'. *Herald Sun*, August 12 1994, p. 15.

Conroy, Paul. 'Kennett in Warning as Strip Raid Row Grows'. *The Age*, August 12 1994, p. 3.

Cooke, Robin. 'Mutoid Waste Recycledelia and Earthdream'. In G. St. John (ed.), *FreeNRG: Notes from the Edge of the Dance Floor* Melbourne: Common Ground Publishing, 2001, pp. 131–156.

Coppola, Francis. [Director]. *Apocalypse Now* [film]. San Francisco, CA: Zoetrope Studios, 1979.

Cosgrove, Stuart. 'Liner notes to Techno! The New Dance Sound of Detroit'. 10 Records (Virgin). DIXG 75, 1988a.

Cosgrove, Stuart. 'seventh city techno', *The Face*, Vol. 9 (May), 1988b, pp. 86–89.

Courier Mail. 'Do Your Kids Walk or Ride to School by Themselves? You Could Be Breaking the Law', August 5 2016. Retrieved 14 December 2016 from http://www.couriermail.com.au/news/queensland/do-your-kids-walk-or-ride-to-school-by-themselves-you-could-be-breaking-the-law/news-story/d45f1daefac034cb0a7aef961285c88b.

Crettenden, Ian. *1996 Census of Population and Housing: Melbourne ... A Social Atlas*, 1998. Retrieved 8 Sep 2016 from http://www.ausstats.abs.gov.au/ausstats/subscriber.nsf/0/CA25687100069892CA256889001C9F9E/$File/melb.pdf.

Criminal Justice and Public Order Act (UK). 1994. s63.1.

Danforth, Alicia et al. 'MDMA-assisted Therapy: A New Treatment Model for Social Anxiety in Autistic Adults. *Progress in Neuro-Psychopharmacology and Biological Psychiatry*, Vol. 64, 2016, pp. 237–249.

Das, Sushila. 'State to Act on King Street Fights'. *The Age*, October 24 1995, p. 6.

Dawkins, Urszula. 'A Random Revolution'. *RealTime*, Issue 110, 2012, p. 24. Retrieved from http://www.realtimearts.net/article/issue110/10748.

Donaghy, Bronwyn. *Anna's Story*. Sydney: HarperCollins, 1996.

Dovey, Kim. *Fluid City: Transforming Melbourne's Urban Waterfront*. Sydney: University of New South Wales Press, 2005.

Drever, Andrew. 'End of the Earthcore', *The Age*, November 28 2008. Retrieved 1 December 2016 from http://www.theage.com.au/news/entertainment/music/end-of-the-earthcore/2008/11/27/1227491711042.html.

Dreyfus, Suelette &Assange, Julian. *Underground: Tales of Hacking,*

Madness & Obsession on the Electronic Frontier, 2001. Retrieved 28 November 2016 from http://www.underground-book.net/.

Duff, Cameron, Johnston, Jennifer, Moore, David & Goren, Netzach. *Dropping, Connecting, Playing and Partying: Exploring the Social and Cultural Contexts of Ecstasy and Related Drug Use in Victoria*. Melbourne: Victorian Government, 2007.

Duffett, Mark. 'Average White Band: Kraftwerk and the Politics of Race'. In S. Albiez & D. Pattie (eds.), *Kraftwerk: Music Non-stop*, New York and London: Continuum, 2011, pp. 194–213.

Edgar, Ray. 'Street Cred to a Tee'. *The Sydney Morning Herald*, 25 November 2012. Retrieved 25 August 2016 from http://www.smh.com.au/entertainment/about-town/street-cred-to-a-tee-20121124-29zop.html.

Ellis, Rennie. *Decadent: 1980–2000*. Melbourne and London: Hardie Grant Books, 2014.

Faulkner, Jane. 'King St Crackdown: Plan Takes Shape'. *The Age*, 30 October 1995, p. 1.

Fitzgerald, John. An Assemblage of Desire, Drugs and Techno. *Angelaki: Journal of the Theoretical Humanities*, Vol. 3, No. 2, 1998, pp. 41–57.

Fitzsimons, Scott. *EXCLUSIVE: Why Stereosonic Boss Richie McNeill Quit The Business*, 1 December 2014a. Retrieved from http://themusic.com.au/interviews/all/2014/12/01/why-stereosonic-boss-richie-mcneill-quit-the-business-part-one/.

Fitzsimons, Scott. *EXCLUSIVE: The Birth Of Dance Festivals In Australia: Richie McNeill Part Two*, 2 December 2014b. Retrieved from http://themusic.com.au/interviews/all/2014/12/02/the-birth-of-dance-festivals-in-australia-richie-mcneill-part-two/

Fitzsimons, Scott. *EXCLUSIVE: How Stereosonic & Richie McNeill Survived The Festival Turf War*, 4 December 2014c. Retrieved from http://themusic.com.au/interviews/all/2014/12/04/exclusive-how-stereosonic-and-richie-mcneill-survived-the-festival-turf-war/

Foster, Ruth. *Knowing in my Bones*. London: Adam & Charles Black, 1976.

Forster, Clive. *Australian Cities: Continuity and Change* (3rd ed.). South Melbourne: Oxford University Press, 2004.

Ghodse, A. Hamid & Kreek, Mary-Jeanne. 'A Rave at Ecstasy'. *Current Opinion in Psychiatry*, Vol. 10, No. 3, 1997, pp. 191–193.

Gibson, Chris. Subversive Sites: Rave Culture, Spatial Politics and the Internet in Sydney, Australia. *Area*, Vol. 3, No. 1, 1999, pp. 19–33.

Gibson, Chris. 'Appropriating the Means of Production: Dance Music Industries and Contested Digital Space'. In G. St. John (ed.), *FreeNRG: Notes from the Edge of the Dance Floor*. Melbourne: Common Ground Publishing, 2001.

Gibson, Chris & Pagan, Rebecca. *Rave Culture in Sydney, Australia: Mapping Youth Spaces in Media Discourse*, 2003. Retrieved from http://www.snarl.org/youth/chrispagan2.pdf.

Graeme Butler & Associates. *Palace Theatre, Bourke Street, Melbourne: Heritage Assessment for the City of Melbourne 2014*, 2014. Retrieved from https://www.melbourne.vic.gov.au/about-council/committees-meetings/meeting-archive/MeetingAgendaItem Attachments/672/12013/DEC14%20 FMC1%20AGENDA%20ITEM%20 6.4.pdf.

Gregg, Melissa & Wilson, Jason. (2010). Underbelly, True Crime and the Cultural Economy of Infamy. *Continuum: Journal of Media & Cultural Studies,* Vol. 24, No. 3, pp. 411–427.

Griffin, Tom. *Playgrounds: A Portrait of Rave Culture.* Carlton, Vic: Mango Press, 2005.

Groening, Matt et al. *The Simpsons: Homerpalooza (The Simpsons Seventh Season)*, 19 May 1996, Beverly Hills, CA: 20th Century Fox Home Entertainment.

Guilliatt, Richard. 'Nightclubbing: Clubs Stage Daring Rescue Bid on Melbourne's Nightlife. *The Age*, 21 October 1983, p. 32.

H2O. *Melbourne Old Skool by H2O*, 8 January 2008. Retrieved from http://www.inthemix.com.au/forum/archive/index.php/t-214798.html.

Hannah, Rell. *Music Wars: The Sound of the Underground.* Pomona, QLD: Central Station Publishing, 2017.

Harley, Ross & Murphie, Andrew. 'Australian Electronica: A Brief History'. In S. Homan & T. Mitchell (eds.), *Sounds of Then, Sounds of Now: Popular Music in Australia.* Hobart: ACYS Publishing, 2008, pp. 93–111.

Harrison, Grant & Siedle, Paul. *Chasers 10 Years: Celebrating the Sights & Sounds of a Decade 1985–1995.* Melbourne: Chasers, 1995.

Hawley, Janet. 'They Work, They Pray, They Wash…' *The Age*, 1 October 1988, p. 320.

Henderson, Nick. *Interview with Gavin Campbell and Robert Goodge for Treaty 25th Anniversary*. Unpublished transcript lent to author. Canberra: National Sound and Film Archive of Australia, 2016.

Hindmarch, Carl [Writer, Director & Producer]. *Pump Up The Volume: The History of House Music* [documentary film]. London: Channel 4, 2001.

Higginson, Lisa. 'Sales Demise Lends A Hand'. *The Weekly Review*, 2 July 2014, p. 9.

Homan, Shane. 'Sydney's Phoenician Club, the NSW Premier and the Death of Anna Wood'. *Perfect Beat*, Vol. 4, No. 1, 1998, pp. 56–83.

Hore, Monique. Melbourne Coffee Obsession Sees Cafe, Restaurant Boom in City. *Herald Sun*, 15 February 2016. Retrieved 12 September 2016 from http://www.heraldsun.com.au/news/victoria/melbourne-coffee-obsession-sees-cafe-restaurant-boom-in-city/news-story/b8d7198055d0f7629f16bf737bcfa310.

Hurley, Michael. Aspects of Gay and Lesbian Life in '70s Melbourne. *The La Trobe Journal*, No. 87, 2011, p. 44. Retrieved 16 Feb 2017 from http://latrobejournal.slv.vic.gov.au/latrobejournal/issue/latrobe-87/t1-g-t5.html.

Hurley, Michael. 'We're Not All Straight in the Garden State'. In S. Blackburn (ed.), *Breaking Out: Memories of Melbourne in the 1970s*. Willoughby, NSW: Hale & Iremonger, 2015, pp. 252–271.

Iveson, Kurt & Scalmer, Sean. 'Carnival at Crown Casino: S11 as Party and Protest'. In G. St. John (ed.), *FreeNRG: Notes from the Edge of the Dance Floor*. Melbourne: Common Ground Publishing, 2001, pp. 223–235).

James, Rhys [Director & Producer]. *Locked Off* [documentary film]. London: Vice Media, 2016. Retrieved 25 May 2016 from http://www.vice.com/en_uk/video/locked-off.

Jarvis, Nick. *The most notorious warehouse parties of all time*, 5 February 2014. Retrieved 1 December 2016 from http://inthemix.junkee.com/the-most-notorious-warehouse-parties-of-all-time.

Jenkins, Jeff. *Molly Meldrum Presents 50 Years of Rock in Australia*. Melbourne: Wilkinson Publishing, 2007.

Johnston, Chris. 'Man of Techno', *The Age*, 1 October 1999, p. 57.

Johnston, Chris. 'The Razor Gang. *The Age*, 30 March 2012. Retrieved from http://newsstore.fairfax.com.au/apps/viewDocument.ac;jsessionid=8C1192FBA4691FC89E55A5B11391B84D?sy=afr&pb=all_ffx&dt=selectRange&dr=1month&so=relevance&sf=text&sf=headline&rc=10&rm=200&sp=brs&cls=672&clsPage=1&docID=AGE1203302AFBJ73DSRJ.

Johnston, Damon & Cummins, Andrew. 'Strip Search Police Face Sack'. *Herald Sun*, 12 August 1994, p. 7.

Kesa, Ingrid. *Tripping Down Memory Lane with a '90s Rave VJ*, 27 October 2015 Retrieved from http://thecreatorsproject.vice.com/en_au/blog/taking-a-trip-down-memory-lane-with-seminal-90s-melbourne-rave-vj-adem-jaffers.

Kennedy, Heather & Lambert, Catherine. 'The Deadly Agony of Ecstasy'. *Herald Sun*, 29 October 1995, pp. 4–5.

Kiss 90fm. *kiss this*. May 1996, Melbourne: Kiss 90fm.

Lambert, Alex. 'Narratives in Noise: Reflexivity, Migration and Liminality in the Australian Psytrance Scene'. In G. St. John (ed.), *The Local Scenes and Global Culture of Psytrance*. New York: Routledge, 2010, pp. 203–219).

Landry, Charles. *The Creative City: A Toolkit for Urban Innovators*. London: Earthscan, 2006.

Larkin, John. *Victorian Country Pubs*. Adelaide: Rigby, 1980.

Lee, Jenny. *Making Modern Melbourne*. Carlton, Vic: Arcade, 2008.

Liticia. 'DJ Lani'. *Techno Renegade*, January 1998, p. 14.

Longmire, Anne. *St Kilda: The Show Goes On. The History of St Kilda Vol. III, 1930 to July 1983*. Hawthorn, Vic: Hudson, 1989.

Lowenstein, Richard [Director]. *Dogs in Space*. Melbourne: Burrowes Film Group, 1986.

Lowenstein, Richard [Director]. *We're Livin' on Dog Food* [documentary film]. Melbourne: Ghost Pictures, 2009.

Lucas, Clay. 'Palace Fire Deliberately Lit'. *The Age*, 12 July 2007. Retrieved 26 Aug 2016 from http://www.theage.com.au/news/national/palace-fire-deliberately-lit/2007/07/12/1183833645175.html.

Lucas, Clay. 'New Year's Booze Ban Set to Stop Out-of-control Party'. *The Age*, 17 August 2014. Retrieved 6 July 2017 from http://www.theage.com.au/victoria/new-years-booze-ban-set-to-stop-outofcontrol-party-20140817-1053mm.html.

Luckins, Tanja. 'Pigs, Hogs and Aussie Blokes: The Emergence of the Term "Six O'clock Swill"'. *History Australia*, Vol. 4, No. 1, 2007, pp. 8.1–8.17.

Luckman, Susan. 'Rave Cultures and the Academy'. *Social Alternatives*, Vol. 17, No. 4, 1998, pp. 45–49.

Luckman, Susan. 'Practice Random Acts: Reclaiming the Streets of Australia'. In G. St. John (ed.), *FreeNRG: Notes from the Edge of the Dance Floor*. Melbourne: Common Ground Publishing, 2001, pp. 205–221.

Luckman, Susan. 'Doof, Dance and Rave Culture'. In S. Homan & T. Mitchell (eds.), *Sounds of Then, Sounds of Now: Popular Music in Australia*. Hobart: ACYS Publishing, 2008, pp. 131–149.

MacIntyre, Iain. *Tomorrow is Today: Australia in the Psychedelic Era, 1966–1970*. Adelaide: Wakefield Press, 2006.

Maunder, Trish. 'Outdoor Rave Guide', *The Age*, 27 November 1998, p. 46.

McDonnell, John. 'Scene and Heard: Italo-disco. *The Guardian*, 1 September 2008. Retrieved from http://www.theguardian.com/music/musicblog/2008/sep/01/sceneandhearditalodisco.

McFarlane, Ian. *Encyclopedia of Australian Rock and Pop*. Allen & Unwin, 1999.

Retrieved from http://web.archive.org/web/20040419084449/www.whammo.com.au/encyclopedia.asp?articleid=551.

[McrGrooveHeritage]. *How People Originally Cut Shapes To House In The UK (Features Foot Patrol) – Manchester 1986* [Video file]. 17 July 2013. Retrieved 3 June 2016 from https://www.youtube.com/watch?v=vBYvWPdUOHM.

Melbourne City Council. (1993). *Central City Heritage Study Review: Final Report*. Retrieved 31 Mar 2017 from https://www.melbourne.vic.gov.au/SiteCollectionDocuments/central-city-heritage-study-review-1993-p2.pdf.

Melbourne Underground Development. *Artistic Manifesto*. Melbourne: M.U.D., nd.

Meyer, Tim. *Every Picture Tells a Story* [Video file], 27 November 2008. Retrieved 15 September 2016 from https://www.youtube.com/watch?v=IBT_K_-jFoY.

Midro, Jason. '*The Changing of the Guard!' DJ Will E Tell to Jason Midro* [Video file], 14 December 2015. Retrieved from https://www.youtube.com/watch?v=S7KGZ9w8zOQ.

MILESAGO. *Venues*, nd. Retrieved 6 July 2017 from http://www.milesago.com/Venues/venuesframe.htm.

Miller, Alexandra. *Australia's Daily Alcohol Toll: 15 Deaths and 430 Hospitalisations*, 31 July 2014. Retrieved 6 July 2017 from https://theconversation.com/australias-daily-alcohol-toll-15-deaths-and-430-hospitalisations-29906.

Mills, Tammy & Houston, Cameron. 'Victoria Police Apologise for Tasty Raid'. *The Age*, 5 August 2014. Retrieved 1 December 2016 from http://www.theage.com.au/victoria/victoria-police-apologise-for-tasty-raid-20140804-100gzg.

Mithoefer, Michael et al. 'Durability of Improvement in Post-traumatic Stress Disorder Symptoms and Absence of Harmful Effects or Drug Dependency after 3,4 Methylenedioxymethamphetamine Assisted Psychotherapy: A Prospective Longterm Follow-Up Study'. *Journal of Psychopharmacology*, Vol. 27, No. 1, 2013, pp. 28–39.

Ministry of Sound. 'Liner notes to Melbourne Sound Sessions/ Bounce Sessions'. Ministry of Sound. MOSA190, 2014.

Mittman, JD [Director] & Flavell, Keren [Producer]. *Sounds Like Techno*. Melbourne: Australian Broadcasting Corporation, 2003. Retrieved from http://www2.abc.net.au/arts/soundsliketechno/html.

Montano, Ed. 'Stereosonic and Australian Commercial EDM Festival Culture'. In G. St John (ed.), *Weekend Societies: Electronic Dance Music Festivals and Event-Cultures*. New York: Bloomsbury Academic, 2017, pp. 45–67.

Mothersole, Dave. *Unveiling the Secret—The Roots of Trance*. 14 April 2010. Retrieved 26 August 2016 from http://www.bleep43.com/bleep43/2010/4/14/unveiling-the-secret-the-roots-of-trance.html.

Murray, Enda. 'Sound Systems and Australian DiY Culture: Folk Music for the Dot Com Generation'. In G. St John (ed.), *FreeNRG: Notes from the Edge of the Dance Floor*. Melbourne: Common Ground Publishing, 2001, pp. 57–70.

Nietzsche, Friedrick. *The Birth of Tragedy and The Case of Wagner* (W. Kaufmann, Trans.). New York: Vintage Books, 1967.

Nowell, David. *The Story of Northern Soul: A Definitive History of the Dance Scene that Refuses to Die*. London: Pavilion, 2012.

O'Neill, Shannon. '"Copyright doesn't mean shit to me": Sampling and Appropriation in Australian Electronic Music and Sound Art'. In G. Priest (ed.), *Experimental Music: Audio Explorations in Australia*. Sydney: UNSW Press, 2009, pp. 75–93.

Phillips, Dom. 'Future Sound of Melbourne "Chapter One"' [review]. *mixmag*, March 1996.

Phillips, Walter. '"Six O'clock Swill": The Introduction of Early Closing of Hotel Bars in Australia'. *Historical Studies*, Vol. 19, No. 75, 1980, pp. 250–266.

Poe, Jim. *Inside 'Techno City': Melbourne's clubbing history with Dave Pham*. 2014. Retrieved 24 October 2016 from http://inthemix.junkee.com/inside-techno-city-melbournes-clubbing-history-with-dave-pham/24630.

Poe, Jim. *Oral History of the Sydney Rave Scene, 1989–1994*. 27 July 2016. Retrieved 16 July 2017 from https://www.redbull.com/au-en/oral-history-of-the-sydney-rave-scene-1989-1994.

Poe, Jim. *An Oral history of Melbourne's Rave Scene, '88–'97*. 13 July 2017.

Retrieved 13 July 2017 from https://www.redbull.com/au-en/melbourne-rave-scene-oral-history-1988-1997.

Priest, Gail. 'Sounding Sight, Space and Bodies: A Survey of Mixed Media Explorations'. In G. Priest (ed.), *Experimental Music: Audio Explorations in Australia*. Sydney: UNSW Press, 2009, pp. 196–215.

Priest, Gail & Chan, Sebastian. 'Part 1: The Emergence of Popular Unpopular Electronic Music'. In G. Priest (ed.), *Experimental Music: Audio Explorations in Australia*. Sydney: UNSW Press, 2009, pp. 94–103.

Race, Kane. *Pleasure Consuming Medicine: The Queer Politics of Drugs*. Durham, NC: Duke University Press, 2009.

Rennison, Kristina. 'Little Nobody Andrez'. *Techno Renegade*, Vol. 2, No. 3, 1998, p. 14.

Reynolds, Simon. *Energy Flash: A Journey through Rave Music and Dance Culture*. London: Faber and Faber, 2013.

Riddell, Pat. 'Just the Sonic'. *Tekno Renegade*, No. 11, July 1999, pp. 18–19.

Rietveld, Hillegonda. 'Trans-Europa Express: Tracing the Trance Machine'. In S. Albiez & D. Pattie (eds.), *Kraftwerk: Music Non-stop*. New York and London: Continuum, 2011, pp. 214–230.

Ross, Liz. 'From Lesbian Activist to Revolutionary Socialist'. In S. Blackburn (ed.), *Breaking Out: Memories of Melbourne in the 1970s*. Willoughby, NSW: Hale & Iremonger, 2015, pp. 232–251.

Sacks, Oliver. *Hallucinations*. London: Picador, 2012.

St John, Graham. 'Doof! Australian Post-Rave Culture'. In G. St. John (ed.), *FreeNRG: Notes from the Edge of the Dance Floor*. Melbourne: Common Ground Publishing, 2001a, pp. 9–36.

St John, Graham. 'Techno Terra-ism: Feral Systems and Sound Futures'. In G. St. John (ed.), *FreeNRG: Notes from the Edge of the Dance Floor*. Melbourne: Common Ground Publishing, 2001b, pp. 109–127).

St John, Graham. 'Doof! Australian Post-Rave Culture'. In G. St. John (ed.), *FreeNRG: Notes from the Edge of the Dance Floor*. 2001c, pp. 11–56. [eBook]. Retrieved 28 April 2017 from http://www.undergrowth.org/freenrg_notes_from_the_edge_of_the_dancefloor.

St John, Graham. (ed.). *The Local Scenes and Global Culture of Psytrance*. New York: Routledge, 2010.

St John, Graham. *Global Tribe: Technology, Spirituality and Psytrance*. Sheffield, UK: Equinox, 2012.

San Miguel, Dolores. *The Ballroom: The Melbourne Punk and Post-punk Scene*. Melbourne: Melbourne Books, 2011.

Shand, Adam. *Big Shots: Inside Melbourne's Gangland Wars*. Melbourne: Penguin, 2010.

Shand, Adam. *Carl Williams: The Short Life and Violent Times of Melbourne's Gangland Drug Lord*. Melbourne: Penguin, 2012.

Shaw, Kate. 'Independent Creative Subcultures and Why they Matter'. *International Journal of Cultural Policy*, Vol. 19, No. 3, 2013, pp. 333–352.

Shepherd, Garry. *Technotopia: Commerce House*. 2007. Retrieved from http://pandora.nla.gov.au/pan/33581/20070817-1208/mc2.vicnet.net.au/home/cybafaer/web/cyb905/commerce_house.html.

Sicko, Dan. *Techno Rebels*. Detroit, MI: Wayne State University Press, 2010.

Silvester, John & Rule, Andrew. *Underbelly: The Gangland War*. Smithfield, NSW: Floradale and Sly Ink, 2008.

Siokou, Christine. Seeking the Vibe. *Youth Studies Australia*, Vol. 21, No. 1, 2002, pp. 11–18.

Siokou, Christine & Moore, David. '"This is not a rave!" Changes in the Commercialised Melbourne Rave/Dance Party Scene'. *Youth Studies Australia*, Vol. 28, No. 3, 2008, pp. 50–57.

Siokou, Christine, Moore, David & Lee, Helen. '"Muzzas" and "Old Skool Ravers": Ethnicity, Drugs and the Changing Face of Melbourne's Dance Party/Club Scene'. *Health Sociology Review*, Vol. 19, No. 2, 2010, pp. 192–204.

Spencer, Amy. *DIY: The Rise of Lo-Fi Culture*. London: Marion Boyars, 2008.

Strong, Peter. 'Doofstory: Sydney Park to the Desert'. In G. St John (ed.), *FreeNRG: Notes from the Edge of the Dance Floor*. Melbourne: Common Ground Publishing, 2001, pp. 71–89.

Sydney Morning Herald. 'Suspicious Fire Razes St Kilda's Palace', 11 Juy 2007. Retrieved 26 August 2016 from http://www.smh.com.au/national/suspicious-fire-razes-st-kildas-palace-20070711-n65.html.

Sydney Rave History. Flyers. 2015. Retrieved 6 July 2017 from http://www.sydneyravehistory.com/flyers.

Tamulavage, Diane. *Shifting the spotlight to females in EDM: Reid Speed*. 4 March 2014. Retrieved 1 December 2016 from http://www.youredm.com/2014/03/04/shifting-spotlight-females-edm-reid-speed/.

Teh, Katherine. 'Harem Dens and Oil Lamps'. *The Age*, 26 August 1988, p. 42.

Teh, Katherine & Gowdie, Cathy. 'Police Search Nightclub in Drug Raid. *The Age*, 5 December 1988, p. 19.

Teriyakianarkisaki. 'History'. nd. Retrieved 28 November 2016 from http://web.archive.org/web/20031002131125/http://www.teriyakianarkisaki.com/history/1996.html.

Thomson, David. 'Architects Combine Kitsch and Theatre in The Metro'. *The Age*, 18 November 1987, p. 39.

Thornton, Sarah. *Club Cultures*. Cambridge, UK: Polity Press, 1995.

Toltz, Joseph. '"Dragged into the Dance"—The Role of Kraftwerk in the Development of Electro-Funk'. In S. Albiez & D. Pattie (eds.), *Kraftwerk: Music Non-stop*. New York and London: Continuum, 2011, pp. 181–193.

Tomazin, Farrah. 'RaveSafe'. *groo:vine*, No. 9, June 1999, p. 5.

Tomazin, Farrah, Donovan, Patrick & Mundell, Meg. 'Dance trance', *The Age*, 7 December 2002. Retrieved 7 June 2016 from http://www.theage.com.au/articles/2002/12/07/1038950203557.html.

Tramacchi, Des. Chaos Engines: 'Doofs, Pyschedelics and Religious Experience'. In G. St John (ed.), *FreeNRG: Notes from the Edge of the*

Dance Floor. Melbourne: Common Ground Publishing, 2001, pp. 171–187.

Trevor. *Rowland S. Howard: A Tribute.* 2010. Retrieved from http://messandnoise.com/features/3853723.

Tropea, Richard. 'Tape 23. Recording of Kate Bathgate's "Beat In The Street", guest Dj H20'. (2016). Retrieved from https://www.mixcloud.com/richardtropea/tape-23-recording-of-kate-bathgates-beat-in-the-street-guest-dj-h20/.

Tsolidis, Georgina & Pollard, Vikki. 'Being a "wog" in Melbourne—Young People's Self-fashioning Through Discourses of Racism', *Discourse: Studies in the Cultural Politics of Education*, Vol. 30, No. 4, 2009, pp. 427–442.

Turkle, Sherry. *Alone Together: Why We Expect More From Technology and Less From Each Other.* New York: Basic Books, 2012.

Van der Kolk, Bessel. *The Body Keeps the Score.* London: Penguin, 2015.

Vice Media. *THUMP Specials: Rave Days—The Birth of Melbourne's Rave Scene.* 2015. Retrieved 9 January 2017 from https://thump.vice.com/en_us/video/thump-specials-rave-days-the-birth-of-melbournes-rave-scene.

Victorian AIDS Council. *Gay Health Update.* No. 101, 10 July 1987.

Victorian Heritage Council. 'Victorian Heritage Database Report: Commerce House', 2017a. Retrieved 6 July 2017 from http://vhd.heritagecouncil.vic.gov.au/places/64987/download-report.

Victorian Heritage Council. 'Victorian Heritage Database Report: Riverside Inn, Richmond', 2017b. Retrieved 6 July 2017 from http://vhd.heritagecouncil.vic.gov.au/places/8874/download-report.

Victorian Ombudsman. *Report: Investigation of Police Raid on the Commerce Club (Tasty Night Club) on Sunday 7 August 1994.* Melbourne: Victorian Government, 1994.

von Wayward, Melynda. *The History of the Melbourne Punk Scene 1977–1987.* 2004. Retrieved 12 September 2016 from http://www.punkjourney.com/.

Walking Melbourne. 'Commercial Travellers Association: 318-324 Flinders Street, Melbourne', nd. Retrieved 6 July 2017 from http://www.walkingmelbourne.com/building247.html.

Warshaw, Matt. *The Encyclopedia of Surfing.* Orlando, FL: Harcourt, 2005.

Whiteoak, John. 'Italo-Hispanic Popular Music in Melbourne Before Multiculturalism'. *Victorian Historical Journal*, Vol. 78, No. 2, 2007, pp. 228–250.

Wikipedia. 'Leeroy Thornhill', 2016. Retrieved 14 August 2016 from https://en.wikipedia.org/wiki/Leeroy_Thornhill.

Wikipedia. 'List of Electronic Music Genres', 2017. Retrieved 26 April 2017 from https://en.wikipedia.org/wiki/List_of_electronic_music_genres.

Williamson, Kathleen. 'Propagating Abominable Knowledge: Zines on the Tekno Fringe'. In G. St John (ed.), *FreeNRG: Notes from the Edge of the Dance Floor.* 2001, pp. 58–86) [eBook]. Retrieved 29 April 2017 from http://www.undergrowth.org/freenrg_notes_from_the_edge_of_the_dancefloor.

Wilmoth, Peter. 'Nightstyle'. *The Age*, 12 March 1985, p. 21.

Wilmoth, Peter. 'Tsars of the Night Brigade'. *The Age*, 19 July 1988, p. 11.

Wilmoth, Peter. 'Mr Nightlife'. *The Age*, 19 September 2004. Retrieved from http://www.theage.com.au/articles/2004/09/16/1095221723753.html.

Wilson, Brian. *Fight, Flight, or Chill: Subcultures, Youth and Rave into the Twenty-first Century*. Montreal: McGill-Queen's University Press, 2006.

Wilson, Greg. *Cutting Shapes—How House Music Really Hit The UK*. 18 July 2013. Retrieved from http://blog.gregwilson.co.uk/2013/07/cutting-shapes-how-house-music-really-hit-the-uk/.

Wodak, Alex & Warhaft, Gideon. 'Is Ecstasy Really That Dangerous? All Your Questions Answered', 8 December 2015. Retrieved 1 December 2016 from https://www.theguardian.com/commentisfree/2015/dec/08/is-ecstasy-really-that-dangerous-all-your-questions-answered.

World Bank. 2016. Retrieved 25 November 2016 from http://data.worldbank.org/indicator/IT.NET.USER.P2?cid=GPD_44&locations=AU.

Wright, Briony & McShane, Liam. 'Through Music Comes Life…'. *Tekno Renegade*, No. 11, July 1999, pp. 20–21.

Zalewski, Tony. *Deconstructing Indiscriminate Violence: A Mixed Methods Study in Nightclub Security* (PhD thesis), Monash University, Melbourne, 2013.

Endnotes

Introduction

1. Behlendorf, 1994.
2. Thornton, 1995, p. 117.
3. Thornton, 1995, p. 121.
4. Thornton, 1995, p. 117.

Chapter 1: Dancing Queens

1. Brewster & Broughton, 1999, p.138.
2. Brewster & Broughton, 1999, p.56.
3. Collin, 1997, p.11.
4. Brewster & Broughton, 1999, p.148.
5. Brewster & Broughton, 1999, p.156.
6. Brewster & Broughton, 1999, pp.154, 159.
7. Brewster & Broughton, 1999, pp.156, 161.
8. Hindmarch, 2001, 7:30.
9. Collin, 1997, p.15.
10. Collin, 1997, p.15.
11. Brewster & Broughton, 1999, p. 205.
12. Brewster & Broughton, 1999, p. 207.
13. Brewster & Broughton, 1999, p. 207.
14. Collin, 1997, p.12.
15. Brewster & Broughton, 1999, p. 291.
16. Reynolds, 2013, p.18.
17. Hindmarch, 2001, 9:15.
18. Wilmoth, 2004.
19. Wilmoth, 1988.
20. Wilmoth, 2004.
21. Ellis, 2014, pp. 22–23, 32–33, 60–61, 144.
22. McDonnell, 2008.
23. Catalda Verrina, 2015, p. 154.
24. Sicko, 2010, pp. 24, 26.
25. Button, 1986.
26. Whiteoak, 2007, p. 246.
27. Tsolidis & Pollard, 2009, p. 429.
28. Lee, 2008, p. 112.
29. Tsolidis & Pollard, 2009, p. 430.
30. Tsolidis & Pollard, 2009, p. 430.
31. Lee, 2008, pp. 114–115.
32. Brewster & Broughton, 1999, p. 213.
33. Hurley, 2011, pp. 46, 51, 55; Hurley, 2015, p. 260.
34. Hurley, 2011, pp. 55–56.
35. Hurley, 2011, pp. 56–57.
36. Ross, 2015, p. 247.
37. Hurley, 2015, p. 263.
38. Hurley, 2015, p. 263.
39. Hurley, 2011, p. 56.
40. Victorian AIDS Council, 1987.
41. Childs, 1972.
42. Hurley, 2011, p. 46.
43. 'also: celebrating 30 years', 2010, p. 15.

44 Gibson & Pagan, 2003, p. 10; Harley & Murphie, 2008, p. 101; Mittman & Flavell, 2003, Australian Scene (1).
45 Hurley, 2015, p. 258.
46 Hurley, 2011, p. 49.
47 'also: celebrating 30 years', 2010, p. 14.
48 'also: celebrating 30 years', 2010, p. 20.
49 Chamberlain, 2016.
50 Race, 2009, pp. 22, 24.
51 Race, 2009, p. 24.
52 'also': celebrating 30 years', p. 12.
53 Phillips, 1980, pp. 250, 251, 254, 259.
54 Phillips, 1980, p. 251.
55 Luckins, 2007, p. 8.3.
56 Larkin, 1980, quoted in Luckins, 2007, p. 8.1.
57 Luckins, 2007, p. 8.7.
58 MILESAGO, nd.
59 Phillips, 1980, p. 266.
60 Longmire, 1989, p. 230; *The Age*, 24/07/73, p. 12.
61 Adams, 2010.
62 Adams, 2010 and Hore, 2016.
63 Thomson, 1987.
64 Graeme Butler & Associates, 2014, p. 77.

Chapter 2: Punks and Pineapple Heads

1 Longmire, 1989, p. 2.
2 von Wayward, 2004.
3 Forster, 2004, pp. 32–34.
4 Lowenstein, 1986.
5 Trevor, 2010.
6 Lowenstein, 2009, 60:10.
7 Lowenstein, 2009, 59:56.
8 Lowenstein, 2009, 12:25.
9 Andrews & Blades, 2009, p. 37.
10 von Wayward, 2004.
11 Mittman & Flavell, 2003, Man & Machine (2).
12 Harley & Murphie, 2008, pp. 94–96.
13 Harley & Murphie, 2008, p. 97.
14 Andrews & Blades, 2009, p. 50.
15 McFarlane, 1999.
16 Shaw, 2013, p. 348.
17 Guilliatt, 1983.
18 Wilmoth, 1985.
19 San Miguel, 2011, p. 170.
20 Rietveld, 2011, p. 215.
21 Rietveld, 2011, pp. 216, 226; Toltz, 2011, p. 181.
22 Wilmoth, 1985.
23 Henderson, 2016.
24 Henderson, 2016.
25 Johnston, 2012.
26 Johnston, 2012.
27 Johnston, 2012.
28 Johnston, 2012.

Chapter 3: Pleasure Seekers

1 Mittman & Flavell, 2003, Detroit Roots (4).
2 Collin, 1997, p19.
3 Hindmarch, 2001, 25:20.
4 Hindmarch, 2001, 27:30.
5 Reynolds, 2013, p.22.
6 Hannah, 2017, pp. 41–42.
7 Hannah, 2017, p. 43.
8 Hannah, 2017, p. 1.
9 Hannah, 2017, p. 3.
10 Hannah, 2017, p. 43.
11 Hannah, 2017, pp. 44, 46.
12 Hannah, 2017, p. 45.
13 Hannah, 2017, pp. 50, 54, 57.
14 Hannah, 2017, pp. 59, 75.
15 Nowadays, *Vault* is located outside the Australian Centre for Contemporary Art in Southbank.
16 Poe, 2017.
17 Hannah, 2017, p. 78.
18 Reynolds, 2013, p. 31.
19 Mittman & Flavell, 2003, Man & Machine (1).
20 Reynolds, 2013, p. 31.
21 Reynolds, 2013, p. 31.
22 Mittman & Flavell, 2003, Detroit Roots (6).
23 Reynolds, 2013, p. 31.
24 Reynolds, 2013, p. 31.
25 Collin, 1997, p. 25.
26 Collin, 1997, p. 26.
27 Collin, 1997, p. 26.
28 Collin, 1997, p. 28.
29 Mithoefer et al., 2013; Danforth et al., 2016.
30 Luckman, 2008, p. 140.
31 Collin, 1997, p. 30.
32 Collin, 1997, pp. 41 42.
33 Collin, 1997, p. 46.
34 Hindmarch, 2001, 64:40.

35 Collin, 1997, p. 50.
36 Hindmarch, 2001.
37 Collin, 1997, p. 58.
38 Hindmarch, 2001, 69:10.
39 Thornton, 1995, p. 155.
40 Collin, 1997, p. 75.
41 Collin, 1997, p. 68.
42 Collin, 1997, p. 85.
43 Hindmarch, 2001, 84:10.
44 Tramacchi, 2001, p. 173.
45 Nietzsche, 1967, p. 36.
46 Ayto, 1999, p. 434.
47 Spencer, 2008, p. 323.
48 Collin, 1997, p. 195.
49 'Wizz' or 'whizz' is British street slang for the drug speed.
50 Hindmarch, 2001, 89:40.
51 The Inter City firm are a crew of football hooligans associated with West Ham United, so-called because they rode the Inter City trains to away matches.
52 Collin, 1997, p. 102.
53 Collin, 1997, p. 92.
54 Reynolds, 2013, pp. 81–82.
55 Melbourne Underground Development, nd.
56 Reynolds, 2013, p. 54.
57 Collin, 1997, pp. 131–132.
58 Wilmoth, 1988.
59 Mittman & Flavell, 2003, Australian Scene (1).
60 Mittman & Flavell, 2003, Australian Scene (1).
61 Teh, 1988.
62 Other clubs playing acid house at this time include Metro and IDs Nitespot. See, for example, *The Age*, 20/01/89, p. 36.

Chapter 4: Children of Ecstasy

1 Sicko, 2010, p. 35.
2 Rietveld, 2011, p. 226.
3 Sicko, 2010, p. 49.
4 May quoted in Cosgrove, 1988a.
5 Mittman & Flavell, 2003, Detroit Roots (5). See Cosgrove, 1988b for the original interview.
6 Sicko, 2010, p. 68. Thornton also makes this claim in *Club Cultures* (p. 74).
7 Rietveld, 2011, p. 227.
8 Sicko, 2010, p. 70.
9 Aitken, 2011.
10 Sicko, 2010, pp. 28–29. Sicko also makes this claim of Cybotron's 'Alleys Of Your Mind' however he notes that 'Sharevari' was released first (p. 44).
11 Duffett, 2011, p. 209.
12 Mittman & Flavell, 2003, Detroit Roots (5).
13 Mittman & Flavell, 2003, Detroit Roots (5).
14 Mittman & Flavell, 2003, Detroit Roots (6).
15 Mittman & Flavell, 2003, Australian Scene (1).
16 Sydney Rave History, 2015.
17 Sydney Rave History, 2015.
18 Sydney Rave History, 2015.
19 Gibson & Pagan, 2003, p. 10.
20 Harley & Murphie, 2008, p. 98.
21 Harrison & Siedle, 1995, p. 10.
22 Hawley, 1988.
23 Teh & Gowdie, 1988.
24 Duff et al., 2007, p. 8.
25 Ghodse & Kreek, 1997 cited in Duff et al., 2007, p. 8.
26 Brabazon, 2002, p.22.
27 See, for example, Siokou, 2002, p. 16.
28 Reynolds, 2013, *p.* xxxvii.
29 Siokou, 2002, p. 15.
30 Mittman & Flavell, 2003, Australian Scene (1).
31 Collin, 1997, p. 97.
32 The Bus Stop is a dance from the 1970s, revived in Melbourne during the late 1980s.

Chapter 5: Pure Ravers

1 Walking Melbourne, nd.; Victorian Heritage Council, 2017a.
2 Walking Melbourne, nd.
3 Walking Melbourne, nd.
4 Shepherd, 2007.
5 Shepherd, 2007.
6 Shepherd, 2007.
7 Shepherd, 2007.
8 Shepherd, 2007.
9 Collin, 1997, p. 194.
10 Collin, 1997, p. 194.

11 Collin, 1997, pp. 194–195.
12 Thornton, 1995, p. 4.
13 San Miguel, 2011, p. 178.
14 [Ben Pitcher's Industry Insider], 2013.
15 [Ben Pitcher's Industry Insider], 2013.
16 Priest & Chan, p. 97.
17 Mittman & Flavell, 2003, Future Music (2).
18 Priest & Chan, p. 97.
19 Mittman & Flavell, 2003, Australian Scene (2).
20 Higginson, 2014.
21 *Tekno Renegade*, 02/99, p. 23.
22 Fitzsimons, 2014a.
23 *groo:vine*, 02/99, issue 5, p. 9.
24 Midro, 2015.
25 Midro, 2015.
26 Midro, 2015.
27 Midro, 2015.
28 Midro, 2015.
29 *groo:vine*, 02/99, issue 5, p. 9.
30 Midro, 2015.
31 Coppola, 1979.
32 Longmire, 1989, p. xii.
33 Longmire, 1989, p. 146.
34 Longmire, 1989, p. 7.
35 Longmire, 1989, p. 104.
36 Longmire, 1989, p. 203.
37 Lucas, 2007.
38 Sydney Morning Herald, 2007.
39 Lucas, 2007.
40 Lucas, 2007.

Chapter 6: Techno Renegades

1   Ellis, 2014, p. 66.
2   St. John, 2012, pp. 27, 30.
3   St. John, 2012, pp. 34–35.
4   St. John, 2012, pp. 34–39.
5   St. John, 2012, pp. 41–42.
6   St. John, 2012, p. 41.
7   Mothersole, 2010.
8   St. John, 2012, pp. 45, 48.
9   Cohen, 1999.
10 Cohen, 1999.
11 Edgar, 2012.
12 Edgar, 2012.
13 Mittman & Flavell, 2003, Australian Scene (3).
14 Fitzsimons, 2014a.
15 Possibly DJ Moneypenny, a 'regular fixture in late eighties New York' according to Brewster & Broughton (1999, p. 406).
16 Boudry, 1995.
17 Victorian Heritage Council, 2017b.
18 Hakim Bey quoted in Gibson & Pagan, 2003, p. 12.
19 Gibson & Pagan, 2003, p. 12.
20 Gibson, 1999, p. 23.
21 James, 2016, 6:30.
22 http://www.rba.gov.au/publications/smp/boxes/2011/aug/c.pdf, accessed 5 September 2016.
23 Mittman & Flavell, 2003, Australian Scene (5).
24 For a map of rave locations that I have uncovered in my research, see http://www.technoshuffle.com.au/rave-map.
25 Dovey, 2005, p. 125.
26 Dovey, 2005, p. 126.
27 Dovey, 2005, p. 125.
28 In 2018 this address no longer exists. It is close to the corner of Docklands Drive and St Mangos Lane in Docklands.
29 Tropea, 2016, 37:40.
30 Griffin, 2005, p. 93.

Chapter 7: Global Villagers

1   Melbourne Underground Development, nd.
2   Melbourne Underground Development, nd.
3   Crettenden, 1998.
4   Reynolds, 2013, p. 115.
5   Reynolds, 2013, pp. 120–144; Collin, 1997, p. 248.
6   Reynolds, 2013, pp. xxvi, 162.
7   Reynolds, 2013p. 119.
8   *Mixmag* 6/93, quoted in Collin, 1997, p. 247.
9   Collin, 1997, p. 255.
10 TVU stands for Unlimited Television Inc., a community television station launched in 1987 and screened on Channel 31.
11 H2O, 2008.
12 Mittman & Flavell, 2003, Australian Scene (5).

13　Button, 1986.
14　Courier Mail, 2016.
15　*Techno Renegade*, 10/98, p. 14.
16　St. John, 2012, p. 249.
17　Boudry, 1998.
18　Cooke, 2001, p. 134.
19　Cooke, 2001, p. 134.
20　Cooke, 2001, p. 143.
21　Cooke, 2001, p. 143.
22　Priest, 2009, p. 198.
23　Priest, 2009, p. 199.
24　Priest, 2009, pp. 200, 201, 203.
25　Kesa, 2015.
26　Dawkins, 2012.
27　Reynolds, 2013, p. xxix.
28　Siokou, 2002, pp. 11, 13, 15. Siokou found that 25 percent of respondents had never tried ecstasy.
29　Siokou, 2002, p. 16.
30　Siokou, 2002, pp. 14–15.
31　Siokou, 2002, p. 15.
32　Boudry, 1995.
33　Faulkner, 1995.
34　Das, 1995.
35　Thornton, 1995, p. 99.
36　In 1992 a number of people returning from a Happy Valley outdoor rave party south of Sydney died in car accidents. Sydney DJ Abel described the first Happy Valley party in 1991 as 'our generation's Woodstock.' See Poe, 2016.
37　Tomazin, 1999.
38　Duffett, 2011, pp. 204, 207, 208.
39　Kiss 90FM (1996).
40　*groo:vine*, 11/98, p. 10. The Visions of Shiva was a short-lived collaboration between Harald Blüchel (aka Cosmic Baby) and Paul van Dyk. They released two singles: 'Perfect Day' in 1992 and 'How Much Can You Take?' in February 1993.
41　*groo:vine*, 11/98, p. 10.
42　Liticia, 1998.
43　Mittman & Flavell, 2003, Australian Scene (5).
44　Meyer, 2008.
45　*groo:vine*, 03/99, p. 8.

Chapter 8: Melbourne Shufflers

1　See, for example, Foster, 1976, pp. 17–20 and Van der Kolk, 2015, pp. 242–243.
2　MacIntyre, 2006, p. 44; von Wayward, 2004.
3　Brewster & Broughton, 1999, p. 107.
4　Brewster & Broughton, 1999, p. 93.
5　Brewster & Broughton, 1999, pp. 86, 88.
6　Brewster & Broughton, 1999, pp. 103–105.
7　Brewster & Broughton, 1999, pp. 104–105.
8　Brewster & Broughton, 1999, p. 90.
9　Brewster & Broughton, 1999, pp. 87, 90, 101.
10　Nowell, 2012.
11　Nowell, 2012.
12　Carroll, nd.
13　Australian Broadcasting Corporation, 2015.
14　Warshaw, 2005, p. 605.
15　Warshaw, 2005, p. 605.
16　See, for example, Australian Broadcasting Corporation, 2015.
17　Coles, Knispel & Knispel, 2005, 37.00.
18　Wilson, 2013.
19　Wilson, 2013.
20　[McrGrooveHeritage], 2013.
21　Wilson, 2013.
22　Wilson, 2013.
23　Brewster & Broughton, 1999, p. 113; Wilson, 2013.
24　Wilson, 2013.
25　Wilson, 2013.
26　Coles, Knispel & Knispel, 2005, 48.40.
27　Coles, Knispel & Knispel, 2005, 49.30.
28　Wikipedia, 2016.
29　Brewster & Broughton, 1999, p. 101.
30　Brewster & Broughton, 1999, p. 107.
31　Coles, Knispel & Knispel, 2005, 25:00.
32　Baldwin, 2010, pp. 152–153.
33　Brocker, 2011, p. 102; Rietveld, 2011, p. 221.
34　Duffett, 2011, pp. 197, 199, 200.
35　Reynolds, 2013, p. 225.

36 Bathgate, 1993.
37 Bathgate, 1993.
38 Reynolds, 2013, p. 226.
39 Phillips, 1996.
40 Andrez, 1998.
41 Riddell, 1999.
42 Riddell, 1999.
43 *groo:vine*, November 1998, p. 5.
44 Tomazin, Donovan & Mundell, 2002.
45 A good place to start is http://www.melbourneshuffle.com.au/.
46 Coles & Knispel, 2005, 7:30.
47 Coles & Knispel, 2005, 7:53.

Chapter 9: Gatecrashers

1 Melbourne City Council, 1993.
2 Victorian Ombudsman, 1994, pp. 4, 5.
3 Conroy, 1994.
4 Johnston & Cummins, 1994; Connellan & Delianis, 1994.
5 Connellan & Delianis, 1994.
6 Mills & Houston, 2014.
7 Victorian Ombudsman, 1994, pp. 1, 2, 65.
8 Victorian Ombudsman, 1994, p. 27.
9 Victorian Ombudsman, 1994, pp. 26–28.
10 Victorian Ombudsman, 1994, pp. 30.
11 Victorian Ombudsman, 1994, pp. 30; Zalewski, 2013, p. 134.
12 Das, 1995; Zalewski, 2013, p. 136.
13 Victorian Ombudsman, 1994, pp. 31.
14 Fitzgerald, 1998, p. 50. The quote is from an anonymous rave promoter.
15 Donaghy, 1996, pp. 85, 91; Homan, 1998, p. 79.
16 Gibson & Pagan, 2003, p. 14.
17 Homan, 1998, pp. 57, 65.
18 Gibson & Pagan, 2003, pp. 11, 13.
19 Gibson & Pagan, 2003, pp. 14, 19.
20 *Sydney Morning Herald*, 06/06/91, quoted in Gibson & Pagan, 2003, p. 16.
21 Homan, 1998, p. 60.
22 Luckman, 2008, pp. 144–145; Mittman & Flavell, 2003, Australian Scene (6).
23 Criminal Justice and Public Order Act (UK), 1994.
24 Donaghy, 1996, pp. 151–152.
25 Donaghy, 1996, pp. 11, 16, 38.
26 Donaghy, 1996, p. ix.
27 Donaghy, 1996, p. 166.
28 Miller, 2014; Wodak & Warhaft, 2015.
29 Kennedy & Lambert, 1995.
30 Kennedy & Lambert, 1995; *Herald Sun*, 29/10/95, p. 44.
31 Kennedy & Lambert, 1995.
32 Thornton, 1995, pp. 6, 122, 132.
33 Fitzgerald, 1998, p. 49.
34 Gregg & Wilson, 2010, p. 411.
35 Gregg & Wilson, 2010, p. 414.
36 Shand, 2012, p. 91.
37 Shand, 2012, pp. 59–61.
38 Silvester and Rule, 2008, p. 2.
39 Shand, 2012, pp. 64–66.
40 Shand, 2010, pp. 41–42.
41 Shand, 2012, pp. 60, 62.
42 Silvester and Rule, 2008, pp. 2–3.
43 Shand, 2012, p. 1.
44 Jarvis, 2014.
45 Siokou & Moore, 2008, p. 51.
46 Poe, 2017.
47 Homan, 1998, p. 72.
48 Gibson & Pagan, 2003, p. 21.
49 Shaw, 2013, p. 338.
50 Gibson & Pagan, 2003, p. 21.
51 Reynolds, 2013, p. 527.
52 Siokou & Moore, 2008, p. 51.
53 St. John, 2001, p. 12.
54 Mittman & Flavell, 2003, Australian Scene (9).
55 I have Aaron Roach to thank for this witticism.
56 Gibson & Pagan, 2003, p. 21; Luckman, 1998, p. 48; Montano, 2017, pp. 48, 57.
57 Fitzgerald, 1998, p. 53.
58 Brookman, 2001, p. 61.
59 Mittman & Flavell, 2003, Australian Scene (9).
60 Sicko, 2010, p. 97.
61 Sicko, 2010, p. 100.
62 Sicko, 2010, p. 100.
63 Poe, 2017.
64 Bridges, 2005, pp. 225–226.
65 Laurent Garnier described Melbourne's techno scene as 'world class'—see *Techno Renegade*, 11/97, p9. Luke Slater dubbed Melbourne 'techno city'—see Johnston, 1999.

66. Thornton, 1995, p. 66.
67. Mittman & Flavell, 2003.
68. Mittman & Flavell, 2003, Future Music (5).
69. Fitzsimons, 2014b.
70. Fitzsimons, 2014b.
71. Fitzsimons, 2014b.
72. Montano, 2017, p. 55.
73. Fitzsimons, 2014b.
74. Richie McNeill, cited in Montano, 2017, p. 56.
75. Montano, 2017, p. 52.
76. Fitzsimons, 2014c.
77. Fitzsimons, 2014a.
78. Montano, 2017, p. 50.
79. Montano, 2017, pp. 47,48, 50.

Chapter 10: Two Tribes

1. Siokou et al., 2010, p. 195.
2. Siokou et al., 2010, p. 193.
3. See, for example, Siokou et al., 2010, pp. 197-198. I will add that any alleged lechery on the part of the muzza pales against the sad yet predictable tales I've heard of some DJs abusing their power, fame and white male privilege to prey on young women.
4. Siokou et al., 2010, p. 196.
5. Coles, Knispel & Knispel, 2005, 25:30.
6. Siokou et al., 2010, p. 192.
7. Thornton, 1995, p.11.
8. Thornton, 1995, pp. 11–12.
9. My phrase, not Thornton's.
10. Siokou et al., 2010, p. 201.
11. Siokou et al., 2010, pp. 194–195. Chris Brookman's research on Sydney ravers found that as the scene commercialised, an emerging pick-up culture threatened the 'non-sexual element' of raving although whether this was due to muzzas is unclear. See Brookman, 2001, p. 56.
12. Brookman, 2001, p. 32.
13. Brookman, 2001, p. 37.
14. Brookman, 2001, p. 37.
15. Fitzgerald, 1998, p. 42.
16. Hindmarch, 2001, 115:00.
17. Groening et al., 1996.
18. Wikipedia, 2017.
19. Reynolds, 2013, p. 544.
20. *Tekno Renegade*, 03/99, p. 41.
21. Griffin, 2005, pp. 14–15, 26–27, 53, 54, 55, 63, 83, 127.
22. Duff et al., 2007, pp. 7–8.
23. Siokou & Moore, 2008, p. 55.
24. Siokou & Moore, 2008, p. 55.
25. Gibson, 1999, p. 21.
26. Shaw, 2013, pp. 344–347. My map of nineties rave venues shows a similar picture. See http://www.technoshuffle.com.au/rave-map.
27. Forster, 2006, p. 176; Shaw, 2013, p. 347.
28. Landry, 2006, p. 6.
29. Richie McNeill, quoted in Montano, 2017, p. 56.
30. Shaw, 2013, p. 348.
31. World Bank, 2016.
32. Vice Media, 2015, 12:48.
33. Gibson, 1999, p. 19.
34. Turkle, 2012, p. 16.
35. Dreyfus & Assange, 2001, p. 207.
36. Dreyfus & Assange, 2001, pp. 207, 211.
37. Dreyfus & Assange, 2001, pp. 226, 231.
38. Dreyfus & Assange, 2001, p. 239.
39. Ollie Olsen quoted in St. John, 2012, p. 120.
40. Wright & McShane, 1999.
41. Wright & McShane, 1999.
42. Mittman & Flavell, 2003, Man & Machine (1).
43. *Tekno Renegade*, 03/99, p. 36.
44. St. John, 2012, p. 52.
45. Andrez, 1995.
46. Fitzsimons, 2014.
47. St. John, 2012, p. 249.
48. St. John, 2012, p. 48. *Techno Renegade* magazine started using the label 'psy trance' in 1998.
49. Rennison, 1998.
50. Rennison, 1998; Mittman & Flavell, 2003.
51. *Listen Up*, 05/95, p. 8.
52. Mittman & Flavell, 2003, Future Music (1).
53. Strong, 2001, p. 72.
54. St. John, 2012, p. 252.
55. Brown, 2015.
56. St. John, 2001c, p. 24.
57. St. John, 2001c, pp. 24–25.

58 St. John, 2001c, p. 25.
59 *groo:vine*, 03/00, p. 9.
60 Earthcore was a four-way collaboration between Fitzgerald, Boursine, Christian Diaz and Pip Darvall. See Maunder, 1998.
61 Earthcore took a five-year hiatus after Spiro Boursine declared it dead in November 2008. See Drever, 2008.
62 *Techno Renegade*, 11/97, p. 12.
63 St. John, 2001b, p. 113.
64 Lambert, 2010, p. 210.
65 St. John, 2012, p. 257–259.
66 St. John, 2012, p. 258.
67 Krusty, 2008, quoted in St. John, 2012, p. 257.
68 St. John, 2012, p. 260.
69 See, for example, St. John, 2010 and St. John, 2012.
70 St. John, 2001a, p.10.
71 Berstan, 2003.
72 Murray, 2001, pp. 64–66.
73 Murray, 2001, p. 66; Strong, 2001, p. 74.
74 Murray, 2001, pp. 65–67; Strong, 2001, p. 75.
75 Williamson, 2001, p. 73.
76 Mittman & Flavell, 2003, Australian Scene (6).
77 St. John, 2001a, p.22.
78 Luckman, 2001, pp. 207–208.
79 Luckman, 2001, p. 211.
80 *groo:vine*, 03/99, p. 7.
81 Iveson & Scalmer, 2001, pp. 227–228.
82 Teriyakianarkisaki, nd.
83 Teriyakianarkisaki, nd.
84 Strong, 2001, p. 77.
85 Teriyakianarkisaki, nd.
86 Teriyakianarkisaki, nd.
87 Hindmarch, 2001, 36:40
88 Gibson, 1999, p. 24.
89 Mittman & Flavell, 2003, Man & Machine (6).
90 Mittman & Flavell, 2003, Future Music (1).
91 Priest & Chan, p. 96.
92 Priest, 2009, p. 102.
93 Mittman & Flavell, 2003, Man & Machine (3).
94 Ministry of Sound, 2014.
95 Reynolds, 2013, p. 721.
96 Reynolds, 2013, pp. 681, 686.
97 Facebook post, 27/09/15.
98 Barrie, 2016.
99 Lucas, 2014.

Index

0055 rave 161, 267
22,000 Volts 174
2XLC 94
3PBS 49, 144, 145, 203
3RRR 68, 90–91, 144–145
808 State 124, 223
8411 Community Centre (Manchester) 207

A
Abrahams, Josh 50, 92–93, 113, 123, 162, 189, 192, 217–222, 233, 237, 247, 284; img 71
Acid Deathbed 185
Adamski 73, 79
Adcock, Scott (aka Beam Me Up Scotty) 101, 181, 277
Adrian Age 171
Afrika Bambaataa 53, 58, 93, 259
Agent Mad 250, 251, 264
A Guy Called Gerald (Gerald Simpson) 121, 208
AIDS 34–37
Alert, Scott 260
Aletti, Vince 25
Alexander, Peter 229
Alfredo 73–74

Alien Nation 277
Allen, Shaneen 64
Allkins, Stephen 36
A London Acid Party 106
Alternative Lifestyle Organisation (ALSO) 35–38, 166, 170; img 24, 25
Amadeus 106
Amnesia (Ibiza) 73–74
Amnesia (Melbourne) 245
Anderson, Laurie 214
Anderson, Mark 57
Andy Van (Andrew Van Dorsselaer) 126
Anna's Story 235
Antediluvian Rocking Horse 273, 279
A Number of Names 95
Aphex Twin 151
Apollo 249–250; img 45
Artificial (Nicole Skeltys) 275, 279
Assange, Julian (aka Prof, Mendax) 268–269, 271
Atkins, Juan 93–96
Aurora 192
Australian Recording Industry Association (ARIA) 63, 221
Ayoubi, Jason 250, 266
Azwan Transmissions 223

B
Baby Lemonade 123, 158
Bamford, Alan 49
Banks, Mike 246
Basement Jaxx 250
Bass Culture 243
Bass Station 260
Bathgate, Kate 144–145, 155, 170, 188, 214
Bauhaus (club) 70
Bayertz, Simon 63
BBE 250
Beastie Boys 59
Beat in the Street 144, 155, 166, 188, 214
Bee Gees 26
Behlendorf, Brian 13
Beginning, The 97
Belleville Three 96, 107, 213
Bellotte, Pete 27
Bergen, Andrez (aka Little Nobody) 274–275, 283
Berserker 192
Bertie's 39
Bertie Street warehouse 267; img 67
Bertschik, Steve 223–224
Beyer, Adam 167
Big Day Out 224, 249
Biology 108–111, 114, 141, 147, 156; img 28
Biomechanoid 276
Birthday Party, The 47, 55, 56, 125
Biz-E 97
BlastOff Sound System 157–158; img 30
Bleeps International 121
Booth, Peter 118
Borrow, Toby 245
Bosh 277
Boudry, Emmy 151–154, 163–165, 192–193, 261; img 61
Boursine, Spiro 276–279
Boys Next Door 45–47
Brack, John 38
Brand X 151
Brewster B. 16–17, 31, 39, 69, 87, 98, 113, 126, 128, 164, 186, 205, 247, 248, 254, 258; img 79
Bridge Road Club 159
Bring a Torch 160
Brophy, Philip 46, 49
Brown Alley 257–258, 260
Brown, James 55 56, 209
Burns, Mel 206
Burns, Robbie 140, 209–210, 259, 265, 276, 280, 287

Burt, Warren 182
Butler, Bruce 272
Byrne, Timmy 30, 70, 100, 145, 285–286

C
Cadillac Bar 89
Campbell, Gavin 54–57, 59, 60–65, 107, 138, 228–230; img 49, 50
Can (band) 93
Cara Caama 191–192, 193, 279, 281
Carbone, Davide 88–91, 100, 106–108, 110, 122, 123, 132–133, 134, 139, 144, 149, 155, 161, 173, 218–222, 229, 282, 287; img 53, 57, 71
Carron Tavern 130, 155
Carter, Derrick 251
Cartwright, Adrian 160, 181, 223–224, 261, 267
Castle, Ray 273
Cave, Nick 45, 47
Ceberano, Kate 64
Central Station Records 68–70, 87, 88, 134, 144, 145, 149–150, 164, 219
Champion Hotel 44
Chaps and Babes 33, 54
Charm (Daniel Wittenberg) 152, 163; img 58
Chasers 41, 59, 62–63, 84, 85, 88, 98, 107, 121, 130, 131, 134, 191, 201, 205, 206
Checkpoint Charlie 84, 88, 99, 119, 130, 132, 141, 182
Chemical Brothers 41, 223, 224
Cheren, Mel 25
Chesworth, David 49
Chevron 33, 54, 62–63, 64, 84, 85, 88, 91, 98, 99, 121, 131, 206, 239, 266
Cinnaman 285
Cizevski, Avairs 29
Class War 160
CJ Bolland 167, 172, 245, 246, 249, 251
Clarke, Hewan 208
Clink Street 81
Clinton, George 58, 93
Club Filter 50, 270–272; img 46, 74
Club Labrynth 83, 171, 172, 215
Code of Practice for Running Safer Dance Parties 242
Coe, Chris 282
Collector's Corner 51, 71
Collins, Andrew Peter 34, 36–37
Colossal 151
Colston-Hayter, Tony 77, 79, 107

Commerce Club 115, 116–128, 131–132, 134, 228, 230, 266
Commercial Travellers Association of Victoria (CTA) 116–118, 128
Continental Baths 66
Cooke, Robin 180–181, 195
Cooper, Tyree 71
Coppel, Michael 249
Cosmic Baby (Harald Blüchel) 191, 212, 214–215, 270
Cotela, Frank 252
Course, John 70, 90, 99, 126, 139
Cox, Carl 140, 243, 244, 247, 248, 250
Craig, Carl 246
Cream 247, 251
Criminal Justice and Public Order Act (CJA) 234
Crystal Ballroom (aka Seaview Ballroom) 44–45, 47, 55, 57
Culpan, Julian (aka Mute Freak) 282
Cure, The 58, 129
Curtis, Colin 208
Custard Shop 147
Cyber 114
Cyber Dada 184, 185
Cyberdelia 184
Cyberthon 184–185, 268
Cybotron (Detroit) 93

D
Daemion, Amiel 222
Daft Punk 250
Dahl, Steve 27
Daley, Paul 251
Dancenet 151
Daniels, Colin 150
Danny D 165
Darn Tootin' 269
Davis, Richard 93
Dead or Alive 58, 130
Dee Dee 282–283
Def 201
Delianis, Paul 229
Dent, Simon 106
Depeche Mode 53, 58, 94
Devil Fish 273
Dewhirst, Ian 'Frank' 202
de Wulf, Frank 140, 223
Digby, Simon 248
Digweed, John 212, 240, 260
Dimattina, Melanie 264
'Disco Demolition Derby' 27

Disco Mix Club (DMC) 70, 192
DMC Records 150
Digitise the World 184, 185
Disko, Fred 114, 142–143, 273
DJ Choci 119
DJ Harvey 119
DJ Pierre 17, 71
DJ Reverse 119
DJ Slack 282–283
DJ Sneak 250
docks, the (aka Docklands) 19, 165–167, 197, 221, 241, 250–251, 257, 265–266, 269; img 76
Dogs In Space 45, 163
Dollman, Sioux 169, 174; img 5
Dome 239, 256
Don't Shoot the Messenger 185
doof 265, 275–281, 282
Do the Right Thing 200, 209
Dr Cid 114
Dream nightclub 141–144, 264, 268
Dr John 122
Dr Motte 246
D-REK 175
Dr Yunupingu 63
du Heaume, Miles 124

E
Ears, The 148
Earthcore 107, 276–279; img 47, 48, 77, 78
Earthdream 180
Eat the Rich 160
ecstasy 72–76, 79, 81, 99–105, 106, 109, 119, 147, 171, 174, 186, 190–191, 216, 229, 233–240, 261–263, 271
EDM 19, 20, 285–286
Einstürzende Neubaten 51
Ellis, Rennie 30, 142
Emerald Forest 176, 179
enjoy 139; img 27
Erez, Dror 252
Esplanade Hotel (the Espy) 180, 241
ESP: The Sleeper Awakes 158
Essendon Airport (band) 49, 63
Euphemism 150
Every Picture Tells a Story 169–171, 173, 174, 176, 177, 185, 195, 196–197, 267, 283; img 36, 37, 38, 42, 43
Exodus 79
Experimental 151
Eye-Q 216

F
Farley, Terry 74
Fatboy Slim 41, 223
Festival Hall 36, 246
Finemore, Scott 260
Fischer, Adam '8bit' 282
Fitzgerald, Joe 237–239, 262
Fitzgerald, Karl (aka Swytek) 107, 277
Flagstaff Gardens 246, 281
Floatation 153
Foot Patrol 208
Frantzeskos, George 28, 58, 231
Frantzeskos, Sam 28–31, 33, 39, 41–42, 53, 58, 231–232, 243
Freeland, Adam 251
Freequency (Sydney Park) 234, 280, 282
Frew, George Nelson 29
FSOM 218–222, 250, 275; img 71
f.u.n. 97
Fung, Trevor 74
Furst, Rob 57
Future (London) 74
Future (Melbourne) 167, 240, 250–252, 264, 266
Future Music Festival 252
Future Sound of London 218

G
Gangemi, Attilio 185
Garnier, Laurent 140, 167, 245
Gatecrasher 247, 251, 253, 286
George Hotel (Seaview Hotel) 43
German Paoli 142
Gina G (Gina Gardiner) 127, 243
Glass, Philip 214
Glastonbury 119
Global Village 9, 174–181, 187–188, 192, 194–196, 212, 236, 266, 278, 283; img 8–14, 39–41, 63, 64
Global Warming 282
Goa Bro 114
Goa Gil 142
Goa trance 142–143, 192, 272–273
Godin, Dave 202
Goegan, Bernie 147
Goldman, Paul 55
Goldsmith, Brian 29–30
Goldsmith, Oliver 245
Goldsworthy, Kane 200
Goodge, Robert 63
Grainger, Percy 48
Grant, Stuart 46

Grasso, Francis 22, 23–24
Green Ant 193, 277
Green, David 107
Greer, Kylie 193
Greville Records 51
Gstaad 123
Gudinski, Michael 150, 250
Guetta, David 243

H
Haçienda 208
Hakim Bey (Peter Lamborn Wilson) 159
Halcyon Nights 250, 251
Hales, Geoff (aka Rip Van Hippy) 111–112, 273
Hamnett, Katherine 107
Hansen, John 183
Happy Valley 190
Hardfloor 273
Hard Kandy 260
Hardware, Hardware Corporation 129, 154–157, 166–167, 170, 188, 194, 215, 236, 240, 246, 248, 251, 252, 261, 262, 263–264, 266, 267; img 32, 33, 34, 35, 69
Hardware Club 60
Hardware Records 157
Hardy, Ron 67, 71
Haring, Keith 60, 178
Harmony 164–165; img 31
Harrison, Grant 98, 108–109
Harthouse 216
Haven 21, 23
Hawke, Bob 63
Hawtin, Richie 167, 245, 273
Healy, Jeremy 250
Heaven 17 94
Heckmann, Thomas P. 275
Heeney, David 150
Hellfire Club 142, 144, 148
Hess 154, 155, 163, 165
Hi-Fi Bar 282–283
HIV see AIDS
HMC (Carmello Bianchetti) 126, 170
H2O (Terrence Ho) 85, 98, 104, 105, 110, 113–114, 120–122, 134, 147, 149–150, 155, 157–158, 170, 174, 190, 212, 215, 231, 253, 259, 262, 283; img 54
Hogan, Dominic (aka Lumukanda) 144, 273, 276
Hogan, Mark 151–154, 163, 165, 188; img 58
Hollenbach, Misha 107

Holloway, Nicky 74–76
Honeysmack (David Haberfield) 250, 275, 283
Hordern Pavilion 35
Houghton, Brett 55
Howard, Rowland S. 45, 47
Huber, Brian 275
Hughes, Gary 114, 127, 166, 170
Hughes, Michael 145
Hugo Klang 47–50, 143
Human Backs 124
Human League 53
Hunt, Warren 193
Hunters and Collectors 54, 56
Hurley, Steve 'Silk' 17, 68, 85
Hutchence, Michael 65, 112, 131, 182

I
Ibiza (island) 73–74, 85, 142, 207
IDs Nitespot 70, 84
If? Records 275
Illusion 132–133
Imagineering 282
Inflation 29, 30, 33, 40, 41, 53, 57, 58, 86, 88, 98, 131, 141, 175, 231; img 51
italo disco 16–17, 31–32, 53, 88, 95, 143, 286
Itch-E and Scratch-E 221
Ito 249
Ippoliti, Camillo and Fab 58

J
JAB 148
Jackson, Herb 71
Jackson, Janet 200
Jackson, Michael 200
Jackson, Paul 60
Jaffers, Adem 182–185, 268
Jaffers, Jeff 114, 182, 184–185
Jam & Spoon 216
James, Mark 83–84, 91, 98, 108–109, 127, 131, 134, 137, 139, 141, 144, 150, 164, 167, 179, 191, 197, 232, 236, 237, 241, 243–244, 248, 250–251, 254, 264, 266; img 55
Jefferson, Marshall 68, 85, 283
Jellyheads Collective 280
Joe 90 170
John, Driena 111, 168, 206
John, Heidi and Richard 80–85, 108–115, 118, 119, 127, 147, 154, 155, 159, 161, 164, 166–181, 185, 187–188, 190, 192, 194–197, 206, 242, 244, 263–264, 288; img 52
John, Jade 111, 176–179, 194
Johnston, Chris 64, 112, 115, 273
Jolson, Jerome 249
Jones, Grace 30, 35
Jooce 133
Joy Division 142
Juice Records 126

K
Kaczor, Richie 25
Kapiniaris, George 32
Karmagenics 193
Kate S 192
Keating, Paul 96
Keiller, Rupert 223–224
Kells, Brent 175
Kelly, Sean 40–41, 53, 57–59, 65, 99, 104
Kemistri 3 113, 218
Kennett, Jeff 229, 241
Kenny Ken 171, 173
Kevorkian, François 25
Kid Paul 216
Kirby, Geraldine 36
Kiss FM, kiss 90fm 145, 191, 221, 285
Klein, Jill 148
Knipe, Jayse 165, 228
Knox, Macgregor 61
Knuckles, Frankie 65, 66–67, 97, 120, 250
Kogakis, Jake 145
Koto 143
Kraftwerk 53, 58, 93–95, 124, 213, 214, 259
Kraze 97
Kryal Kastle 267
Krusty (Eugene Gaffney) 277, 278, 280, 281
Kurihara, Masayuki 273
Kwashook, Raelene 206
K-YZE 200

L
Lab-4 211
Lani G (Lani Greer) 191–194, 227, 230, 266, 269; img 73
Laser Dance 143
Last, Nigel 83
Laurent 143
Law, Steve (aka Zen Paradox) 71, 273, 276, 283
Laz, Desiree 226, 262
Lees, Vivian 249

Leftfield 151, 251
Leslie Street warehouse 192; img 68
Lester, Thaddeus 106
Levan, Larry (Lawrence Philpot) 24, 28, 56, 66, 67, 220
Levine, Ian 203
LFO 121, 170
Liano, Bettina 107
Liano, Teresa 65
Lieb, Oliver 135, 245, 250
Light Car Club of Australia (LCCA) 60–61, 118
Light Productions 98
Lindsay, Pat 267
Little Bands 45, 47, 60, 282
Little Reata 282
Locomotion 57
Loft, The 23–24, 26
Lounge 50, 270, 272, 286
Love Parade 246, 286
Lowenstein, Richard 45
Loyde, Lobby 125
LSD (aka acid) 24, 44, 71, 73, 76, 85, 88, 102, 104, 114, 132, 153, 229, 238, 262
Luhrmann, Baz 222
Lunacy 88, 100, 132; img 26
Lunatic Fringe 108, 155

M
Madasss! 193; img 44
Mad Rod (Singtoh Roddajun-Dogon) 50–53, 85, 105, 106, 118, 119, 141, 144, 145, 243, 244, 248, 267, 269, 270–272, 286–287; img 46, 74
Maher, Richard 69, 240, 246, 265
Maine, Andrew 60
Main, Paul 62, 63
Mancuso, David 23–24, 25, 56
Mandate 17, 33, 52, 70, 87
Mantronix 17, 259
Mansion 245, 256, 260, 266
Marcus 37, 99
Mardon, Marie 84–85
Mark and Emmy, see Mark Hogan, Emmy Boudry
Marinelli, Paul 68
Marmion 216, 223
Masaray 273
Massive Attack 224
Masters at Work 12
Matilda's 55
Max Q 112, 148, 182

May, Derrick 93–96, 122, 246, 259
Maze 116–128, 132, 134, 141, 147, 206, 228, 230–231; img 29, 53, 54
McClelland, Ken 34
McClelland, Kim 15–16, 92, 138, 179, 186–187, 189, 190, 208, 224–225, 257, 269, 277, 287; img 18, 65
MC Hammer 200
McNeill, Kevin 155–156
McNeill, Richie see Richie Rich
MDMA see ecstasy
Mecca (Blackpool) 203
Melbourne Bounce 19, 285
Melbourne Fringe Festival 164
Melbourne Showgrounds 157, 239
Melbourne shuffle 19, 198–218, 224–226
Melbourne Shuffler 206, 211, 225, 226, 256
Melbourne Underground Development (M.U.D.) 80, 169, 173–174, 176, 179–180, 192, 194–196, 267, 278; img 6, 7
Meltdown 183, 184
Merda 148
Meridian 55
Merzbow 144
Metro 41–42, 201, 224, 231, 243, 266
MFS 216
Mickey's Disco 54
Middleton, Steve 185
Midro, Jason 134–136, 192, 195, 196, 260, 281; img 61
Millar, Liz 144, 170
Mills, Jeff 167, 240, 246, 250, 251
Minchell, Paul 29
Ming D 166
Miss Krystal Pussy Cha Cha (Kristina Prpa) 149
Miss Moneypenny 150–151
Moby 41, 151
Models 54
Mokbel, Tony 240
Monkey 260
Moran, Jason and Mark 239–240
Moroder, Giorgio 27, 31
Mothersole, Dave 143
Mr Fingers 71
Munster Terrace 180
Murphy, John 44, 47, 49
Murphy, Scott 150
Music Box 67, 71
Mushroom Records, Mushroom Distribution Services (MDS) 63, 150–151, 215, 273, 285

Mutoid Waste Company 180
Mystic Force (Russell Hancorne) 165, 273
Mystic Madness 276

N
Napster 259
Natural 1 105, 146–148, 162, 170, 176, 178, 187, 198–202, 205, 209, 210–211, 216–217, 221, 225, 239, 241, 246, 247, 264, 280; img 80
Nebula 276
Nervous 151
Network 121
Neu! 93
New Order 94, 129–130
New York, New York (club) 29
Nexus 158; img 30
Nigel B. 107
Nightclub Owners Association (NOA) 231–232
Nitzer Ebb 142–143
No (band) 50
Non Bossy Posse 275
northern soul 122, 202–204, 208, 210, 218
NSW Code of Practice for Dance Parties 241–242
Nu Groove 121
Nui 70

O
Oakenfold, Paul 74, 84, 85, 145, 273
Obese Records 150
Octave Records 149–150
O'Hara, Liam 184
O'Loughlin, Paul 137
Olsen, Ollie 44–45, 47–50, 71, 85, 95, 104, 111–112, 114, 119, 123, 127, 131–132, 142–144, 147, 148, 152, 182, 185, 206, 247, 268, 272–274; img 58
One Stop DJ 150
Ong, Andrew 241
Onyx 200
'Operation Ecstasy' 100
'Operation Maze' 230
Orchestra of Skin and Bone 50
Ostoja-Kotkowski, Josef Stanislav 182
Ozone 282

P
Painters and Dockers (band) 125
Palace nightclub 113, 136–140, 141, 188, 191, 209, 214, 215, 223, 244, 260; img 27, 56

Paladin 260
Palumbo, Jo 68–70, 87, 149
Panic 176
Paradise Garage 24–25, 67, 73, 127
Parliament-Funkadelic 93
Patsy and Elizabeth 106
Patton, Tony 84
Peach, Vince 203
Peanuts Gallery 28–29, 58
Pearce, Craig N. 55
Pee Wee Ferris 139
Peter Mac 17
Phoenician Club 233–234
Phreakin 260
Phuture 71, 130
Pickering, Mike 208
Pier (Cleethorpes) 202, 210
Pipersberg, Eric 145
Plank, Duncan 138–139, 173, 211, 215, 225, 233, 257
Playgrounds: A Portrait of Rave Culture 167, 262
Pleazure 179; img 39, 70
Pokeys 33
Portelli, John 107
Postcode 3000 228, 266
Power House 100, 108, 156, 266
Poyser, Max 117
Prime Suspect 271
Primitive Calculators 44–46, 50
Prince of Wales (St Kilda) 33, 50, 212
Prince Patrick Hotel 108
Principle, Jamie 67–68
Prodigy, The 41, 173, 210, 224, 246
Psyburbia 281
Psychic Harmony 268; img 40
Psycorroboree 277
Psy Harmonics 273–274, 275
Psyko Disko 143, 273
Psyko, Steve 114, 143, 273
psytrance 143, 274, 275, 277, 278
Public Address 107
Pullen, Stacey 246
Pulp 78
Pumpkin Dave 122
Pura 275
Pure 137–140, 141, 144, 150, 181, 209–210, 219; img 56
Purvis, Warwick 58

Q
Quadrant 151–153; img 58–60
Quadrophonia 139
Quay, Charlie 59

R
Rados, Alan 68
Raff, Peter 145, 252
Rainbow Serpent Festival 277–278, 287
Rampling, Danny 74, 75, 98, 145
Rat Pack 171
RAT parties 35, 97
Ravesafe 190
raves.com.au (RDC) 269
Raw Hide see Red Raw
Razor 60–65, 70, 87, 115, 118, 131, 138, 228; img 50
Read, Chopper 54
Reals, The 48
Reclaim the Streets (RTS) 281
Reels, The 54
Red Raw 35–38, 166; img 24
Regular Records 272
Renegade 147–148
Rhythmatic 91, 132, 144
Rhythm and Soul 150
Rhythm Records 149, 150
Richie Rich (Richie McNeill) 129–136, 138, 139, 145, 149, 150–151, 152–157, 158, 163, 164–165, 166–168, 170, 176, 179, 192, 194, 206, 210, 215–216, 218, 223, 228, 231–232, 241–242, 244–245, 249–253, 261–265, 266, 267, 273, 283; img 57
Richmond Recorders 125
Right On One Productions 152–153
Rising High 151
Riverside Inn 158–159
RMITV 185, 268
Roach, Aaron 145, 188, 190, 236, 258, 260–261, 284
Robbins, Steve 86–91, 98, 103, 107, 110, 131, 131, 134, 137, 139, 149, 155, 165, 218–222, 283, 287; img 51, 54, 71
Roland TB-303 49, 67, 71, 126, 183, 219–221, 273
Roland TR-808 49, 67, 126, 202, 219
Roland TR-909 67, 202, 221
Romper Stomper 175, 201
Rosner, Alex 23
R&S 151
Rubell, Steve 28
Rudeboy 118–124, 127, 133, 134, 142, 149–150, 155, 157–158, 160, 165, 170, 232, 270–272, 283; img 46, 53, 74
Run DMC 59
Rush, Joe 180
Rushton, Neil 94

Russell, Noel 29
Ryan, Siobhan 61
Ryrie, Kim 48

S
Sadie's Bar 282
Salt-N-Pepa 59
Sanction 90, 98, 99
Sandilands, Nimmo 64, 70, 84, 85, 106, 122–123, 125, 138, 149, 155, 157, 159, 161–162, 171, 206, 216, 245, 266, 281
Sandy, Jarvis 110
Sarah HB 171
Sasha 240, 260
Saturday Night Fever 26, 54, 200
Saunderson, Kevin 93–96
Savage 260
Scarlet Garden 223
Schaeffer, Pierre 48
Schlager, Braden 123–126
Schulze, Klaus 214
Schumacher, Thomas 282
Seaview Ballroom see Crystal Ballroom
Sebastian's 39
Sedition 57–58
Second Summer of Love 75
Sektor 3 228
Severed Heads 50, 183
SFX 253
Shaolin Wooden Men 247
Shamen, The 172, 244
Shaft, Mike 207, 208
sharpies 125, 200–201, 204, 218
Shed 14 166–167, 215, 232, 240, 246, 250, 266
Shelter Foundation 170
Shepherd, Garry 117, 161
Shock 151, 285
Shoom 74–75
Shulgin, Alexander 72
Shut Up and Dance 121, 172
Sidney, Sid 64, 100–101, 122, 138, 139, 141, 206, 215
Siedle, Paul 59, 70, 98, 131
Sikora, Mateusz 275
Singer, Gary 229, 230
Singh, Charanjit 95
Skinny Puppy 143
Slater, Luke 283
Slater, Nigel 145
Slieker, Simon 209, 282
Snoopy's Discotheque 31
Soft Cell 53

Somerville, Jimmy 250
Sonic Animation 223–224, 250; img 72
Sonic Voyagers 275
Soulenoid 275
Soundboy 150
Spanky (Earl Smith) 71
Sparks, Will 285
Spicer, Ian 118–123, 127–129, 132, 134, 147
Spiral Tribe 79, 280
SPK 50
Stef 64, 110, 112, 114, 175, 179
St Kilda Festival 164
St Kilda Sea Baths 54, 114, 252
Stammers, Tim 62
Stereosonic 252–254, 256
Stobart, Tim 125
Stockhausen, Karlheinz 48
Stonewall Inn 21–22, 33
Storey Hall 260
Strange 174–175, 178
Street rave 163–164, 192, 261; img 61, 62
Strictly Rhythm 151
Studio 54 25, 26, 28–29, 41
Stynes, Jim 263
Subterrain 58, 59, 65
Sugar (Felix Hamer) 277, 281
Summadayze 251, 253, 254, 256
Superstition 216
Sweatbox 97
Sweethearts 33
Swelter 55–57, 60, 62
Sydney Mardi Gras parade (1978) 33, 35
Sydney rave scene, the 97–98, 159–160, 164–165, 221, 234, 265

T

Taipan Tiger Girls 47
Tasty raid, the 227–231, 236
Taylor, Jules 60–61
Taylor, Seth 216, 246, 260
Taxi & Kano 122
Temple 228
temporary autonomous zone (TAZ) 159, 242
Tenuta, Dominic 31
Teriyaki Anarki Saki 282–283
Terry, Todd 12, 112
Third Eye 112, 126, 143, 148, 183–184, 272
Thompson, Terry 249
Thornhill, Leeroy 209
Throbbing Gristle 51, 142
Thrush and the Cunts 45, 60

Thumpin' Tum 39
Tiger Lounge 44
Till, Andrew 114, 142, 144, 148, 158, 272, 276, 279
Till, Darren 147–148
Till, Diane 148
Till, Gus 111–113, 148, 182
Tilman, Anders 142
Time (club) 201
Time Square 59, 98
Tittl, Larissa 99
Thrussell, David (aka Snog, Black Lung) 144, 275
Tok H 130
Tollic, Peta 29
Tone Loc 97
Tonka 79, 119
Totem OneLove 251, 252, 253
Trainspotting 14
Transelements 277
Tranzmission 145, 214
Trax (hacker) 271
Trax Records 17, 68, 207
Treble, Andrea 55
Trip (club) 75, 119
Tronik Voodoo Exorcism 145
TR-Storm 275
Tru, Henry 175, 194–195
Try Youth and Community Services 155–156, 170, 261
Tsk Tsk Tsk 46, 49–50
TVU Warehouse 164, 174, 266
Twisted Wheel 202–203
Two Tribes 250, 252, 263
Tyler, Jeff 165, 194, 260

U

Ultra Nate 250
Underbelly 239–240
Underground (club) 29–30; img 49
Underground Resistance 151, 245–246
Underworld 14, 151, 224
Unity Productions 97
University Club 33, 62, 117
Uppiah, Guy 57, 62, 107

V

van Dyk, Paul 215–216, 256–257, 259
Väth, Sven 215–216, 245, 249
Venuto, Frank 193, 277
Vegas, George 170
Velvet Lounge 282

Vertigo Hypo 123
Vibe Tribe 280, 282
Vicious Vinyl 126, 243
Viridian 250
Vogel, Peter 48
Voiteck 250, 275, 283
Voodoo (Phil Woodman) 169, 174–176, 178, 180, 190, 194–197, 205, 212, 267; img 1–4

W
Walker, Johnnie 74
Walker, Ken 69
Walker, Stephen (The Ghost) 90
Wall, Tracey 166
Walters, Debbie 36
Waltzing Matilda Hotel (Springvale) 16–17
Warehouse (Chicago) 66–67
Warehouse (Melbourne) 134
War of the Worlds 129
Welcome 2000 251
Werder, Felix 48
Westend Forum 230–231
Westgate Sports and Entertainment Centre (Altona) 196, 267; img 6, 7, 65, 66
West, Ken 249
WetMusik 135, 260
Where the Wild Things Are 240
Whirlywirld 44, 47–48, 50
Whisky A Go Go 39, 54
Whitlam, Gough 34, 46
Whittle, Robin 273
Whiz (club) 245
Wieczorek, Joe 79, 81–83, 159, 171, 172–173, 215
Wigan Casino 203, 210
Wild Colonial Club 204
Wilkinson, Kellie 114
Will E Tell 129, 133–136, 137, 139, 154–155, 157, 163, 165, 166, 170, 194, 196, 245, 260, 264, 283; img 57
Williams, Carl 240
Wilson, Greg 207–208
Winter Daze 35, 37
Wolstencroft, Richard 142
Women's Own Warehouse 36, 166; img 25
Wood, Anna 233–237, 241
Woodliffe, Jonathan 210
Woodman, Dan 175
Woodman, Phil see Voodoo
Wrong Shop 147

X
Xpress 98

Y
Yellowcake rave 280
Yothu Yindi 63
Young Charlatans 45, 48
Young, Claude 245, 283

Z
Zen Paradox see Steve Law
Zoff, Leo 72
ZuZus 84–85, 88, 106, 119, 141, 266

Discography

A list of song, EP and album titles referred to in the text. It is not intended as a representative list of music from the period.

808 State, 'Pacific State', Creed, 1989: 124

A
Adonis, 'No Way Back', Trax, 1986: 207
Afrika Bambaataa & The Soulsonic Force, 'Planet Rock', 21 Records, 1982: 58

B
Baz Luhrmann, 'Everybody's Free (To Wear Sunscreen)', EMI, 1999: 222
The Beatles, 'Lucy In The Sky With Diamonds', Parlophone, 1967: 88
Black Box, 'Ride On Time', Out, 1989: 79
Braden Schlager, *Schlager On The Moon*, Valley Of The Moon Midi, 1990: 125

C
Carl Cox, 'I Want You (Forever)', Perfecto, 1991: 244
CJ Bolland, 'Horsepower', R&S, 1991: 172
Cosmic Baby, 'Fantasia', Logic, 1994: 214
Cosmic Baby, 'Treptow', Logic, 1994: 214
Cream, 'Sunshine Of Your Love', Polydor, 1967: 10

The Crystals, 'Da Doo Ron Ron', London, 1963: 10
Cybotron, 'Alleys Of Your Mind', Deep Space, 1981: 95

D
Farley 'Jackmaster' Funk feat. Darryl Pandy, 'Love Can't Turn Around', London, 1986: 207
Darude, 'Sandstorm', 16 Inch, 1999: 212, 217
The Dave Clark Five, 'Bits and Pieces', Columbia, 1964: 204
The Dave Clark Five, 'Reelin' And Rockin'', Columbia, 1965: 10
Donna Summer, 'I Feel Love', Casablanca, 1977: 27
Donna Summer, 'MacArthur Park', Casablanca, 1978: 54
Doug Lazy, 'Let It Roll', Grove St., 1989: 121

E
Electribe 101, 'Talking With Myself', Club, 1988: 90

Energy 52, 'Café Del Mar', Eye Q, 1993: 12
Eruption, 'All You B**tards', Impact, 1995: 100
Eternal, 'Eternal', ULR, 1992: 243

F

The Farm, 'All Together Now', Produce, 1990: 233
Frankie Bones, 'Dantes Inferno', Nu Groove: 122
FSOM, *Melodia*, Candyline, 1992: 220
FSOM, *Wear 'n' Tear*, Candyline, 1992: 220
FSOM, *Beyond*, Candyline, 1993: 218
FSOM, 'Welcome', Candyline, 1993: 218, 222
FSOM, 'Welcome (Thomas P. Heckmann Remix)', If?, 1995: 275
FSOM, *Chapter One*, Volition, 1995: 221

G

Gat Décor, 'Passion', Effective, 1992: 149
Gina G, 'Ooh Aah … Just A Little Bit', Warner Bros., 1996: 127
Gloria Gaynor, 'I Will Survive', Polydor, 1978: 25
Groovematic, *Witness The Strength*, Vicious Vinyl, 1990: 126
GTO, 'Pure (Energy)', Go Bang!, 1990: 99, 122
A Guy Called Gerald, 'Voodoo Ray', Rham!, 1988: 121, 208

H

Hanson & Davis, 'Tonight (Love Will Make It Right)', Fresh, 1985: 207
A Homeboy, A Hippy and A Funki Dredd, 'Total Confusion', Tam Tam, 1990: 113
HMC, *The 100% Juice EP*, Juice, 1992: 126
Hugo Klang, 'Mad Bakes The Problematic Head', Not on label, 1983: 49
Humanoid, 'Stakker Humanoid', Westside, 1988: 182

I

Inner City, 'Big Fun', KMS, 1988: 96
Isis Overload, *Isis Overload*, Not on label, 1991: 126

J

Jamie Principle & Frankie Knuckles, 'Your Love', Trax, 1987: 67–68
Jay Justin, 'Everyone Let's Stomp', HMV, 1963: 204

Jocelyn Brown, 'Somebody Else's Guy', Vinyl Dreams, 1984: 58
Joey Beltram, 'Energy Flash', Transmat, 1990: 172
Joey Negro, 'Do It Believe It', Nu Groove, 1990: 122
Josh Abrahams & Amiel Daemion, 'Addicted To Bass', Prozaac, 1998: 222

K

Kariya, 'Let Me Love You For Tonight', Sleeping Bag, 1988: 121
The KLF, 'What Time Is Love?', KLF Communications, 1988: 99
Kraftwerk, *Autobahn*, Philips, 1974: 213
Kraftwerk, *Trans-Europe Express*, Kling Klang, 1977: 58, 93, 213
Kraftwerk, *Die Mensch-Maschine*, Kling Klang, 1978: 213

L

Led Zeppelin, 'Whole Lotta Love', Atlantic, 1969: 23
LFO, 'LFO', Warp, 1990: 171
Little Pattie, 'He's My Blond-Headed Stompy Wompy Real Gone Surfer Boy', HMV, 1964: 204
LL Cool J, 'I Can't Live Without My Radio', Def Jam, 1985: 59
LMFAO, 'Party Rock Anthem', Interscope, 2011: 225
Loose Joints, 'Is It All Over My Face?', West End, 1980: 25
Lost Tribe, 'Gamemaster', Hooj Choons, 1998: 217
Lovedoll & Bronxy, *Beatfreaks*, Not on label, 2015: 222
Lucid, 'I Cant Help Myself', Delirious, 1997: 12

M

Man 2 Man meets Man Parrish, 'Male Stripper', Bolts, 1986: 17
Manuel Göttsching, *E2-E4*, Inteam, 1984: 24
Marmion, 'Schöneberg (Marmion Remix)', Superstition, 1994: 223
Marshall Jefferson, 'Move Your Body (The House Music Anthem), Trax, 1986: 68, 85, 207
Max Q, *Max Q*, CBS, 1989: 112
Max Q, 'Monday Night By Satellite', CBS, 1989: 182

MK, 'Somebody New', KMS, 1989: 122
Mig 31, 'Mig 31', Pirate, 1991: 192
Mr. Monday, 'Future', Elevation, 1990: 219

N
Neal Howard, 'Indulge', Network, 1990: 122
Nightmares On Wax, 'Aftermath', Warp, 1990: 171
A Number of Names, 'Sharevari', Capriccio, 1981: 95

O
Orbital, 'Belfast', FFRR, 1991: 14, 154, 233

P
Phuture, 'Acid Tracks', Trax, 1987: 71
Phuture, 'We Are Phuture', Trax, 1988: 130
Pulp, 'Sorted for E's and Wizz', Island, 1995: 78
The Prodigy, 'Charly', XL, 1991: 172, 209
The Prodigy, 'Everybody In The Place', XL, 1991: 209

R
Rhythim is Rhythim, 'Nude Photo', Transmat, 1987: 93
Rhythim is Rhythim, 'Strings Of Life', Transmat, 1987: 93
R Kelly, 'She's Got That Vibe', Jive, 1991: 12
Robert Miles, 'Children', DBX, 1995: 12
Ron Trent, 'The Afterlife', Warehouse, 1990: 121
Rozalla, 'Everybody's Free (To Feel Good)', Pulse-8, 1991: 233

S
SCNDL & J-Trick, *Bounce Sessions*, Ministry of Sound, 2014: 285
Second Phase, 'Mentasm', R&S, 1991: 172
S-Express, 'Theme From S-Express', Rhythm King, 1988: 12
The Shamen, 'Ebeneezer Goode', One Little Indian, 1992: 172
Shut Up & Dance, 'Raving I'm Raving', Shut Up And Dance, 1992: 172
Skyy, 'First Time Around', Salsoul, 1980: 25
Sonic Animation, *Time Is An Illusion*, Sonic Animation, 1995: 223
Sonic Animation, *Theophilus Thistler... An Exercise In Vowels*, Global, 1999: 224

Spencer Davis Group, 'Gimme Some Lovin'', United Artists, 1967: 10
Steve 'Silk' Hurley, 'Jack Your Body', Underground, 1986: 17, 68, 85, 207
Sven Väth, *Accident In Paradise*, Eye-Q, 1992: 215

T
T99, 'Anasthasia', Who's That Beat?, 1991: 172
Technotronic, 'Pump Up The Jam', ARS, 1989: 130
Third Eye, 'The Real Thing', Regular, 1990: 112, 183
Third Eye, 'Pray', Regular, 1991: 183
Third Eye, *Third Eye*, Regular, 1991: 112
Third Eye, *Ancient Future*, Psy-Harmonics, 1993: 272
Tricky Disco, 'Tricky Disco', Warp, 1990: 122

U
Underworld, 'Born Slippy', Junior Boy's Own, 1995: 14
Union Jack, 'Two Full Moons And A Trout', Platipus, 1993: 223
Unique 3, '7 A.M.', 10 Records, 1989: 171
Unique 3, 'Weight For The Bass', 10 Records, 1990: 171

V
Various, *House Sounds of Chicago*, London, 1988: 75
Various, *Techno! The New Dance Sound Of Detroit*, 10 Records, 1988: 94
Various, *Zeitgeist — Spirit Ov Thee Times*, If?, 1995: 275
Various, *This Is Melbourne Bangers*, Ministry of Sound, 2013: 285
The Village People, 'YMCA', Casablanca, 1978: 27
The Visions of Shiva, 'Perfect Day', MFS, 1992: 191
The Visions of Shiva, 'How Much Can You Take?', MFS, 1993: 191

W
Westbam v Red Jerry, 'Wizards Of The Sonic (Matt Darey Remix), Wonderboy, 1998: 213

Y
Young Charlatans, 'Shivers', demo recording, 1978: 45
Yothu Yindi, 'Treaty (The Filthy Lucre Remix)', Razor Recordings, 1991: 63

Z
Zen Paradox, *Eternal Brainwave*, Psy-Harmonics, 1993: 273

The Author

Paul Fleckney is a writer, educator and researcher. He teaches urban planning at the University of Melbourne.

Paul grew up in England and became fascinated in rave during 1988's 'Second Summer of Love'. Too young to experience the acid house explosion firsthand, he read the hysterical headlines in the press and watched the pantomime of moral panic play out on TV. A keen techno music fan, Paul remembers well the bitter disappointment he felt when he first stepped inside a nightclub. He pronounced rave dead, buried beneath a thousand commercial 'choons' and a sticky beer-stained carpet. But then, a conversation with Melbourne DJ Brewster B. in 2013 renewed his interest in rave. As Paul listened to Brewster's fascinating and outrageous stories, he realised that through writing about rave he could share in a subculture that had not only eluded him for twenty-five years but also had transformed the lives of thousands of young Melburnians.

Photo by: Kim McClelland